TRANSLATING PAIN:
IMMIGRANT SUFFERING IN LITERATURE AND CULTURE

MADELAINE HRON

Translating Pain:
Immigrant Suffering
in Literature and Culture

UNIVERSITY OF TORONTO PRESS
Toronto Buffalo London

© University of Toronto Press Incorporated 2009
Toronto Buffalo London
www.utppublishing.com
Printed in Canada

ISBN 978-0-8020-9919-8

∞

Printed on acid-free paper

Library and Archives Canada Cataloguing in Publication

Hron, Madelaine, 1976–
  Translating pain : immigrant suffering in literature and culture / Madelaine
Hron.

  Includes bibliographical references and index.
  ISBN 978-0-8020-9919-8

  1. Fiction – Minority authors – History and criticism.   2. Emigration and
immigration in literature.   3. Suffering in literature.   4. Immigrants in
literature.   5. Emigration and immigration – Psychological aspects – Cross-
cultural studies.   6. Fiction – 20th century – History and criticism.   I. Title.

  PN491.5.H768 2009   809.3'9353   C2008-905675-2

University of Toronto Press acknowledges the financial assistance to
its publishing program of the Canada Council for the Arts and the
Ontario Arts Council.

This book has been published with the help of a grant from the Canadian
Federation for the Humanities and Social Sciences, through the Aid to
Scholarly Publications programme, using funds provided by the Social
Sciences and Humanities Research Council of Canada.

University of Toronto Press acknowledges the financial support for its
publishing activities of the Government of Canada through the
Book Publishing Industry Development Program (BPIDP).

Contents

Acknowledgments

'I am part of all that I have met,' Tennyson's Ulysses explains when returning from his odyssey. Likewise, this book has been shaped by many people. Foremost, 'life piled on life,' I am humbly grateful to all the immigrants and refugees who inspired this book into being by sharing their stories with me. This venture was also only possible thanks to the support of my academic 'homes,' the University of Michigan, Carnegie Mellon University, and Wilfrid Laurier University, and the generous funding of the Social Sciences and Humanities Research Council of Canada, the Václav Havel Dissertation Fund, and the Center for Arts in Society at Carnegie Mellon. Several chapters derive from articles in other publications, and permission to reprint is gratefully acknowledged. An early version of chapter 4 first appeared in *Disability Studies Quarterly* 25:4 (2005); chapter 6, in *French Literature Series* 32 (2005) published by Editions Rodopi, and portions of chapters 9 and 10, in the *Slavonic and East European Review* 85:1 (2007).

I am especially thankful for certain travel companions who guided me along the way, be it with pearls of wisdom or peals of encouragement: Zdena Brodská, Bev and Ken Curtis, Jitka and Roger Dobberstein, Frieda Ekotto, Wendy Garrity, Philippa Gates, Jiří Gruntorád, Tim Haggerty, George Lang, Mariam Pirbhai, Andreea Ritivoi, Charles Sabatos, Anton Shammas, Tobin Siebers, Paul Tiessen, Eleanor Ty, and Madeleine Vala. I am also indebted to the writers who personally explored their work with me, especially Dany Laferrière, Lubomír Martínek, Iva Pekárková, and Jan Vladislav. I thank Susan Gorman, Kristen Poluyko, Sylvia Terzian, and Michele Kramer for proofing versions of the manuscript, Noeline Bridge for indexing it, and Kate Baltais for her wonderful work as my copyeditor. I am grateful to John

Roscoe for his great book cover designs. I also thank everyone I worked with at the University of Toronto Press, especially Jill McConkey, Daniel Quinlan, Barb Porter, and the typesetter, True to Type. Finally, this voyage would have been impossible without my mother and Terri, who weathered it with me with much love, patience and good humour. I dedicate this book to my father, *'ma tati,'* who died, leaving us *'to seek a newer world,'* just as this quest of mine began.

An Affective Introduction

sorte nec ulla mea tristior esse potest
(there can be no fate sadder than my own*)

– Ovid, *Tristia*

This book originates in real life. When I was an undergraduate on exchange in Montreal, I volunteered in a program aimed to help immigrants better acculturate to life in Canada. This program sought to assist newly arrived immigrants in a number of practical ways, for instance, acquiring language skills, resolving legal or financial matters, and most importantly, adjusting to cultural differences. I spent many hours in training sessions, learning about cultural diversity; I was taught, for example, never to touch the heads of Indian children and where to buy exotic types of rice. I will never forget the excitement and trepidation I felt as I met with my first client: Azadeh, a refugee from Iran.[1] I felt anxious but ready for our encounter. I had brushed up on recent Iranian politics, was ready to engage in *taghruf* small talk, and even knew where to buy pomegranate sauce for the famous Persian *fesenjan* dish. While initially my new-found friend was impressed that I knew something about Persian culture, and was certainly appreciative that I could fill out various forms for her or procure her familiar food, soon our meetings took an unexpected turn: Azadeh just longed to talk to me. She did not really want to talk about Canada and its cultural differences, or Iran and its politics. Primarily, she wanted to

---

*All translations in this book are mine, unless stated otherwise.

express something else – her feelings of loneliness, homesickness, fear, and confusion in this strange new country. I didn't quite know how to respond to Azadeh's sadness; after all, I hadn't been trained in any form of psychological counselling. So I just listened, as best I could, trying to console her with my presence. As I engaged with other immigrants, be it Desta from Ethiopia or *ti moun* from Haiti, all of them echoed and repeated Azadeh's longing. So many of the immigrants I met could spend hours attempting, in broken French, to articulate their feelings to me: feelings of nostalgia, isolation, fear, frustration, and loss. As I cultivated my new role – that of empathic listener and witness to these immigrants' experiences – I began to realize that, despite their linguistic and cultural differences, all of them shared a similar story: a story of concealed sadness and suffering, which I came to understand as the pain of immigration.

At the same time as I was volunteering with these immigrants, I was also pursuing my studies in Francophone minority literatures at the Université de Montréal. It soon became apparent to me that in the academic sphere, as in the training session at the volunteer centre, cultural differences and successful integration – indicated by terms such as 'multiculturalism,' 'pluralism,' and 'hybridity' – were the circulating currency in contemporary discourse. I thoroughly enjoyed learning about the diversity in minority literature and was fascinated by the creativity of literary analyses, but I was also perturbed. It seemed to me that, in all our analyses of 'resistance,' 'subjectivity,' and 'agency,' we were missing much of the meaning of these narratives. Like the immigrants' verbal accounts, these literary texts were laden with suffering, tragedy, and feelings of alienation, anguish, and loss. As I pursued my research and readings, I came across example after example of what I now define as 'immigrant suffering.' Yet, these themes were often dismissed in class discussions, or only briefly acknowledged with concerned nods and uneasy silences, similar to my own face-to-face responses to immigrants' unhappiness. As there was little theoretical vocabulary to discuss these painful, 'real-life' issues, they were generally set aside. This book, *Translating Pain: Immigrant Suffering in Literature and Culture,* the result of many meaningful personal encounters and equally revealing readings, is my humble attempt to draw scholarly attention to the sufferings of immigration in contemporary literature and culture.

Uniquely, then, *Translating Pain* explores an aspect of the immigration experience that, until now, has not been seriously considered in literary studies: immigrant suffering. This book examines the affective, or emotional, dimensions of the immigration experience. The study of 'immigrant psychology' is an emerging field of research; its implications have yet to cross the disciplinary boundaries of medicine, psychology, and sociology. Only recently have cultural theorists, feminist critics in particular, drawn attention to 'the politics of emotions,' and even to 'the politics of pain' (see, e.g., Ahmed, Abu-Lughod and Lutz, Berlant, Brown); as of yet, there has been no investigation of their role in immigrant discourse. Similarly, notions of 'social suffering' or 'cultural appropriations of suffering' have been circulating in sociology and in media studies (Bourdieu, Farmer, Kleinman, Moeller), but they have yet to seriously enter literary discourse, and postcolonial, diasporic, or immigrant studies especially.[2] Current cultural criticism emphasizes the vital issues of nationality, race, gender, and socioeconomic status in understanding minority subjects. The interpolation between these paradigmatic issues with affectivity, however, or by extension, with the sociocultural politics of emotions, remains, at the present time, 'undertheorized' territory in literary studies. Interdisciplinary in scope, *Translating Pain* draws on various fields of research – including ethnopsychology, sociology, medicine, trauma studies, political philosophy, and cultural theory – to examine the question of suffering in contemporary immigrant literature and in current cultural discourse.

Translating Pain therefore offers a much-needed critical, cross-cultural study of the affective dimensions of the e/immigrant experience in literary production. In so doing, it asks important questions about the pain-filled performance of decolonization, globalization, and multiculturalism in immigrant-receiving countries. It addresses the questions of representation, language, cultural performance, and embodiment in contemporary culture. Most importantly, it inquires how the subject in pain or in the position of victimization may gain agency or representation in social discourse.

Translating Pain not only seeks to better understand the affective experience of immigrant suffering, but it also deliberates its sociocultural and political effects. Shifting from culture to literature and from affect to effect, *Translating Pain* works towards a more global and comprehensive understanding of the real-life immigrant experience, through the lens of fictional representations, be they literary narratives or cultural myths that circulate in current popular culture. The intent is to unravel some of the fallacies, contradictions, and confusions that stem from the collective dishonesty that surrounds immigration, whether in public policy or in literary studies.

From Real Life to 'Fictions'

Most of us understand that, in 'real life,' immigrants experience difficulties when arriving in a new country, difficulties like getting used to another climate, a new environment, and different social or cultural customs. Many of us would recognize that immigrants might also experience adversities, such as economic hardships and racial discrimination or social tensions arising from linguistic, ethnic, and cultural differences. However, few of us are aware of the long-term suffering that immigrants may experience even years after their arrival in a new country, or even as second- or third-generation immigrants. Psychiatrists have shown, for instance, that immigrants of diverse ethnicities, in several general generations, have a higher risk of schizophrenia and other psychoses.[3] Family doctors have noted that immigrant mothers presented two to three times more cases of *hyperemesis gravidarum*, a medical condition during pregnancy which manifests itself by very severe nausea that can require hospitalization (e.g., Groleau; Vikanes et al.). Both psychologists and physicians have pointed to various other diseases and conditions that affect immigrants in particular, ranging from long-term trauma post-traumatic stress disorder (PTSD) and depression to rarer disorders such as *folie à deux* or the Persephone syndrome.[4]

Translating Pain posits that our limited understanding of immigrant suffering may have effects in real life: in public attitudes towards immigrants, and as a result, in public policy. Despite the general acknowledgment of immigrant hardship, most of us know that real life attitudes towards immigrants are not simple; rather, they often prove problematical, if not hostile. For instance, in the summer of 2006, Canada faced evacuating up to 50,000 of its citizens from Lebanon, all of whom were trying to escape the war there. Some Canadians were angered that the government was using their hard-earned tax dollars to rescue Canadians who had been living in Lebanon for many years, and so had not contributed to Canada's economy. These critics felt that these Lebanese-Canadians had made a choice to live in Lebanon, and so now had to face the consequences for it. The logic of these critics completely dismissed the real life fear, trauma, and violence experienced by these escapees, as well as the long-term devastation, repression, and social upheaval they would face if they remained in Lebanon. In this case, the victims of this discrimination were Canadian citizens living abroad, although many of them were first- or second-generation immigrants. The situation of immigrants is therefore often complex, especially when we consider different types of immigrants, such as 'illegal' migrants, currently a highly contentious issue in the United States, Canada, and Europe.

Many real life attitudes towards immigrants – as well as their repercussions in law and public policy – derive from 'fictions' that circulate in the public sphere, 'fictions' that hinder our understanding of the immigrant experience, in particular our understanding of immigrant suffering. Critics of the 2006 Lebanese-Canadian evacuation, for instance, had a somewhat fictionalized view of what it means to be a 'good' or 'successful' Canadian citizen: they presumed that in the current era of globalization, Canadian citizens must remain living and working within Canada's borders. Although many Lebanese-Canadians may have been aid workers, diplomats, or businesspeople promoting Canadian values or commerce abroad, these factors were dismissed, supplanted by the belief that Lebanese-Canadians had made a 'choice' to leave, that they may be opportunists and even cheats, traitors, or absconders, who took up Canadian citizenship for specious reasons. Thus, various fictions about nationality, citizenship, and 'successful' immigration came into play here, as did, of course, questions of suffering. Critics of the evacuation could not empathize with the sufferings of their compatriots abroad when war broke out, or more generally, they could not contemplate their precarious position as alienated transnationals, dislocated between both nations, with sympathies and loyalties to both countries. Instead, many critics harboured the fiction that they themselves were the victims of the situation: by saving these 'defectors,' they would later suffer financially.

Translating Pain attempts to demystify some of the diverse fictions circulating about immigrants, and deliberates how they affect public perceptions of the immigrant experience, especially that of immigrant suffering. Chapter 1 addresses such popular myths as the 'myth of success' or the 'choice' to emigrate. It points out problematical legal categories and public policy terms about immigration, as well as current theoretical tendencies in academic discourse that obscure or fictionalize the immigrant experience. In particular, this book calls attention to the impact of narrative, and of fiction, in shaping our understanding of the immigrant experience. I argue that many of the misconceptions about immigrant suffering arise from the generic 'immigrant narrative,' which naturalizes immigrant pain as a necessary part of the immigration process.

Throughout these pages, I consider various 'fictions' about immigration and immigrant pain in diverse cultural contexts and accounts to identify their real-life sociopolitical ramifications. The bulk of *Translating Pain* explores immigrant fiction, or literature, by immigrant authors about immigration. The crux of this study concerns how immigrant writers might convey their sufferings of immigration in their fiction, given contemporary socio-cultural assumptions and literary conventions.

Popular assumptions about immigration also often affect immigrants themselves. Immigrants may internalize the conventional image of the successful immigrant, and so feel compelled to play down their suffering of immigration, be it in their new country or in their home country, so as to measure up to the stereotypical fiction of success. Similarly, immigrant writers might find themselves conforming to standard models of the immigrant narrative, or popular notions about immigration, so as to meet the expectations of their readership, and more importantly, the demands of the publishing market. If their fiction does not correspond with certain conventional criteria or market demands, it may not be published. Representing the pain of immigration therefore undermines various assumptions associated with immigration. In literary fiction, especially, expressions of suffering destabilize many of the conventions of the traditional immigrant narrative, itself instrumental in fashioning the contemporary understanding of the immigrant experience.

How do immigrant writers express the pain of immigration in their fiction? How do they convey intangible emotions resulting from such experiences as alienation, racial discrimination, and economic hardship with words, plot, and narrative, often in the language of their new culture? These questions demarcate the fundamental inquiry of this book. Accompanying them are further, supplementary questions, related to the 'fictions' I've outlined above. How do writers respond to assumptions about immigration? Do they resist cultural stereotypes or literary conventions? How so? Perhaps, however, the crucial question is the one that moves from fiction to real life: how might authors express their immigrant pain so that their suffering is heard and heeded in the dominant discourse? This critical question establishes an eventual sine qua non between affect and effect: it suggests that understanding the affective dimensions of immigration, as fictionalized in immigrant texts, might have effects in the public forum. Indeed, can experiencing the sufferings of immigrants in a fictional context help us to better understand immigrants in real life and, perhaps, prevent hostility towards them? *Translating Pain* attempts to answer these significant and complex questions from as broad a cross-cultural perspective as possible.

From Fiction to Real Life

Translating Pain: Immigrant Suffering in Literature and Culture explores how different groups, distinct in their sociocultural experiences, social class, gender, race, and ethnicity, translate the suffering of immigration. Specifically, the study compares the complex articulations of immigrant pain in (1) francophone North African (or Maghrebi), (2) Haitian, and (3) Czech texts by authors who emigrated to France and North America. My cross-cultural analysis – of Maghrebi, Haitian, and Czech immigrant texts – interconnects diverse geographies, ethnicities, religious world-views, and even postcolonial and postcommunist polities. As a scholar of comparative literature, I have often lamented academic departmentalization; in my studies of minority literatures, be it in the Slavics department, the French department, or the American Studies department, discussions on similar issues rarely transcended the department's mandate, although there was often fertile common ground for further analysis. This book therefore seeks to cross the boundaries of national literatures: it juxtaposes immigrant issues from three different regions (North Africa, the Caribbean, and Eastern Europe) and brings together postcolonial and postcommunist concerns. It also examines the intersection of different world-views (Muslim, creole, and secular humanism) with global capitalism. By adopting such a wide-ranging scope, this book vies to comprehensively understand the immigrant experience. It seeks to discern both the universal and commonly shared aspects of immigrant suffering, as well as to examine its socioculturally inflected dimensions. Is the suffering of immigration an essential experience that transcends cultures and boundaries? Or is it inflected culturally and politically? How does the pain of immigration translate in different contexts or for disparate target audiences?

The lynchpin of *Translating Pain* is the concept of translation. In real life, newly arriving immigrants find themselves figuratively 'translating' into citizens of the host country: they must transform their images of home, their idealized notions of the new country, their former values, customs, and, above all, their culture, into the context of the target host country. In their fiction, writers also 'translate' their experiences of immigration into narrative. In so doing, they must meet the expectations of their target market and target audience. Often, these writers must take up a different language, that of the host country, and so their works are often literal translations from their native language. Finally, the fictions we tell ourselves about immigration, or the various narratives circulating about immigration, often bear effects in the public forum; they often 'translate' into popular assumptions, cultural attitudes, and even public policies. On various levels, then, the framework of translation offers an effective means of conceptualizing the various processes described in this book.

Regarding immigrant texts as translations proffers important insight into the role of immigrant fiction in contemporary culture. Translation theorists generally define the function of translation as rewriting, interpretation, or critique. Conceiving of immigrant literature in this light – as a rewriting, interpretation, and critique of the target majority culture – offers a viable model for reading the cultural performance of these texts in current discourse. Moreover, translation theory also emphasizes the concepts of fidelity and betrayal, exhibitionism and erasure, and remembering and forgetting in the translation of texts; all of these factors play a significant role in the writing of immigrant fiction. Lastly, translation studies, perhaps more than literary studies, draws particular attention to the politics and economics of cultural production; it exposes these texts as market commodities, dependent on the demands of cultural consumerism and global capital.

Translation theory proves especially useful when considering the translation of pain into language and narrative. In recent critical theory there has been a deconstructionist tendency to read illness, pain, or trauma as 'ineffable' or 'unrepresentable.' My analysis counters these claims; it does not contend that pain is 'untranslatable' in fiction or cultural production. I revisit the reasoning of often-cited critics such as Woolf, Scarry, or Caruth, and draw on theorists such as Wittgenstein, to demonstrate that pain may be communicated in language. My work reclaims an often-overlooked concept developed by Roman Jakobson: 'intersemiotic translation.' Building on Jakobson's notion of intersemiotic translation, I theorize that pain, and even socioeconomic hardships or racial discrimination, are structured as 'languages,' and as such, may be translated into the symbolic language of words.

Translating Pain considers how writers may create effective inter-semiotic translations of their immigrant suffering, given the constraints of language, culture, genre, and the assumptions of the target audience. I posit that, in order to translate their pain effectively, immigrant writers must engage in a particularly performative rhetoric that both reappropriates and resists generic narrative models and cultural assumptions. This rhetoric must be persuasive: it must affectively influence readers, so that, in effect, they translate this suffering in the context of their own life experience. Three sections of literary analyses – on Maghrebi, Haitian, and Czech immigrant literature – delineate various rhetorical strategies that immigrant writers might employ to convey their sufferings of immigration. Although the rhetorical strategies are idiosyncratic and certainly culturally contextual, the themes I examine – the rhetoric of body; the cultural translation of beliefs, values, or myths; and the role of silence, humour, and allusion – are germane to numerous texts.

Part II, on Maghrebi literature, explores the rhetoric of bodily pain: how the sufferings of immigration may be conveyed by corporeal references, allusions to injury, pain, or malady, as well as in metaphors of disease. Intriguingly, the body of the Maghrebi immigrant is often stripped of any ethnic or cultural connotations, or any references to the religion of Islam, so that the immigrant pain is more acceptable to Western audiences. My readings of such various authors as Mehdi Charef, Malika Mokeddem, Leïla Sebbar, Ahmed Zitouni and Fawzia Zouari demonstrate that these writers exhibit their cultural and social dis-ease by explicitly inscribing bodily disease thematically and stylistically into the corpus of the text. The many instances of accidents, sexual mutilation, self-inflicted pathologies, and the etiologies of disease in these immigrant texts express how an embodied discourse criticizes the labour oppression, gender inequity, and racial and ethnic marginalization of Maghrebi immigrants. However, I also question the limits of explicitly embodied discourse, problematizing the 'zeroism' or seemingly pathologically performative victim position that it entails for the immigrant individual, as well as the 'fake pain' and imposture it might occasion. Moreover, this section offers a thorough overview of French-Maghrebi writing. Not only do I consider such established writers as Charef, Sebbar, Mokeddem, Chraïbi, or Ben Jelloun, I also examine the works of lesser-known first-generation authors such as Kassa Houari, Mustapha Raïth, and Kamal Zemouri; overlooked women authors such as Sakinna Boukhedenna, Hafsa Zinai-Koudil, and Minna Sif; recent women writers such as Fadela Amara, Samira Bellil, and Zouari, and dismissed or controversial 'Beur' authors, such as Mehdi Belhaj Kacem, Ahmed Zitouni, Paul Smaïl, and Youcef M.D.

In Part III, in an analysis of Haitian immigrant literature, I investigate how the pain of immigration might be understood through sociocultural signifiers, in this case the slippery, hybrid signifier of Haitian *vodou*. First, I reveal the multiple social, political, and cultural misrepresentations of *vodou* in Haitian and in target North American culture. Then I investigate how Haitian immigrant authors appropriate the trope of *vodou* in their fiction, focusing on the '*vodou*-themed' works of such diverse Haitian authors as Emile Ollivier, Gérard Etienne, Dany Laferrière, Stanley Péan and Edwidge Danticat. As in popular culture, the uses of *vodou* in Haitian fiction remain ambiguous. Conveyed with humour, satire, and allusion, *vodou* references can serve a multiplicity of purposes, including as nostalgic referents of the Haitian homeland, as vehement resistance against dictatorial oppression, or as advocacy for greater cultural tolerance and pluralism in the host country. I probe the difficulties of employing such a polyvalent cultural signifier as *vodou*, along with the use of myth, humour and satire, to convey immigrant pain. I question whether, in light of such implicit references, the implied pain of immigration may not be mistranslated and misunderstood.

In Part IV, I examine the return of the emigrant 'home,' to the country of origin, focusing on the return of Czech emigrants after 1989. In Czech literature of exile, the hardships of immigration were repressed for a number of possible literary, sociohistorical, and psychocultural reasons. This absence of pain played a crucial role in the reception of Czech emigrants returning home after 1989. Exploring narratives of return by emigrants such as Milan Kundera, Jan Pelc, Iva Pekárková, Jaroslav Formánek, and Lubomír Martínek, I inquire whether the pain of immigration can ever be healed or treated upon return, or whether, seemingly absent, it continues to haunt the immigrant texts in allusive deviations and allegorical detours. Part IV ultimately shows that a rhetoric of pain, in particular, an explicit and performative rhetoric of pain, might grant immigrant minorities easier entry into the public forum, and more effective representation in public discourse.

In my analyses, it becomes apparent that, when expressing their sufferings, the protagonists in these fictions seek acknowledgment of their difficult immigrant experiences and their oft-marginalized personhood. In real life, immigrant writers similarly seek recognition and acceptance in the public forum. Translating the pain of immigration thus represents an attempt at gaining legitimacy and significance in social discourse. Moreover, it can even become a means of asserting collective rights. The struggle for civil rights is, above all, a discursive struggle. As Michel Foucault has shown, sites of discursive struggle encompass numerous aspects – the body, language, culture, social interactions – in the manifold relations of power that constitute the social body.

Translating Pain contends that pain plays a particularly significant role in the discursive struggle for minority rights. Philosophers such as Friedrich Nietzsche have argued that pain performs a crucial function in social discourse. Current feminist critics such as Wendy Brown or Lauren Berlant have similarly exposed the politics of pain in contemporary U.S. identity politics, just as theorists from Denis Vasse to Paul Farmer have attempted to theorize the implications of social suffering. Drawing on these theories, and applying them to literary analyses, *Translating Pain* establishes that affect may have effects: an effective rhetoric of pain may grant the immigrant minority subject voice, agency, and mobility in the public forum. In certain problematic instances, pain may even become the way in which immigrants define their identities. My cross-cultural analyses, therefore, investigate both the possibilities and limitations of this rhetoric of pain in immigrant fiction and evaluate its real-life sociopolitical implications.

In the end, the representation and rhetoric of immigrant suffering in these various fictions only has effects if translated into real-life actions. Personally, I hope that this book – in its pedagogy of immigrant suffering – translates into a better understanding of the 'real-life' immigrant experience. It is affectively written for the Azadehs, Destas, and *ti mouns* of the future.

PART I

Translating Immigrant Suffering

1 'Perversely through Pain':
Immigrants and Immigrant Suffering

Give me your tired, your poor
Your huddled masses yearning to breathe free
The wretched refuse of your teeming shore.
                    – Emma Lazarus, 'The New Colossus'

In their painful flight, their thoughts turned to the America never seen,
land of promise, sweet land of liberty – which would reward all sufferers,
redress all grievances. America [...] which they would come to love not
because of its streets paved with gold, but perversely through the pain it
caused in thrusting upon them the obligation of becoming an individual.
                    – Oscar Handlin, *The Uprooted*

Can one be a foreigner and happy? The foreigner intimates a new idea of
happiness. Between flight and origin: a fragile limit, a provisory homeostasis [...]. The strange happiness of the foreigner is to maintain this
eternal flight or this perpetual transience.[1]
                    – Julia Kristeva, 'Y a-t-il des étrangers heureux?'

The Immigrant

I begin this book with a varied set of quotations about immigration to
showcase that, from late nineteenth-century America to recent reflections by a French-Bulgarian scholar, the experience of immigration has
often been misrepresented. Most saliently, in a number of cultural discourses, the suffering of immigration is often dismissed.

Even after a century, Emma Lazarus' famous words (1883), inscribed on a plaque at the foot of the Statue of Liberty, convey the popular view of immigration: that of embracing the flood of subaltern victims in a redemptory gesture, the nation taking up a saviour role. Implied is the notion that once these destitute migrants, or 'wretched refuse,' reach their new homeland, all their hardships will cease; they can finally 'breathe free' – as immigrants.

In his groundbreaking study of nineteenth-century immigration, Oscar Handlin (1952) repudiates this facile image of immigrant assimilation; he outlines the various difficulties that early migrants faced upon arrival in the United States of America. As Handlin explains, it is 'perversely through pain' that immigrants become individual citizens. Immigrant pain is likened to a normative requisite, if not a necessary obligation, of citizenship and individualism, as generic as the streets paved with gold in this idealized land of liberty and promise.

Handlin's celebration of rugged individualism and redemptive adversity persists to this day. In her 2000 apology of 'happy estrangement,' for instance, Julia Kristeva posits that foreigners in France need only embrace their uniqueness and mobility to enjoy a precarious happiness. In our age of multiculturalism and globalization, we prefer to extol the 'difference,' 'hybridity,' and 'mobility' of the nomadic, cosmopolitan hero, rather than fixate on the sufferings of the unhappy immigrant.

These short excerpts are but a few examples of the broad spectrum of popular narratives circulating about immigrant suffering in society today. Echoing Lazarus, popular opinion often suggests that upon entry into the new, host country, the grievances of immigrants should cease. If immigrants complain too loudly in the public forum about their hardships, they are apt to elicit such hostile responses as 'if it is so bad here, why don't you return to your homeland?' or 'it was your choice to come here!' Although most people would admit that immigration is not a painless process, like Handlin (and most sociologists and psychologists today), they would also view these difficulties as necessary developmental 'stages' or 'phases' of an immigrant's 'acculturation' or 'adjustment.' Even former immigrants are apt to minimize the difficulties of their peers with such remarks as 'it was also hard (or even harder) for me when I first came' or 'if you work hard enough, you will succeed (and be stronger for it).' In academic discourse, the prevailing currency of multiculturalism has a tendency to downplay these struggles of immigration, in favour of ideals of 'cosmopolitanism,' 'transnationalism,' and 'global citizenship,' or the 'mobility' and 'hybridity' hailed by Kristeva. As a result of these diverse cultural narratives about immigration, our understanding of the immigrant experience – and in particular that of immigrant suffering – is severely curtailed.

This chapter should perhaps open with a quote by the renowned early immigrant writer Anzia Yezierska: 'Without comprehension, the immigrant would forever remain shut – 'a stranger' [...] ('How I Found America' 167). For the goal of this chapter is to offer further understanding of the immigrant experience, and in particular the pain of immigration. However, before outlining the various forms of sufferings that immigrants may face, this chapter first takes pause to consider various narratives circulating about immigration – from sociolegal definitions to trends in academic discourse – to locate the migrant suffering silenced within them. The overarching claim in this chapter, one that I will return to throughout the book, is that our cultural understanding of the pain of migration is largely shaped by definitions, stereotypes, popular assumptions, and generic narrative structures that demarcate and describe the immigrant. Understanding these generic conventions will lead not only to greater comprehension of the immigrant, but may also serve to alleviate migrant suffering.

Migration Today

In 2005, United Nations estimates show that there were more than 190 million migrants worldwide, or that one out of 32 people in the world was living outside the country of their birth. In 2000, in the United States, 10.4 per cent of the resident population was foreign-born, thus first-generation immigrants; in Canada, this proportion was 17.4 per cent. In contrast to these high immigrant-receiving countries, in France, for instance, only 6.3 per cent of citizens were foreign-born; in the Czech Republic, a mere 2.1 per cent (OECD Tables A.1.5, A.1.6, B.1.6). However, these numbers omit 'irregular immigration' or migrants who never achieve legal status.[2] Nor do these figures adequately represent the critical problem of displaced persons or refugees in the world. In 2005 there were officially more than 34 million uprooted people worldwide and 13 million seeking asylum as refugees (UNHCR). That same year, European Union countries had 374,000 applications for asylum, but granted asylum to only 24 per cent of applicants (UNHCR). By contrast, in 2005, Iran and Pakistan, considered to be some of the more unstable regions in the world, together hosted more than 21 per cent of the world's refugees, or 2.2 million people (UNHCR note 10).

These statistics reveal that mass migration represents one of the characteristic features of contemporary globalization. As John Berger sums up, 'migration can more and more be portrayed as "the quintessential experience" of the age, as market forces, ideological conflicts and environmental change now uproot such vast numbers of people' (55). Globalization, with its expansion of markets and greater mobility of capital, culture, and technology, results in a greater movement of people, because of such factors as the relocation of cheap labour, professionals, and academics, as well as the displacement of workers' families or corporations, and mass migration caused by political instability, conflicts and wars.

These statistics, of course, do not reveal the vast human suffering that such mass migration represents, be it violence, poverty, or injustice, or the more personal hardships, such as the decision to leave one's homeland to the hostility one faces upon arrival in a new country. Statistics confirm that, with the growing numbers of migrants in the world, anti-immigrant feelings are increasing in most countries. In October 2007, the PEW Research Center found that 62 per cent of Canadians believe that 'we should further restrict and control immigration,' as did 75 per cent of Americans, 68 per cent of French, and 75 per cent of Czechs (PEW 6). Similar increases in anti-immigrant feelings were reported by the European Monitoring Centre on Racism and Xenophobia.[3]

Painless Definitions

Labels and definitions further conceal the hardships that immigrants face. First coined in the early nineteenth century to refer to migrants to the United States, 'immigrant,' broadly applied, designates a person who migrates to reside in a country other than the one of his or her birth. In current usage, however, the characterization of the 'immigrant' varies widely across disciplinary boundaries. Generally associated with politics, demography, sociology, and economics, the 'immigrant' often represents the case of exception, or the case of the 'ethnic' or 'non-White' other. In legal terminology, the immigrant is strictly opposed to the refugee; while in literature the immigrant is often conflated with the stranger, exile, or émigré. Each of these definitions grants important insight into the popular understanding of the immigrant experience.

The Immigrant vs the Refugee

Let us begin with legal terminology, where the 'immigrant' is clearly differentiated from the 'refugee.' Intriguingly, it is also either an excess or absence of suffering that differentiates these two groups of persons. Legally, a 'refugee' is a person seeking asylum in a foreign country because of persecution, war, extreme poverty, or natural disasters. In most industrialized countries, however, asylum claims are usually only granted for political or religious reasons, as expressed both in the U.N. charter and the Geneva Convention. In the U.N. Charter, refugees are defined as persons 'fleeing persecution, attack or discrimination because of race, religion, nationality or membership in a certain group,' who according to the Geneva Convention, can demonstrate 'a valid reason [to flee] based on a well-founded fear.' Legally, then, a fear of imminent suffering – most often a direct and dangerous threat to one's life – lies at the basis of a refugee asylum claim. By contrast, a claim for immigrant status, such as the U.S. Green Card, requires that applicants demonstrate their merit – their financial independence, employment potential, viable language skills, and stable family status – so as to prove that they will have the fewest problems possible in the host country and will assimilate as easily as possible.

Sociological literature develops the distinction between immigrants and refugees by distinguishing between voluntary and involuntary migration, often by differentiating between 'push' and 'pull' (Ben-Sira 8). 'Refugees' are commonly defined as involuntary migrants 'pushed' by life-threatening and coercive political conditions, while 'immigrants' are known as voluntary resettlers 'pulled' by expectations of a better future and attractive economic opportunities. Here again, we see a 'pain-filled' distinction between the voluntary and involuntary migrant: between past suffering and future opportunity.

In real life, however, it is not always easy to distinguish forced migration from voluntary resettlement, or between immigrants and refugees. For example, Vietnamese 'boat-people' were identified by the U.S. government as 'political refugees,' while Haitian 'boat-people' are classified as 'illegal economic immigrants,' even though both groups experienced persecution and traumatic flight from an oppressive regime. As Haitian writer Edwidge Danticat explains, 'those fleeing Haiti today are panic-stricken souls fleeing a political reign of terror – not, as the Clinton Administration likes to label them, "economic refugees"' ('Let My People Stay' 124). The immigrant writers that I will be discussing in the rest of this book point to the problems inherent in these definitions. Legally, Haitians and Algerians are most often considered to be economic migrants, although their literary works depict civil war and persecution. On the other hand, Czechs were usually viewed as political refugees by immigration authorities, although many of them left communist Czechoslovakia to seek a better standard of living in the West. Almost all of the authors I am considering from the Maghreb and Haiti were deemed economic migrants; the notable exception is Gérard Etienne, who was considered a political refugee because he was tortured under the Duvalier regime. By contrast, most of the Czech writers I am considering were able to gain political refugee status.

Czech author Iva Pekárková offers intriguing reflections on the distinctions between the immigrant and the refugee, which I have outlined above. Pekárková herself spent several months in an Austrian refugee camp before receiving a Green Card, an experience she recounts in her novel, *The World Is Round* (1994). Despite living in a refugee camp, Pekárková refuses to consider herself a refugee because, as she explains, 'I was not forced to flee from persecution or tyranny; I was running towards freedom and opportunity. I had not suffered enough to deserve to be called a refugee.'[4]

Pekárková's remarks on 'suffering enough' point to the distinction between immigrants and refugees: the degree of pain associated with the experience. In *The World Is Round*, Pekárková satirizes this legal language game: she shows how refugees must master the art of inventing an amply heart-wrenching story to be granted asylum on political and humanitarian grounds in foreign countries (55–6). By contrast, applicants for immigrant status must demonstrate that they won't trouble the host society in any way; that they are model citizens with no grievances. Once in the host country, this discourse of 'painlessness' persists. Jindřiška, the heroine in *Gimme the Money* (2000), Pekárková's immigrant novel set in New York City, sums up 'the immigrant motto: put up or shut up' (78). Pekárková here points to the difficulties both immigrants and refugees face with respect to the sufferings of acculturation. Immigrants who experience hardships often feel they have no right to complain about their difficulties since their resettlement was their own choice. Refugees, on the other hand, are compelled to feel grateful that they were saved from their previous painful situation, and so often dare not speak of the pain of immigration.

Immigrant et al.

The thorny legal distinctions between refugee and immigrant become even more complicated when these terms are translated into popular cultural discourse, because such a variety of designations are conflated with the immigrant condition, such as 'migrancy,' 'diaspora,' 'emigration,' or 'exile.' Furthermore, in literary studies, the canon of texts I analyse in this book has alternately been characterized, in different contexts, as 'migrant literature,' 'postcolonial literature,' 'multicultural literature,' 'exile literature,' 'émigré literature,' or as 'dissident literature.'

First and foremost, it is important to recognize that there are very few literary texts written by actual refugees; novels such as Pekárková's *The World Is Round* are relatively rare. When we consider the real-life conditions of refugees, the reasons for this paucity become clear: most refugees living in refugee camps or as asylum seekers do not have the material conditions, time, energy, or even desire to write about their experiences. Many of them may be illiterate or lack the literary skills to describe everyday life in a refugee camp, or as a landed asylum seeker, in a way that is engaging enough to capture a publisher's attention and be marketable in bookstores. While the refugee experience has been represented by writers, filmmakers, and artists, who themselves are not refugees, I would argue that even these representations of refugees are often conflated with or supplanted by representations of the immigrant experience. For instance, the 'Lost Boys of Sudan' are familiar 'refugee' figures in contemporary popular culture, as they have been represented in books (e.g., Eggers' *What Is the What*) and documentaries (e.g., *Lost Boys of Sudan* or *God Grew Tired of Us*), and have themselves penned testimonials about their experience (e.g., Nhial's *Lost Boy No More* or Deng's *They Poured Fire on Us*). 'The Lost Boys' refer to children who fled to Kenya during the Second Sudanese Civil War (1983–2003); many of them spent more than ten years in the 1980s and 1990s wandering from refugee camp to refugee camp. However, when we read these texts or screen these films, we notice that these children's refugee experience is curtailed to a few pages or a few film sequences; what is emphasized is their immigration experience – their arrival and acculturation into the United States. Moreover, although these refugees' situation was most dire a decade or two ago, their story has only gained prominence today, in light of the Darfur genocide (2003 to present). In certain respects, the Lost Boys' successful 'happy ending' immigrant stories offer us a fictional solution to the atrocities in Darfur.

Similarly, the immigrant condition is often conflated with the migrant condition. The term 'migrant' generically refers to a person who moves from one place to another, whether internally within a country, or from one country to another. In popular culture, however, this label is associated with migrant workers – workers engaged in remunerated activities in a country where they are not nationals – and even more commonly with illegal workers, who do not have the proper authorization to work in a foreign country, and so have no legal status there. In literary studies, 'migrant literature' refers to texts about displacement and movement. While most of these texts are about immigration, they can also include cases of emigration, migration, nomadism, wandering, or travel, as is the case in Formánek's *Beze stop* or Martínek's *Opilost z hloubky*.

The experiences of immigration and emigration are likewise confused. Immigration refers to a person's settlement and acculturation into a new country, and foregrounds the relationship with this new country. By contrast, emigration refers to the movement out of one's country, and the relationship to one's former homeland. A first-generation immigrant is thus always also an emigrant. However, as I further elaborate in chapter 9, perhaps because of Western-centrism, the emigrant experience is often disregarded in popular culture, legal discourse, and academic discourse. There is, for instance, no established genre of the 'emigrant novel,' which would correlate with the well-recognized genre of the immigrant novel.

In literary studies, immigrant texts are also further described, in disparate contexts, as 'ethnic,' 'multicultural,' 'postcolonial,' or 'diasporic' texts. Designations of 'ethnic' or 'multicultural' are usually deployed to foreground cultural elements in these texts. Although most texts reflect a specific ethnocultural perspective, appellations of 'ethnic' and 'multicultural' are more commonly used to denote texts by visible minorities. 'Postcolonial texts' refer to texts produced by people from formerly colonized countries, such as Haitians and Maghrebians, in the case of this book. Finally, 'diaspora,' a term originally used to refer to the experience of Jews, is now used to refer to many cultural groups that have been dispersed from their homeland

and have settled in substantial numbers abroad. Again, however, only certain ethnic groups, usually visible minorities, are considered 'diasporic'; for instance, while we speak of the Indian, African, Nigerian diaspora, there is no equivalent 'Czech diaspora.' Rather, Czechs, Russians, and other white Europeans are usually designated as 'émigrés' when they emigrate from their native land. Non-white, non-Western others are not.

Lastly, the terms 'émigré' and 'exile' must be added to the repertoire of immigrant nomenclature. Both of these titles bear certain political and class connotations. As further elaborated in chapter 9, the label 'émigré' emphasizes the process of emigration, rather than that of immigration; it refers to a person forced to leave his or her country because of repressive political circumstances, as a political exile. In the case of Czechs leaving Czechoslovakia between 1948 and 1989, all of them were deemed émigrés and, as such, political refugees by Western authorities. All Czechs could petition for entry into Western countries by seeking asylum as political refugees (though many of them chose to be sponsored by families who had already settled there). Yet, not all departing Czechs were political exiles, or 'dissidents,' persons vocally or actively challenging the Communist political regime; many of them were simply seeking better economic conditions or reunion with their family abroad. Czech literature written abroad, in the period 1948–1989, is very rarely considered 'immigrant literature'; rather, it is designated as either 'dissident literature' or 'exile literature.' As in the Czech case, the immigrant experience is often supplanted by the exilic condition, especially when writers and intellectuals are concerned.

The Academic Exile vs the Immigrant

In literary and cultural criticism, the figure of the immigrant is most often eclipsed by that of 'the exile,' or of the 'academic exile,' as I would term him. The 'academic exile' is an intellectual who claims to be a political exile (although he or she may not be, legally, a 'political refugee'), or who defines his or her condition – that of being an 'outsider' – as one of exile. In comparison with the immigrant experience, the exilic condition, rich in historical and metaphorical connotations, paradoxically, represents a privileged position in its political and intellectual dimensions. Historically, exile denotes a form of banishment and ostracism imposed as societal punishment, be it in Ancient Greece or in eighteenth-century Europe, or as a response to religious or political persecution. Only influential persons were generally exiled, such as kings (from Tarquin to France's Charles X) to important public intellectuals (Ovid, Dante, or Hugo). If ordinary persons irritated rulers or monarchs, they would generally be dispossessed of their property or simply killed off. In contemporary forms, political refugees, especially intellectuals, are considered 'exiles,' when forced to migrate across political and geographical boundaries where they can more freely express themselves. Exile also carries metaphorical connotations – as a pervasive feeling of alienation, estrangement, or angst – which is taken up by various intellectuals to describe their home-less existential condition; this form of 'inner exile' need not involve geographical displacement.

In academic circles, exile comes to represent an elevated position associated with intellectual value, which often completely replaces the figure of the immigrant. Edward Said perhaps best exemplifies the intellectual currency of the exilic condition in his *Reflections on Exile*. Said correlates exile with 'novelists, chess players, political activists, and intellectuals' because of their 'accomplished mobility' (363). Although Said admits 'that anyone prevented from returning home is an exile' (362), he rather unconvincingly distinguishes between exiles, refugees, expatriates, and émigrés. In his description, neither émigrés nor expatriates have political motives for their departure, and refugees are simply relegated to mobs undeserving of interest, characterized as 'large herds of innocent and bewildered people requiring urgent international assistance' (362–3). Notably, Said's synopsis here completely omits the figure of the immigrant.

The exilic condition elevates the role of the 'non-native' academic to that of a particularly objective and discerning critic of current affairs. As Said puts it, exile represents a privileged intellectual locus of 'picking a quarrel with where you come from,' which he heralds as 'a potent, even enriching, motif of modern culture [...] Exiles cross borders, break barriers of thought and experience' (365). In so doing, 'non-native' academics – be they 'diasporic exiles,' 'post-colonial exiles,' or exiles from former communist countries – hold greater authority in academic scholarship, by virtue of their experience of exile.

Moreover, the idealized portrait of the academic exile – the intellectual experiencing existential angst or 'inner exile' – draws heavily on the image of the victimized artist. For Said, an exile suffers because of his difference; he endures 'an anomalous and miserable life, with the stigma of being an outsider' (362). Yet, with 'a touch of solitude and spirituality' (362), his experience also verges on the sacred. Said's image of the exile is a self-aware individualist who is discriminated, but thus defined, by his condition of otherness., As Myriam Chancy points out, however, Said's 'nostalgic incarnation of a poet-figure' or 'idealized insurgent' clearly derives from a position of privilege that often is brushed aside by academics: 'privilege goes unrecognized by Said: his/her solitude and spirituality is gained from not having to be concerned with mere survival; she or he lives in a contemplative state not unlike that reserved for the upper class in the Victorian age' (*Searching for Safe Spaces* 3)

In many ways, the figure of the academic exile combines the conventional representation of the 'romantic victim' and the 'modern artist.' Both of these concepts are associated with high modernism, and notions of class privilege, spiritual solitude, and literary authority. As V.S. Naipaul explains (1992), 'writers domiciled overseas [...] commonly imagine and describe themselves as living in exile because it is a term privileged by high modernism and associated with the emergence of the metropolis as a crucible for a more international, though still European or American-based culture' (cited in Nixon 25). Intimated in Naipaul's remarks lies the irony that, by adopting the trope of exile, academic intellectuals take on many of the values – class privilege, artistic distance, and Eurocentrism – that so often they vehemently criticize from their position as postcolonial or diasporic critics.

In contrast to the exalted image of the exile is the mundane image of the 'immigrant,' which is associated with menial and physical labour in fields, factories, or the service sector. As Belinda Edmondson argues, in *Making Men*: 'unlike the exile, the immigrant author brings no cultural capital to bear in her invocation of literary authority. In contrast to the glamorous image of the educated – if tortured – exile, thinking and writing in a 'cultured' cosmopolitan center where he can finally be understood, the image of the immigrant calls to mind very different scenarios: depressing urban sweatshops and low-status jobs; physical, not intellectual, labor' (141). Moreover, as Edmundson explains, an exile is often related to nationalism, while immigration and nationalism seem divorced from each other. Because of their objective distance and critical spirit, exiles seem to have an advantageous perspective on the home and host countries and thus are concerned with 'the loftier aims of exile [...] the meaning of the native land' (141). By contrast, the immigrant's motives are often reduced to economic gain, their 'focus is on 'making it' in the metropole' (141).

Most basically, unlike immigrants, exiles are often perceived in terms of loss and dislocation, condemned to enduring an ambiguous state of 'in-betweenness.' Todorov defines the exile as a 'being who has lost his country without thereby acquiring another, thereby living in a double exteriority' (249). These feelings of lack, displacement, and/or duality are dismissed in the case of the immigrant, who is generally understood in terms of gain and success – the immigrant acquires greater security, prosperity, status, or more generically, a 'better life' in the immigration process.

Notably, almost all of the writers I consider in this book would not be defined as 'exiles.' The exception of course, is Milan Kundera. Indeed, Kundera's status as academic 'exile' grants him more status and intellectual privilege than any of the other 'ordinary immigrant' writers I examine in this book. On close inspection it becomes evident that Lubomír Martínek's writing, for instance, is much more philosophical or intellectual than Kundera's; or that Edwidge Danticat, because of her advocacy on behalf of Haitian immigrants, is much more of a public intellectual than Kundera ever was. Yet, although the Cold War has been over for more than a decade, Kundera continues to be deemed by many Westerners as an alienated Czech intellectual, 'exiled' in Paris.

The distinction between 'immigrant' and 'academic or intellectual exile' is highly questionable in today's global economy. From a legal standpoint, most academics are not political refugees, who claim asylum upon landing in their new country; rather, they request permanent residency and then citizenship like any first-generation immigrant. Moreover, there are very few academics who refuse Western citizenship, so as to remain, in effect, truly exiled in their host nation. In the Canadian and U.S. academy especially, to claim most grants (SSHRC, Guggenheim, NSERC), an applicant must be a permanent resident or citizen; I highly doubt that most academics in Canada or the United States can afford to refuse to become citizens. Like any immigrant, then, the academic gains intellectual capital, social status, and economic advantage, as well as stability, security, and increased mobility, by moving to European or American universities. Within the academic community, despite certain losses, academics find a form of 'home,' or belonging, acceptance, and freedom. Finally, to succeed in the academy, the intellectual must integrate Western academic discourse to the same extent that the immigrant must acculturate to values of the host nation. However, by affirming a sociocultural distinction between the exile and the immigrant, the academic intellectual manifestly grants himself power and authority in social discourse.

The Immigrant Narrative

Fundamentally then, it is the fictions circulating about immigrants that most profoundly shape our understanding of the immigrant experience. I would argue that the most basic of these fictions is the generic immigrant narrative, which originated in the late nineteenth century when large waves of (mainly European) immigrants arrived in North America.

Recognized as an established genre by literary scholars, this generic narrative is perhaps best defined by William Boelhower in his structural analysis, 'The Immigrant Novel as Genre' (1981). While Boelhower's analysis ostensibly concerns U.S. immigration, its basic features delineate most Western immigrant narratives. The following macro-proposition succinctly sums up the structure of the generic immigrant narrative: 'An immigrant protagonist(s), representing an ethnic world-view, comes to America [or a new country] with great expectation, and through a series of trials is led to reconsider them in terms of his final status' (6). The immigrant novel bears several key components: a hero, a journey, and a series of trials. Each of these informs our general understanding of the immigrant experience, in particular, the hardships of immigration.

First, the immigrant genre requires a hero. Immigrant heroes, however, are no ordinary heroes, distinguished by their laudable deeds. Rather, they are characterized first and foremost by their difference: they represent an 'ethnic world-view.' Thus, from the outset, immigrants are others. What is more, immigrant heroes are not viewed as individuals, but rather as representatives of a foreign ethnic collective. As Boelhower informs us: 'what is essential [is that] they are *foreigners* (aliens) and immigrants (uprooted); they are *naïve, ignorant* of American life in all of its facets, have a *language* barrier, are *unassimilated* and crucially, *hopeful* initiates' (6; my emphasis). In this generic model, immigrants are incomplete or inadequate 'initiates,' characterized by their lack, whether that be social ignorance or linguistic and cultural incompetence.

Second, like most stories, this narrative entails a journey. Such a journey may involve a spatiotemporal trajectory from the home to host country or a series of movements: departure, passage, and finally, arrival. More importantly, however, the immigrant narrative reflects a particular type of journey – a Bildungsroman, an educational journey where the immigrant learns to assimilate various sociocultural norms. In his structural analysis, Boelhower shows how immigrant heroes must transform linguistic, social, and cultural patterns to conform to those of the host culture (7) and revise their previous, idealized vision of the host nation (5). In the traditional immigrant journey, then, it is assumed that immigrants will eventually 'arrive' and successfully integrate or assimilate into their new host society.

Finally, the central component of the immigrant narrative is 'a series of trials.' It is through trials that immigrant heroes proceed on their journey, encounter cultural differences, or separate from their former values, to finally be acculturated as full members of the host society.

Certainly, Boelhower's structure of the immigrant narrative – as a journey from home to host country – is more applicable to early immigrant narratives, such as Mary Antin's *The Promised Land* (1912), *or* Abraham Cahan's *The Rise of David Levinsky* (1917) Anzia Yezierska's *Bread Givers* (1925). Yet, all of these novels also put into question the assimilation that is supposed to resolve the immigrant story. In contemporary immigrant novels, integration, acculturation, or resolution is interrogated even more forcefully. In such twentieth-century immigrant classics as Amy Tan's *The Joy Luck Club* (1989), Bharati Mukherjee's *Jasmine* (1989), or Eva Hoffman's memoir *Lost in Translation* (1989), successful 'arrival' is always postponed, and final closure is deferred. Unlike their earlier counterparts, contemporary immigrant texts do not dwell too much on the immigrant departure or passage to the host nation; rather many focus solely on life in the new country, sometimes long after arrival, especially those novels written by second- or third-generation writers.

Yet, even contemporary texts continue to conform to Boelhower's basic formulation of the immigrant novel: that these narratives represent 'a pluricultural reality' (6). As such, they also reflect contemporary sociocultural discourse about otherness, ethnicity, multiculturalism or cosmopolitanism. Within this discourse, the enduring sufferings of the immigrant signal the failure of the narrative of the pluralistic nation. As such, these sufferings are all too easily dismissed.

Effects of the Immigrant Narrative: Popular Misconceptions

Although straightforward, the immigrant narrative becomes more complex and problematical when we consider its assumptions, connotations, and possible effects in the public forum, especially as far as the hardships of immigration are concerned.

To begin with, the immigrant hero is primarily defined by his or her otherness, not by virtue of any heroic attributes. On the contrary, the immigrant hero seemingly often lacks basic social skills, which he or she must acquire in the immigration process. This stereotypical representation is precarious when translated into the social sphere. Any hardships or difficulties that immigrants encounter in a 'real-life' environment may be attributed to their deficient status, their linguistic or social inadequacies, and their cultural difference or the characteristics of their ethnic group, rather than being viewed as problems caused by external socioeconomic or political conditions, or alternately, by the hostile environment of their host nation. As a simple illustration of this dynamic, we only have to consider the situation of numerous physicians, lawyers, or postsecondary-school-educated immigrants to Western nations, who, although they may be fully qualified to practise medicine, law, or engineering in their home countries, are forced to re-do their degrees or certifications, at great expense and effort to them. In many cases, especially if they have a family to support, they cannot afford the time or money to requalify themselves, and they take up lower-paying, less-recognized jobs instead. Should they become unemployed, homeless, or ill, they may be viewed either as a social burden or as immigrants who have failed to 'fit in' or acculturate. All too often, it is easier to 'blame the immigrant' for his or her difficulties, rather than addressing the underlying causes of these hardships.

Perhaps most importantly, the immigrant narrative obfuscates immigrant suffering as a necessary series of trials. Such a 'series of trials' proves to be a basic requirement in most narrative forms, from the fairy tale to the tragedy. In his analysis of fairy tales, for example, Vladimir Propp shows that at a most basic level, the hero must always suffer a number of obstacles in a story. Similarly, Aristotle describes *pathos* as one of the foundations of the tragic structure. A series of trials is thus a required element of intrigue: such 'painful acts' grant a number of *peripeteia* to the plot and shape the character of the hero who overcomes them. Because of its generic structure, the immigrant narrative risks being conflated with other prototypical narratives of suffering, whether it be the classic American 'rags-to riches' story or the Christian narrative of redemption.

As a result of being a necessary part of the immigrant story, the hardships, difficulties, and sufferings of immigration risk being essentialized, banalized, or relativized. Oscar Handlin's remark – that successful integration is accomplished 'perversely through pain' (297) – exemplifies this normalization of suffering. As he suggests, it becomes almost an 'obligation' to suffer so as to become an individual, and thus an American citizen. Statements alluded to previously – such as 'It was their choice to come here' or 'If they don't like it here they can just go back were they came from' – also point to the inevitability of hardship in the immigration process. Notwithstanding their 'choice' to emigrate, few immigrants willingly choose to suffer alienation, discrimination, or poverty. Ironically, because of their 'choices,' immigrant hardships are all too often relativized and regarded as minimal when compared with the conditions that immigrants may have experienced beforehand in their home countries. It is once again much easier to dismiss the suffering of immigration as a universal or relative phenomenon, rather than to contend with alleviating specific difficulties that immigrants may face.

Furthermore, because suffering is viewed as an inherent part of the immigrant narrative, it easily becomes regarded as part of the immigrant group experience and internalized as necessary by immigrants themselves. Oftentimes these assumptions are echoed by long-time immigrants, in remarks such as 'I remember that well' or 'I went through that too.' In such perspectives, suffering can quickly become hierarchical: 'You think you have it bad? When I came ...' As a result of the multiple dismissals of their difficulties, immigrants themselves often also minimize, relativize, or suppress their sufferings of immigration, rather than face manifold criticism of their experience.

Finally, innate in the immigrant narrative is the notion that any hardships immigrants face will eventually subside and end as the immigrant story successfully concludes. Therefore, it is crucial to understand and account for the *telos*, or end purpose, of the immigrant narrative. On the one hand, it represents a Bildungsroman of acculturation and thus aims to show successful integration into society. On the other hand, it performs and reproduces the pluricultural ideals in contemporary society.

Certainly, there are immigrants who successfully integrate in their host environment. All too often, however, the immigrant story is condensed to a simplistic triumphant struggle over all obstacles, be they language barriers, ethnic discrimination, or past trauma. For, if all immigrant stories are success stories, we are also successful as a society – we are hospitable, undiscriminating, classless, and pluralistic; we have a thriving economy, are generous to the poor, and proudly embrace racial, ethnic, and gender differences. The immigrant success story thus conceals the difficulties that immigrants face, the violence perpetrated on them by society, the economic system, or legal policies. The media, of course, emphasize certain instances of immigrant distress, such as shocking cases of hate crimes and murder. These exceptional events, however, expediently obfuscate other more banal occurrences of immigrant poverty, violence, or injustice; current policies of cheap labour, detentions, or forced expulsion; and, most importantly, the everyday experiences of immigrant suffering.

The fiction of immigrant success is closely linked to the capitalist 'myth of success.' Related to the myths of the American Dream, open opportunity, and easy social mobility, the 'myth of success' refers to a complex set of values that leads people to believe that 'everyone can succeed, if only they try hard enough.' As Richard Weiss has shown in his *The American Myth of Success: From Horatio Alger to Norman Vincent Peale* (1969), in the United States, this myth is modelled on behavioural patterns derived from American Puritanism and the Protestant work ethic – the ethical maxims of industry, frugality, and prudence. Throughout the nineteenth and twentieth centuries, this myth continued to be promoted in the social sphere, particularly in literature. Texts ranging from famous early writing (e.g., Benjamin Franklin's *The Way to Wealth*, 1814) to Horatio Alger's famous children's stories (e.g., *Struggling Upwards*, 1890), to inspirational writing of the 1950s (e.g., Norman Vincent Peale's *The Power of Positive Thinking*, 1952), to contemporary self-help books, all teach us 'to think our way to success.' Although the 'myth of success' is most closely associated with the United States, it is also reflected in attitudes towards immigrants in other parts of the world. Members of the host nation often believe that immigrants can succeed, if only they are determined and diligent enough.

A variant of this 'myth of immigrant success' is the well-circulated notion of 'model minorities,' elaborated in the work of William Peterson in the late 1960s. Model minorities refer to ethnic, racial, or religious minority groups, such as Asian Americans, who are stereotypically considered to achieve more successful integration. Such success is typically measured by their socioeconomic capital, education, and low crime rate. The hierarchies and assumptions of 'model minorities' can incite conflict or ill-sentiments between minority groups, as well as difficulties for members within these model groups, if they do not reflect the stereotypical image of the model of the well-adapted immigrant.

All too often, when immigrants do not conform to the 'myth of success' and are not successful at adapting as 'model minorities,' their problems are deemed their fault, caused by their own lack of effort. In return, immigrants sometimes end up blaming themselves for their failures or their economic or social problems. Many become increasingly disillusioned and depressed when they finally grasp that financial success or social mobility is not easily achievable in their new environment. The 'myth of success' is internalized by immigrants themselves, who are compelled to play down their suffering of immigration, whether in their host country or in the country of their origin, so as to conform to the image of the successful immigrant.

In many discourses, because of the generic features of the immigrant narrative, immigrant pain is often dismissed. In popular culture, immigrant suffering is sublimated by the progressive 'narrative of the nation,' which advocates naturalization, assimilation, and adaptation. The 'myth of success' misleads many people into thinking that through sacrifice and hard work they will eventually gain success. In the United States, some people continue to view immigration as a liberating rite of passage to the American Dream. Others believe that, upon arrival, the hardships of immigrants will eventually disappear as immigrants assimilate in their new home.

The immigrant's educational journey of integration is not only translated in popular assumptions, but in academic discourse as well. Most psychosociological models reinforce developmental stages of adjustment that culminate in the final stage of successful integration. Similarly, certain tendencies in literary theory tend to privilege such notions as ethnic performance, resistance, hybridity, mobility, or multiculturalism that reinforce the ideals of a 'pluricultural reality,' but which concomitantly also dismiss the realities of contemporary global migration and the sufferings of immigration. Since this book is largely concerned with immigrant literature, I would now like to examine some of these tendencies in literary theory and consider their implications in critical analysis.

'Happy in Theory'

In a 2000 presentation at a UNESCO conference on movement and migration, 'Y a-t-il des étrangers heureux?' (Are There Any Happy Foreigners?), Julia Kristeva posits that foreigners[5] should be happy – because of their liberating, mobile migration and their singular, authentic experience of alienation. In her essay, Kristeva counters essentialized notions of home, rootedness, and static identities to advocate the possibilities created by mobility and difference. As in her other work,[6] Kristeva argues that foreignness should be celebrated, as it reveals the uniqueness in each individual. Celebrating such 'singularity,' she suggests, is perhaps the only way to prevent the pitfalls of either assimilation or communalism (53). Foreignness proves theoretically 'good,' Kristeva argues, as it makes individuals aware of their personal differences, and such differences disallow an assimilationist collective 'we' (53). Furthermore, guaranteeing this 'unalienable right' to difference promotes the values of universal human rights (63), which recognize the worth of each person's individual rights. Kristeva concludes that she 'believes in' the singular, risky happiness that only strangers can experience (54); according to her, foreigners need only embrace their precarious singularity in order to be happy.

Although Kristeva presents us with a laudable defence of difference, I find it perturbing that in her theorization of a happy estrangement, she minimizes the hardships that foreigners experience. While she does admit that foreigners are sometimes viewed as 'intruders responsible for urban evils' or 'adversaries who should be eliminated to pacify the national collective' (53), she offers no viable solutions to these hostile responses, other than that we must realize that difference distinguishes all of us. While she acknowledges that foreigners habitually bear the 'scars' of discrimination (54) or that they represent a social 'excess' (53), whose appearance often 'burns happiness' (54), sadly, she sees their 'scars' as an affirmation of diversity, which proves 'the inexistence of the banality of humankind' (54). While she concedes that foreigners 'live hatred' (55), she suggests that such hatred grants foreigners a 'consistency' (56): 'living painful and familiar hatred' offers the foreigner 'the opportunity to affirm herself as present to one's self and to others'; it makes her 'real,' 'authentic' and 'existing' (56). In the rest of the article Kristeva applauds mobility, but here she reduces migrants' suffering to fixed markers – 'scars,' 'consistency,' the 'authentic,' and 'real.'

Equally disturbing are Kristeva's comments on the psychological, linguistic, and economic dimensions of the immigrant experience. Language is a mere 'prosthesis' (59) that allows the foreigner to be linguistically liberated and capable of great intellectual and/or obscene audacity (59). Labour is heralded as a global merchandise that can be exported everywhere without tax (61), and since the immigrant 'has nothing and is nothing, he can sacrifice everything. And the sacrifice begins with work' (61). Finally, in highly nationalistic countries such as France ('nowhere is one *more* a foreigner than in France' claims Kristeva), the foreigner, who will 'always remain incurably different and unacceptable' (63), prompts philosophical and ideological debates about otherness, citizenship, and human rights.

Kristeva's emphasis on the 'singularity' of the foreigner, much like Said's notion of 'exile,' depicts otherness as an exclusionary or exceptional state. In our global world, however, when one out of every 32 people is a first-generation immigrant, this contention is clearly misleading. Migration, foreignness, or exile is thus not a special privileged status, but increasingly, a common and complex feature of our global world.

In her defence of difference, Kristeva paints the portrait of the happily estranged 'cosmopolitan hero.' She blatantly and intentionally misunderstands the difficulties that immigrants encounter daily. This misunderstanding, typical of certain discourses of multicultural cosmopolitanism, seriously affects the understanding of immigration itself. It sets aside many of the realities of the contemporary world – economic forces and sociopolitical conflicts – as well as the viable prospects for happiness of the more than 34 million migrants or 140 million 'foreigners' in the world today. It remains questionable how many of these individuals can happily enjoy the singularity, difference, and mobility that Kristeva proposes. As Hardt and Negri point out, the ever-increasing numbers of deterritorialized migrants in today's global economy speak more of marginalization and oppression than they do of liberation: 'certainly from the standpoint of many around the world, hybridity, mobility, and difference do not immediately appear as libratory in themselves. Huge populations see mobility as an aspect of their suffering because they are displaced at an increasing speed in dire circumstances [...] In fact, a stable and defined place in which to live, a certain immobility, can on the contrary appear as the most urgent need' (154–5). As Hardt and Negri reveal, Kristeva's ideals of 'eternal flight' or 'perpetual transience' are not viable choices for many migrants in our global world; rather, these conditions are symptomatic of the suffering brought on by their migration.

Certain trends in current literary theory – in postcolonial, diasporic, cross-cultural, or transnational studies – similarly celebrate notions of 'singularity,' 'difference,' and 'mobility' (as well as complementary concepts of 'hybridity,' 'resistance,' and 'cosmopolitanism'), at the expense of other, much more undefined 'subaltern' states of dependence, despondence, or impotence. It is repeatedly forgotten that difference, hybridity, and mobility often originate from painful events – such as discrimination, interracial conflict, or destitution – and reflexively refer back to them, revealing the difficulties of always being 'singularly' othered or securely belonging somewhere in the world. For many immigrants, notions such as 'hybridity,' 'mobility,' and 'difference' are not connotative of any form of redemptive transcendence; nor can they be translated into any theoretical form of 'happy estrangement.' Rather, many of these libratory terms, so blithely circulated in contemporary theory to reflect an idealized form of multiculturalism, more accurately translate the sufferings of immigration.

Ostensibly, Kristeva's notion of estranged happiness in mobility, transience, and flight seeks to deconstruct the notion of 'home' or belonging – in many ways, the goal of the immigrant process of integration. 'Home' is a concept often disregarded in contemporary critical theory. Adorno claimed, 'the highest form of morality is not to feel at home in one's own home' (cited in Nafisi 94). 'Home' has often been associated with static immobility, uniformity, and essentialism, as well as narrow perceptions of nationalism and patriotism. Nigel Rapport and Andrew Dawson argue, in *Migrants of Identity*, that the processes of globalization (creolization, hybridity, synchronicity) have dismantled traditional conceptions of individuals as members of fixed and separate societies and have rendered the traditional idea of 'home' obsolete. Globalization implies a world of movement where identity is created through stories (Berger), myths (Levi Strauss) or, more commonly in postmodern theory, in performativity (Butler). As Angelika Bammer succinctly sums up, 'Home is neither here nor there [...] it's a hybrid, *both* here *and* there – an amalgam, a pastiche, a performance' (cited in Nigel and Rapport 7).

Certainly, in the current era of globalization, 'home' can no longer be regarded as a stationary, homogeneous point of view. Despite this, however, human beings still need a 'home'. – a safe and secure living space. In this sense, home might be the centre of one's social life, a safe and familiar environment that confers order in people's lives and control over their identities. More than a dwelling place, home is the locus of individuals' significant daily activities where they create their identities, stories, and performances. Home is belonging. Academic theorists and intellectual exiles find a space of belonging in the academic community, in their intellectual circles, or in their writing. Many immigrants, however, may still long for a similar sense of community and acceptance in their sociocultural environment and in public discourse.

From Kristeva's notion of 'happy estrangement' or Said's figuration of the 'exile' certain tendencies in academic discourse – be it a discourse of facile liberatory cosmopolitanism or of the victimization of the public intellectual – wholly dismiss the figure of the 'immigrant.' Instead, both the 'estranged foreigner' and the 'alienated social critic' are formulated outside the generic immigrant narrative; instead of being commonplace migrants, these privileged positions represent 'singular' or exclusionary experiences, which offer extraordinary possibilities of transcendence and transformation. Clearly, in our global world of mass migration – where one in 32 people is a foreigner (or first-generation immigrant), one in 140 a refugee, and one in 100 displaced by conflict or civil unrest (Burnett 195) – this assumption is tenuous at best. Because of their supposed lack of a 'homing desire,' however, these privileged figures are able, reiterating Kristeva, to maintain their precarious, estranged, happiness.

As we have seen, there is little place in popular discourse for the suffering of the immigrant. In contrast to the figures of the 'refugee,' the 'involuntary migrant,' or the 'exile,' the 'immigrant' is not, by definition, supposed to be suffering, either before or after arrival in the new country. While the generic immigrant narrative does recognize immigrant hardships, it minimizes or normalizes them so as to conform to the discourse of multiculturalism – a discourse that is even more celebrated in contemporary academia.

Importantly, in my discussion of the problems inherent in these categorizations, I have attempted to show that, in many instances, the immigrant figure often is also a refugee, an involuntary migrant, or an academic exile. Boundaries between these definitions are often blurred. In many cases, these categories serve to further distance or particularize the suffering of immigration – while the foreigner, the refugee, and the exile are said to be suffering, the immigrant (who represents many of us) is not really viewed as suffering; he or she is merely adapting. Because of these blurred boundaries, and the dismissal of the pain entailed, my formulation of the 'immigrant' includes both refugees and exiles and works to render these groups, and their multifaceted sufferings, closer to us.

Immigrant Pain

Having discussed various misrepresentations inherent in the defini-tion of the immigrant and subsequently in the characterization of immigrants' suffering, I hope that by now I have tweaked your curios-ity enough to ask: what is the suffering of immigration?

Unlike in popular discourse, the suffering associated with migra-tion has long been recognized in medicine. In 1678, a young Swiss doctor named Johannes Hofer documented the case of a foreign student who was experiencing a serious, life-threatening form of homesickness. Hofer coined the term 'nostalgia' to refer to this patho-logical condition. Hofer's findings on this new 'disease' were later corroborated by various doctors in the eighteenth and nineteenth cen-turies (e.g., Verhovitz, Jaspers, Zwinger), who elaborated on its symp-toms, causes, and treatments.[7] In the 1760s, German and French doctors further classified nostalgia as a mental condition or nervous disorder.

It was not until the twentieth century, however, that physicians rec-ognized that many immigrants suffer a wide variety of psychological and physical disorders resulting from immigration. Nostalgia is no longer considered a mental disorder; however, particular immigrant groups have been linked to higher incidences of such diseases as schizophrenia and depression, as well as rarer disorders (e.g., Hutchinson and Haasen; Zolkowska et al.; Vikanes et al.). Intriguingly, one of the first psychiatrists to describe the psychic state of the immi-grant was none other than Frantz Fanon, whom I will discuss in chapter 3. Today, immigrant psychology, and even ethnopsychology or ethnopsychiatry, are growing fields in medicine. Currently, scientific studies are increasingly showcasing the cultural attributes of certain psychological problems or focusing on the particular psychology of specific ethnic groups.

Most basically, the sufferings of immigration may best be described as 'pain.' Medical experts define pain as: 'an unpleasant sensory or emotional experience associated with actual or potential tissue damage or described in terms of such damage' (IASP S216). Derived from this definition, 'immigrant pain' may be characterized as 'an unpleasant emotional experience' or 'damage' associated with the process of immigration. The damage incurred by immigration may be physical, emotional, or psychosocial. Most psychologists agree that immigration is a complex psychosocial process, because of its irregular development, its compound causality, cultural specificity, and its multifaceted symptoms.[8]

Generic Models

Generally, most psychologists and sociologists view the difficulties of immigration in terms of development towards 'healthy' integration – be it in terms of adjustment steps,[9] stages of individuation,[10] or phases of cultural transformation.[11] Grinberg and Grinberg, for example, forerunners in the field of migrant psychology (1989), break the immigrant's journey into three stages, moving from an acute, explicit pain, to controlled 'suffering' in subdued or latent pain, to finally, an absence or loss of pain (79–89). Of course, when viewed as a part of the process of immigration, immigrant pain risks being reduced to a trope of the generic psychosocial narrative, in much the same way that immigrant suffering is considered a necessary component of the immigrant narrative structure. Such linear development, artificially constructed, presumes progress and ultimate resolution, and reflects the national narrative of assimilation.

More convincing is Abdelmalek Sayad's formulation of the immigrant condition as a 'double absence.' In *La Double Absence* (1999), Sayad characterizes the immigrant subject as both an immigrant and an emigrant, who remains psychically both in the former home and the new, host country, or in both the past and the present. This ambiguous state of twin identities and binary thinking is the greatest challenge facing immigrants. At the heart of this 'double absence' is the anguish that many immigrants feel at being suspended 'in-between,' in a virtual existence between two worlds. This 'in-between,' where time and space become chaotic, often becomes a locus of impotence for immigrant subjects, where little agency, voice, or movement is possible. Contemporary immigrants, many of whom can return to their homes for visits, often find themselves trapped in a liminal locus of inertia.[12] Sayad's paradigm is especially pertinent for immigrant writers, who often recreate their home worlds and childhoods in their fiction, parallelling the present with the past, and inhabiting both of these worlds virtually.

Compound Causes

In this 'in-between' state of emigration and immigration, the causes of immigrant pain often prove difficult to determine. Grinberg and Grinberg explain that 'a constellation of factors combine to produce anxiety and sorrow' (14). The pain of immigration may be associated with circumstances related to the event itself: arrival and contact, departure and separation, or culture shock and cultural adaptation. Suffering might also result from traumatic events before emigration, such as violence, persecution, or war. Finally, immigrant hardships can continue for many years after immigration, arising from alienation, racism, poverty, or violence.

When integrating into a new society, immigrants undergo a variety of changes, and these might affect each person differently. Such changes range from biological, physical, and environmental adjustments (exposure to unfamiliar diseases, nutrition, climate, or living conditions) to sociopolitical, economic, or cultural differences (altered power relations, family and social structures, different languages, religion, traditions). Immigrants respond differently to these changes, depending on their values, attitudes, and motives, or their family relationships, societal status, and class mobility. Immigrant psychiatrist Salman Akhtar (1999) contends that a sense of 'efficacy,' a feeling of purpose and fulfilment, is particularly important for an immigrant's well-being. Such 'efficacy' manifests itself especially in terms of gainful employment, matching the immigrant's professional qualifications. As Akhtar explains, 'to be vocationally impotent is to psychically wither away' (25). In sum, if immigrants feel they are valued and useful members of their host society, they are less likely to succumb to depression or be overwhelmed by the hardships they encounter.

Immigrants must often heal the scars of their past while rebuilding their lives in immigration. Numerous psychologists have studied the problematical adaptation of refugees or immigrants from war-torn, violence-ridden, or repressive societies.[13] In all the cases I study, immigrants are affected to a certain degree by past traumas. For example, Haitians are traumatized by the tyranny of the Duvalier regime, just as Algerians are distraught because of the violence of the fundamentalist civil war. Maghrebi and Haitian writers are haunted by the legacies of colonialism, just as Czech writers are tormented by the effects of totalitarian communism. In immigrant literary texts, these traumatic sequelae, represented by fragmented memories, flashbacks, nightmares, or hallucinations, often eclipse the difficulties of integrating into the host country.

Furthermore, many immigrants suffer because of the protracted immigration process itself. In many countries, it can take years for immigrants to have a hearing before a refugee board, and further years before they can officially become citizens. During that time, immigrants live in 'limbo,' often unable to gain fitful employment, seek adequate medical treatment, travel out of the country or reunite with their families. In his book *Torture in the Age of Fear* (2005), Ezat Mossallenejed, a torture survivor who formerly worked for a refugee assistance program and as president of the Canadian Centre for Victims of Torture, goes so far as to claim that the 'limbo' for refugee and immigrant claimants, in fact, in many ways resembles the 'limbo of torture,' or the anxiety-ridden waiting period before one's next torture session.

Moreover, immigrants experience hardships, such as poverty and discrimination, long after their initial arrival. Social suffering remains perhaps the most pervasive, and yet most overlooked, form of 'damage' inflicted on immigrants. As Paul Farmer has compellingly argued in 'On Suffering and Structural Violence' (1996), there is no accepted definition of 'structural violence' as he terms it – latent forms of suffering that are a 'recurrent and expected condition' (262) – for those many anonymous victims who have little voice in the social sphere. Nor is there a viable framework, a 'multiaxial model' that combines social class, gender, and cultural differences to study the 'dynamics and distribution of such affliction' (280). In the literary texts I analyse, it is clear that social suffering is the most significant cause of immigrants' hardship, and that immigrant writers struggle to express the pain circumscribed by such 'structural violence.'

All of these causes of suffering combine to shape the immigrant experience. The case of French Algerians, for example, demonstrates how these different forms of suffering – immigration changes, traumatic memories, and structural violence – manifest themselves in a complex matrix of symptoms. Algerian immigrants are often refugees who fled from a country characterized by political violence, seeking political freedom and/or economic opportunities in France. Instead of gaining anything through immigration, they are often displaced in slums and reduced to France's cheap labour force. Because of this sociopolitical, familial, and economic violence, the second- and third-generation (Beur) youth often seem unable to adjust to French society. In all, immigrant pain may be best characterized as a cumulative series of traumatic events resulting from the immigration process itself, past violence, and/or socioeconomic and cultural disparity in the receiving country.

Psychological Symptoms

Most of the suffering associated with immigration is psychological. Sociologists and psychologists agree that 'migration can produce profound psychological distress even among the most motivated and well prepared individuals, and even among the most receptive circumstances' (Portes and Rumbaut 56). Psychologists characterize such psychological distress in terms of confusion, anxiety, maladjustment (Abe and Zane), stress, readjustment (Ben-Sira),[14] psychological or emotional disturbance (Kuo and Tsai; Palinkas), or trauma and crisis (Grinberg and Grinberg). Former refugees, who experienced persecution, violence, or trauma in their countries of origin often suffer from symptoms of chronic post-traumatic stress disorder (PTSD), including depression, self-injury, disassociation, depersonalization, isolation, and persistent mistrust. Certain rare mental disorders – such as *folie à deux* (when two people supposedly share the same hallucination) or Persephone's syndrome (unhealthy attachment between mother and daughter) – are more prominent in certain immigrant populations (see Lerner et al.; Dunkas and Nikelly).

Generally, however, the condition most often ascribed to immigrants is that of loss. Immigration involves many losses, including the loss of home, familiar food, native music, accepted social customs, maternal language, childhood surroundings, and loved ones. Immigrants mourn for these objects of loss, and they also grieve lost aspects of their old selves. Sometimes this mourning is incomplete, leading to depression, notions that are further elaborated in my chapter on Maghrebi immigrants.

Shortly after arrival, immigrants experience the 'shock of arrival,' characterized by feelings of disorientation, frustration, and panic. Expected to adopt two sets of social codes and relations simultaneously, immigrants often experience confusion and/or anxiety. As they face the wholesale loss of their most meaningful and valued objects, they also develop insecurity about their identities. Identitary instability is perhaps the most widespread theme in immigrant novels. Some immigrants do not know who they are anymore, while others feel as if they are hiding a secret, a different identity or special knowledge. Some dissociate[15] to counteract their anxiety or confusion, while others respond in a manic way, harming others or themselves. For example, in Jaroslav Formánek's *Beze stop* (Without a

Trace, 2001), the hero's identity is erased, fused with that of the nameless, homeless, jobless, or dispossessed. In contrast, Jan Pelc's *... a výstupy do údolí* (...And Entries into the Valley, 2000) seethes with riotous violence, as the hero is unable to deal with his turbulent emotions.

Immigrants escaping violence often find themselves tormented by guilt for having left for a more prosperous and safe environment. Many immigrants feel remorse for having abandoned their family and friends, and they feel culpable about having betrayed their country. In their analysis of Israeli immigrants, Knafo and Yaari stress the impact of Jewish history and Zionist principles on guilt-ridden Israeli emigrants (238). As shall be seen in the Czech case, guilt similarly affected many Czech emigrants. This guilt is often manifested in persecutory or prison dreams; interestingly, the nightmares of Czech refugees before 1989 were usually about being returned to Czechoslovakia and confined there (Cernovsky).

In the long term, immigrants often face continuing isolation and alienation, which might lead them to completely lose their sense of self or succumb to depression or schizophrenia. For example, in the novel *Journal 'Nationalité: immigré(e)'* (1987), by Sakinna Boukhedenna, the second-generation immigrant protagonist Sakinna, alienated from both France and Algeria, claims that her identity is simply that of 'immigrant' (e.g., 100, 103, 105, 126). Disassociated from all persons and places, she even claims that she 'does not exist'; she is 'nothing' (73). Feelings of alienation are often accompanied by symptoms of depression, such as feelings of emptiness, uselessness, lack of energy, restlessness, or irritability. In immigrant novels, such symptoms are often reflected in disjointed prose or in repetitive descriptions. Sometimes immigrants also develop more serious mental conditions such as schizophrenia or other psychoses. Mehdi Belhaj Kacem's *Cancer* (1994), for example, textually embodies paranoid mania, or 'social cancer' as the narrator terms it. In a 1992 study of mental health among Cuban and Haitian refugees to the United States, Portes and Rumbaut connect high levels of mental disease to emigration. In another study, Kushner (1989) documents that, since the 1850s, suicide rates among migrants to the United States have been higher than those of the native-born population. Reflecting these real-life statistics, suicides also feature prominently in immigrant fiction.

Physical Manifestations

The pain of immigration is not limited to psychological disorders or emotional distress; sometimes it manifests itself explicitly through physical symptoms. As Grinberg and Grinberg explain, feelings of loss and anxiety are often felt 'as something nearly physical [...] on the border between the physical and the mental' (65). Often, immigrants succumb to so-called somatic illnesses, which the Grinbergs relate to 'psychoses of the body' (145). Such somatic illnesses include anorexia, bulimia, ulcers, or asthma, which are deemed partially psychological in nature. Overall, immigrants are generally more susceptible to diseases than are mainstream populations. Researchers link these higher incidences of diseases among immigrants to cultural differences: in certain cultures there is a greater likelihood of becoming ill.[16] Others argue that certain diseases may directly derive from the immigration process itself and the difficulties it entails.[17]

Aside from physical diseases, immigrants often signal their suffering in bodily functions such as eating or sleeping. Sleep problems such as insomnia or excessive sleeping might signal a protective mechanism against distress, or a sign of depression and dissociation. Accepting or rejecting the food of the host countries also indicates the immigrant's feelings about the acculturation process. In *Immigration and Identity: Turmoil Treatment and Transformation* (1999), Salman Akhtar points to the role of the body as one of the unaddressed realms of immigrant psychology, especially with respect to race and ethnicity (39). He urges clinicians to focus more on bodily manifestations of pain, in scars, skin disorders, eating disorders, or disease, and urges physicians to investigate the function of the body in different cultures, be it the role of bodily exposure or discernible rituals involving the body in different cultures. Although some physical signs of immigrant distress are plainly visible, they are often dismissed as unrelated to the process of immigration.

Linguistic Problems

Clearly language is an immense barrier for immigrants not fluent in the language of the host country. Immigrants experience frustration as they attempt to communicate their feelings of sadness or unhappiness through language. Even immigrants acquainted with the host language must adapt to linguistic codes such as different accents, speech registers, and non-verbal behaviours. As Edward T. Hall explains, in *The Silent Language* (1980 [1959]), a large portion of communication is also shaped by the 'vocabulary of culture' (57), which, for example, structures the language of social contact and interaction, territoriality and the use of space, and conceptual models and patterns of organization. As a result of these communication differences and difficulties, the immigrant may feel lost; to paraphrase Grinberg and Grinberg, immigrants, 'invaded' by 'chaotic messages,' may feel 'eaten up' or victimized by an unfamiliar and hostile world (78).

In medical psychology, research on language disorders specifically associated with immigration is just beginning. Although psychologists have correlated diagnoses of depression or schizophrenia among immigrants with language problems (see, e.g., Haassen et al.), there is still much research to be done on immigrant psychology from a linguistic point of view. Psychiatrists are beginning to realize the impact different linguistic patterns may have on the diagnosis and treatment of aphasia or dysphasia.[18] Psychotherapists are just now becoming aware of the crucial importance of the mother tongue in counselling and therapy; a recent study confirms that one's native tongue allows 'access to deeper layers of psychic material when its loss has inflicted psychic damage' (Mander 102). I predict that future psychological studies will show that immigrants often manifest linguistic disturbances, such as agrammatism, changes in syntactic structure, or word formation, as symptoms of psychological distress. Certainly, my experience in working with immigrants or reading immigrant narratives shows that such linguistic 'damage' is symptomatic of immigrant suffering.

Ultimately, however, immigrants are always confronted with the difficulty of conveying their pain in language – be it the language of words, the language of the body, or the language of psychological signs and symptoms. Immigrants in need of mental health care must also learn to negotiate the cultural language of the medical health system of the new culture, along with the political and social structures that circumscribe it. In all, in order to express their pain, immigrants must learn to translate it.

2 'Suffering Matters':
The Translation and Politics of Pain

What literature has to tell us about suffering, in short, depends on basic decisions about what counts as literature and whose suffering matters.

– David B. Morris, *The Culture of Pain*

Saepe etiam lacrimae me sunt scribente profusae: 'I often weep when writing so' (4:3, 95). Thus wrote the poet Ovid two millennia ago in his *Tristia*, as he contemplated his exile, a fate he described as 'worse than death' (3:1, 53). Although he frequently laments that words fail him (3: 4, 46), that he's forgetting Latin (5:7, 56–64), or that words cannot contain all his suffering (1:5, 55), Ovid nonetheless repeatedly manages to describe the cultural hostility and alienation he experiences (5:7, 5:10), the bodily pain that reflects his mental anguish (3:8, 24–34), and the immediacy and continuity of his torment as 'teardrops overflow to wet the page' and 'cold sorrow drips in his heart like rain' because 'his old wounds feel fresh again' (4:3, 96–8). Despite his eloquence, Ovid's 'many grievances' (5:1, 37) went unheeded; he remained condemned to a fate that he defines as unique in its hardship: 'No destiny can be sadder than my own' (5:12, 6).

Now, two millennia after Ovid, how are contemporary immigrants to express their sufferings of immigration – so that they be heard and heeded in the public forum? This is the fundamental question that drives this chapter and grounds this book. As we have seen in the previous chapter, immigrants experience a variety of hardships, including mental disorders and somatic pain, social alienation and economic discrimination. Yet, the sufferings of immigration are often dismissed in popular culture, and even in academic discourse, because, most basically, the sufferings of immigration are normalized so as to propagate the ideals of the multicultural nation. Ovid's poetry points to an even more basic problem facing immigrants, immigrant writers in particular, who attempt to articulate their pain of immigration in words: the sufferings of exile have been expressed for more than 2,000 years, by numerous illustrious writers. Any reference to them today, in the contemporary subgenre of immigrant fiction, risks being dismissed as generic or passé. As David B. Morris so aptly points out, in his examination in *The Culture of Pain*, 'What literature has to tell us about suffering, in short, depends on basic decisions about what counts as literature and whose suffering matters' (25).

This chapter investigates how immigrant writers might make their suffering of immigration matter to us, as readers, while also exploring the matter of suffering in contemporary social discourse. In so doing, the chapter first delves into the difficulties of expressing pain in language. While some scholars claim that pain and trauma defy representation (Scarry, Caruth), I argue that, indeed, pain can be communicated in language (Wittgenstein), especially if we consider such expressions of pain as 'translations' (Jakobson). Translation theory proves particularly useful when examining the complex difficulties that immigrants face in conveying their suffering in words – the constraints of language, culture, genre, and the assumptions of the target audience. Examining these various paradigms permits a better understanding of how immigrant writers might most effectively translate their hardships of immigration, so as to make these sufferings matter to us, both in fiction, and perhaps most importantly, in social discourse. The difficulties of making suffering matter raise critical questions about effective rhetorics of pain, minority representation, and subsequently, the political role of pain in social discourse. The second part of this chapter then delves into the politics of pain in the social order, from Nietzsche's philosophy to contemporary identity politics. In so doing, I investigate the implications, possibilities, and limitations of effective translations of immigrant pain in contemporary social discourse.

Pain and Trauma

Ineffable

Virginia Woolf's essay 'On Being Ill' (1926) is often cited by critical theorists as verification of the ineffability of pain: 'English [...] has no words for the shiver and the headache [...] let a sufferer try to describe a pain in his head to a doctor and language at once runs dry' (84).

In current critical theory, particularly in trauma studies, the communicability of pain is frequently questioned; any expression of pain is considered 'under erasure' or deficient and incomplete, in that it defers meaning. Elaine Scarry has powerfully argued, in *The Body in Pain*, that extreme pain is not only inexpressible, but the event of pain inevitably destroys language itself: '[Pain's] resistance to language is not simply one of those incidental or accidental attributes, but it is essential to what it is' (5). Scarry posits that pain, notably excessive pain, points to an originary signification of sorts, in a 'prelanguage of cries and groans' (6). Pain represents the ultimate *différand* that cannot be deconstructed, but rather deconstructs the sufferer's world. Ironically, in the second part of her work, Scarry proceeds to reconstruct the sufferer's world, through cultural symbols ranging from the Bible to the work of Karl Marx.

Scarry's deconstructionist tendencies are reflected in much trauma theory today, a fact that is perhaps not surprising when we consider that the first literary critics to espouse trauma theory were Paul de Man's students at Yale (Caruth, Felman). In literary criticism, trauma has been famously defined by Cathy Caruth as 'a response, sometimes delayed, to an overwhelming event or set of events, which takes the form of repeated intrusive hallucinations, dreams thoughts or emotions,' which has often been conflated with the 'ineffable' or 'unrepresentable' because of the insistence on one aspect of trauma – that of disassociation: 'the event is not assimilated or experienced fully at the time but only belatedly' (4–5). As a result of these deconstructionist and disassociative tendencies, there is a tendency among trauma theorists, as Radstone sums it up, 'to associate not with the effects of triggered associations, but with the ontologically unbearable nature of the event itself' (89). By fixedly focusing on this event 'too terrible to utter aloud,' there is, as exemplified in the first paragraph of Judith Herman's canonical *Trauma and Recovery*, undivided attention 'on the meaning of the word *unspeakable*' (1).

Most problematically, the 'event' of primary concern for literary trauma theorists today relates to 'historical trauma' – or a traumatic event, to cite Kaja Silverman, whose 'historical ramification extends far beyond the individual psyche' and thus 'interrupt or even deconstitute what a society assumes to be its master narratives and immanent necessity'(55). In trauma studies, this singular event is, invariably, the Holocaust. A recent trauma studies conference I attended offered a salient, albeit disturbing, example of this problematical privileging of Western history. In keynote discussion sessions, renowned trauma scholars Janet Walker and Dominic LeCapra had little to say to scholars who, for instance, were studying trauma in post-genocide Rwanda or post-Taliban Afghanistan; their comments referred these scholars back to Lanzmann's *Shoah*. Moreover, throughout the conference, Janet Walker could only make a few brief asides to the part of her book that dealt with incest narratives; most of her remarks had to be contained to her analyses of Holocaust films. How, then, to fit expressions of immigrant suffering into current literary criticism about pain and trauma?

The Challenge of Immigrant Suffering

In many ways, the sufferings expressed in immigrant narratives challenge underlying assumptions in current trauma studies and in literary criticism about pain. As pointed out in the previous chapter, the International Association of the Society of Pain Subcommittee on Classification defines pain as 'an unpleasant sensory or emotional experience associated with actual or potential tissue damage or described in terms of such damage' (IASP S216). Medical practice, therefore, associates pain with *damage* or an *unpleasant sensory or emotional experience*, which may be caused by tissue damage, but which may also allude to other forms of damage. My work contextualizes such damage in terms of the process of immigration. The damage incurred in immigration can result from culture shock, from difficulties of acculturation, or from social violence, such as poverty, crime, or racism, upon arrival in the host country. As cited above, the damage caused by these personal and social phenomena need not necessarily be physiological, but can be emotional or psychological as well.

Moreover, the immigration process can be considered traumatic. Saliently, many immigrants may have experienced trauma in their home country or during their flight to the host country, and as a result may develop various traumatic *sequelae*, or symptoms of post-traumatic stress disorder, such as fear, hallucinations, depersonalization, or dysphoria. Judith Herman outlines a variety of such symptoms in *Trauma and Recovery* (121), and defines those who suffer PTSD as persons who have 'a history of subjugation to totalitarian control over a prolonged period (months to years)' (121). While Herman points to such examples as prisoners of war, concentration camp survivors, members of religious cults, and victims of domestic or sexual abuse, when we consider immigration, it is clear that many immigrants, such as Haitians, Algerians, or Czechs, lived for years as subjects of totalitarian regimes, be it the Duvalier dictatorship or the former Communist regime. Likewise, for many immigrants, arrival may be considered, to reiterate Caruth, an event that is 'not assimilated or experienced fully at the time but only belatedly' (4), just as the process of immigration may be viewed as an 'overwhelming event or set of events' (5). In many ways, then, the hardships that immigrants experience – including linguistic difficulties, cultural negotiations, isolation, economic struggles, social alienation, hostility, and violence – may be deemed traumatic events, which, when prolonged or repeated, have a profound impact on the psyche.

Communicable

Most importantly, this book counters the claim that pain is inexpressible; rather it explores how such pain is in fact expressed in language. In so doing, it reflects the theorizations of Ludwig Wittgenstein, who posits that there is no prelinguistic 'private language,' but that even the subjective experience of pain may be communicated to others through a shared code of signs, such as crying or grimacing, as well as through acquired verbal signs. In his *Philosophical Investigations*, Wittgenstein explores the fundamental question: 'Could someone understand the word "pain," who had never felt pain?' (105, sec 315). Wittgenstein relates the sensation to a blind person's inability to conceive of the colour red or to the failure of an individual unfamiliar with cheese to imagine its taste. Unlike 'cheese' or 'red,' however, 'pain' refers to an experiential phenomenon that is experienced by most people to some degree.[1]

Wittgenstein argues that sensations such as pain may indeed be communicated through verbal expressions and through a shared, learned, behavioural code. For instance, he cites the example of a hurt child, who cries when it is a baby, but as this child matures, verbal expression replaces crying (89, sec. 144). Wittgenstein is careful to note, however, that correlating a cry with a simple verbal expression is misleading; rather, this cry is a proposition, an expression of thought (104, sec. 317), which can only point to a painful place (101, sec. 302); it is up to the listener to imagine it. Wittgenstein emphasizes that only the subject in pain cannot doubt the actuality of his or her pain, while the onlooker can only infer it, perhaps doubting it, perhaps believing it

(90, sec. 246). An onlooker can respond to expressions of pain with belief, disbelief, or suspicion (sec. 310), and can either demonstrate empathy by grimacing in return (sec. 310) or conceal any empathy by not displaying emotion (sec. 311).

In line with Wittgenstein, then, my book argues against any 'private language' of pain, but affirms that painful sensations can be communicated to someone who is not experiencing them. My work also upholds, however, the experiential value of pain: pain matters – or gains significance – only insofar as the sufferer perceives it and acknowledges it. To others, or post facto, pain can never be 'known,' it can merely be 'interpreted.' Thus, my work does not wholly dispute Scarry's claim that language cannot fully capture the original essence of pain. However, my book does claim that the subjective phenomenological experience of suffering[2] can be expressed by objective signs (albeit sometimes more overt signs than covert ones), as presented in immigrant narratives, but that we must learn to better understand and interpret these expressions of pain.

The broad scope of literary traditions and variety of texts that I examine in the rest of this book reveal that, indeed, suffering can be expressed in language. That being said, the rest of this book also demonstrates that expressing pain is neither easy nor transparent. Rather, given the limits of language, conveying one's sufferings is often problematical. Unlike oral testimonials, written expressions of pain cannot be accompanied by gestures, tone, or dramatization. Moreover, linguistic referents related to pain are limited. Pain is most often described by its effects – duration, intensity – as well as by its location. The McGill Pain questionnaire, for instance, one of the main models for evaluating pain in medicine, offers only seventy-seven words, in twenty categories, to describe pain in the English language, while also providing five descriptors of pain intensity and another nine for pain duration. Linguistically, pain can also be conveyed by similes, comparative metaphors, and allusions. More importantly, however, the expression of pain is further limited by cultural, generic, and social conventions.

At this point, I think it is useful to review Woolf's canonical essay 'On Being Ill' (1926), which, when read in its entirety, is much more concerned with the sociocultural and generic role of illness in literary discourse than it is with the deficiency of language to express pain. Throughout her text, Woolf deploys a variety of similes and metaphors to describe her suffering. That being so, she also argues that there is a dearth of literary narratives of illness, in contrast to lyrical love poetry, for instance. Almost a century later, Woolf's remarks seem outdated – in our culture, the pathography, or narrative of illness, is an established genre, popularized by AIDS narratives, cancer autobiographies, and TV dramas such as *ER, Chicago Hope,* or *Grey's Anatomy.* In Woolf's time and culture, however, illness was suppressed for a number of factors including, as Lucy Bending has pointed out, 'taste, decorum and fear' (84): 'It both could and could not be written about, since social conventions and physical and linguistic incapacity silenced individuals, whilst novelistic conventions [...] turned it into an empty convention' (82). Bending's own work on physical pain in nineteenth-century literary texts deftly demonstrates that the literary expression of pain is limited not only by language, but also by social attitudes and generic literary conventions.

In immigrant narratives, the issues of culture, genre, and social expectations are similarly and crucially important in both the transmission and reception of the sufferings of immigration. In many cases, such literary and sociocultural conventions prove even more problematical than the linguistic limits of expressing pain. To better address this compound matrix – of language, culture, and genre – in the expression of pain, I now propose to consider these expressions of pain in terms of translation theory.

The Translation of Pain

Throughout the rest of this work, I will be considering immigrant expressions of pain as 'translations,' because I think that the framework of translation best elucidates the complex articulation of pain in immigrant texts. Translation theory not only proves particularly useful when considering the transmission of pain into language, but it also emphasizes the roles of culture, social expectation, and literary conventions that affect the expression of immigrant pain in its reception in the new country. In sum, my work considers the ways in which immigrants translate the source language of pain into the target language of the host country.

In many ways, translation aptly reflects the immigrant experience. Just as the language of the host society may not be transparent for immigrants, neither is the time, place, or culture they inhabit; immigrants survive always in the ghostly shadow of their former selves: their source cultural language of home. As they acculturate to their host country, immigrants must also translate themselves, changing, adapting, and recreating themselves in continua of transformation. The sufferings that immigrants experience in immigration demand translation. The pain immigrants feel is not transparent; it originates from deep within the body and the mind. When attempting to convey this pain, immigrants seek to identify it, describe it, understand it, but also to transform it. Moreover, by eliciting their pain, immigrants might also hope to treat, or even, heal it.

Translation is particularly useful when considering the expression of pain. Expressing pain is not a transparent act; yet, neither is it ineffable. Translation does not presume transparency; yet, at the same time, it does counter inexpressibility. In no case does a translation connote exact equivalency; rather, it advances notions of difference, interpretation, and mediation. Translation employs language that is always shadowed by loss – that of an 'other' text, an 'other' voice, an 'other' world. As Benjamin argues, translation passes through continua of transformation – to translate is to transform. My understanding of translation is 'equivalence in difference,' as Jakobson defined it (233), that is, difference that begets interpretation and critique.

In translation studies, 'translation' is usually defined as the conversion of a sign into some further alternative sign (Jakobson 232), from a source language to a target one. Standard translation focuses primarily on the rendition of verbal signs. Manifestly, pain does not originate with verbal signs. Nonetheless, pain can be conceived of as a system of signs: pain is manifested by body signs – by non-verbal neurological, physical, and/or psychological symptoms. Furthermore, social suffering, such as sexism, racism, or socioeconomic hardship, is also intimated by decipherable signs. In so doing, the translation of pain may be deemed to be a form of 'intersemiotic translation' (or transmutation), defined by Jakobson as 'an interpretation of verbal signs by means of signs of nonverbal sign systems' (233). Here, Jakobson is referring to the translation of language into music, art, dance, or other forms of expression. As Dinda Gorlée points out, in this case of 'figurative' translation, the target code is a language 'only in a metaphorical manner of speaking' (162). In like manner, if we can figuratively conceive of pain as a language, we can also engage with the intersemiotic translation of pain. My work, then, takes up Jakobson's notion of intersemiotic translation in reverse: it examines how the source language of pain may be interpreted into a verbal sign system of the target host country – in all, how immigrant writers might *translate* their pain into the written word.

Like translators, writers are faced with the difficulties of finding linguistic equivalencies for their pain – be it to describe their pain, convey its intensity, explain its cause, or specify its location. The scarcity of a direct language of pain does not mean that there is no viable mode of expression for their pain; rather, like translators, writers must engage in a variety of representational tactics to render their suffering understandable to readers. For instance, like Ovid in this chapter's introductory passage, some writers might choose to relate their pain in similes or lyrical laments, while others might insinuate it covertly in ellipses or humorous asides. Throughout this book, then, I examine various representational strategies – or forms of rhetoric – that writers might deploy to convey the sufferings of immigration.

Culture

The framework of translation also calls attention to the crucial role of culture in the expression of immigrant suffering. Culture not only affects the prose of immigrant writers, but also reflects the immigration experience; the process of acculturation may be viewed as a form of cultural translation. Moreover, it must be remembered that just as language is a social construct, so too is pain; pain is shaped by a specific culture, time, and place, and its interpretation is determined by sociocultural and political contexts.

As David Morris explains, in *The Culture of Pain*, pain is always historical: 'it is never simply a sensation but rather something that the time-bound brain interprets and that the time-bound mind constructs: a specific human artifact bearing the marks of a specific human history' (29). These sociocultural dimensions of pain cannot be underestimated in the case of the translation of immigrant pain. While some cultures, such as those influenced by Buddhism, view suffering as an inevitable part of life; in Christian contexts, by contrast, some forms of suffering are considered redemptive, just as others are considered sinful. In the case of immigrants, as discussed in the previous chapter, the oppression of certain political refugees, such as Czechs under communism, was regarded differently in public policy than, for instance, the 'economic opportunism' of Haitian boat-people.

In addition to translating the feeling of pain into symbolic signifiers, immigrant writers must also engage in some form of cultural translation. Cultural translation, as defined by Eugene Nida and Charles Taber

(1969), involves 'translation in which the content of the message is changed to conform to the receptor culture in some way, and/or in which information is introduced which is not linguistically implicit in the original' (199). As this definition demonstrates, cultural translation focuses on the target culture; its aim is to offer target recipients with as transparent a text as possible. In so doing, there is some attempt to educate target readers about elements from the source culture; however, there is also emphasis on adjusting those cultural elements so that they are not too foreign or obscure for the receiving culture to understand.

Cultural translation also deftly reflects the cultural adjustments or acculturation that immigrants face when adapting to the host culture. Already in 1944, in *The Stranger: An Essay in Social Psychology*, sociologist Albert Schutz explained that immigrants must conform their 'thinking as usual' (503) to the cultural patterns of a foreign group: 'The approaching stranger has to "translate" its terms into terms of the cultural pattern of his home group, provided that, within the latter, interpretive equivalents exist at all' (504). Interestingly, while Schutz suggests that cultural translation operates largely within the realm of language and verbal expression – in words with several connotations, idioms, and technical terms, as well as in gestures and facial expression – he also points to a category that he names language 'fringes' – the stuff of poetry, cultural memory, and historical experience (504–5). While linguistic differences and behaviour form a large part of cultural adaptation, it is the 'language fringes,' or disparate cultural understandings, that often are the hardest to convert adequately into another cultural environment.

Fifty years after Schutz, Homi Bhabha similarly described culture as the assorted 'shreds, patches and rags of daily life' (145) and posited that 'cultural performativity' was the 'space of the people' that countered the 'pedagogical' narrative of the nation (146). To theorize this resistant notion of cultural performativity, Bhabha also draws attention to the importance of 'cultural translation' (163), advocating an engagement with 'hybrid sites of meaning,' the 'foreignness of languages,' 'incommensurable differences,' and 'the double, the untranslatable – alien and foreign' to counter the authoritative and oppressive narrative of the nation (167–8).

Undeniably, the biggest threat facing cultural translation is wholesale assimilation – the loss of one's cultural identity and social and historical roots, and the erasure of one's source cultural language. In order to 'translate themselves' successfully, immigrants can either replace their culture with its equivalent in the host country, or learn to integrate their culture within the scope of the narrative of the nation. Immigrant writers face a similar choice when conveying their suffering in fiction. The easiest way to translate their sufferings would be to strip them of any cultural referents whatsoever. Another possibility is to find a cultural equivalency for their pain in the target language, a difficult operation to achieve, especially if one is a foreigner. A final option is to transpose the cultural elements directly into the host country. Such a transposition, or the transfer of elements from the source text into the target text, with minimal or no modification, would markedly preserve one's cultural identity. In this optimal case of cultural preservation, however, it is questionable whether the reader-recipient could grasp the meaning of these cultural signifiers. If a Maghrebi writer contextualizes his sufferings of immigration in terms of Scheherazade, would the narrative be understood as a means to escape death, as in the case of *The 1001 Nights*? Or how might the reader respond to a Christmas fairy tale about 'Uncle Knapsack'? Would they grasp the references to Duvalier's *tonton makoutes*? Paradoxically, as Bhabha argues, it is only through 'this foreign perspective, that it becomes possible to inscribe the specific locality of cultural systems [...] to perform the act of cultural translation' (146), which has the performative power to shape and even counter the pedagogical narrative of the nation.

Genre

In the case of immigrants, one of the main pedagogical features of the narrative of the nation is shaped by genre, specifically the genre of the immigrant narrative. Immigrant narratives are clearly subjected to structural codes or genres, also defined as 'literary or aesthetic categories' (Genette 414). Even when immigrant writers do not write within the genre of the 'immigrant narrative,' they are regularly relegated to this category, whether by the publishing industry or by the receiving readership. As Jacques Derrida states, 'every text participates in one or several genres: there is no genreless text: there is always genre and genres, yet such participation never amounts to belonging' (212). All too often, then, fiction written by immigrants is viewed as 'belonging' to the genre of the immigrant novel.

The importance of genre cannot be underestimated in the context of the translation of suffering and in its sociocultural interpretations. As

Morris explains, 'subtly or overtly, then, genre moulds facts and events to fit its contours, and a narrative of suffering will undergo subtle changes depending on whether it takes the form of a documentary film, a television miniseries, or a comic book [...] The shaping force of genre extends beyond form to meaning. In fact, audiences depend on generic patterns to provide a framework for interpretation' (34). As we have seen in the previous chapter, the genre of the immigrant novel largely influences popular understanding of the immigrant experience and the sufferings of immigration.

To reiterate, the generic immigrant narrative neutralizes immigrant suffering as a necessary part of the immigration process. In the standard immigrant narrative, as formulated by Boelhower, for instance, the structural elements – the ethnic hero, the journey of acculturation, and the trials that the hero must endure – all contribute to shaping popular misconceptions about the immigrant experience. All too often, given the emphasis on the immigrant journey, difficulties upon arrival are minimized in comparison with life in the home country. Immigrant heroes, described by Boelhower as 'naïve,' 'ignorant,' 'unassimilated,' 'hopeful initiates' (6), may be blamed for their hardships, because – as failed heroes – they lack the linguistic, social, or cultural skills to successfully manoeuvre in society. The hardships that immigrants encounter may be readily attributed to their deficient hero status, their manifest difference, or the characteristics of their ethnic group, rather than viewed as problems caused by their surrounding environment. Most saliently, in this narrative, immigrant suffering is reduced to 'a series of trials' to be resolved upon the immigrant's successful integration into the host society. As such, suffering functions as a necessary plot requirement, as in many fairy tales (Propp), Bildungsromane, 'rags-to riches stories,' or even in the prototypical Christian narrative of redemption. When regarded as a necessary plot convention, immigrant suffering risks being banalized and essentialized, rather than being deemed as a reflection of the immigrant condition. Reduced to a generic – even necessary – cliché, the suffering of immigration risks being completely dismissed. Finally, let us not forget the pedagogical purpose of the immigrant narrative: to demonstrate 'pluricultural reality' (Boelhower 6), with the immigrant hero's eventual acculturation.

As I have shown in the previous chapter, this generic immigrant structure informs many popular myths today, ranging from the myth of the American Dream, of open opportunity and social mobility, to the capitalist 'myth of success' that 'everyone can succeed, if only they work hard enough.' In academic discourse, the privileging of such concepts as hybridity, multiculturalism, and cosmopolitanism, or of facile hierarchies, such as that of the 'model minority,' disregard the sufferings of immigration. In the end, then, the *telos* of the immigrant narrative – acculturation into a pluralistic society – in fact, reflects the pedagogical narrative of the host country, as do many of the popular and academic misconceptions about immigration that reproduce it.

Target Language

These various cultural assumptions draw attention to the crucial role of the target culture in receiving and interpreting expressions of immigrant suffering. Ultimately, the translation of immigrant pain is most affected by the 'language' of the target country – its culture, its social expectations, its ideological assumptions, and its generic literary conventions. While some immigrant writers' target audience may consist of readers in their home country (as will be explored in chapters 9 and 10), many immigrant writings published in the West have their target readers in the host country, or readers in Western immigrant-receiving nations. Invariably, cultural myths about immigration circulate in both the home and host target audiences, and writers must shape their narratives so as to either reproduce or resist these cultural assumptions.

In the process of immigration, immigrants generally, like immigrant writers specifically, must also 'translate themselves' so as to satisfy the cultural, linguistic, and social expectations of the host country. As psychologist Zeev Ben-Sira argues, successful integration takes place when the demands of both immigrants and the host nation are met; these may include economic, affective, or social-political demands.[3] Immigration obviously affects the host society as a whole. It alters the social and ethnic composition of cities and neighbourhoods, and occasionally immigration even alters the composition of an entire society. Behaviour patterns in public places, at work, at home, and within the realms of economics and politics are affected by the arrival of immigrant populations. Some groups in the host society are likely to confront the changes resulting from an influx of immigrants (such as unemployment, wage cuts due to the availability of cheap labour, shifts in their urban landscape; or the need to accommodate cultural differences) with discrimination or animosity. These, in turn, are liable to provoke intergroup tensions and polarization, as we see currently in the United States and in Western Europe.

It is the receiving country that determines the nature and extent of immigrant sufferings. The host environment largely influences what types of hardships immigrants will face, and the types of physical, emotional, and/or social manifestations of pain they might experience. The target country, especially its medical and legal institutions, will be largely responsible for doubting or recognizing immigrant suffering and effectively treating it. Thus, sociocultural attitudes towards immigration cannot be underestimated, as immigrants attempt to translate their experiences to the host audience. Citizens, both in the home country and in the host country, might not be aware of the many difficulties of immigration. Some may view First World nations as the 'Promised Land' of 'milk and honey' when contrasted with the 'dirt and crime' of the developing world. Others may feel that immigrants should feel grateful for being allowed to emigrate to a 'better place' with 'more opportunity.' If immigrants complain about their immigrant hardships, these complaints may be easily dismissed or deemed to be the result of their 'choice' to immigrate. In host countries with strong national sentiments, such as France, immigrants are never expected to 'fit in'; it is presumed they will always remain 'different' from the 'pure-bred' citizens. By contrast, in countries composed of generations of immigrants, as in the case of the Canada or the United States, the hardships of immigrants might be considered a natural and commonplace requirement of the immigrant experience, as we have seen in reference to the immigrant narrative.

In many ways, then, immigrants may be considered to be sacrificial victims who, via the generic immigrant narrative, suffer in order that social discourse might continue. According to René Girard, writing in *Violence and the Sacred*: 'sacrificial substitution' (5) 'prevents the spread of violence by keeping vengeance in check' (18) and serves 'to restore harmony to the community' (7). In Western Judeo-Christian societies, the most salient example of this sacrificial suffering is Christ's sacrifice for humanity: Christ's sacrifice gained redemption for Christian believers in eternal life. Immigrants are similarly expected to suffer and sacrifice themselves through hard work, so as to be ultimately 'redeemed,' if not immediately, then surely in future generations, when their children are 'native' citizens. As we have seen in the generic immigrant narrative, however, immigrants are neither epic heroes nor saviour-figures; they are often not even individualized, but represent an 'other' ethnic collective. Moreover, they are often portrayed as deficient subordinates, who must give up much of their culture to conform to the expected reality of the nation. Finally, immigrants' sufferings seem banal in light of all the generic stories of suffering to be assimilated every day.

In all, immigrant writers face considerable obstacles in attempting to translate their pain of immigration in their fiction – obstacles related to the complexity of language, culture, genre, and assumptions of their receiving country. Their translation invariably contends with the complex task of resisting, reformulating, or reproducing prescriptive literary and sociocultural models, so as to either transform or conform to sociopolitical and cultural expectations. If their cultural translation and performance is successful, immigrant writers may effectively have the possibility of gaining voice and agency in social discourse, and they may even potentially be able to effectuate changes in the social order.

Having considered the ways in which the translation of pain is subject to the structures of language, let us now consider the effects of such language: rhetoric (effective aesthetic expression), genealogy (effective legitimation in discourse), and politics (effective representation in society) – to examine the potential effects of the translation of immigrant suffering.

The Rhetorics of Pain

For their pain to be heard and heeded by their target audience, writers must communicate their sufferings as effectively as possible. Writers must therefore engage in a rhetoric of pain. Rhetoric is generally defined as the 'art of using language so as to persuade or influence others' (*OED*). Ever since the time of the Ancient Greeks, literary theory has recognized the transformative power of rhetoric or the stirring of emotions to produce effects. As Aristotle explained, by eliciting emotions, rhetoric causes listeners 'to change their opinion in regard to their judgments' (R1378a). In many ways, then, rhetoric is closely related to translation, as, most basically, rhetoric 'creates meaning' (Booth). As Kenneth Burke explains, 'wherever there is persuasion, there is rhetoric. And wherever there is 'meaning,' there is 'persuasion" (696). The texts I consider clearly attempt to persuade their readers of the existence and meaningfulness of the sufferings of immigration. Moreover, as I.A Richards also points out, 'rhetoric is the study of misunderstanding and its remedies' (3). It may even be argued that immigrant writers may be seeking not only to diagnose their misunderstood sufferings of immigration, but also that their fiction vies to treat or remedy these sufferings.

Elaine Scarry contends 'to be in great pain is to have certainty; to hear that another person has pain is to have doubt' (7); thus communicating pain always involves persuasion, argumentation, or rhetoric on the part of the sufferer. The most unambiguous expression of pain is clearly the straightforward, declarative statement: 'I'm suffering.' However, rarely can this simple statement convey the intensity of the subject's suffering, nor is it likely to affect the reader on an emotional or intellectual level. Therefore, some form of rhetoric, or effective language is necessary to translate this pain successfully. As we have seen in the introduction to this chapter, for instance, Ovid describes the suffering of his exile in exaggerated terms; he portrays himself weeping when writing, his tears overflowing and wetting the page, or he compares his sorrow to dripping water or to fresh wounds (4:1, 96–8). When read aloud in Latin, the prolonged vowels interspersed by staccato-like consonants resemble long, drawn-out sobs, punctuated with hiccups (e.g., *umidaque est fletu littera facta meo*).

Writers have a wide variety of rhetorical strategies at their disposal to convey their suffering. Some of these strategies may be particularly explicit, such as Ovid's highly melodramatic verses of lament, while other forms of rhetoric may be implicit, such as metaphors, allusions, or humour that only intimate but do not make explicit immigrants' suffering. The scope and effects of these rhetorical strategies, however, again largely depend on the limits and possibilities of language, culture, and genre, as well as on the knowledge of the target audience. For instance, if the target audience is not familiar with a specific metaphor, or culturally does not share the same form of humour as the writer, such more implicit rhetorics of pain may be misunderstood or dismissed. In like vein, if melodramatic exaggeration becomes repeatedly reproduced in immigrant texts, they may be deemed sensationalist, cliché, or generic, and be similarly dismissed.

For the literary scholar, the rhetorics of pain are most apparent in the use of language – the grammatical syntax, style, and arsenal of literary techniques. As we have seen in Ovid, both the lachrymose lexicon and the analogously mournful rhythm create a sense of despair. In other instances, writers might convey their anger, frustration, or anxiety through exclamations, rhetorical questions, or repetitive declarative statements, or they may allude to psychological problems, such as trauma, confusion, or alienation, through repetition, fragmentation, or the use of ellipses. Certain works are characterized by literary devices that point to a particular rhetoric of pain. For instance, in *Journal 'Nationalité: immigré(e)'* (1987), writer Sakinna Boukhedenna often reveals her unhappiness using the *epimone*, or the frequent repetition of a phrase or question for emphasis, or *epiplexis*, posing questions to incite reproach rather than to elicit answers. In contrast, Mehdi Belhaj Kacem's *Cancer* (1994) abounds with technicques used to degrade the reader, such as *tapinosis*, undignified diction employed to debase a person or thing, and *bdelygmia*, a litany of abuses conveyed in a series of critical epithets or descriptions of attributes.

Rhetoric is not manifested solely through language; in certain forms of rhetoric, culture, genre, and reader expectations are also instrumental. Throughout the *Tristia*, for instance, Ovid makes numerous intertextual references to Latin texts such as the *Aeneid*, to Roman gods, and to the political events of his day, to further persuade readers of his grief. While some of these allusions might be familiar to Western readers, in another cultural context much of this rhetoric may be lost. For instance, if the target audience is unfamiliar with the cultural concepts of '*dor*' or '*saudade*'[4] then the Romanian or Brazilian writer, in this case, is forced to translate these notions into the cultural language of the host nation. Allusions to religious or cultural beliefs – to a *bokò* or a *djinn*,[5] for example – pose even greater problems to readers unfamiliar with Haitian *vodou* or Arabic cultural traditions. Genre also determines the rhetoric possible in a particular text. In legal affidavits, for instance, it is required that political refugees list their past trauma as dispassionately and accurately as possible; in an autobiographical testimonial, however, the reader might expect some form of revelatory, intimate confession.

Throughout this work, then, I explore a wide variety of rhetorics of pain. While I am interested in the linguistic aspects of these rhetorics of pain, I am primarily concerned with their cultural and generic dimensions, as I aim to examine how these cultural rhetorics are both shaped by and shape the target audience. To this end, this book explores the rhetoric of pain in a variety of cultural contexts – in North African, Caribbean, and Eastern European immigrant literature – so as to examine the rhetorics and translation of pain in the broadest scope possible. In so doing, I focus both on more explicit rhetorics of pain, as well as on more implicit ones. Part II examines the rhetorics of bodily pain in Maghrebi immigrant literature; examples of this depiction of explicit pain range from graphic scenes of corporeal violence to lurid imagery of disease. By contrast, Part III probes on more subtle cultural rhetorics of pain, specifically those implied by allusions to *vodou* in Haitian immigrant texts. Finally, the last part of the book explores the seemingly 'silent' rhetorics of pain, or the rhetorics of avoidance, allusion, and distancing in the case of Czech exile literature.

This book seeks, most of all, to investigate the intended and actual effects of these rhetorics of pain. The writer's target audience is manifestly essential in such deliberations. Again, while some authors may be addressing the general public in the host nation, others may be writing for the immigrant community abroad or for readers in their home country. In so doing, writers may be attempting either to assimilate into the host nation, or at the other extreme, they may be vociferously resisting any such acculturation. The rhetorics of pain thus vary extensively in their intended objectives. While some writers may be seeking to grant their readers a rational, intellectual, or even scholarly understanding of the pain of immigration, others may be attempting to provoke an emotional response in their readership, hoping to incite them to feel their pain empathetically or even experientially. While some writers may be writing essentially for themselves, as a form of healing or therapy, others might wish to inflict pain on their readers or rouse their feelings of remorse and responsibility.

As Richard E. Young submits, 'rhetoric is the art, method, and theory of bringing about psychological change' (xiv). Although it is difficult to ascertain the 'psychological change' intended for readers by each individual author examined in this book, I would argue that their rhetorics of pain generally tend towards two divergent ends. At one extreme are immigrant writers seeking sympathy, mutual understanding, and a sense of belonging or social integration. These writers would exemplify a view of rhetoric as formulated by Kenneth Burke: 'the ideal of rhetoric is consubstantiality; that is sympathetic understanding among all men' (55). In this view, the purpose of rhetoric would be emotional and intellectual identification, as well as positive, if not harmonious, social transformation.

At the other extreme are immigrant writers who advocate resistance and difference in their rhetoric of pain. Some immigrant writing may be antagonistic to the host nation, critical of or resistant to normative social discourse, or seeking to assert or reinforce the writer's specific cultural or ethnic identity. Such an oppositional rhetoric of pain is perhaps best described by George Lamming, in his The Pleasures of Exile (1992). Arguing that violence is an inevitable part of the postcolonial nation-building experience, Lamming clamours for 'present exercises in anger' (44) to both represent and resist this violence. He argues that a rhetoric of violence is necessary to heal the wounds of the violated subject: 'It seems to me that there is almost a therapeutic need for a certain kind of violence in the breaking. There cannot be a parting of the ways. There has to be a smashing' (45). Lamming posits this rhetoric of violence as a means of curbing and transforming the structural external violence that postcolonial subjects may face. Immigrants, as well, might turn to aggressive rhetorics to resist their oppression, or even therapeutically, to purge themselves through such rhetorics of violence.

The intended effects of rhetorics of pain may thus range from emotional and intellectual attachment to differentiation and retribution – from a politics of 'ideal consubstantiality' to a politics of 'violence.' In the end, perhaps the most powerful function of these rhetorics of suffering is their sociopolitical and cultural role. Apart from their aesthetic, literary, and sociocultural effects, rhetorics of pain might also serve a purpose in the public forum. Adeptly employed, rhetorics of pain might offer the immigrant subject representation, agency, voice, and even power in social discourse. I now turn to the role of pain in discourses of power to examine the possibilities, and limits, of such politics of pain for immigrant writers who engage in rhetorics of suffering.

The Politics of Pain

Pain has always played an important role in social discourse. We can easily bring to mind sacrificial rites in ancient cultures, spectacles of pain in the Roman Coliseum, the torture techniques of the Inquisition, or even current 'intelligence operations' of Americans at Abu Ghraib or Guantanamo Bay. Having already briefly discussed the role of sacrifice as a means of restoring social harmony (see, e.g., Girard), I would now like to address the role of pain in gaining and maintaining power, by referring to the theories of Friedrich Nietzsche. Nietzsche's work offers important criticism about the role of pain in social discourse and the uses and abuses of pain as an instrument of power. In particular, his discussions of the ascetic priest or in his formulation of the 'power of the weak' and his notion of *ressentiment*, Nietzsche grants us insight into the ways in which individuals may gain power and authority. Nietzsche's observations about the politics of pain inform the theorization of such scholars as René Girard, and they have been further developed in feminist criticism to examine current practices in American identity politics. Nietzsche's theories of the politics of pain and contemporary theories about the role of pain in U.S. identity politics are both crucial paradigms to consider when analysing how the suffering minority subject, such as the immigrant, may gain effective authority, agency, and voice in social discourse.

The Role of Pain in Social Discourse

Nietzsche argues, most comprehensively in *On the Genealogy of Morals* (GM), that the interpretation of suffering plays a crucial role in the discourse of power. For Nietzsche, 'Why do I suffer?' represents humankind's fundamental existential question. The answer to this question – the interpretation of suffering – intimates the explanation, justification, and narration of 'the meaning of life': '[Man] did not know how to justify, explain, affirm himself, he suffered from the problem of his meaning [...] his problem, however, was not suffering itself, but rather the absence of an answer to his questioning cry: "*Why do I suffer?*"' (GM 3.29). On an individual level, a rationalization for one's suffering might be formulated by a coherent and convincing personal narrative. Similarly, on a collective level, so that the given interpretation of suffering is adequate, it must be generally agreed upon and sustained; thus it requires consensus and constant reaffirmation. The task of the social order is to offer an accepted, authoritative explanation and justification for suffering – in much the same way as the individual must fashion a rational and persuasive narrative to rationalize his or her own individual suffering. The social order thus establishes itself as an authorial and authoritative power. Once a social explanation for suffering is legitimized, any attempts to deconstruct it or deviate from it prove threatening, as they risk destabilizing this authoritative power.

The social order maintains its power partly by inflicting pain as punishment. As Nietzsche states that pain is the *mnemotechnics*, the means by which memory is created: '"Something is branded in, so that it stays in the memory: only that which hurts incessantly is remembered" this is a central proposition of the oldest (and unfortunately also the most enduring) psychology on earth' (GM 2.3). Here, Nietzsche alludes to public displays of pain as such as torture, hangings, or executions. In such public shows of punishment, both the insubordinate individual who suffers excruciating bodily pain and the collective masses who witness these painful events learn to 'remember' the narrative of the social order and the memorable structures that enforce it. Today we no longer attend public executions or tortures; nonetheless, the media ensure that we remember the nation's narrative, whether through pain-filled scenes of the 9/11 demolition of the Twin Towers or scary images of 'Arab terrorists' brandishing guns. In contrast, by omitting to show certain details, such as the plight of Haitian refugees in detention in U.S. prisons, or the treatment of 'suspected terrorists' such as Canadian citizen Maher Arar, the media conveniently make us forget those elements that do not fit cohesively into the national narrative. In the case of immigrants, certain institutions either legitimate or discredit immigrant suffering, including legal institutions, medical institutions, and literary and cultural institutions. As such, the suffering in immigrant novels reflects the ways in which institutions maintain their power by interpreting pain, and the ways in which immigrants either struggle or succumb to these interpretations in their own politics of pain.

Pain as Power: The Ascetic Priest

Nietzsche puts forth two main models by which the individual can engage in the politics of pain to gain power. The first is that of the ascetic priest, who in many ways deploys and reproduces Christian ideology to gain power. In Nietzsche's view, Christianity perpetuates a particularly abusive interpretation of suffering. Founded on the binaries of good and evil, virtue and sin, and just and unjust suffering, Christianity contends that suffering is the ultimate good and that weakness is strength. Central to Christian belief is that Christ, the Son of God, died for the sins of humankind in a final sacrificial act of unconditional love, thus redeeming humanity for all time. The highest form of virtue, goodness, or justice in Christian morality, therefore, is to suffer for others. Nietzsche finds this concept of salvific suffering wholly repugnant; for him, it creates a society of passive victims who find power in weakness. Such a world-view is antithetical to Nietzsche's ideal of the noble man, who finds strength in self-creative power.

Nietzsche especially attacks the ascetic priest, who elevates 'selflessness, self-denial and self-sacrifice' to 'an ideal, a kind of beauty' (GM 3.18), and for whom 'pleasure is felt and *sought* in ill-constitutedness, decay, pain, mischance, ugliness, voluntary deprivation, self-mortification, self-flagellation, self-sacrifice' (GM 3.11) – in all who finds 'triumph in the ultimate agony' (GM 3.11). The ascetic priest employs pain to justify his own worth and maintains power and authority by validating his suffering or by discrediting the suffering of others. The ascetic priest turns the direction of the suffering upon himself, and poisons himself and others by advancing such notions as guilt, debt, atonement, deprivation, or self-blame. Nietzsche condemns the ascetic priest as a *'life-inimical* species' (GM 3.11), who denies life itself in all of its sensual and physical pleasure, and worse, who corrupts and poisons the minds of others around him.

Nietzsche's comments about Christianity and the ascetic priest are relevant to these immigrant novels, as we consider the politics of pain, and thus power, that they propagate. As I have shown in the genre of the immigrant novel, 'a series of trials' is often deemed necessary or a prerequisite for success. When reading these texts, we should ask ourselves if these immigrants establish their identities and authority by appealing to suffering as an ascetic ideal, a higher good. Do some authors gain authority and power by their valorization of suffering? Do the characters in these novels elevate 'self-lessness, self-denial and self-sacrifice' as 'an ideal, a kind of beauty' (GM 2.18)? Or, in another vein, how many of these immigrants are infected by internalized guilt and self-blame by 'priests' currently in power? We might, for instance, relate these 'priests' to the former colonizers, who inflicted a sense of internalized oppression on colonized peoples, or the Communist regime, which denounced emigrants as traitors to the nation and attempted to cultivate emigrants' sense of guilt and betrayal. Nietzsche's portrait of the ascetic priest thus points to problems of self-perpetuated, passive victimhood as an instrument of power. When reading these novels, therefore, it is important to consider whether the representation of pain grants these authors special power or moral authority.

The Power of the Weak: Ressentiment

Nietzsche also identifies a politics of pain that the 'weak' may deploy to gain power, in his notion of *ressentiment* – a precarious politics of power, with both destructive and creative potential. Generally, Nietzsche condemns *ressentiment,* or resentment stemming from a sense of inferiority and frustration, which often leads to revenge, cruelty, and violence, and in which the individual defines himself or herself with respect to the other. For Nietzsche, *ressentiment* forms the basis of 'slave morality' which exists in contrast to the 'master morality,' of the noble man: 'while the noble man lives in trust and openness with himself [...] the man of *ressentiment* is neither upright nor naïve nor honest nor straightforward with himself. His soul squints' (GM 1.10). Ironically, though, as Tobin Siebers (1988) has shown, Nietzsche himself never escapes his own *ressentiment* in his reaction to Christianity, or in his polemics against it.

In some of his discussions, however, Nietzsche attributes to *ressentiment* certain positive qualities related to his own philosophy of self-creation. The most salient examples of *ressentiment*'s creative possibilities are found in his description of 'the slave revolt in morals' – the revolt that would enable those marginalized in society to resist the subordination and violence inflicted on them:

> The slave revolt in morals begins when *ressentiment* itself becomes creative and ordains values: the *ressentiment* of creatures to whom the real reaction, that of the deed, is denied and who find compensation in an imaginary revenge. While all noble morality grows from a triumphant affirmation of its self, slave morality from the outset says no to an 'outside,' to an 'other,' to a 'non-self': and this no is its creative act. The reversal of the evaluating gaze – this necessary orientation outwards rather than inwards to the self – belongs characteristically to *ressentiment*. (GM 1.10)

This 'slave revolt,' which has its foundation in *ressentiment*, urges individuals to identify the sources of their resentment and to work against them in a vehement 'no' directed at everything outside, thus overcoming them in an act of dissent. *Ressentiment* therefore bears creative possibilities: described as a creative moment, it originates from a rise of consciousness and leads to acts of resistance that brings about a transformation of societal values. Moreover, Nietzsche points out that *ressentiment* does not necessarily always entail direct revolt, but also manifests itself in 'clever' strategies, which include a 'perfect understanding of how to keep silent, how not to forget, how to wait, how to make himself provisionally small and submissive' (GM 1.10). Nietzsche suggests that, if the weak learn to correctly employ the strategies of *ressentiment*, they might even overcome the noble race: 'A race of such men of *ressentiment* is bound to become eventually cleverer than any noble race' (GM 1.10). In fact, Nietzsche even goes so far as to term 'the instincts of reaction and *ressentiment* as the real instruments of culture' (GM 1.11).

Contemporary theorists similarly emphasize the productive power of *ressentiment* as a rise to consciousness. Eric Gans suggests that *ressentiment* points towards the notion of 'significance' in Western discourse (143). Citing examples from the Bible and Greek mythology, Gans shows how *ressentiment* drives individuals to assert their own significance, precisely in their victimhood, or their apparent secondary status: 'What is intuitively grasped is the self-as-victim [...] it is the victimary position, not the dominant one, that has been from the beginning of central significance' (61). As Gans cautions, however, the value of *ressentiment* does not merely lie in its consciousness-raising potential, but, rather, it rests in its transformative possibilities – in its creative attempts to transcend the victim status (64). To be a 'real instrument of culture,' a creative act of *ressentiment* entails a continuous process of transformation, and of overcoming, those elements within the social order that are deemed non-significant. Such transformation can only be achieved if the subject is no longer dependent on the Other for definition, or operating in response to the Other, to take up Nietzsche's main criticism of *ressentiment* as a reaction (GM 1.10).

Such formulations of *ressentiment* are critical when considering immigrant texts. Marginalized in both social and literary discourse, immigrants often find themselves, as Gans might argue, asserting their significance. Much of their writing manifests a rise to consciousness, affirming the value of the victim position in social discourse. How can these immigrant writers assert their significance without resorting to resentment? As Nietzsche and Gans have argued, for *ressentiment* to lead to a successful revolt, it must be a creative act of dissent that ultimately leads to transcendence. Might we consider some elements in these texts to be creative acts of dissent? Do they rise above resentment, so as to engage in a 'transformation of the old strategies of significance' (Gans 64)? Or do they remain powerless, cultivating their resentment with a rhetoric of pain? How are we to respond to the resentment that does appear in these texts? These are important questions to consider when examining the rhetorics of pain in these texts and their effects in social discourse.

In all, Nietzsche's arguments may easily be elaborated in the context of immigrant suffering. Manifestly, then, the pain of immigration is interpreted differently in social discourses than it is by immigrants in their personal narratives. While social discourse aims to legitimate and reaffirm its interpretation of immigrant suffering in order to maintain social control, immigrant writers must choose to either reflect or resist this normative social interpretation of suffering. In so doing, they are confronted with the politics of pain, or the uses and abuses of pain for either gaining or maintaining power. On the one hand, like the ascetic priest, writers can reappropriate suffering as a means of gaining power and authority, validating self-sacrifice, self-denial, and suffering in general. On the other hand, they might resist power, by engaging in some form of *ressentiment*. While this 'power of the weak' grants writers some possibilities of resistance, self-awareness, and significance, it is not without its dangers – specifically those of creating one's self solely in reaction to others, and of affirming one's authority in victimhood.

Nietzsche's theorizations of the role of pain in social discourse, and the resulting politics of pain, are clearly pertinent today, with respect to the immigrant texts I discuss, and more generally, in light of minority discourse. Contemporary theorists, notably feminists, have referred to Nietzsche's associations of pain and power to explicate current trends in U.S. identity politics in particular, a topic I now wish to address in more detail, so as to draw out further possibilities and limitations of a politics of pain.

Identity Politics and the Limits of Victimhood

Identity politics is a political stance that views group identity as the foundation for social analysis and political action. In line with Nietzsche's theories, certain contemporary feminist scholars have been instrumental in showing that a rhetoric of pain is a fundamental feature of current U.S. identity politics. Lauren Berlant, for instance, has even labelled U.S. identity politics a 'literacy program in the alphabet of pain' ('The Subject' 33), a rudimentary language of victimization, characterized by many instances of suffering, pain, and trauma. As increased globalization leads to diminished national control (exemplified, for instance, by the creation of the European Union), I believe this 'alphabet of pain' is not limited to the United States, but is increasingly becoming a global lingua franca, as I will reveal in the following chapters, with examples ranging from Algeria to the Czech Republic.

To briefly review, this 'pain-filled' identity politics has developed in the past decade, when, as feminists have shown, social discourse moved from the 'politics of redistribution,' which sought to reveal structural inequalities, to a 'politics of recognition' (Fraser), in which political claims are forged by claims of identity, based on singular categorizations and linked to identity politics. The search for authenticity has driven many minority groups to speak from a victim position of woundedness, where pain offers a singular, originary, and thus irrefutable experience. Wendy Brown is perhaps the most important feminist critic to have shown the perilous overvaluation of pain in feminist (and by extension minority) discourse. Brown put forward the concept of 'wounded attachment,' developed from Nietzsche's notion of *ressentiment*, to refer to a process whereby minorities all too often focus exclusively on their woundedness – the particular and particularizing injuries inflicted on them by the oppressive dominant discourse – in order to establish their subject position, voice, and agency in social discourse.

Brown's work reveals the problematical way in which this pain-filled identity politics operates. As Brown explains, narrating experiences of pain, hurt and oppression are increasingly granting minority groups moral authority and legitimacy; progressively, only those who have suffered have the legitimate right to speak on behalf of the group. Because such pain-filled experiences become the basis of knowledge and moral authority, all members of the group begin to particularize and substantiate their wounds, and to own and prove their personal suffering, so as to confirm their identity. As a result, these 'logics of pain' engender a particular form of politics that is profoundly self-centred, focuses fixedly on its woundedness, and celebrates misery. Finally, woundedness, or the structure of wounding that these groups seek to overcome, actually becomes fetishized as a proof of identity, so that, in the end, it becomes hyper-valorized as a means of gaining power. As Brown shows, 'wounded attachments' prove dangerous: referring to Nietzsche's concept of *ressentiment*, they 'rely upon a negative stance that only says "no"; its only creative deed is to refuse' (Bell 61). In sum, in this discourse of victimization, experiences of pain become the impetus for creating a subject position, leading to the danger that pain becomes so overinscribed that subject positions are always already determined by it. Moreover, when adopting these positions of pain, victim-subjects seemingly never escape their position of ascetic suffering or resentful victimization.

Brown's work also offers a caustic critique of the victimization that this politics of pain entails, a critique almost as scathing as Nietzsche's. In this discourse of 'wounded attachments,' Brown argues, individual subjectivity is not defined by the ability to act, work, or think; rather, it becomes defined by whether the individual has endured violence intimately, as a passive victim. Such self-perpetuating passivity clearly relates to the permanent weakness that Nietzsche despises in the petty victims of social order, as well as to their resentment, which seems to be their only slavish morality. Furthermore, subjects in pain are likely to remain in this painful position, in a groove of self-repetition and habituated resentment, as it is this inaccessible locus of personal pain that grants them power and authority to speak as subjects, and more fundamentally, creates their identities and subject positions. Brown's critique speaks directly to my own work – to what extent do immigrant texts define immigrant subjectivity as a self-perpetuating, passive victimhood? To what extent do they remain imbedded in a locus of woundedness – or claim, maintain, and perform pain to gain an identity?

Also important, Brown stresses, is the relativization of pain that victim politics engenders. Since everyone poses as a victim, pain becomes a common denominator, and all personal stories become equated with narratives of individual personal trauma. Since everyone wants to participate in political discourse, everyone seeks to hold and own his or her own singular wound, which gives him or her both power and identity. Competition arises as every group attempts to legitimate its particular wounds and grant validation to the mechanics of its trauma. The pain of other groups is all too often dismissed as members attempt to justify their own pain. No one heeds the pain of others; pain becomes reified, banalized – and denied. So, while pain grants subjects a voice in dominant discourse, ultimately these individual voices of pain are drowned out by the cacophony of other voices clamouring their suffering. Again, one may ask, to what extent does the pain of immigration grant immigrants a privileged identity? Or by contrast, to what extent is their suffering dismissed and denied in light of the many other, always more shocking instances of trauma in the world?

Invariably, in such politics of pain, certain types of pain are privileged as opposed to other types, resulting in a hierarchization of pain. The more traumatic and shocking the pain, the more recognition and power can be gained. As Beverly Skeggs explains, in 'The Rhetorical Affects of Feminism,' the shock of trauma often eclipses less sensational forms of violence: 'The currency of distress has led to a displacement whereby awareness of everyday structural adversity on a daily basis is eclipsed by the accounts of exceptional, personal, traumatic pain' (28). Skeggs contrasts the role of trauma, an exceptional, singular event, to the quotidian suffering that people experience because of poverty, inequality, and injustice. In my opinion, this criticism gives perspective to more recent theoretical work on trauma studies (and now, 'terror studies'), which all too often emphasizes singular shocking suffering and therefore shifts the emphasis away from everyday oppression. For immigrants, certainly, everyday subordination plays a greater role in their lives than sensational traumatic events, and yet, immigrant narratives most often highlight these extraordinary circumstances.

Finally, feminist theorists have also questioned the effects of such politics of pain in the realm of legal and public policy, and social discourse more generally. In 'The Subject of True Feeling,' Lauren Berlant seriously interrogates 'the politics of true feeling' as a regime of truth and knowledge: 'What does it mean for the struggle to shape collective life when a politics of true feeling organizes so much analysis, discussion, fantasy, and policy [...] when feeling, the most subjective thing [...] takes over the space of ethics and truth?' (35). Instead of facts, empirical evidence, or established patterns, in this pain-filled discursive formation, it is 'true feeling,' and especially the 'shock of pain,' that produces clarity, despite the fact that such shock can also generate confusion, panic, or inaccuracy (35). In law, then, Berlant shows that pain as a sign of injustice provides an unreliable basis for justice claims, most saliently 'because [only] some groups can articulate their identities with reference to wounds and pain (and only some would want to do so)' (29). In the context of immigrant texts, therefore, it is vital to bear in mind that certain types of pain remain unspoken, and certain immigrant groups remain unheard. As we shall see in the chapters on Czech exile literature, the sufferings of Czech emigrants were intentionally silenced in their fiction, as well as deliberately stifled by the reading audience. More saliently, it is crucial to remember that certain types of suffering do not make it into literary fiction, such as the experience of modern slaves or illegal labourers. In contrast to the ubiquitous genre of the immigrant novel, there is no comparable genre of the illegal migrant narrative.

In the end, as Berlant posits, such a politics of pain, in effect, serves to corroborate the national narrative and its assumed aims of justice, morality, and goodness. In this discursive formation, 'feeling bad becomes evidence for a structural condition of injustice,' and 'feeling good becomes evidence of justice's triumph' (35), a dichotomy that reaffirms the 'redemptive notion of law as the guardian of public good' and the telos of the nation-state: 'to eradicate systemic social pain' (34).

Such a formulation, however, is a myth, as Berlant points out, a particularly seductive one at that, especially for more privileged members of society. It appeases the guilt of these privileged and partial parties and mitigates their responsibility in dealing with social ills; for, eventually, the nation will fix all these social problems. Moreover, all of these 'bad feelings' experienced by others can easily be distanced, either reduced to subjective experiences or reified into a generalized reflection of social dis-ease. In this discursive formation, all 'subaltern pain is deemed in this context universally intelligible, constituting objective evidence of trauma reparable by the law' (34). Thus, as pain becomes the basis of justice claims, truth, and knowledge in legal discourse and public policy, it becomes normative, universally intelligible, and generic – and serves to validate the ideal, reparative role of social institutions.

Translating the Politics of Immigrant Pain

In sum, Nietzsche and contemporary feminist theorists put forward challenging criticism of the politics of pain – be it the limitations of pain as truth and knowledge, the perils of perpetrating passive victimhood, the shock of trauma in contrast to ordinary oppression, or the relativization or normalization of pain. Given these numerous difficulties, how do immigrant writers translate the politics of pain in their work? Do they reproduce the problems inherent in current identity politics or do they somehow evade them? In all, the suffering in immigrant fiction cannot be read indiscriminately, but rather, in terms of the effects it produces and the power it holds in social discourse.

    When considering the role of these immigrant texts in social discourse, it is crucial to stress that, unlike Nietzsche's ascetic priest or the many feminists privileged enough to articulate their 'wounded attachments,' the immigrants I examine in these texts are generally not in positions of power. On the contrary, North African and Haitian immigrants represent groups often excluded and marginalized in the social order; on the whole, they stand for the silenced, powerless victims of current global politics. Immigrant writers from these regions are unlikely to gain social recognition or influence when writing about their hardships of immigration, nor are they likely to gain literary authority by writing texts labelled as 'personal narratives' or classified under the generic rubric of 'immigrant novels.' Most of the works I analyse are not considered canonical literature, but, rather, are dismissed as marginalia. Many are out of print only a few years after their publication. To emphasize my point, it is perhaps vital to note that only five of the more than forty novelists that I investigate in the following chapters have been translated into English (Kundera, Etienne, Danticat, Laferrière, and Sebbar).

As for the sufferings of immigration translated in these texts, rarely are they shocking or scandalous enough to jolt us into an awareness or concern for immigrant hardships. Loneliness, alienation, poverty, hunger, exploitation, discrimination, racism – most of these misfortunes can be easily dismissed as characteristic features of the human condition. The few traumatizing incidents of rape, mutilation, or suicide in these texts might similarly be dismissed in light of the graphic scenes of war, sexual abuse, and murder that we vicariously experience every day through the media.

In the end, I would argue that these immigrant writers find themselves writing about immigrant pain not in accordance with the ever-increasing politics of pain, but rather in spite of it, in the face of it, and in reaction to it. Just as they are faced with translating their sufferings into the conventions of language, culture, and genre, immigrant writers are faced with the problem of expressing their pain in our current era of trauma victimization and identity politics of pain.

Indeed, how are immigrants to translate their hardships of immigration in light of the contemporary currency of distress – this 'alphabet of pain,' 'wounded attachments,' and the 'politics of true feeling'? What of the other many constraints they face when translating their pain – be they generic, linguistic, cultural, or sociopolitical? What rhetorics of pain are they to deploy so that the sufferings of immigration may be heard and heeded? These are the questions I will attempt to answer as I examine the rhetoric of pain in various cultural contexts.

PART II

Embodying Pain:
Maghrebi Immigrant Texts

3 'Mal Partout': Bodily Rhetoric in Maghrebi Immigrant Fiction

Il a mal au ventre, dans la tête, dans le dos, il a mal partout. Il souffre atrocement, son visage est éloquent, c'est une souffrance qui en impose.
– Qu'est ce que c'est mon ami ?
– Je vais mourir, monsieur le docteur.
La voix est cassé, imperceptible.
– Où as-tu mal ?
– Partout, monsieur le docteur.[1]

> – Frantz Fanon, 'Le "syndrome nord-africain"'

'Mal Partout'

In 1952, some years before writing the canonical *Black Skin, White Masks* (1968), Frantz Fanon penned a brief article on a 'syndrome' affecting immigrant patients from the Maghreb – Tunisia, Algeria, and Morocco – living in France. Fanon observes that they all exhibit a similar set of symptoms: they insistently complain of indefinable, yet ubiquitous, body pain, that they often dramatize performatively (239). The conclusions of Fanon's diagnosis? Maghrebi immigrants are deprived of expressing their affectivity (247). Until they are allowed to express their affective experience, they will continue to somatize their sufferings of immigration, be it their isolation (243), insecurity (245), sexual frustration (244), or their socioeconomic preoccupations (243).

Thirty years later, neuropsychiatrist Robert Jarret characterizes the symptomatic 'bodily performance'[2] of Maghrebi patients as '*mal partout'* – 'pain-everywhere': 'I won't even elaborate on the *mal partout* that we have all had occasion to observe in the case of Maghrebi migrants. The complaint is monotonous, stereotypical, insistent, annoying; verbal expression is often poor, and the imagery almost non-existent' (1721).[3] Like Fanon (239), Jarret describes the symptomatology of this *mal partout* as ambiguous and its etiology, as indeterminate. Vague, poorly expressed, and lacking in imagery, this pain appears as 'inclassable' in terms of nosology, the medical categorization of diseases (Jarret 1721). Nonetheless, Maghrebi patients plaintively and persistently insist on the presence and intensity of their pain, to the point that their complaints prove 'stereotypical' and 'annoying.'

Jarret also notes that Maghrebi patients embody 'hysterical theatrics' – screams, stereotypical exclamations, vertigo, and dramatic falls – to emphasize their suffering, 'putting on a performance in the theatrical sense of the word' (1721). Patients fluctuate between such hysterical theatrics and adynamia, depression, and apathy. As a result of these 'ritualistic bodily performances,' like in the 1950s (Fanon 239), Maghrebi patients in the 1980s are also often dismissed as 'pretenders, hysterics, hypochondriacs, psychoneurotics, etc.' (Jarret 1721).

Intrigued by his patients' ubiquitous and often theatrical bodily pain, Jarret explores its etiology and pathogenesis – why Maghrebi immigrants perform such generalized or dramatic bodily pain. Jarret posits that immigrants may turn to their bodies because they are marked by ethnocultural stereotypes. He hypothesizes that this somatization may be cultural in origin. He also suggests that patients engage in a sort of 'rite of allegiance with the doctor who actualizes the complaint' (1721), as the doctor must recognize their suffering, diagnose it, and adequately treat it.

In the end, though, like Fanon, Jarret correlates this corporeal rhetoric to the Maghrebi immigrant condition. For example, he suggests that Maghrebi immigrants use the body as a 'defensive cultural tool against acculturation' in an attempt to be 'authenticated, distinguished as individuals, as suffering subjects,' as well as demanding 'reparative healing on an unattainable, socioeconomic level' (1721). In his English abstract, Jarret sums up the situation, stating that 'the necessity to communicate, to exist again, finds its justification through the channel of corporal complaint [...] particularly for the Maghrebian, the damaged body-tool needing repair is a current representation which has the meaning of a cry for help' (1723). The body, evoked as a broken 'body-tool,' effectively translates the status of many Maghrebi immigrants as disenfranchised workers in French society. Their pain-filled 'cry for help' points to the emergency of their situation and their urgent need for relief. However, corporal complaints not only serve to communicate immigrants' pressing sociocultural marginalization, they may even enable immigrants to 'exist again.' As their pain is recognized and treated by the medical establishment, Maghrebi patients may find acknowledgment for their personhood, and even, perhaps, their social suffering, that is otherwise lacking in their social environment. Thus, some patients may effectively create a new identity for themselves through their corporeal suffering.

Numerous physicians and psychologists have observed the somatic pain of Maghrebi immigrants, although few have related it as eloquently to the immigrant condition as have Fanon or Jarret. Discussions of generic *mal partout* are complemented by studies of its symptomatic aspects, such as its urogenital manifestations or male sexual impotence.[4] Notably, Tahar Ben Jelloun (1977), one of the most respected French-Maghrebi novelists, wrote his doctoral thesis in psychiatry on the affective and sexual problems of first-generation immigrants.[5] In the past twenty years, the ethnopsychology of Maghrebi immigration has become an established field in medical practice; such ethnopsychiatrists as Tobie Nathan (1986, 1988), Claude Mesmin (1993, 1995) and Nathan (2001), and Abdessalem Yahyahoui (1989) have researched the particularities of the Maghrebi medical condition, including elective mutism, intergenerational disorders, and diverse neuroses or psychoses, often in terms of Arab, Muslim, or Kabyle cultures, as well as in terms of the immigrant condition.

The 'Diagnosis': Bodily Rhetoric in Maghrebi Immigrant Fiction

In literature, as in psychology, the reader is similarly often overwhelmed by the numerous instances of bodily pain and injury in Maghrebi immigrant texts. Immigrant workers are frequently portrayed as disabled or maimed; immigrant heroes are repeatedly marked by wounds or scars; and most plots delve into circumstances of brutality and violence. In Mehdi Charef's classic, *Le Thé au harem d'Archi Ahmed* (1983), for instance, we are shocked by violent scenes of suicide and drug overdose. The recent Beur (second-generation French-Maghrebi) best-seller, *Dans l'enfer des tournantes* (2002), by Samira Bellil, concentrates almost exclusively and graphically on the trauma of rape. The body, therefore, and in particular the wounded body, represents an important theme in Maghrebi immigrant fiction.

Many Maghrebi writers describe their work in terms of bodily rhetoric. Tahar Ben Jelloun, for example, sums up his first immigrant novel, *La Réclusion solitaire* (1976), as a body in disguise, 'ce livre est un corps travesti' (126). Writer and artist Mustapha Raïth explains that the rise to consciousness of the immigrant is explicitly visceral: 'It's physical, from the gut, the consciousness of this fatally incurable uprooting that brings about a merciless struggle' (7). In his novella *L'Entre-Deux Vies* (1999), Bouabdellah Adda sums up his authorial position as 'writing so as to no longer know who I am, my hero or my pain' (79).

Conspicuously, despite the pervasiveness of bodily imagery and rhetoric in Maghrebi immigrant fiction, unlike in psychology, there has been no in-depth examination of this phenomenon in literary criticism. Certainly, various literary scholars have pointed to instances of the body or woundedness in specific Maghrebi texts; however, no one has yet comprehensively examined the role of the body in Maghrebi immigrant fiction, or deliberated its import for literary criticism.

Like Fanon, I posit that Maghrebi immigrant literature, and immigrant literature as a whole, cannot be understood if its affective dimensions remain dismissed. This part of the book, therefore, offers a preliminary 'diagnosis' of various fictional manifestations of bodily pain in Maghrebi fiction. This chapter surveys the generalized sense of *mal partout* or *malaise* in Maghrebi immigrant texts. The following chapters focus on more specific corporeal symptomatology – such as injury, disability, mutism, hysteria, depression, or disease – that affect particular segments of the French-Maghrebi population, depending on their occupation, social class, and generational and gender status. Like medical researchers, upon presenting my 'diagnosis,' I also submit an 'etiology' of sorts: I theorize why Maghrebi immigrant writers so often draw on the body and somatize their sufferings of immigration. Unlike psychologists, however, who are primarily concerned with understanding the psyche of actual patients, my analysis investigates the body as an effect of language – or as rhetoric – in fictional representations. Concomitantly, I examine the function and effects of this bodily rhetoric in Maghrebi immigrant fiction, while alluding to its role in literature more generally.

'Malaise Partout':
Generalized Dis-ease in Maghrebi Immigrant Texts

Maghrebi immigrants occupy a precarious position in France. As a result of decolonization in the 1960s and 1970s, and the Algerian civil war in the 1990s, there are an estimated five million Maghrebi immigrants in France today. It is difficult to determine exact population statistics for Maghrebi persons living in France, however, because the French government prohibits utilizing ethnic or religious affiliation in census data. Additionally, because of the many difficulties of acquiring legal immigrant status, many Maghrebis have never become citizens; although they have resided in France for most of their lives. Over the years, several governmental measures have sought to restrict the immigrant population in France, and as a result, many Maghrebi individuals find themselves living and working in France illegally. Generally, Maghrebis are marginalized in French society, confined to HLM (low-cost housing) on the outskirts of large cities, relegated to low-paying jobs, restricted to inferior schools, and largely underrepresented in politics and the media.

It is important to recognize that there are discrete generations of Maghrebi immigrants, each of which experiences the immigration process differently, depending on age, class, and gender status. The first generation of immigrants, male Magrebian workers, came to France between the 1940s and the 1970s as manual labourers. Many of these Maghrebi men were joined by their wives and children after 1974, when a French family reunion law allowed women to rejoin their husbands working in France. Since the 1980s, the Beurs, or second-generation French-Maghrebis, have become an increasingly important minority group in French cosmopolitan society. As I will flesh out in the following chapters, each of these groups – the 'fathers,' 'mothers,' and immigrant 'children'[6] – engage in a different bodily rhetoric to emphasize their particular difficulties of immigration, as 'labouring bodies,' 'gendered bodies,' or 'ethnic bodies.'

The position of Maghrebi immigrant writers proves particularly problematical. As Alec Hargreaves has pointed out, the term *écrivain immigrant* – immigrant writer – is rarely deployed to characterize these authors, as it implies a paradox of sorts: *écrivain* denotes a relatively esteemed social position, while *immigrant* is generally associated with a low-class, blue-collar social sector (7). When immigrant writing first appeared in France, in the 1980s, it was often categorized as *éthnographie de banlieue,* or 'ghetto ethnographies.' In the past twenty years, French-Maghrebi writing has gained considerable recognition; however, it still has not attained the status of mainstream French literature. A cursory visit to most bookstores reveals that Maghrebi authors are frequently not shelved alongside French writers as *littérature française,* but are relegated to *littérature étrangère,* the foreign literature sections of the store, usually under the heading 'Maghreb.' Moreover, only the best-known Maghrebi authors are found in general bookstores; the majority of books analysed in this chapter, for example, are only available in specialized libraries.

Stemming from this marginalization, a feeling of generalized sociocultural dis-ease permeates Maghrebi immigrant texts, which closely relates to the French word *malaise,* a condition attributed to the *banlieues* since the 1980s (Amara 64). At first glance, the titles of many of these immigrant novels draw attention to immigrants' feelings of spatiotemporal dislocation, cultural loss, and identitary confusion. Consider the following titles: *Une fille sans histoire* (Girl without History), *Zeida de nulle part* (Zeida from Nowhere), *L'Entre-Deux Vies* (Between Lives), *Journal 'Nationalité: immigré(e)'* (Journal 'Nationality: Immigrant'), or *Les ANI du Tassili.* In the last example, 'ANI' stands for *'arabes non-identifiés'* ('unidentified Arabs'), which, much like the U.S.'s 'non-resident aliens,' suggests UFOs, or OVNI in French. All of these titles denote feelings of loss – be it a missing past, missing spatiotemporal markers, or missing national affiliation – and connote an alienated sense of identity.

Stylistically, these texts are generally characterized by ambiguity, denoting the subjective and epistemic uncertainty of Maghrebi immigrants. Immigrants' initial disorientation – their long-term dislocation and iterative exclusion – is manifested textually by ambiguous and incomplete sentences, repetition, and rhetorical questions. In all, a discernible rhetoric of *pathos* permeates these texts. In Ancient Greece, the classical rhetoric of *pathos* emphasized a speaker's psychological state and sought to evoke an emotional response from the reader, be it anger, pity, or patriotism. The literary critic often notices classical figures of speech associated with *pathos* in these Maghrebi texts, especially those expressions linked to uncertainty. For example, the reader often finds repetitions for rhetorical effect, such as *diacope* and *epimone*, persistent pleas or reiterated expressions of deep feeling. Inner turmoil is connoted by *ellipses* and *aposiopesis*, a sudden breaking off in speech to portray overwhelming emotion. There are many instances of *adynaton*, which refers to the impossibility of expression, as well as *aporia*, expressions denoting confusion or doubt. In particular, I was struck by how many Maghrebi novels begin with negative constructions, most notably with the words *je ne sais pas* – 'I don't know.'

The introductory passage of Sakinna Boukhedenna's *Journal 'Nationalité: immigré(e)'* (1987) exemplifies the dysphoric and aporetic style that characterizes many Maghrebi immigrant texts. Boukhedenna writes:

> I'm *bored* and *tired* of watching *time pass by*. I'd rather live, be well 'in my skin.' Besides, I don't know why I'm *feeling so bad inside*. I'm *tired* of *trying to make myself understood*. I know *it's not working*. Why always *put up pretenses* to people *who don't care* about what I say? It's *very difficult, I'm no longer managing. I'm on my last legs*. I'm twenty years old, there are those who say those are the best years. *I'm unstable on all levels*.[7] (7, italics and underlining mine)

As her rhetorical question suggests, the narrator presumes she has an audience, and so performatively emphasizes her emotional distress in a pathos-laden address. In addition to the trademark 'I don't know' (indicated with underlining), her opening is littered with expressions of anxiety, apathy, ambiguity, depression, and loss (indicated with italics) that denote her social and existential *malaise*. The pervading mood in this passage is clearly dysphoric or depressed.

The style of Maghrebi immigrant novels often resembles the language of the depressed, as defined by Julia Kristeva. In her treatise on depression, *Black Sun* (1989), Kristeva describes the linguistic symptoms of depression as 'arbitrary or empty' language (51) or as 'meaning without signification' (49). As Kristeva sums up, 'the speech of the depressed is to them like an alien skin' (53), a particularly apt analogy in the case of immigrants who often write in an alien language. Notably, Kristeva posits that the only means to understand the indistinct language of the depressed is through the semiotic signs of the body. She terms this new semiotics 'the continuum of the body'

(62) and suggests that this 'body continuum' reveals itself verbally in the tone of voice, gestures, breathing, and in written language, through grammatical syntax, the logic of argument, rhetorical devices, phrasing, and rhythm (65). As Kristeva explains, 'one must learn to understand [this body language] in order to decipher the meaning of affect' (55). In Boukhedenna's dysphoric introduction, the feeling of depression is emphasized by the 'textual continuum of the body,' or the rhetorical elements inscribed in the corpus of the text. Moreover, a close examination of the passage reveals the presence of the body; the narrator's body confirms that she is not 'well in her skin.'

The dysphoria in Maghrebi texts is further reflected by the setting. Many novels are set in the *cités* or *banlieues*, suburbs of low-cost housing on the periphery of major French cities. Described as poor, dirty, violent, and gloomy, the characterizations of the *banlieues* draw attention to the miserable living standards of many Maghrebi immigrants. As Michel Laronde has pointed out, descriptions of the *banlieues* alternate between mud (*boue*) and cement (*béton*) (99). Laronde theorizes that these two polarities metaphorically refer to the role of Maghrebi culture in French society: mud denotes the dissipation of Beur culture, and cement, its solidification. On a more basic level, however, mud and cement allude to two forms of suffering that Maghrebis experience in immigration: the sinking mud may connote immigrants' depression and despondency, while the cement may refer to their confinement on the margins of society, or their fixed reification within the social order. Furthermore, the cement that imprisons the *cité* is often 'tagged' with graffiti, or scarlike markers of the violent, traumatic experiences that damage the Beur community every day. As Charef explains, 'the cement wall reports menaces, lies, and distress, signalling SOS in the shape of a fist' (25). Oftentimes, immigrant suffering is inscribed in descriptions of the *cité* environment, for example: 'The cracked paint, vanished in places, emphasized the fissures of the cement, like an aged face that had gone old before being born. Gaping holes marked the facade, much like a sick face pocked by leprosy'[8] (Kettane 39). In this example, drawn from Nacer Kettane's *Le Sourire de Brahim* (1985), the building's facade is personified as prematurely old and pocked, diagnosed as sick from leprosy, an untouchable, highly contagious disease. The infected face of this dilapidated building effectively translates the pessimistic outlook on the future that many Maghrebi immigrants espouse.

Most conspicuously, the *malaise* of Maghrebi immigrants is also emphasized thematically: in particular, in the theme of violence. Violence, often explicit corporeal violence, pervades many of these texts, in graphic scenes of delinquency, drugs, sexual abuse, and death. Medhi Charef's *Le Thé au harem d'Archi Ahmed* (1983), for instance, is framed by a scene of a young druggie passively inhaling gas in the basement and the suicide of a young mother, Josette, on New Year's Eve, who jumps out of her window (10, 165). These drastic measures point to the extreme despair experienced by the inhabitants of the *cité* and to the only possibilities that seem viable to them. Most Beur novels are framed with at least one violent death. Indeed, in many novels, the only possible resolution of the narrative is death, often premeditated suicide.[9]

It may even be argued that corporal violence, death, and victimization are generic components of the Beur novel and film, in particular. Charef's novel *Le Thé au harem* and Mathieu Kassovitz's film *La Haine* (1995), the first literary and cinematic Beur hits respectively, established the generic Beur narrative; they were subsequently followed by numerous duplicates. After *La Haine*'s box-office success, numerous films reproduced both its structure and themes, such as Jean-Louis Richet's *Etats des lieux* (1996), *Ma 6-T va craquer* (1998). Narratively, Charef's and Kassovitz's classics basically describe the violent, albeit ordinary, life of alienated male youths in the *cités*, who, by virtue of their marginalization, abuse, and delinquency, are both victims and victimizers. Rachid Djaïdani's novel *Boumcœur* (1999) demonstrates the difficulty of transcending this prototypical narrative model. In *Boumcœur*, Djaïdani attempts to turn his protagonist, Yaz, into a hero, ironically, by rendering him more of a victim. In this rather convoluted and unrealistic plot, Yaz is tricked, imprisoned, and ransomed by his best friend, Grézi. It is only when Yaz is freed and Grézi is imprisoned that they can both write up an interesting story about life in the *cité*, as they planned to do at the outset of the text. During his harrowing imprisonment in a cellar, Yaz, as an epic hero, confirms his heroic status by enduring great bodily suffering and mental anguish.

An 'Etiology' of Bodily Rhetoric

As we have seen in this diagnostic survey, the body – stylistically, textually, or thematically marked in the corpus of the text – often effectively translates the suffering of immigration in Maghrebi immigrant fiction. Yet, the body of the Maghrebi immigrant is not a neutral concept; on the contrary, it is a culturally constructed signifier that is often pejoratively racialized. As Fanon notes in 'Le "syndrome nord-africain"' the bodies of Maghrebis are 'dissimulated by social truth by the attributes of *bicot, bouinole, arabe, raton, sidi, mon z'ami*' (237), all derogatory terms for Arabs. Why, then, do immigrant writers so often turn to bodily rhetoric to signal their sufferings of immigration? Do they do so simply to resist such racist reification? Or does the body offer something more? These are some of the questions I explore in this 'etiology' of the body in Maghrebi immigrant literature.

In the affective domain, the medical establishment has clearly pointed to the significance of the body in understanding patients' emotional states. As Fanon, Jarret, and other psychologists have shown, patients often somatize their psychological suffering because, as Kristeva suggests, they cannot express their emotions using sentential language, but rather they manifest them through bodily language. Furthermore, medical researchers have shown that the memory of trauma and violence often resides in the body. As Elaine Scarry explains, 'what is "remembered" in the body is well remembered' (109). Maghrebi immigrants, for example, may be affected by traumatic events in their homeland, such as the Algerian civil war, as well as by the violence that they suffer in French society, and thus turn to language about the body to convey painful, embodied experiences. However, a further examination of the body, especially as far as language, culture, and materiality are concerned, grants further understanding of the role of the body in Maghrebi literature.

Numerous theorists have pointed to the primacy of the materiality of the body on even more fundamental levels. Nietzsche, for instance, argues that all self-awareness derives from the body: 'I am body entirely and nothing beside [...] behind your thoughts and feelings, my brother, stands a mighty commander, an unknown sage – he is called *Self*. He lives in your body, he is your body' (*Thus Spoke Zarathustra* 61, 62). He even suggests that every aspect of society and culture derives its meaning from the body: 'every table of values, every "thou shalt" known to history or ethnology requires first a physiological investigation and interpretation rather than a psychological one' (GM 5). As a result, Nietzsche contends that any philosophical investigation must 'start from the *body* and employ it as guide' (*Will to Power* 289). Nietzsche's arguments about the materiality of the body have been echoed by theorists such as Foucault or Bakhtin, and remain pivotal paradigms in such fields as feminist theory, disability studies, or more generally, cultural studies. As Mikhael Bakhtin argues, 'one cannot draw an absolute distinction between body and meaning in the area of culture' (cited in McNally 6). The only way to expose these 'bodies of meaning' is, according to Bakhtin, 'to return both a language and a meaning to the body [...] and simultaneously return a reality, a materiality, to language and to meaning' (*Dialogic Imagination* 171).

The 'bodies of meaning' associated with the Maghrebi body are particularly complex and contradictory. In the area of culture, however, the Maghrebi body often denotes a site of epistemic reification or ethnocultural discrimination. Yet, at the same time, the reality and materiality of the immigrant body also represents a locus that enables both language and meaning, and thus functions as a site of both possibility and resistance.

The Socioculturally Constructed Body

It is important to recognize that for Maghrebi immigrants, the body is not neutral; rather, it is a culturally constructed signifier. In traditional Islamic culture, for example, researchers have shown that the male body is associated with virility, power, and authority. Similarly, the female body connotes honour, purity, and reproduction, both biological reproduction and the transmission of traditional cultural values. The cultural role of the body is further emphasized in the public spaces of traditional Arab culture such as the *hammam*, mosque, or *souk*. As Khuri has shown, the *hammam*, or public baths, call attention to the body as hygienic and purified, especially as far as religious ablutions are concerned; the mosque stresses the sanctity of the body and its role as an instrument of worship; and finally, the souk, or marketplace, highlights the role of the body as a means of communication, social interaction, and economic exchange.

In immigration, however, many of the traditional Arab-Islamic connotations of the body are lost. The spaces of traditional Maghrebi culture are replaced by the work environment of the factory, shopping malls, or the milieu of the *cités*. As I will elaborate in subsequent chapters, in these forums, the body often functions as a body of labour, an object of exchange, and even a vehicle of delinquency and violence. For instance, many first-generation Maghrebi males came to France as manual labourers or assembly workers; in immigration their bodies become reduced to broken tools of labour or powerless cogs in the assembly line. Similarly, in France, Maghrebi women cannot maintain their traditional role of mother, wife or daughter; therefore, their bodies often figuratively connote sociocultural impurity or dangerous contamination by foreign influences.

Perhaps more importantly, in France, the bodies of Maghrebi immigrants are culturally constructed as ethnic or racialized bodies by their hosts, most of whom are White. Because of racist discourse, immigrants often find themselves reduced to the category of the body, and often unconsciously, they internalize this racial discourse. Immigrant writers frequently refer to their physical otherness and draw attention to the manifest racial differences in their appearance. For example, Paul Smail begins his novel, *Vivre me tue* (Living Is Killing Me,[10] 1997), by explaining that he cannot find a job because 'there will always be a candidate who is less tanned than I, whose hair is less frizzy, whose skin is less grainy, whose nose is less crooked [...] I'm not a human resource; my mug is too ugly.'[11]

In the case of postcolonial Maghrebis, such racist discourse points to the colonial past. In colonial discourse, the racialized body of the colonized other serves to contrast with the rational consciousness of the civilized White colonizer. As Frantz Fanon puts it, in colonial rhetoric, 'the Negro symbolizes the biological' (*Black Skins* 167). Colonial reasoning reduced Blacks, women, and other visible minorities to ontological bodies and attributed to them primitive, instinctive, animal passions. Orientalist discourse, in particular, influenced the colonial depiction of Maghrebi peoples. As Said has shown, orientalist stereotypes portray women as exotic, highly sexualized beings, while men are reduced to violent, animal savages. By contrast, the rational (White) male body became the epitome of 'reason' and 'enlightened civilization,' represented as detached from base passions or animal instincts, and increasingly divorced from the physical realm of routine work and other physical hardship.

Conventional immigrant discourse reproduces many of these standard colonial stereotypes, albeit with a difference. The heroic male body is replaced by the image of the productive, civilized model citizen, or by extension, the heroic host nation, idealized as a rational, civilizing, and liberating saviour-entity. In many ways, the generic immigrant narrative continues to reiterate colonialism's civilizing mission. 'White man's burden' has transfigured into 'democracy's burden,' as multitudes of destitute migrants from the developing world are welcomed into countries of the developed world to become educated and assimilated into a progressive social order and Western values. In this civilizing discourse, the immigrant is still relegated to a subordinate role, opposed to citizen, and is often positioned either in the realm of nature, matter, animals, proletarians, or othered as a culturally exotic or ethnically informative 'specimen.'[12]

In fiction, classroom scenes often exemplify this civilizing immigrant discourse, while also pointing to numerous stereotypes associated with immigrant bodies. Azouz Begag's *Le Gone du Chaâba* (1986), for example, describes the education of poor children living in a shanty town; they are instructed to wash before coming to class, and their hands are duly inspected upon arrival for signs of uncleanliness. If they cannot shed their filthy animal habits, they are beaten into being better civilized. Similarly, in Ferrudja Kessas' *Beur's Story* (1990), the heroine's sister is forced to remove the henna from her hands at school; however, 'as the henna did not wash off, she was dispatched to the nurse, as if she had the plague' (163). In Kessas' text, the immigrant child is not only associated with animal-like uncleanliness, but also with dangerous disease. However, her hands are clearly not dirty, but painted, albeit with exotic, cultural markers of otherness. These manifest signs of difference must be eliminated if she is to become a civilized French citizen. Interestingly, as a result of the negative reactions that she faces at school, the heroine, Malika, chooses not to paint her hands with henna during the school year, thus succumbing to the racist rhetoric that she encounters about her body. The Maghrebi body, then, as a culturally and racially constructed signifier, plays an ambiguous role for Maghrebi immigrant writers. By drawing attention to the ethnic body, authors can resist racist discourse. Yet, in so doing, they also run the risk of reproducing ethnic stereotypes.

Constant Referent

Socioculturally, the Maghrebi body thus represents a problematical locus. However, when stripped of its cultural connotations, the body offers the migrant subject tangible presence and epistemic certainty. The reality of the body functions as a stable spatiotemporal referent.

In its materiality, the body may be considered as the only unchanging constant in migrants' displaced lives. As Jarret explains, 'the representation of his body is the only reality the "migrant" cannot escape from' (1723). As Abdelmalek Sayad argues in *La Double Absence*, one of the biggest difficulties immigrants face is their dislocation both in time and space; immigrants live in the dual space of the memory of their absent home and the present reality of the new country as both emigrants and immigrants. In such dislocation, the body might be the only 'home' that immigrants have. As numerous postcolonial theorists have pointed out, in diaspora the only 'home [is] in the body.'[13]

Maghrebi immigrants in particular find themselves socioculturally dislocated, belonging to neither Arab nor French culture. As Boukhedenna points out in *Journal 'Nationalité: immigré(e),'* many immigrants consider themselves 'victims of a lack: lacking [their] cultural identity' (74). As a result, they feel as if they are 'nothing,' 'from nowhere' (73). Boukhedenna concludes that their only identity is their immigrant status: 'We are of Immigrant Nationality. Neither French nor Arab, we are exile' (126).

The dislocation of Maghrebi immigrants is further exacerbated by their marginalized position in French society. Physically ostracized into HLM (low-cost housing) ghettos on the periphery of urban centres, many immigrants feel they inhabit a 'no man's land,' that they have been refused 'membership' from the 'elitist club' of society, to take up a metaphor from Bouzid in *La Marche* (The March, 1984).[14] For many Maghrebi immigrants, this privileged 'membership card' that Bouzid seeks is French citizenship – a status often denied them. Many Maghrebi immigrants live in the country illegally, as *clandestins* or *sans-papiers* (as illegal immigrants or those without papers). Illegal migrants experience acute daily anxiety, as well as the chronic shame of living a sham life.

Adda's novella, *L'Entre-Deux Vies* (1999), poignantly reveals the trauma of illegal immigrants. When the protagonist realizes that he has been denied temporary residency – 'MOM! DAD! I'M AN ILLEGAL!!' (75) – he feels as if he is dissolving, and becoming bodiless: 'everything crumbles into what is no longer a head or no longer a body' (75). At the same time, his reaction is profoundly visceral; he feels the need to 'vomit his fear,' yet his fear 'has disappeared and dissolved into his body' (75). Adda finely contrasts the narrator's 'paper' identity with his bodily presence. In legal language, Adda's hero ceases to exist; as a 'scribbled,' 'stricken out' 'scrap of paper' (75) he has no identity. Nonetheless, he remains physically present in France, although he must constantly conceal his body and his sufferings of immigration: he is forced to 'lie, hide ... never revealing anything and keeping fear deep inside' (75). As in Adda's text, the referent of the body is often the only trace of the illegal immigrant's existence.

Universal Signifier

As I have shown in numerous examples in Maghrebi fiction, the body plays a critical role in the linguistic expression of suffering. Fundamentally, in language, the materiality of the body functions as a universal signifier of pain. Bodily signs – scars, injuries, or physical ailments – prove universally intelligible markers of suffering. Moreover, body language represents a fundamental means of communication. New immigrants, who have difficulty expressing themselves in the language of the host country, can generally communicate with gestural expressions. Translating abstract emotional states, such as depression, sorrow, or mourning, can be particularly difficult linguistically, given cultural equivalencies or idiomatic expressions, such as 'being blue' or 'being down.' However, generally everyone can relate to a pain in the belly or an ache in the head. As Wittgenstein argues, everyone understands a cry as a sign of pain; it designates 'the primitive, the natural expression of the sensation' (89 sec. 244). Furthermore, a strident cry of pain signals distress, a pressing plea for urgent help. The more distressing or explicit the cry, the more likely it is to provoke a reaction from the listener, and elicit help or rescue. Unlike psychological states or social problems, which must be worked through or endured, physical pain demands more immediate aid and assistance.

Psychiatrist Hossaïn Bendahman argues that, for immigrants, the somatization of pain signifies 'a lack' of linguistic inscription or cultural identification with the host country: 'When the mother tongue is lacking, and no longer allows for cultural or social inscription [...] somatization is deployed so as to better convey suffering' (218).[15] Writers may similarly express a lack of language or cultural equivalents, especially when trying to convey painful emotions. As author Abdelkader Djemaï explains, 'we feel pain; we want to say something; there is a lack. Writing comes with this lack. It's an intimate, open wound.'[16] It is also important to recognize that, unlike newly arriving immigrants, writers do not generally lack linguistic skills or familiarity with their target culture. On the contrary, a writer's choice of words is usually deliberate and often rhetorical, in that it aims to produce effects. Djemaï's powerful description of writing as an 'intimate, open wound,' clearly impacts readers emotionally, if not viscerally, and invites us to witness the woundedness of Djemaï's work as an intimate confidante.

Explicit corporeal rhetoric thus not only serves to signal suffering, but it may also solicit an affective reaction. In the same way that a strident cry engages a listener to help a distressed victim in real life, in fiction, particularly powerful forms of bodily rhetoric may elicit a response from the reader, such as recognition, sympathy, or even relief. Linguistically, the body proves to be a universally translatable signifier, and when rendered explicit and affective, it also conveys an urgent message of distress, which solicits an immediate response.

Tool of Resistance

An etiology of the body reveals that immigrant writers may engage in bodily rhetoric for various reasons. They may refer to the body because it incarnates much of the trauma that they may experience in immigration. They may draw on the body to reflect their lack of linguistic and cultural inscription in French society. Dislocated from their homeland, disassociated from both French and Arab culture, and socially, even legally, excluded in French society, immigrant writers may draw on the body as the source of stable identity.

In another vein, immigrants may return to the body because, all too often, they themselves are relegated to the locus of the body, discriminated as ethnic others or cultural subordinates, reduced to a lower, more physical, violent way of life. By writing, immigrant authors deconstruct the opposition between the civilized citizen and the alienated body of the Other. They reclaim the immigrant body within the domain of literature – the realm of 'high,' 'artistic' culture and the sphere of reason that colonist ideology attributes to the autonomous, self-creating, bourgeois male – and so recuperate their embodied identity, self-expression, and agency.

Finally, immigrant writers may draw on the universal signifier of the body to convey their emotional distress and social alienation as clearly, critically, and efficiently as possible. Physical bodily pain renders the sufferings of immigration concrete and tangible, graphically explicit, and even viscerally understandable for the reader. Ultimately, therefore, corporeal rhetoric – in its cultural, linguistic, and materials valencies – serves as a tool of resistance. Although the causes and effects of such rhetoric may be manifold, ultimately, its purpose most often points towards resistance.

The resistance characterized by bodily rhetoric is perhaps best defined by Ross Chambers' notion of oppositionality. As Chambers explains, in *Room for Maneuver: Reading (the) Oppositional (in) Narrative* (1991), oppositional manoeuvres 'cannot – and do not attempt to – change the structure of power in which it operates [...]; it merely exploits that structure of power for purposes of its own' (11). Above all, Chambers stresses that oppositional manoeuvres represent survival tactics; they make the system 'live-able' (7) in that they help 'maintain some sense of dignity and personhood' (7). Immigrant fiction, in general, may be considered to be a survival strategy; by writing, immigrants attempt to gain dignity and personhood in social discourse that has largely excluded them.

Similarly, Maghrebi immigrant writers deploy bodily rhetoric to performatively affirm the presence of the body of the Maghrebi immigrant in French social discourse, while also vying to grant it a 'sense of dignity.' In other words, they seek to establish, as Nietzsche might put it, the materiality of the Maghrebi body, both as a legitimate and physical presence in French society, while also vying to create a legitimate literary corpus in French literature. As Bakhtin might argue, the Maghrebi immigrant body bears a wide spectrum of sociocultural meanings: it might point to the immigrant's psychological condition, geographical marginalization, socioeconomic exploitation, or racial reification.

In all, as a form of rhetoric, the generic *mal partout* and thematic *malaise* in Maghrebi fiction, seeks various effects. Ultimately, many of its aims relate to the immigration process itself: it may seek to convince the reader of the sufferings of immigration, to affirm them, resist them, or even, to heal them. Yet, when is this rhetoric, in fact, effective?

At the outset of this chapter, I noted that, in the medical sphere, by virtue of its repetition and theatrical dramatization, frequent fictional instances of bodily pain become dismissed as stereotypical, even 'annoying,' clichés. My literary analysis in this chapter has similarly pointed to various generic expressions of bodily pain in Maghrebi fiction, but it has also examined the ambiguous role of the body in

Maghrebi culture, as a site of both reification and resistance. At this point, the discerning critic cannot help but query: what are the possibilities of a rhetoric of bodily pain? What types of corporeal rhetoric may be resistant or effectively affect the reader? When does fictional *malaise* and *mal partout* give way to essentialized 'clichés' or, by contrast, to sensationalist 'theatrics'? Finally, when does a cultural performance of pain become a 'syndrome' or even, a discourse of victimization? These are some of the questions I will address in the following chapters as I consider the effects, possibilities, and limitations of bodily rhetoric to translate the pain of immigration.

4 In the Maim of the Father: Disability and Bodies of Labour

Handicapé et reclus chez lui, mon père n'existait plus aux yeux des autres.

— Fawzia Zouari, *Ce pays dont je meurs*

'There had to be an accident' ('Il aura fallu l'accident') (53) says the narrator of Fawzia Zouari's novel, *Ce pays dont je meurs* (1999), as she describes the seemingly inevitable accident that condemns her father to a wheelchair. Once crippled, the father becomes an abject object that cannot be looked upon, either by society or by his own family: 'Handicapped and confined to the house, my father did not exist in the eyes of others. [...] I didn't dare fix my gaze on him for too long a time' (55–6).[1]

The body of the first-generation male Maghrebi immigrant remains largely invisible in French-Maghrebi immigrant texts and in contemporary literary theory. Yet, all too often, the body of the Maghrebi father is shamelessly visible – for it is often portrayed as disabled. From Charef's classic, *Le Thé au harem d'Archi Ahmed* (1983), to Zouari's more recent novel, the immigrant father is regularly depicted as mentally challenged or physically handicapped. If not literally disabled, the father's agency and voice are figuratively disabled in immigrant texts by his conspicuous silence or absence. In this chapter, I fix my attention on the ambiguous representation of first-generation French-Maghrebi males in immigrant fiction, focusing, in particular, on their relationship to disability.

Disability, as disability studies repeatedly emphasizes, is a social construction, much like gender or ethnicity. Impairments of the body or mind do not necessarily render one disabled. Rather, disability, or the attribution of corporeal deviance, is a product of cultural rules and social relations. As Rosemarie Garland Thomson elaborates, 'disability is a representation, a cultural interpretation of physical transformation or configuration, and a comparison of bodies that structure social relations and institutions' (6).

In France, disability studies is not as established a field of inquiry as it is in North America. Nonetheless, a few centres devote attention to the study of handicapped persons (*l'étude de la condition des personnes handicapées*), on readaptation (*études en réadaptation / sciences de la réadaptation*) or on rehabilitation, incapacity, or invalidity (*réhabilitation, incapacité, invalidité*). Interestingly, a large number of publications on disability concern *pretium doloris* – work accidents and disability insurance. In France, disability is often situated in the context of jurisprudence, economics, and medicine. North American disability studies, of course, tends to emphasize the social construction of disability as a product of cultural rules and social relations.

Thomson points out that disability must be moved from the realm of law and medicine to the realm of political minorities, 'recast from a form of pathology to a form of ethnicity' (6). Intriguingly, in the case of male Maghrebi immigrants, the physically disabled body is clearly associated with a specific ethnicity and a specific gender, and thus reflects a particular form of identity politics. How, then, should we read the disabled body in Maghrebi immigrant narratives? What are the various meanings attributed to it? What type of discourse does disability enable – what are its possibilities? What are its limits? These are some of the questions I raise as I explore the multiple, contradictory meanings of the disabled body in Maghrebi fiction, so as to ultimately probe its role in identity politics.

'Bodies of Labour'

When socially contextualized, the disabled bodies of first-generation Maghrebi immigrants expose inequalities in representation, labour, race, and citizenship in French society in the mid-twentieth century. The first generation of Maghrebi immigrants, male workers, came to France between the 1940s and the 1970s, as manual labourers. On a most basic level, these immigrants may be reduced to bodies of labour, or *corps-labeur*, to use the term employed by Abdelmalek

Sayad in *La Double Absence* (1999). In his sociological study, Sayad shows how these immigrants are so often absent in social discourse, and excluded from civil, national, and labour rights, although they are manifestly present in the social order, as labouring bodies.

Analyses of first-generation immigrant workers are also largely absent in contemporary literary criticism, especially in contrast to the figure of the father in literature set in the Maghreb. From early articles to recent theses (Bahri), major critics have focused on the role of the father in Maghrebi texts, particularly on his patriarchal role, addressing such issues as 'the revolt against the father' (Déjeux 285), 'the silence of the father' (Boubeker 182), or 'the illusory quest for the father' (Bonn 84). Novels set in the Maghreb tend to depict the father as a sadist, a negative body (*Corps-négatif*) (Khaïr-Eddine), or a 'being [...] that vegetates and only desires to vegetate' (*un être [...] qui végète et ne désire que végéter*) (Chraïbi 85). As Samira Doudier explains, the father is either a castrating or destructive figure in literature set in the Maghreb, and is either criticized or dismissed without any particularity whatsoever; he is typically characterized as 'fallen, old, impotent, weak, ridiculed, emblematic of a recent, degenerate, postcolonial and underdeveloped society' (107). As all of these studies focus on the father as symbolic of the decay of traditional Arab-Muslim patriarchal order, or the erasure of the so-called law of the father, few of them consider the experience, let alone woundedness, of the father as an individual subject.

In contrast to the copious criticism of the father in native Maghrebi literature, or perhaps in light of it, analyses of first-generation male immigrants, portrayed as workers or fathers in French-Maghrebi immigrant texts, are surprisingly scarce. The stories of embodied suffering of this immigrant generation thus remain largely dismissed. The notable exceptions to this literary criticism, such as Susan Ireland's 'First-Generation Immigrant Narratives' (2001), do not explicitly examine disability; however, they must necessarily allude to it (37–8). For example, Ireland's article, which focuses on oral narratives and prominent first-generation texts, attempts to 'give voice' (32) to this 'silent generation' (22). Ireland inadvertently points us to such authors as Ben Jelloun, who states that 'the denunciation of the political system is expressed through the immigrant body' (*La Plus Haute des Solitudes* 71). As Ireland surveys the experience of first-generation immigrants, she inevitably and 'forcefully brings out the reasons for [immigrants'] psychosomatic illnesses (usually impotence) – isolation, separation from their families, abstinence from sex, humiliation at work, accidents at work and unemployment' (32).

Medical discourse, however, has long noted the somatized suffering of French-Maghrebi workers, as I have explained in the previous chapter. Notably, Ben Jelloun's *La Plus Haute des Solitudes* (1977), stems from his doctoral dissertation on the psychiatric evaluation of first-generation Maghrebi patients. Ethnopsychologists such as Jarret have pointed out that the ubiquitous psychosomatic suffering of Maghrebi patients (*mal partout*) largely derives from their immigration experience. As Jarret concludes, 'particularly for the Maghrebian, the damaged body-tool needing repair is a current representation which has the meaning of a cry for help' (1723). Jarret's description of bodily pain as a 'damaged body-tool' closely relates to Sayad's notion of the Maghrebi immigrant worker as *corps-labeur*.

Intriguingly, in immigrant texts, first-generation Maghrebi workers are often reduced to body-tools, or bodies of labour. Karl Marx, contrasting the work of artisans and factory workers, argued in *Das Kapital* that concrete labour activities take on increasingly abstract forms until they are eventually repressed, reduced, and disregarded as interchangeable fragments of homogeneous labour. In immigrant novels, we witness such homogenization as all the immigrant fathers eventually resemble each other. On the assembly line, many immigrants are only identified by the anonymous label *Momo* (a generic nickname for Mohammed; Zouari 71), or worse, taken for Haitians or Africans, *coco* or *mon-z-ami* ('coconut/penis' and 'mah friend'), while being condescendingly talked to in *petit nègre* (pidgin Negro; Houari 56). Furthermore, especially in novels focusing on second-generation immigrants, the first-generation immigrants, 'fathers,' are reduced to stock characters in the home as well, simply referred to with such epithets as *Le Vieux* (Old Man; Sif), or *Le Père* (The Father; Charef), or *'Le gros, l'ogre, le father* [sic]. *Rarement papa, encore moins El-hadj'* (The Fat One, the Ogre, the Father. Rarely Daddy or even more rarely El-Hadj; Raith 189). Here, the father's lack of identity reflects the mechanized homogenization of the assembly line that defines much of his existence.

The worker is also often described by references to the body, or by corporeal metaphors, often related to labour. To cite a poignant example of such a 'body-tool' metaphor, I refer to Myriam Ben's short story, 'L'émigré' (1993), where the protagonist compares his first day as an agricultural worker to open-heart surgery: 'Thus I assisted at my first open-heart surgery. They plugged in the electrodes. No, no. That time didn't plug in the electrodes. They opened my heart. No, I'm mistaken. No, that time they opened the heart of the land itself, the heart of the earth and of a river' (147).[2] In this multilayered quote, the hero conflates the act of tilling the ground with a medical operation – the extraction of his own heart. In this image, the immigrant, his labour, his country – everything except his confused conscience – is reduced to a violated body. As in a gruesome medical procedure, the heart, the metaphorical seat of one's life, one's story, and one's meaning, is gouged out from all of these bodies. In much of the experiences of first-generation immigrants, the heart of the matter is excised from these immigrant texts; all that is left is the materiality of their bodies, bodies of labour.

To arrive at the heart of the matter – the stories and experiences of first generation immigrants – I turn to Yamina Benguigui's *Mémoires d'immigrés* (1997). In this series of socioanthropological interviews, Benguigui offers an excellent overview of the concerns facing these 'fathers,' as she terms them. As manual labourers, first-generation immigrants worked long hours in strenuous, physically demanding jobs, and often lived in unsanitary housing conditions. If they became ill or injured, they rarely had recourse to medical care, disability compensation, or benefits, as labour unions were either not open to foreigners or were only just being founded. Most lived with the fixed idea of return (11, 19) and chose not to settle or integrate entirely into French culture. Their relationship to language was also precarious; many were illiterate and therefore essentially mute in the public forum (9, 17, 35), unable to complain or bear grievances in social debates.

Strikingly, the interviews point to the physical suffering these labourers incurred because of their working conditions. At the time of the interviews, as older men, they were all broken, discarded bodies of labour. We observe men whose bodies are gnawed by silicose and deafness (39), and men who became lame (62) or paralyzed when machines fell on them (64). With few workers' rights, pension disability insurance, unions, or recourse to strikes (40), these broken bodies were unemployed and forgotten.

Yet, despite their many hardships, most of these immigrants chose not to exhibit their wounds of immigration, especially to their children (41). As one of Benguigui's interviewees explains, he did not want his children to develop hatred towards their country, but rather to become good, happy citizens (41). Many allude to the image of the utopian male body that is strong and resistant to pain, and most agreed that their self-worth, status, and identity is defined wholly by work. One of the interviewees makes this self-definition clear, when referring to the day he was forced to retire: 'What was terrible, was the day I became incapable of working. [...] I had always worked, twice as hard as the others, firstly to evolve, then to be considered like the French who had the same qualifications as I had, and finally, for my children, for my sons, so that they would be proud of their father, so that they understand that I had done everything to integrate [...] I don't understand what it means, in the end, to integrate' (31–2).[3]

For these first-generation immigrants, 'integration' seems directly related to labour. It reproduces the traditional model of immigrant success, the progressive capitalist myth of 'poor boy makes good,' that through honest, hard work, immigrants will succeed as citizens. The broken bodies of these immigrant workers reflect the failure of this success story and point to the dehumanization and exploitation of labour within the economy.

The Possibilities of Disability:
First-Generation Immigrant Texts

In Maghrebi immigrant fiction, 'fathers' are rarely given a chance to speak at length, as they are in Benguigui's interviews. To create a composite sketch of 'fathers' in Maghrebi immigrant literature, I combine two sources of immigrant fiction: first, first-generation Bildungsroman texts that follow the journey of immigrant workers to France, and describe their attempts to make their fortunes in their adopted country, such as Houari's *Confessions d'un immigré* (1988), Raïth's *Palpitations intra-muros* (1986), and Zemouri's *Le Jardin de l'intrus* (1986); and second, contemporary novels that focus on the second-generation of immigrants, or Beurs, as they are called in France. The term 'Beur,' derived from immigrant slang called *verlan*, is used to refer to second- or third-generation Maghrebian immigrants, or the children of working-class North African immigrant parents, who were born or schooled in France. Beur novels refer to fathers only in passing, and, adopting an intergenerational and retrospective perspective, are laden with sceptical hindsight – see Charef's

Le Thé au harem d'Archi Ahmed, Imache's *Une fille sans histoire* (1989) or Zouari's *Ce pays dont je meurs*.

A careful examination of first-generation Bildungsroman immigrant novels reveals many of the same themes as in Benguigui's interviews – illiteracy, poor housing conditions, and ultimately, injury and disability. Many novels also point to the silence and shame that circumscribe the workers' wretched living conditions. For example, in Houari's *Confessions d'un immigré* (1988), the protagonist Selim concludes that it is because of 'excessive shame' ('par excès de pudeur') that his father hid the state he was living in (51). The father's shame is largely induced by his inability to be a successful provider for his family. As the story progresses, Selim himself becomes unemployed and slips into similar depression and silence, and throughout the narrative attempts to express his suffering. Unlike Selim, his father is not given a chance to tell his story, and, largely expunged from the novel, is reduced to shame, silence, and absence – typical attributes of the Maghrebi father figure.

In most first-generation texts, the many hardships experienced by immigrant workers serve to destabilize the traditional narrative of success. Most novels such as Zemouri's *Le Jardin de l'intrus* (1986) present dystopic versions of the 'poor boy makes good' narrative model. In Zemouri's text, set in the 1950s, we learn that the father's job is the creation of fertilizer from excrement at l'Entreprise de Purification de la Seine (19), an ominous foreshadowing of harrowing events that subsequently ensue in the novel. By the end of the story, the father loses his job, becomes ill and dies, while the mother is condemned to a sanatorium. With the rise of the Front Libération Nationale (FLN) or Algerian Liberation Movement, the narrator, Lamine, is too terrified to leave his low-cost housing (HLM) and dreams of returning to Algeria, but, figuratively paralyzed, is unable to act.

In early immigrant arrival stories, then, illness, injury, and disability serve to put into question successful integration within French society, and draw attention to the exploitation and oppression of Maghrebi workers. Disability makes visible what often remains invisible in social and literary texts – the forgotten role of labour in the Maghrebi experience. Yet, despite their ailments, in these Bildungsroman texts, first-generation immigrants are not constructed as disabled. On the contrary, even the most dystopic arrival stories describe the valiant efforts of immigrant workers, who despite their sacrificial wounds, are portrayed as a heroic, albeit doomed figures.

Intriguingly, in some first-generation novels, disability designates a coveted locus of possibility – a means of escaping or evading the system of labour. For example, in Raïth's *Palpitations intra-muros* (1986), the father actually becomes angry because the doctor 'had not diagnosed the disease he thought he had' (198). In this case, the father was hoping for a leave of absence or at least compensation for his illness. In Houari's rather utopic text, *Confessions d'un immigré*, the mutilated hand of Said, the friend, signals the idyllic hope of compensation, rest, and even return 'home.' Said, the narrator, expresses his resentment of Tayeb, an unsuccessful miner who became a celebrity when his leg was crushed in a mining accident; Tayeb then returned to Algeria to live contentedly from his workers' compensation. Said claims to know people who put one of their hands under a pile of bricks or even cut off a hand just to receive such compensation (52). He also believes that 'those who lose a limb in a work accident often feel blessed by God, because they finish with exile, once and for all' (52).[4] In these cases, an injury offers immigrant workers a means by which to transcend their working status and attain a different identity, albeit the identity of a sick individual.

In a chapter of *La Double Absence* devoted exclusively to the prevalence of injury among sick immigrant workers, Sayad offers a similar hypothesis: injuries offer immigrant workers a means of engaging with social discourse. As Sayad explains, in the social sphere immigrant workers are largely ignored as *corps-labeur*, 'labour-bodies' (288). Sickness, injury and mutilation, however, force the medical establishment to take notice and treat their sufferings. Financial or social institutions are often also implicated, as they must offer immigrants compensation for their injuries, largely incurred because of socioeconomic and/or labour exploitation. Immigrants must often wrangle with medical and social institutions to make them aware of the severity of their injuries, and so are compelled to express their experiences in the public forum. Immigrants attempt thereby to treat more than their physical wounds; they take up illness for more than therapeutic purposes ('à des fins qui ne sont pas toujours thérapeutiques') (267). Instead, immigrant workers may take up a sick status as a means of resisting their marginalization in society and their objectification as mere bodies of labour. What is more, disability compensation offers them a means of reparation for past ills, and sometimes even assures them a more financially stable and work-free future. As Sayad sums up, 'what is astonishing and problematic (scandalous even) to the point of being considered a pathology or an *abnormality* even, is the way in which the sick immigrant uses his sickness (and the medical juridical process) to settle a dispute that is said to be of a social nature' (267, italics in original).[5] As Sayad intimates, such 'sick manoeuvring,' or the appropriation of disability as a locus of possibility, might be viewed as scandalous, abnormal, and even 'freakish' in mainstream French society.

The representation of disability in arrival stories of first-generation immigrants might also seem 'freakish' to the general French readership, as injury signals a locus of possibility, both literally and figuratively. On a literal level, injuries enable immigrant workers to fight for compensation for their hard work, and sometimes disability insurance grants them a means of exiting the labour force. On a metaphorical level, disability bears numerous possible connotations about the immigrant condition. It serves to disable the traditional narrative of success and facile immigrant integration. It calls attention to the stereotypical image of the active, fit, and autonomous citizen, typically used in contrast with the clichéd representation of the socially disengaged and isolated disabled citizen (Marks 170). Disability emphasizes the immigrant's role as that of a productive undamaged object of labour. It points to the immigrants' vulnerability in the economic system, and their exclusion, invisibility, and marginalization in social discourse. Even when they are healthy and able-bodied, these workers remain disabled by their immigrant status.

In literary examples, the appropriation of disability in many ways functions as a means of 'flaunting the narrative prosthesis,' to refer to a theory proposed by Mitchell and Snyder (8). On the one hand, 'textual prosthesis,' much like a prosthetic device, Mitchell and Snyder argue, seeks 'to return the incomplete body to the invisible status of a normative essence' (8). 'Flaunting' one's prosthesis, or undressing the wounds of one's disability, on the other hand, exposes disability's troubling presence, and 'provides literary works with the potency of an unsettling cultural commentary' (8). Here, as immigrants flaunt their injuries, they exhibit the various 'social prostheses' that render their exploitation and marginalization normative and invisible.

An Impossible Disability: Beur Texts

In Beur texts disability functions quite differently – it is no longer a locus of possibility but, rather, of impossibility. Charef's *Le Thé au harem d'Archi Ahmed* (1983) offers us the archetypal image of the disabled Maghrebi father. Narrator Mehdi's father is brain-damaged; 'he lost his mind' ('il n'a plus sa tête') (41), after falling off the roof in a work accident. A walking 'vegetable,' the father cannot articulate his own condition, and he remains silent throughout the novel. His inner state can only be inferred from the 'the same eternal expression in his gaze, a mix of emptiness and distance' (41). Were it not for his son's intervention, the father would be wholly absent from the novel; however, Medhi must pick him up at the local bar, because he is too drunk to find his way home. When not completely drunk, the father is depicted as inertly watching television.

Mehdi's disabled father embodies many of the stereotypical representations of fathers in Beur novels – absence, silence, and debauchery. In Beur novels, fathers are often reified as absent, reduced to silence, and readily related to dissolute actions. In Charef's novel, the father's disability emphatically calls attention to the father's demoted role in the family unit and his diminished capacity in the social sphere. Clearly, the disabled father is no longer an authority figure; on the contrary, he is likened to a meek child: 'He is the Benjamin of the family, the smallest, the youngest' (159). Furthermore, the location of the father's injury – the head – is also not concidental. Neuropsychiatrist Jarret notices that Maghrebi workers often express their psychic pain through the head, by feigning headaches, vertigo, and theatrical falls (1721). Jarret attributes this focus on the head as their difficulty in transitioning from 'using their muscles' to 'using their brains,' and their loss of authority as the 'head of the household' and 'source of tradition' (1721). On the one hand, the father's disabled condition may be viewed as an evasion or escape from family responsibilities, which then fall onto the children. On the other hand, it also signals the father's loss of traditional authority and patriarchal power.

In Beur texts, then, the visible father-cripple epitomizes the intergenerational perspective on Maghrebi fathers – absence, silence, irresponsibility, impotence, and powerlessness. Rendered invisible, though, is the father's role as a worker; that part of the father's lifestory is amputated in this disabling stereotype. Clearly, the father is silent and absent only because he is brain-damaged because of a work injury. He turns to alcoholism and inactivity only because he has no possibilities for gainful employment when injured. He has no role in the family or in society because there is seemingly no agency possible for disabled people in his social and familial environment.

In some cases, the father's entire life-story, and indeed the fate of his entire family, is wholly conflated with his injury. A scene from Tassadit Imache's *Une fille sans histoire* (1989), where the family gathers around the father when he returns home with his arm in a sling, epitomizes this stereotypical perspective. Here the father's wound becomes the locus of knowledge and identity, both about the father and the family unit. The author emphasizes the intense gaze on the father's maimed hand, an abject object, when she writes, 'He sat down without a word. And they had all leaned in over his hand. Their heads had never been so close. A state of immobility had seized them all' (118).[6] In this significant moment, the family seems to grasp its future of collective immobility. The wound signals the ineffable – their fear of an uncertain future, financial instability, and the loss of a paternal authority figure. Intriguingly, the whole scene is staged in silence; there is no story to accompany the father's woundedness. On the contrary, the father says nothing at all, and thus the family assumes that he experienced no pain: 'And because he never said anything, they concluded that he felt no pain' (112). This example points to the father's missing voice and the intergenerational misunderstanding that derives from it, especially concerning his suffering of immigration. The father's wound proves to be the only sign of his repressed suffering, the only symbol of his silenced story; through the novel, he is otherwise condemned to 'mutism' and 'perpetual absence' (109). For the family, however, the father wholly becomes his injury, a sight/site of abjection and dystopia, as the injury elicits the knowledge of a critical, inevitable change of fortune for the family, a future of uncertainty, instability, and loss.

In many cases, the maiming of the father signals the climactic point of reversal in the narrative – the fatal flaw that leads to tragedy. In Zouari's *Ce pays dont je meurs* (1999), for instance, the narrator bluntly states: 'There had to be an accident' (53). The father's inevitable accident, which confines him to a wheelchair, triggers the cataclysmic reversal in the family's fortune and sets into motion unemployment, poverty, exhaustion, passivity, and, ultimately, their deaths. Following the father's accident, the family's tragic story is dismissed as: 'A father who disappeared in a banal accident. A mother sick missing her country. A life without joy. The anorexic crises of Amira. Money lacking like with all the poor. Nothing that would grant any hope' (144).[7] In this novel, all the family members eventually die: the father dies from a hemorrhage (99), the mother from over-exhaustion, one daughter from self-induced starvation, and the other daughter, the narrator of the story, also chooses to die, because, as she explains, she cannot create any other story for herself (185).

The maiming of the father thus represents a necessary narrative device, the pernicious origin of all of the family's misfortunes. In Zouari's story, after being maimed, the father has no role at all, other than death, a death often glossed over by the narrator as 'a father who disappeared in a banal accident' ('un père disparu dans un accident banal') (144). Although he embodies the family's tragic fatal flaw, the father is barely fleshed out as a character. On being handicapped, the father simply loses all authority and agency: 'He dared not raise his voice against us. Useless, he was quickly persuaded that his authority, in the image of his lower extremities, no longer had any effect' (56).[8] Before the accident, the father is likened to a sexual predator, who wanted 'to imprison the body of his wife so as to take possession of his country' (53). After the accident, he is depicted not only as handicapped, but as a completely sexually inactive. Ultimately, he dies from a hemorrhage, which his daughter attributes to his feeling of sexual impotence and inadequacy: 'I am persuaded that he had died because of the despair of his wife [...] the emptiness of her nights without love-making' (99).

Most generically, the father is likened to an abject object, who inspires neither fear nor pity. We are told that that he provokes only indifference: 'My father did not exist in the eyes of others' (55). While the sight of disabled people is usually viewed with some emotive reaction, either as objects of pity or danger, the figure of the disabled father in Beur texts often provokes little reaction or emotion at all. Even the daughter in Zouari's novel dares not look at her father or his face, which is likened to a black hole: 'I dared not look at him. The dark copper sunburn branded into his inert face reminded me of a former sun turned to ash' (55).[9] When the father finally does die, he is transported to Algeria, literally as a 'piece of luggage, in a box, in cargo, an inanimate form among other such forms' (103). Zouari's description of the father as luggage – 'inert, compressed among a thousand and one objects that he was part of' (103) – is almost as lengthy, and certainly in the same tenor, as is the portrait of her father when alive, as a useless abject object.

Needless to say, I find the depictions of disability in these Beur texts deeply problematical, from a number of theoretical perspectives. On a basic level, not only are these injured fathers reduced to archetypes, but also they are utterly reified as static, absolute body-objects, lacking any voice, agency, or subjectivity whatsoever. The stereotyping of fathers, whether as 'permanently damaged goods,' 'fatally flawed products,' 'isolated misfits,' or 'invisible outsiders,' manifestly exposes mainstream prejudicial attitudes towards disabled people. Thus – very problematically indeed – these second-generation writers depict their fathers in the same discriminatory manner in which they themselves claim to be represented in majority discourse.

Furthermore, from an intergenerational perspective, such objectification clearly creates a visible social differential between first-generation immigrants and those of subsequent generations. In contrast to his mentally disabled father, Medhi appears as a hero, just by virtue of being able-bodied. Thus, instead of advancing ethnic equality, it would appear that some of these texts are perpetrating ablist prejudice.

Obfuscated in this discourse of disability is the fact that the father became disabled because of his working conditions. Unlike their fathers, however, many of the second-generation narrators in these Beur texts remain unemployed. While it is true that in the past thirty years the demand for manual labour in France has decreased, leaving many first-generation immigrant workers unemployed, it must also be recognized that, unlike their fathers, immigrant children have had access to education, and therefore are not illiterate or uneducated and thus are able to work. Yet, in Zouari's story, for example, it would seem that the father's inability to work wholly determines the demise of the entire family.

In my concluding analysis, I point to a final, most perturbing observation: in some cases, Beur heroes usurp the father's disabled position, so as to create for themselves an identity – an identity forged out of victimhood. Such is the case in Zouari's novel, where Amira, the youngest and only French-born member of a traditional French-Maghrebi family, is an anorexic, who ultimately dies from this self-inflicted illness. The handicap of the father or the death of the mother by exhaustion is apparently not interesting enough; to offer a different twist, the author finds it necessary to sensationalize a tragic death by malnutrition in order to create a story of utter suffering and sacrifice. When her father dies, Amira becomes fixated on her father's wheelchair, a space of immobility and disability. Instead of going to work, she sits in his chair, caressing the wheels and playing with her father's beret. Later she is joined by her mother, exhausted from her own work, and they both passively remain there, 'the same murdered hope lodged in their immobile bodies' (147). Eventually, discriminated both at work and at school, willingly unemployed and friendless, Amira embodies the father's disabled position, by her self-induced starvation. In Zouari's novel, Amira's lengthy, sensationalized anorexia certainly eclipses the destitution of the father, whose disability is only mentioned in passing.

In the context of disability, Amira's willed illness brings to mind disability 'passing,' or rather, more accurately, a form of 'disability drag.' Disability theorists often apply the queer theory terms of 'passing' or 'outing' to disabled persons, when they either simulate the 'normalcy' of able-bodied persons, or on the other hand, divulge their disabled status (Brueggemann). In this case, Amira's anorexia may be considered as 'narrative drag,' or 'masquerade,' to employ a term from Tobin Siebers: *allowing expression of a public view of disability for political ends* (9, italics in original). In Zouari's characterization, Amira constructs herself as disabled, so as to claim reparation for discrimination, oppression, or neglect from this disenfranchised locus.

Concluding with Disability

The bodily rhetoric of disability deployed to characterize first-generation immigrants therefore posits both possibilities and limitations in social discourse. To deploy disability terminology, it may enable 'crip culture' or be a disabling 'culture of crippling.' The ubiquitous image of the disabled Maghrebi father enables us to see certain aspects of French society that often remain invisible in literary and social discourse. These bodies in pain lucidly translate the suffering that these first-generation workers themselves cannot express – their objectification as bodies of labour, their socioeconomic exploitation as tools of labour, their absence and silence in the social order, or their inability to transcend their condition because of illiteracy, lack of education, or economic change. Within the family enclave, their wounds speak of their curtailed role as family providers, their loss of respect, honour, and traditional patriarchal authority, as well as their resulting sense of shame, disappointment, and helplessness caused by their failure to integrate successfully in France.

In certain instances, first-generation texts even suggest that injuries and handicaps may offer immigrant workers the possibility of gaining entry, representation, and agency in social discourse, albeit through the medical establishment. In this form of identity politics, based on injury, immigrant workers cease to be bodies of labour, and rather, become bodies broken by labour that oblige society to recognize its economic exploitation and violence, and even compensate them for it. By effectively deploying a politics of pain, certain disabled immigrants – as injured, sick bodies – may gain financial remuneration for socio-economic ills, recognition and treatment in the medical sphere, and even, perhaps, more compassion and acknowledgment in the public forum.

In contrast to this enabling social response, the repeated maiming of the father in Beur texts exposes a disabling form of discourse. The recurring objectification of Maghrebi fathers – be it as silent, invisible, crippled, or abject beings – visibly replicates the typical marginaliza-tion and discrimination of disabled persons. Ironically, Beurs often complain of the racial intolerance and social exclusion they themselves experience. Yet in Charef's novel, the main character's ability and empowerment is clearly contrasted with the father's disability and loss of power. In some cases, then, ability and disability become social differentials, a means of gaining voice, agency, and authority in the narrative. In other cases, as in Zouari's novel, disability becomes an echelon in a hierarchy of differential suffering. Here, in revolt, the pro-tagonist takes up a position of even greater sacrificial suffering than her disabled father, so as to acquire her identity and power from a position of greater victimhood.

In Beur examples, the 'maim of the father' is hardly accidental; rather, it is a deliberate discursive strategy that creates a precarious form of identity politics for Beur immigrants. Certainly, as in texts set in the Maghreb, the 'maim of the father' figuratively represents the loss of the 'name of the father,' or traditional Arab-Islamic culture, in the process of immigration. However, in certain Beur texts, the fic-tional destruction of the father figure enables the creation of Beur sub-jectivity. In this rather crippling politics of pain, Beur identity may be fashioned either from victimization or victimhood. In the end we may ask: must there always be an 'accident'? Must French-Maghrebi authors define their marginalized identity 'in the maim of the father?' How to move from a discourse of disability to one of viable possibility, agency, and ability? These are questions I propose to investigate further as I explore discourses of empowerment, disenfranchisement, heroism, and victimization deployed to represent the able-bodied figures of Maghrebi immigrant women and children.

5 'Ni Putes Ni Soumises?'
Engendering Doubly Oppressed Bodies

We, women living in *banlieue* neighbourhoods, descended from all origins, believers or not, call on our rights to freedom and emancipation! Socially oppressed by a society that shuts us up in ghettos that accumulate misery and exclusion. Suffocated by the machismo of men in our neighbourhoods, who in the name of 'tradition,' deny our most basic rights [...]
- Enough lessons in morality [...]
- Enough*misérabilisme'* (worthlessness/wretchedness) [...]
- Enough justifications for our oppression [...]
- Enough silence [...]
No one will liberate us from this double oppression except we ourselves.
                                        – *Ni Putes Ni Soumises* manifesto[1]

On 8 March 2003, International Women's Day, 30,000 women took to the streets of Paris. It was a movement called Ni Putes Ni Soumises ('Neither Whores Nor Submissives,') that rallied under the manifesto cited above. Most of the demonstrators were young women from the *cités*, who were protesting the violence in the ghetto and its dismissal by French authorities. The group Ni Putes Ni Soumises came into being after the events of 4 October 2002, when Sohane, a 17-year-old girl from the Balzac *cité* of Vitry-Sur-Seine, was burned alive in a dumpster by a 19-year-old youth from a neighbouring *cité*. However, this was not the first incident of graphic corporal violence against Beurettes, or Beur women. In September 2002, a group of nineteen minors from Val-d'Oise were found guilty of gang-raping 15-year-old Samia. That same year, Oufla, a 19-year-old girl, suffered third-degree burns when acid was thrown onto her face and body in the toilets of a Parisian high school in the 14th *arrondissement*.

The brutal physical violence perpetrated against Beurettes engendered a powerful, activist politics of pain – the movement of Ni Putes Ni Soumises. The mutilated bodies of these French-Maghrebi women poignantly served to showcase the complex and compound double oppression that they experience in immigration. By virtue of their bodies – both gendered and racially demarcated – Maghrebi women confront both sexist and racist discrimination. In immigration, because of their ethnic and gendered sociocultural position, female Maghrebi immigrants not only face 'double oppression,' they are also 'doubly exiled': both as foreigners and women, they are discriminated and oppressed by French society, but also, as Arab-Muslim women, they are are alienated and repressed in certain traditional Arab-Muslim discourses.

In this chapter, I explore the problematical representation of women in French-Maghrebi fiction, focusing specifically on the complex bodily rhetoric that is deployed to translate this double oppression. My analysis examines diverse groups of French-Maghrebi women and thus different types of oppression: specifically, I consider 'mothers,' 'daughters,' and what I term 'rebels.' I draw on two types of immigrant novels: first, Beur texts, which point to the experience of Beurette 'daughters' and their first-generation 'mothers,' and second, 'testimonial fiction.' In the 1990s fundamentalism in Algeria gave rise to the 'testimonial novel,' which focuses on the experience of female resistance fighters, who during the course of the novel, often seek refuge in France, and so also obliquely allude to immigrant women.

In fiction, bodily pain intimates a precarious form of rhetoric for women writers. On the one hand, it signals a locus of graphically explicit representation and potential agency, but on the other hand, it also risks reproducing gendered violence and victimization. As Françoise Lionnet has compellingly argued in her landmark 1993 article, 'Geographies of Pain,' 'the body in pain' represents a 'privileged symbolic space [...] to translate cultural conflicts into a visible representational frame' (150). In her analysis, Lionnet examines the problematical position of various female characters who are 'driven to murder as a result of the 'inexpressibility' and cultural invisibility of their pain and dehumanization' (138). In these texts, representations of physical pain manifestly grant women some 'elementary form of recognition and visibility' (138), just as these characters' actions reflect a kind of power, agency, and justice. Yet, at the same time, just as these characters' desperate acts replicate the patriarchal violence perpetrated on them, some critics might argue that writers gain certain voice and authority by reproducing these representations of gendered oppression. Lionnet's article concludes with a forceful caveat about how 'the rest of us, writers and critics' and, I would add, readers, 'who are in command of the interpretive means that can give larger significance to [the] lives' of oppressed persons, choose to represent, read, and respond to these others who occupy a 'position of radical dissymmetry as regards [sic] the rest of us' (150). More than a decade after her ground-breaking article, Lionnet's precient words seem even more relevant today, when the rhetoric of bodily pain has become almost a staple commodity in postcolonial women's writing.

In literary representations, Maghrebi immigrant writers are faced with the difficult task of representing the dual oppression that Maghrebi women face without reproducing its oppressive effects. For example, writers must elaborate on the 'silence' and 'misery' of Maghrebi women without espousing a discourse of '*misérabilisme*,' or reducing women subjects to silent, worthless wretches. They must point to the oppression that Maghrebi women face in some Arab-Muslim contexts, without reducing this subjugation to this singular ethnocultural dimension. The sexually violated female body, in particular, poses a challenge for the writer. On the one hand, writers must represent the sexual objectification or mutilation of the female body as powerfully and as persuasively as possible. On the other hand, in so doing, they risk reproducing this gendered violence or sensationalizing it. In Maghrebi fiction, women are repeatedly reduced to sexual objects, even personified as 'cunts,' and Maghrebi texts are laden with graphic scenes of women being abused, raped, burned, or mutilated. When does such bodily rhetoric resist gendered violence and sexual objectification? When does it reproduce it? Can a rhetoric of bodily pain serve as an effective politics of pain? As the women of Ni Putes Ni Soumises clamour, 'No one will liberate us from this double oppression, except we ourselves.' Does bodily rhetoric, as represented in Maghrebi women's immigrant fiction, signal viable, self-empowering, liberatory potential?

Wives, Mothers, Virgins – or 'Cunts'?

The depiction of women in immigrant fiction – as 'mothers,' 'daughters,' or 'rebels' – reflects the multifaceted history of Maghrebi immigration. Historically, Maghrebi women arrived in France after a 1974 family law allowed wives to join their working husbands in France. Unlike their working husbands, first-generation women, or 'mothers,' did not often leave their homes, and were therefore at the margins of French society, with little access to the outside world except through their children. Their children thwarted any project of return to their native land, and their biculturalism put into question traditional Arab values. Their 'daughters,' second- and third-generation French-Arab women, continue to negotiate their gendered identities in relation to traditional Arab values and those of French culture.

In her interviews, Yasmina Benguigui shows that Maghrebi women share some of the same difficulties of immigration as men, such as bad housing (73) and illiteracy (74). However, Benguigui also stresses that first-generation women, unlike men, are further burdened with 'a double role': as guardians of Muslim traditions and as neophytes in French society (10–11). As explained above, their daughters further experience this 'double exile' – exiled as outsiders in French society and exiled as women in Arab-Muslim culture. In Benguigui's study, the interviewees emphasize the second form of exile, gendered exile, much more often, referring to the cult of virginity, the labour of pregnancy, or the toils of motherhood. One interviewee recalls the shame on her wedding night when her husband was too drunk to consummate their marriage and so she was accused of not being a virgin (85). Another remembers that the only moments of peace she had as a mother were the two days she spent at the hospital after labour (86). Curiously, although some mothers refer to homesickness (90), cultural differences (123), and violent labour strikes (110), the suffering of immigration appears secondary to the difficulties of being an Arab-Muslim woman.

In literature, women's gendered oppression also tends to eclipse their oppression as immigrants. In Beur novels, much like in social discourse, immigrant women usually occupy the traditional roles of mother, wife, and/or daughter. Moreover, these roles are often associated with the stereotypical dichotomy of women as either virgins or whores. In certain instances, this objectification is attributed to Western discourse; in *Shérazade* (1982), Leïla Sebbar draws attention to Orientalist rhetoric, as the heroine's French lover imitates Orientalist depictions of Arab women in nineteenth-century French paintings. More often, the oppression of women is associated with Arab-Muslim culture. In Hafsa Zinai-Koudil's *Sans voix* (Voiceless, 1997), for example, the narrator explains that traditional Arab culture represents an 'immemorial Order' (13) that defines women's gendered role and sexually objectifies them, sometimes even as genitalia.

The sexual reification of women as genitalia is one of the most striking features in French-Maghrebi texts. In many ways, women in some Maghrebi immigrant texts are nothing more than '"black holes" (so to speak),' to quote Lionnet again, 'within and against which all interpretative discourses can only come to a halting stop' (*Geographies* 150). In *Sans voix*, the mother, who perpetrates the 'immemorial Order' reminds her daughter that she is 'nothing but a crack, a "pee-slit"' ('rien qu'une brisure, une "fente à pipi"') (13). In Charef's *Le Thé au harem d'Archi Ahmed* (1983), the male narrator Mehdi similarly describes women as 'hairy holes' (61). Throughout the novel, Mehdi and his buddies repeatedly gang-rape Madeleine, a mentally disabled girl (83), and share and compare women in other sexual adventures (155). Their nonchalant attitude towards women is most perturbing; they unabashedly experiment with Madeleine, prodding her or anatomizing her – likening her clitoris to 'elephant ears,' for example (84). Mehdi, the narrator, explains that this sexual exploitation (which cultivates male machismo and eases men's feelings of inferiority, despair, and boredom) is somewhat justified because women are merely 'holes with hair around them' (*'un trou avec du poil autour'*) (61). In Charef's chilling example, not only are women reduced to monstrous or abject genitalia, but more problematically, this sexual objectification enables sadistic violence against them.

Women thus come to represent '"black holes" (so to speak)' that can easily be penetrated, violated, or abused, without thought, conscience, or impunity. In these explicit examples of sexual objectification, body imagery related to women is bereft of any affective feelings whatsoever. Given such perturbing sexual body imagery, how might writers deploy body imagery to incite feeling, or even, effectuate change? Given its abusive translation in some Maghrebi texts and in patriarchal discourses, can bodily rhetoric effectively translate the sufferings of Maghrebi immigrant women?

Mothers

Representations of mothers in Maghrebi literature are scarce; however, when portrayed, their bodily rhetoric speaks volumes. In contrast to fictions that explore the experience of first-generation males,[2] there are no corresponding novels that focus on the Maghrebi mother.[3]

Rather, descriptions of the mother are generally found in Beur texts, where the mother figure is presented as a foil to immigrant children. Typically, in these cursory descriptions, mothers stand for traditional Arab values that are confronted with the challenges of modernity in immigration. Conspicuously, many of these cultural clashes are enacted by these mothers' bodily performances, which in many ways reflect the 'theatrics' and 'sociosomatic trances' that Jarret describes with respect to some of his patients (1721).

Just as fathers are often described as crippled, mothers are often depicted as hysterics. One of the first scenes from Charef's *Le Thé au harem d'Archi Ahmed* (1983) illustrates the mother's stereotypical hysterical bodily rhetoric, while also pointing to the intergenerational and cultural conflict that mothers often embody. In a scene described from the point of view of her son Madjid, the mother, Malika, confronts the son for coming home late. On a linguistic level, we are told that Malika 'speaks French badly with a funny accent' (16), and we are given an example of her linguistic hodge-podge: '*Ti la entendi ce quou ji di?*' (You udderstad wha me say?). Madjid pretends not to understand her backward babble. More pertinent is Malika's body language; along with her funny French, we are told that she also displays 'Neapolitan gestures' (16). As her son refuses to answer her, she expresses her parental frustration in hysterical exclamations and theatrical gesticulations, for example, 'she beats her thighs' or 'shakes her son' (16). In all, we are told, 'her African origins take over,' and she 'boogies like an Arab' (16). Malika's 'primitive' behaviour thus contrasts with the 'civilized' attitude of her son, who takes up the patriarchal role of the labouring father (he pretends to be exhausted from a long day of work), as well as that of the condescending French citizen. He pretends not to understand his mother's language and, in turn, verbally abuses her or patronizes her. In this scene, the mother is reduced to exaggerated, debased, and even animal-like body language. The scene concludes with the mother threatening the son in fluent Arabic. He, in turn, accuses her of all his problems in immigration, 'knowing that he will hurt his mother' (17). When the son shuts himself up in his room, the mother 'continues her tirade, the one she carries knotted up in her heart,' this time with no audience (17). Her solo performance is interrupted when she is called to help another woman, who is being beaten by her drunken husband.

In Charef's example, the mother's 'boogie' dance and bad French are supposed to offer the reader comic relief. However, they only replicate colonialist discourse, which also derides colonized subjects as backward and primitive; Malika's essentialized Mediterranean, Arab, or African roots do not belong in civilized French society. Also disturbing is the mention of the mother's grief in immigration, and her subsequent attempt to curb the abusive violence that another woman is facing. Disquietingly, in the subsequent scene, some of the actions of the drunken abuser, 'to gesticulate, to menace, to scream' (20), remind us of Malika's bodily rhetoric. Furthermore, we are told that this abuse is a 'permanent spectacle' (19), much like the mother's perpetual tirades and mournful complaints (16). In both these scenes, however, the focus remains on the son's experience and his existential angst; the mother's suffering is secondary. While his mother is dealing with the drunk, our attention is still drawn to Madjid – who remains in his room ruminating on his immigrant condition; he then zones out in front of the television. In the end, despite her stereotypical bodily rhetoric, ambiguous in its comic and condescending effects, the mother does subdue the drunken abuser, and so she is ultimately successful despite her 'backward' behaviour.

In some cases, the mother's 'primitive' behaviour is described as a means of opposing French social structures, as a radical counter-discourse to Western values. Minna Sif's *Méchamment berbère* (1997) offers a laudatory portrait of mother Khadija, who is of Berber origin, and who rebelliously resists the conventions of French society. For instance, the narrator describes Khadija's unconventional tactics at the supermarket: without hesitation, she undresses her children in the aisle and dresses them in new clothes from the racks, or she has them eat, 'serving themselves directly from the shelves; it was much easier than carry-out' (139). The narrator seems to approve of her brazen, criminal behaviour, describing it with humour and characterizing Khadija herself as 'priceless' (*impayable*) (139). In another scene, Khadija confronts government officials who refuse to grant her immigration papers and tell her to return home to Morocco. In crass language, and using scatological imagery, she describes her difficulties of immigration:

I answered the girl at the consulate [...] without embarrassment: 'Fatty, when you'll have your pussy ripped up by six births, when your husband has disposed of you like a piece of rotten flesh to find some fresher meat, when you'll go beg bread for your kids from the French and they give it to you with all their consideration, while your compatriots double-bolt their heart, I wonder if you'll feel like going back to your *bled* to eat croutons soaked with olive oil while praying to the heavens that a charitable neighbour fuck you in exchange for a handful of potatoes to make some broth for the kids.' (138)[4]

In her graphic diatribe, Khadija introduces the suffering body of the immigrant woman in the midst of immigration bureaucracy. With her explicit bodily rhetoric, she shocks her interlocutors, the immigrant official, and readers alike into awareness of the real-life repercussions of immigration policies and the socioeconomic hardships that immigrant women face. With her references to 'ripped up pussies' and 'rotten flesh,' she emphatically stresses the sexual objectification that women suffer. Moreover, she makes clear that her actions are not self-serving but are all for the welfare of her children; she is even willing to prostitute her body to ensure her children's survival. In sum, for Sif, the Berber mother Khadija represents a highly embodied counter-discourse to hegemonic Western culture: her actions flout Western consumer culture, and her graphic language calls attention to many of the problems encountered by Maghrebi immigrant women. Khadija's bodily rhetoric renders the hardships of immigration explicit, memorable, and perhaps offers of a means of surviving them.

Unlike Sif's positive description, the mother's bodily rhetoric more generally proves problematical for her children, especially her daughters. In Charef's example, we observe a son's typical reaction to his mother – which may perhaps be described as a mixed response of patronizing paternalism, ridicule, and indifference. By contrast, daughters often feel more directly threatened by their mothers' language and behaviour. What is more, they refuse to adopt their mothers' rhetoric, because they reject its underlying Arab cultural values and the degrading stereotypes that it entails. In Farrudja Kessas' *Beur's Story* (1990), the daughter describes her mother as a warrior, who was trained in the art of 'murderous words' ('*le verbe assassin*'), for in Algeria, as she explains, a women's best friend is her razor-sharp tongue (25). The daughter 'must shield herself in armour' to protect herself from her mother's 'poisoned arrows' (25). Her mother's 'killer words' demonstrate that 'a woman is nothing but a bitch!' (Une femme, c'est comme une chienne!) (25). In this example, the narrator suggests that her mother merely replicates patriarchal rhetoric that 'condemns her to live out and take up the role assigned to her' (25). The daughter is the victim of her own mother's verbal abuse and the gendered violence that the mother perpetrates.

As Irina Novikova argues, immigrant daughters must sever them- selves from the ways of their mothers to attain integration into the host society. As a result, they often view the mother with disgust, as a locus of failure, danger, and abjection: 'A mother figure looms as the abject in the conversion plot of moving from an immigrant to citizen. Mothers are never instructors, but strange dissociating monstrous figures [...] the site of contamination' (303). Indeed, as in the literary examples cited above, the mother is often relegated to a shocking, grotesque, or mutilated figure, translated through graphic, scatologi- cal imagery associated with sexualized bodies: 'bitches,' 'pussies ripped up by birth,' or 'discarded pieces of rotten flesh'(Kessas 25; Sif 138). Curiously enough, despite their theatrical bodily rhetoric, there are very few descriptions of mothers' actual bodies in these texts – rarely, for example, are their physical features or their faces described. Ironically, although the mothers' only recourse to survive immigration is through reference to their bodies, their bodies are largely missing from these texts. Moreover, by virtue of their typified theatrics and vociferous tirades, most immigrant mothers come to resemble each other. As a result, although explicit, their bodily rhetoric is easily sup- pressed as the rather common literary convention of the emotional or hysterical woman. Saliently, mothers' individual experiences of immi- gration are never fully fleshed out. Rather, the mother figure serves to showcase intergenerational differences inherent in immigration – edu- cation, language, gender, and social class – and so effectively translates what second-generation writers wish to convey about traditional values in immigration, as inflected by gender and ethnicity.

Daughters

In contrast to the synoptic portrait of mothers, Beur novels offer a more nuanced perspective of daughters, or second- and third-genera- tion immigrant women. As an ensemble, these texts explore the theme of 'double exile,' or the dislocation that these women feel in both French and Arab society, and highlight their attempts to negotiate tra-. ditional Arab culture, while also integrating into French society. In most of these stories, Beurette heroines must somehow break away from the social norms of either French or Arab culture. For instance, in Sakinna Boukhedenna's *Journal 'Nationalité: immigré(e)'* (1987), the narrator returns to Algeria to flee racial discrimination in France, only to encounter sexism in Algiers. Kessas' *Beur's Story* (1990) offers another means of escape: entering the French system through education. Finally, the heroine in Leïla Sebbar's *Shérazade* (1982), runs away from home and takes up a multitude of roles, from delinquent to seductress, to break free from her oppression, much like the seductive cunning figure of the *1001 Nights*, but in modern-day disguise.

Boukhedenna's semi-autobiographical novel, *Journal 'Nationalité, immigré(e)'* exemplifies the condition of double exile. Narrator Sakinna defines herself as 'the victim of a lack: cultural identity [...] rejected by the French and native Arabs [...] Neither Arab, nor French' (74). In France, she faces racial and ethnic discrimination; for her, France is 'a country of racism, inhospitality and daily humiliation' (100). At school she is labelled a terrorist (22, 20), deemed smelly and unhygienic by her cooking instructor (26), and insulted by her typing instructor as 'a commie, Black Panther, delinquent, a bitch, a slut, not to mention Algerian' (17). Sakinna chooses to flee to Algeria, believing that there she could 'finally breathe' (100). Yet, in Algeria she faces another type of discrimination: sexual inequality. On the street, she is constantly harassed by men (98), and she must be accompanied by a man both in hotels and on the street (97); at night she fears being either raped or hunted down like a dog by the police (97, 113). Men are not her only oppressors: women also question her virginity (93), and laugh at her at the *hammam* (public baths) (79). She is repeatedly insulted as the 'French slut' (33, 75, 82), or in Arabic as *'Bint haram'* (bastard girl) (98) or *'quahba'* (whore) (85, 95, 98). In a last attempt to find a cultural home, Sakinna espouses the Palestinian cause, only to almost be raped by a Palestinian intellectual (113). In the end, she rejects the oppressive elements of both cultures: 'Arab culture means reducing women to the state she's at, I don't want that Arabness. If being Arab in France means "Bougnoule," and that I must be naturalized to be French, that never' (100). Although she concedes that 'France is racist' (100), she returns there, because at least in France she can 'live alone without a husband, without father or mother' and 'can scream "NO" to racism, "NO" to the exploitation of women' (100). Despite her choice, however, she considers herself as cultureless: an 'immigrant on the path of exile' with the 'identity of an illegitimate woman' (126).

Sakinna's psychological suffering in immigration is most explicitly expressed through her body. For instance, her 'health [is] poorer and poorer' (68), her 'smile is extinguished by exile' (58), and 'her head hurts from all the hate [she] ruminates' (84), as 'every day rolls along like the tears pouring from [her] heart running over with sadness' (68). This bodily rhetoric, characterized by generalized physical symptoms of dis-ease, is a prevalent theme in most Beur women's texts.

In Ferrudja Kessas' *Beur's Story*, heroine Malika also points to her great despair through her body: she cannot sleep, cannot eat, has nightmares, and, 'drunk from solitude and sadness' (25), often faints from exhaustion. Most often, though, she bears her suffering in paralyzed silence, 'her spirit having detached from her battered body' (62). In contrast to Malika's depressed state, her best friend Farida manifests more dramatic manic tendencies. Much more vociferous about her unhappiness, she belligerently quits school to resist her oppressive mother-in-law. Shut up at home, she suffers frenzied psychotic incidents and ultimately hurls herself out the window.

Such bodily rhetoric, however, both in its depressive and violent physical manifestations, is not unique to Beur women's texts. Rather, it clearly reflects the symptomatic *malaise* that I discussed in chapter 3, a *malaise* that characterizes French Maghrebi fiction, first-generation texts and Beur novels by men and women alike. I draw attention to it because it distinguishes an important feature of early Beur women's texts – women's bodily rhetoric is not specifically depicted as sexualized or gendered. Rather, described in generic terms, women's somatic suffering is characteristic of the immigrant condition. Although Sakinna experiences both sexual and racial oppression, her body only translates one type of suffering, the pain of immigration.

Moreover, the discrimination that women encounter in these texts is usually directed at their racialized bodies or cultural identities, and not, conspicuously, at their sexualized bodies or gender identities. Again, in this way, early women's texts are largely undifferentiated from men's texts – the cause of their suffering derives primarily from their physical characteristics, in particular, their racialized features. In *Journal 'Nationalité: immigré(e),'* Sakinna experiences racial discrimination both in France and in Algeria. For example, her teacher in France 'didn't like [her] Afro, although he was sure lice did' (26). In Algeria, she finds out that 'frizzy hair for a woman is shameful and it does not please masculine standards. A girl with frizzy hair is an immigrant, and an immigrant is a slut' (88). Remarkably, although Sakinna experiences explicit sexual discrimination in Algeria, there are few references to her sexualized or gendered body. Rather, this sexual discrimination is made evident through verbal abuse, in expletives such as '*quahba*' (whore) or through men's actions (when she is almost raped). By omitting specific physical references to Sakinna's sexualized body, perhaps the author wishes not to reproduce the sexual objectification that oppresses her.

In early Beur texts, women's bodily rhetoric usually emphasizes one aspect of their 'double exile': their sociocultural dis-ease as second-generation immigrants. In recent years, however, representations of Beur women have shifted away from ethnic discrimination to focus more on women's sexual oppression. In this turn, women's bodily rhetoric has increasingly showcased women as sexualized bodies, and in particular, as sexually violated bodies.

Perhaps the best example of this trend to exhibit sexual violence is Samira Bellil's *Dans l'enfer des tournantes* (In the Hell of Rotations, 2002), one of the best-selling Beur books of 2002. In this semi-autobiographical account, Bellil puts forward the repeated rapes that narrator Samira suffered as a teenager: she was the victim of a number of gang-rapes, termed '*tournantes*' in *cité* slang (in English, roughly translated as 'rotations'). Her account begins with her brutal imprisonment in a basement by a gang and the repeated rapes and tortures that ensue (26–32). Several such horrific incidents are repeated in the novel; every time Samira finds some sort of resolution, she is raped yet again, be it at her boyfriend's house or at the beach (118–19). The narrative describes the shame, disgust, and ostracism that Samira faces at home, at school, and in her neighbourhood; it details her desperate attempts to convince the police and prosecute her assailants; it delves into her growing depression, her descent into drugs and alcohol; and it expresses her growing frustration, rage, and violence. In the end, the narrative resolves successfully; after years of therapy, Samira is able to find a job, stable friends, and reconstruct her traumatic experiences into a book.

Throughout her account, Samira takes up an explicitly bodily based rhetoric. Notably, after her first rape, she is unable to speak about the incident, and even pretends it never happened. However, as she explains, her body takes over to translate her pain: 'The violence and distress that inhabit me need to explode. My body finds a solution. The body is so intelligent! It starts to have epileptic seizures. Not just anything! Sometimes, seven or eight people need to hold me down [...] Thus these crises become my new means of expression' (107).[5]

The body, personified, begins to 'speak' its own violent language in order to translate Samira's rape. Later, it is through violence, alcohol, and drugs that Samira expresses her despair. Ultimately, however, it is by writing her book that she most successfully communicates her trauma and achieves some peace and healing. Nonetheless, on reading this book, we are unsure whether it is the account of a victim or a survivor. The final image in the novel continues to emphasize Samira's horrific victimhood: 'Here, I have presented you with the worst of lived experiences in the cité. This worst [experience] which has made my whole youth topple into horror' (280).[6] In all, given her undivided attention to her sexual exploitation and her victimization, the reader is perhaps left with the final image of Samira as a victim, not a heroine.

This recent bodily rhetoric of sexual abuse clearly and convincingly translates the sexual exploitation, humiliation, and sociocultural problems of contemporary girls in the *cités*. Though graphic and powerful, such bodily rhetoric may, however, also generate certain undesirable effects. Manifestly, the sexual violence that Samira suffers is no longer perpetrated by outsiders to the Beur community, both by the 'native' French and by Arabs in the Maghreb, but rather stems from internal violence within the *cités*. The hardships of immigration and citizenship are thus transformed into the sufferings of ghettoization and gang wars. In some perspectives, then, these problems may no longer be considered to be the problems of the host country, but rather those of a marginalized immigrant community.

In another vein, the figure of Samira as a sexually abused woman may be conflated with the generic image of the female rape victim. As such, the specific ethnocultural dimensions of Beur women's sexual exploitation risk being dismissed. Nonetheless, it is important to remember that this sexual violence reflects the complex sociocultural attitudes of young Maghrebi immigrant men, as well as, obliquely, certain Arab-Muslim traditions nurtured by their parents.

Finally, if such explicit imagery of sexual exploitation becomes a repeated trope, it risks perpetrating further sexual objectification and victimhood. In so doing, it risks being dismissed as a sensationalist stereotype, or even an annoying cliché.

Fictional Rebels

Fictional testimonial novels offer an alternate representation of Maghrebi women; they relate the experiences of former women rebels or resistance fighters who settle in France as refugees. In these testimonials, which surfaced in the 1990s during the recent Algerian civil war, Algerian heroines bear witness to the horrors they experienced in fundamentalist Algeria, while also depicting the subsequent trauma they experienced in immigration as survivors of war. The violence depicted in these women's dreams and memories is overwhelming both in its brutality and its recurrence. As Hafsa Zinai-Koudil enumerates in *Sans voix* (1997), 'kidnappings, murders, coups, rapes ... And the dead add to the dead in a spiral of never-ceasing violence' (132).

Above all, the graphic sexual violence explicitly detailed in these texts is especially perturbing; repeatedly, the reader is forced to visualize abuse, rape, sexual torture, or genital mutilation. Perhaps the most sickening example of such gore may be found in *Sans voix*, where a woman who refused to cooperate with her assailants, who 'chose to be mute' (184), is raped by five men. Yet, the description of a gang-rape is seemingly not horrific enough; the woman narrator then proceeds to meticulously describe what she terms as 'the ultimate horror': 'Because I chose to be mute, they chose to avenge themselves in the most inhuman way possible. First they brutally raped me one by one; I no longer remember if there were four or five of them, and then, when I was half-conscious, they tied up my feet, spread my legs between two trees, and taking off the dog's muzzle, gave him the order to attack. And it was then that the ultimate horror was consummated. Screaming to rip out my lungs, I felt the powerful fangs of the beast dig deep into my genitals, tearing away entire pieces of bloody meat with his maw, and then I fainted' (184–5).[7]

The narrator then interrupts her story to pull up her dress and publicly exhibit 'the real 'cave' at the bottom of her belly' (185) to her interlocutors. She concludes that her story became 'famous and spread through the region'; her nickname, 'The Mute,' derived from the fact she has 'no more lips, the dog ate them' (185). Clearly, the woman rendering this testimonial is not mute; rather, she has a powerful voice that viscerally bears witness to the sadistic brutality of the Front Islamique du Salut (FIS)[8] forces. I find it disturbing, however that this woman's recognition largely stems from her graphic story of sexual mutilation. Her story becomes her physically mutilated body that she must publicly expose in order to be believed by her interlocutors.

As Mildred Mortimer explains in *Maghrebian Mosaic* (2001), women writers often take up imagery of the mutilated body for a number of reasons: 'In most of the texts, the commemoration and mourning take the form of re-member-ing, of putting together maimed and mutilated bodies. Indeed, the theme of the body in pieces recurs insistently in the corpus as a powerful image of the physical and psychological suffering of the victims of terrorism. The repeated use of nouns referring to body parts and of verbs indicating mutilation creates a graphic image of the pain war inscribes on the bodies of ordinary citizens and, at the same time, evokes the dismemberment of the country itself' (182). As Mortimer points out, the image of the mutilated body most effectively conveys the pain of war. Symbolically, the image of violated women's bodies reflects the violence against the nation of Algeria itself. Finally, 're-membering the dismembered body' proves an apt image for the remembering, recovery, and mourning that these women must engage in to find healing for their psychological suffering and trauma. On the one hand, because FIS violence often goes unrecognized, it is understandable that women writers take up such graphic imagery to shock readers into awareness of this aggression. On the other hand, it is disturbing that all of the heroines in these testimonials are survivors of sexual abuse. Seemingly, to be 'Great Heroines,' women must ostensibly first be 'Great Victims.' Moreover, their heroism and victimhood generally derive from sexual oppression.

Furthermore, in this dichotomy, men stereotypically assume the role of the 'Great Enemy.' All their vices and crimes can be reduced to sexual transgressions. For example, in Malika Mokeddem's *Des rêves et des assassins* (1995), the narrator's father is a butcher, who by extension, represents the butchery of the FIS against innocent civilians. All his ideals, we are told, are inextricably linked with sex: 'heroism and nationhood were indissoluble from fornication' (13). 'His disease,' we are told, is 'sex' (11). In this novel, even young boys 'are already censors': 'Barely have they spit up their milk-teeth, they already see women as satanic souls' (79). In all, because of their overdrawn emphasis on sex, some of these novels simply reproduce stereotypical depictions of both men and women and offer a reductionist view of the situation in Algeria and of the experience of these refugees in France.

The position these women espouse in immigration is also disquieting. Their experience in immigration is seemingly completely defined by trauma resulting from their own past victimization or the horrific violence that they have witnessed. Although these women were heroines or rebels in Algeria, in France they are reduced to passive victims with no agency or possibility for healing.

Conspicuously, certain texts, such as Mokeddem's *Des rêves et des assassins*, offer few details about these women's immigrant lives.

Mokeddem simply summarily condenses the immigrant experience of the narrator to 'despair here' or 'BIG BIG NOSTALGIA' (176), stressed by capital letters. The narrator's emotional suffering is reduced to physical bodily pain, described in pithy laconic sentences: 'I can't eat. Can't sleep. Can't move. Have burns in stomach. Cramps below' (222).
. Other testimonials, perhaps delve too excessively into the deep psychological suffering of these women refugees in France. Most women experience signs of post-traumatic stress disorder upon arriving in their host country, suffering nightmares, panic attacks, and hallucinations. Baya, the narrator of Zinai-Koudil's *Sans voix* (1997), constantly repeats the sentence: '*J'ai peur d'apprendre*' ('I am afraid of finding out'), which haunts the entire text.[9] Her fear is usually accompanied by violent bodily reactions, such as delirious insomnia (30), nausea (37), or panic attacks (37). For Baya, there are no stable referents in immigration. Everything is marked by fear, loss, alienation, and ambiguity, which Baya deliriously defines as a life '*entre-deux*' (in-between): 'A cruel game; black-white thoughts. Life and death. A choice-pain, bitter tears. Leave. Live. Return. Die of absence in the cold of exile. Absence-presence, morbid game' (9). Everything seems to expose Baya's pain, with the result that her story becomes 'a chronicle of dramas, lived in flesh and blood' (47).

Yet, Baya's suffering is also self-induced. Baya admits that she could be happy in sunny Paris, however, 'she resists amnesia at the price of pain' (142). Guilt-ridden, she feels she is betraying her country, her family, and friends in Algeria by living a happy life in France; therefore, she chooses to suffer with them in her memories (147). In the end, she concludes, 'the problem' – her double-suffering – 'is too big. Too complicated without a doubt. No one would understand. It's better to shut up, always shut up' (134). Guilt-ridden, unwilling to communicate her pain, unable to fit in, Baya leaves France to return to Algeria, where she hopes 'to exist' as 'more than a ghost'; because in France, as she sums it up, 'she does not exist; she is no one, a being without identity and soul' (158).

The suffering of past trauma thus defines these women in immigration. Such all-encompassing trauma easily becomes dismissed as unrealistic, exaggerated, or sensationalized, as is clearly the case in Latifa Ben Mansour's *L'Année de l'éclipse* (The Year of the Eclipse, 2000). This novel attempts almost too avidly to detail the brutal events surrounding the rape and torture of Habya, a pregnant Algerian. From the outset, the omniscient narrator describes Habya as a mute victim, who cannot express the ineffable violence that she witnessed and experienced at the hands of the FIS; however, it suggests that 'her mouth [was] wounded by the genitals of torturers' (13). The whole novel details the mental and physical suffering that the traumatized Habya witnessed in Algeria and continues to endure in immigration, finally culminating with her dramatic, pathos-laden confession of the murder of her husband and daughter. Although Habya does not want to be just another example of sensationalism and obscenity, like on television (197), her ultimate dramatic testimony is very visual, sensationalist, even superstitious (it was Friday the 13th, at exactly 13:00) and melodramatic (she subsequently faints).

Ben Mansour's novel adopts a rhetoric of pathos and melodrama and insists on Habya's heroic victimhood. For example, in her first words, Habya compares herself to a Christlike martyr (15). Her trauma is often translated as physical pain, such as headaches and fainting or as scatological bodily functions such as urinating or vomiting, which are somehow 'purified' in her 'natural' maternal role: 'The abominable and the pure, together, fed by her flesh' (17). The 'crude human suffering' (208) she bears so stoically is contrasted with the *bobos* ('owies') that 'handicap and destroy' (210) the lives of psychology patients in France in the clinic where she works as a secretary. Ironically, amid the horrors in Algeria, Habya was portrayed as a hero; she was a doctor who saved numerous people, women especially, for example, by granting girls certificates of virginity (55, 211). In immigration, however, Habya becomes a woman crazed by despair, who wants to die or dramatically throw herself out of the window.

Any successful integration of these female Algerian resistance fighters into French society in these novels is seriously undermined. There is seemingly no role, even in fiction, for a female rebel-fighter in the French metropolis. The heroine in Mokeddem's novel refuses to belong to any group in immigration, be it French society or a community of Maghrebi women; she prefers to remain alone, othered in her special victim status. Zinai-Koudil's alienated heroine prefers to return to the horrors of Algeria rather than to live as a ghost in France. As for Ben Mansour, she offers the reader an unrealistic, fairy-tale ending: after finally telling her full story, Habya experiences a '*renaissance*' (the title of the last section), marries the doctor she had worked for, and gives birth to twins.

In all, the rhetoric of the body deployed to depict these rebel women does not seem to resist any stereotypical conventions. On the contrary, it continues to replicate the sexual violence and oppression that these women suffered in Algeria at the hands of reified Muslim fundamentalists. Seemingly, the only power and authority that these women hold in immigration is their victimization, which derives from graphically explicating the sexual mutilation that they have endured.

Real Rebels?

The various forms of women's bodily rhetoric examined in this chapter seem precarious, if not problematical, when the literary critic considers their effects in social discourse. In some instances, mothers' theatrical bodily rhetoric does indeed resist Western capitalist and bureaucratic discourse, and it certainly can make readers poignantly aware of the sexual objectification of Arab women and the sufferings of women in immigration. If deployed as a foil to daughters' experiences, however, such bodily rhetoric risks relegating first-generation women to representatives of oppressive Arab-Muslim traditions. If repeated recurrently, it risks reducing mothers to the conventional stereotype of the emotional or hysterical woman.

Daughters' dual bodily rhetoric does in some ways effectively incarnate Beurettes' problematical 'double exile.' Their rhetoric of somatic malaise clearly draws attention to their sociocultural sufferings as French-Maghrebi immigrants. Yet, as such, it also risks being conflated with the experience of male immigrants, or dismissed as the generic experience of immigration. In contrast, the daughters' more graphic sexualized bodily rhetoric may reduce women to universal victims of sexual abuse or restrict violence against them within the sphere of the ghetto. The twin-fold bodily rhetoric of the rebel-refugees – of sexual violence and traumatic suffering – manifestly confines these supposedly empowered women to enduring victimhood, with little possibility of escape or agency within the social system.

In many instances, these women's heroism may even be deemed a form of 'zeroism' – a term coined by Ross Chambers, to describe patients in AIDS pathographies (*Facing It* 4). In this type of heroism, characters need not act, but only display their disease-ravaged bodies to create a form of social awareness. In French-Maghrebi fiction, it would appear that both Beur heroines (Boukhedenna, Kessas, Bellil) and even former Algerian resistance fighters (Mokeddem, Zinai-Koudil, Ben Mansour) are often reduced to a form of passivity and victimhood, wherein the only marker of their agency and identity is the suffering somatically represented by bodily pain. Problematically, their heroism is not determined by the actions that they perform, but rather, by the suffering that they endure. Whether such zeroism, in the case of able-bodied and illness-free persons, can raise social awareness, or elicit sympathy or action from the reader, remains questionable.

The recurring rhetoric of victimization, especially sexual victimization, is most disturbing in these representations of Maghrebi women. Moreover, the fictional representation of sexual victimization seems to grow increasingly more pathetic, more graphic, and more sensationalist as this trend continues. As I have pointed out, in Arab-Muslim discourse women are sexually objectified, even reduced to genitalia. By repeatedly reproducing this sexual objectification and violence, women have not escaped it or resisted it. On the contrary, it may be argued that some authors draw on it to gain voice and representation in literary discourse.

To conclude on a positive note, however, as evidenced by the Ni Putes Ni Soumises movement, new rebel Maghrebi women are on the rise, who, hopefully, will engender a more resistant form of rhetoric for Maghrebi women. Interestingly, Ni Putes Ni Soumises generated several autobiographies: *Ni putes ni soumises* (2005), by the leader of the movement Fadela Amara, and *Vivre libre* (2003), by supporter Loubna Méliane, as well as Bellil's *Dans l'enfer des tournantes* (2002). In contrast to Bellil's harrowing *récit* of rape, Amara's and Méliane's autobiographies do not stem from personal rape experiences, nor do they remain too fixated on women's suffering, discrimination, or victimization. In so doing, they rarely deploy the forms of bodily rhetoric described in this chapter. When they do refer to generic bodily rhetoric, they differentiate and distance it as the experiences of their former selves, or those of other women in the *cité*. For instance, Méliane reminisces that as a teenager she felt 'mal à l'aise' and, as a result, was always sick from school for days on end, becoming a real 'malade imaginaire' (39). In the present, however, both Méliane and Amara focus on their rise to consciousness, their defiance, their protests, and above all, on their involvement in solidarity movements. Focused on action, the bodily rhetoric of these activist writers may thus be described as that of an 'engaged body in movement.'

Yet, neither Amara nor Méliane dismisses the sufferings that women in immigration face. Amara points to the increased violence of young men, especially brothers, who, like traditional Arab patriarchs, attempt to cloister their sisters at home, but then go out in gangs and sexually abuse girls from different *cités* (34–40). She suggests that Maghrebi girls, who have greater success at school, at work, or with French boyfriends (39), have greater mobility in French society than do their brothers, who often become resentful. She examines the rise of Islamization and France's disengagement with Arab affairs to explain the increased violence in these marginalized ghettos. Finally, Amara points out that 'the worst has been watching men take greater and greater possession of women's bodies' (38). Amara's examples of bodily possession range from women's inhibited freedom of movement to their tendency to wear unprovocative, unisex clothing. As a result, according to Amara, there are only three types of women's bodies existing in the *cité*: submissive bodies of women, who take up the traditional roles of obedient mother or daughter; masculine bodies of women, who join their brothers in gangs and partake in violent rebellion; and transparent bodies of women, who lead a spectral non-existence because of this hopeless situation.

In their texts, however, both Amara and Méliane exemplify yet another form of female body – that of the activist rebel, who incarnates a rhetoric of 'engagement,' 'movement,' and 'change.' Both of these texts are non-fictional autobiographies, however. Such bodily rhetoric now needs to be translated into Maghrebi fiction as well. I would argue that Maghrebi women's fiction needs different types of female bodies – women as activists, media personalities, political leaders, or humanitarians – who engage in a different, more resistant, form of bodily rhetoric.

6 'Pathologically Sick':
Metaphors of Disease in Beur Texts

Comment, coquine! Si je suis malade! Si je suis malade, impudente![1]
— Molière, *Le Malade imaginaire*

Devant cette douleur sans lésion, cette maladie repartie dans et sur tout le corps, cette souffrance continue, l'attitude la plus facile [...] est la négation de toute morbidité. A l'extrême, le Nord Africain est un simulateur, un menteur, un tire-au flanc, un fainéant, un feignant, un voleur.[2]
— Frantz Fanon, 'Le "syndrome nord-africain"'

In the previous chapters, I have pointed out that a generalized sense of dis-ease, or *malaise*, pervades Maghrebi fiction. Symptomatic bodily rhetoric depicts fathers as silent cripples, mothers as bodiless hysterics, or Beur women as victims of sexual abuses. What is more, Kassovitz's film, *La Haine*, and Charef's classic novel, *Le Thé au harem d'Archi Ahmed*, have engendered a generic narrative of Beur youth culture – characterized by corporal violence, drugs, and death – that is difficult to evade.

This chapter explores cases of Maghrebi authors – specifically Smaïl, Kacem, Zouari, and Zitouni – who most explicitly and purposefully take up metaphors of illness or physical disease as central paradigms of their texts. I explore how such a rhetoric of disease reappropriates and resists generic literary conventions to translate immigrants' sociocultural dis-ease. In so doing, I also investigate the effects of this rhetoric of disease/dis-ease with respect to the reader, dominant discourse, and Beur literature itself. If social 'dis-ease' is a stereotypical attribute of the immigrant condition, what happens when immigrant writers themselves start to pathologize their conditions? How can writers reappropriate the metaphor of disease as a means of resistance or self-identification? What possibilities does an explicit rhetoric of disease/disease offer immigrant writers?

Resisting Infection: The Metaphor of Disease

Disease is a precarious metaphor for immigrant writers to espouse. The medical model of disease generally operates on binaries: sickness and health, contamination and purity, or inside and outside. As Susan Sontag has shown, in her book *Illness as Metaphor* (1990), disease is often described in military terms: the body's boundaries are invaded by an alien intruder, who must be battled and resisted to protect the body fortress. Disease is thus a disquietingly productive metaphor when employed in social discourse: it advocates differences between the self and the other, the nation body and the alien invader, the citizen and the immigrant – intimating that if this division between the sick and the healthy is not maintained, the outcome will be lethal.

Moreover, disease has often been linked with immigrants. Historically, disease was frequently attributed a foreign origin. For instance, in the fifteenth century, syphilis was associated with a variety of names, each of which supposed the country of origin: 'the Neapolitan,' 'the French,' or 'the Polish' disease, or 'Canton disease' in China and 'the Chinese disease' in Japan. As Alan Kraut has shown, in *Silent Travelers*, in the United States specific immigrant groups were associated with particular diseases: Asians with bubonic plague, Italians with polio, and Jewish immigrants with tuberculosis. When the AIDS epidemic broke out in the 1980s, Haitian immigrants were pinpointed as the source of the disease (as well as homosexuals, another minority group). Disease is thus often attributed to the 'other,' the unwanted presence in society.

In France, French-Maghrebis were also considered diseased by some groups. The far-right Front National's original 1972 program stated that the party opposed immigration because 'it imperils the health of France.' By 1984 Jean-Marie Le Pen claimed: 'some French regions were literally gangrenous because of the foreign invasion' (cited in Christenfeld). The Front National, which continues to oppose the 'brown plague' (Halimi), is gaining in popularity; from 1974 to 2002 its share of the popular vote rose from 0.7% to 18% (BBC).

Given this discourse, why might Maghrebi authors themselves take up such metaphors of disease? To begin with, by explicitly reappropriating these metaphors of disease, Maghrebi writers may be both reflecting and resisting the pernicious stereotypes that define them, critiquing their social 'dis-ease' and clamouring for healing, recognition, inclusion, and sympathy in dominant discourse. Adopting such a 'sick status' thus might represent an oppositional manoeuvre, which, as Chambers defines it, is a survival tactic that makes the system 'livable' and offers the individual subject 'some sense of dignity and personhood' (*Room for Maneuver* 7).

Furthermore, immigrants might also construct and perform their identities as pathologically 'dis-eased' in order to define and maintain a certain otherness. In *Le poids du réel, la souffrance* (The Weight of the Real: Suffering, 1983), Denis Vasse claims that suffering precipitates a condition of inner alterity in the same way that exclusion or estrangement 'others' the subject externally: 'Suffering always seemingly comes from the foreign. Whether it is comes from the outside [...] or *the inside*, as in the case of disease' (25–6, italics in text). In the following section, I question why immigrant authors might advocate yet another alterity, an inner otherness – suffering and sickness – in their work.

However, such diseased texts might also, inadvertently, sicken readers or further infect them with preconceived stereotypes about immigrants, tainting immigrants as constant complainers, subaltern sufferers, or pathological victims. As discussed in the previous chapter, these immigrants' heroism may be reduced to zeroism, literally here, in the terms that Chambers describes in AIDS pathographies (*Facing It* 4); like AIDS patients at the terminal stages of the disease, their only agency may derive from exhibiting their disease-ravaged bodies. Let us now diagnose how this pathology of disease/dis-ease operates in immigrant texts.

Curing Disease/Dis-ease: Smaïl's Vivre me tue

My first example, *Vivre me tue* (1987), by Paul Smaïl, describes two models of healing one's social dis-ease. The novel follows the reflections of a Beur, whose homosexual brother, Daniel, is desperately attempting to transcend his marginal identity through hyperbolic health. Daniel pushes body-building to the extreme; he even becomes addicted to anabolic steroids to grant his body more 'perfect' definition. Although he becomes a star at a porn club, and is in fabulous physical shape, Daniel's hypermasculization is described in bestial or subhuman terms. For instance, he 'whinnies like a horse' and 'pisses orange' (53). No longer able to have an erection because of the steroids, he performs idealized masculinity using a fake penis. Daniel's attempts to 'perfect' his body prove futile and, in the end, lethal. The novel is framed with Daniel's death from stomach cancer in Germany. In ironic contrast to the hospital's final statement, 'Er hat nicht geleiden' (He didn't suffer), Daniel's real last words are sobs: 'I have hate, I have hate' (56). Smaïl dismisses any physical healing for the marginal identity. His story does, however, suggest a remedy for the pain of such marginalization: narrative and art. The narrator confesses to being contaminated by a 'virus' in his childhood: reading (97). He explains 'that literature in this environment is a pleasure almost as risky as homosexuality' (32). Just as Daniel recreates himself physically, the narrator transforms himself narratively, with adventure stories such as *Moby Dick* or *Treasure Island*. For example, he paraphrases Shakespeare's famous quote, 'If you prick us do we not bleed?' to 'Un Arabe n'a-t-il pas de yeux, un Arabe n'a-at-il pas de mains, des organes, des proportions [...] qu'un français de souche?' (An Arab does he not have eyes, an Arab does he not have hands, organs, proportions [...] like a native French person?) (180). Narrative and art grant him a redemptive cure and offer the 'truth.' While working out, Daniel would listen to a song by The Cure: 'This isn't truth, this isn't right, this isn't love, this isn't life, this isn't right real, this is a lie' (165). Unlike Daniel, too focused on his body to listen to the lyrics, the narrator heeds the healing words of language to reclaim and define his identity.

Smaïl's novel emphasizes that physical resistance to the French social order is futile. The only way to oppose the system is by manoeuvring from within, learning to read its language and adopting it. Indeed, Smaïl's polyvocal style counters normative narrative expectations: it sparkles with intertextual references, English, Arabic, *verlan* (Beur slang), and snatches of song. Smaïl's emphasis on education deviates little from the traditional immigrant narrative, however, which presumes a teleology of education and progress. In the end, the cultivated citizen survives and the dangerous alien outsider dies, exterminated by his own internal disease.

Infectious Disease: Kacem's Cancer

While Smaïl offers us a conventional cure for immigrant disease/dis-ease, Mehdi Belhaj Kacem deliberately reappropriates the abject position of the socially dis-eased individual in his disturbing novel, *Cancer* (1994). This stream of consciousness narrates the pathology of Stamin, an alternative songwriter who is infected with a pernicious form of cancer, 'a willed cancer, cultivated, but at the same time a cancer by birth ... cancer as intense contempt' (12). In an effluvium of gruesome, diseased imagery, we are shown how this cancer manifests itself: for example, Stamin imagines himself cutting off his father's penis and making his mother eat it, or amputating his father's arm with a chain-saw in order to sodomize his victim with it (53–4). In his mind's eye, he proceeds to massacre the rest of his family and his friends. For instance, he envisions his girlfriend hemorrhaging to death after being raped by a monstrous elephant. He fantasizes the destruction of all social institutions – education, work, leisure – and at the end of the book annihilates language itself; debasing language to 'flatulent' monosyllabic sounds, such as 'euh euh euh,' 'hi hi hi,' 'oh oh oh,' or 'moimoimoi.' Sick Stamin refuses any form of healing treatment every-thing is diseased: nature (229), art (55), and even laughter is a placebo. Stamin's sole pleasure is in imagining that he can inflict the most excruciating pain on everybody else. He even wants to eviscerate his readers, 'severing their synapses,' and 'suckling at the perspectives that hold them fast' (37), and 'seriously harm [his/her] mental health' (17). When reading this novel, it is impossible to escape being contam-inated by this insane disease/dis-ease. Through the very act of reading such sickening violence, the reader is also 'infected' by this violence.

In Kacem's *Cancer*, narrator Stamin reclaims the role of an 'infectious agent' assigned to him by dominant discourse, seemingly celebrating the contamination and abjection that this role entails. Just as Kristeva describes abjection as that which 'cannot be assimilated' (*Powers of Horror* 8), a 'place where meaning collapses' (9), Stamin takes up the abject position to resist the assimilation or the meaning granted to him by French society. With his diseased style, it is clear that Kacem attempts to pollute the novelistic genre. Is this text contagious, however? Does the audience feel any sympathetic relationship to this diseased victim? Does this repulsive writing compel readers to con-tinue reading or disgust them so much that they give up? By reappropriating the metaphor of disease, does Kacem succeed in disrupting dominant discourse? Or does this strategy, as a form of role-reversal, merely end up reinforcing the very norms it seeks to subvert?

On a theoretical level, I argue that, much like Smaïl's text, Kacem's *Cancer* operates on a rigid binary, in which one is either immune or diseased, civilized or othered, dead or alive. By attempting to embody the abject, Kacem paradoxically reinforces the very order he attempts to subvert. As David Caron argues in his analysis of AIDS texts in France, as a representation the abject can only figure the ritualized repetition of the act of abjection, in that it reinforces binaries and boundaries (79). Is it possible to embody the abject position, then – 'the quality of the object – that of being opposed to I' (Kristeva, *Powers of Horror* 1) without reinforcing its binary boundaries?

A Self-Inflicted Pathology: Starving to Death

Shifting away from metaphors of transmittable diseases that posit a binary, I now focus on self-inflicted pathologies – specifically anorexia and starvation. In Fawzia Zouari's *Ce pays dont je meurs* (1999) and Ahmed Zitouni's *Une difficile fin de moi* (1998), Beur immigrants choose to starve themselves to death rather than integrate into a society that alienates them. Their self-starvation represents a strategy of resistance, and, what is more, seemingly grants them an identity.

An Exceptional Hunger: Ce pays dont je meurs

In Zouari's novel, *Ce pays dont je meurs,* Amira, the youngest and only French-born member of a traditional French-Maghrebi family, is an anorexic who ultimately dies from her self-inflicted condition. The novel, inspired by a *'fait divers,'* chooses not to depict this death by starvation as a banal occurrence, symptomatic of the immigrant condition, but rather extols it as a heroic act of free will. Amira takes up hunger as a means of distinguishing herself from her family and resisting French society. She thus creates her identity out of threat to that identity – starvation.

The novel, narrated from the perspective of Amira's sister, delves into the details of Amira's estrangement from her family, Arab culture, and French society. As discussed in chapter 4, Amira's father, Ahmed, once a proud man in Algeria, becomes an anonymous assemblyline worker in France, who is injured in an accident and confined to a wheelchair. Paralyzed, he loses all patriarchal authority and voice, and is reduced to an abject object that cannot be looked upon (56). Amira's mother, Djamila, epitomizes the traditional values corrupted in modernity because of excessive materialism and consumerism. Instead of going on pilgrimages to her ancestral tombs (70), she goes on mad shopping sprees to Tati. As Woodman and Heywood argue, anorexia often involves a move to an autonomous identity that involves a rejection of the maternal figure in favour of the cultural codes of the father. In this novel, both parents die, exhausted from attempting to survive in the modern world.

Amira is similarly alienated from both Arab and French culture. She has no knowledge of Arab culture or religion (41). While the family's annual return to Algeria is described as a 'balm for their wounds' (122), for Amira Algeria is full of handicapped people who mistreat the mad and stone women (123). In France, she is equally set apart. Although her sister-narrator stresses that she has white skin, she is nonetheless teased for her 'onion' flesh, as well as her 'pig head' (44). Although she succeeds in school, she is accused of plagiarism (82), supposedly because a little Arab girl could not be smart. Later, after her father's death, discriminated against at work, she quits and spends most of her time sitting in her father's empty wheelchair, an image of utter dejection and lack of agency. Such zeroism is only further developed throughout the novel.

Amira's anorexia proves her greatest 'provocation' (86), and shows her 'difference' (87) and her 'decaying spirit' (86). As the illness progresses, Amira completely loses her identity to become her sick condition, un 'état' (98). Her mother refuses to believe her daughter's illness and calls it an 'unknown disease [...] A French disease' (95). Ultimately, she rejects her daughter because of this disease – 'you are not really sick, you are my daughter by mistake' (131). The narrator's sister is also initially frustrated that Amira adopts 'the same diseases as they [the French] do' (95).

Slowly, however, the sister-narrator comes to understand that Amira's anorexia is 'a way of finding her place, of fighting [...] of treating evil with evil' (133). She realizes that by her revolt, Amira is more Algerian than all of them. While she and her parents have merely attempted to find peace in their new home, Amira rebels against her adopted country (123). In her agonizing death speech, Amira reveals the deadly evil that caused her dis-ease: society's indifference and its lack of concern for the oppressed. This social apathy is clearly shown in the opening and closing sequences, when the authorities unconcernedly wheel Amira's corpse away, with 'mechanical gestures'; 'no one turns around [...] the retired placidly continue watching their dogs piss' (11). The family's tragic story provokes no pity; rather, it is dismissed as a stereotypical immigrant narrative: 'a father disappeared in a banal accident. A mother sick missing her country. A life without joy. The anorexic crises of Amira. Money lacking like with all the poor' (144).[3] The book concludes with the sister-narrator's promise to die too, because she finally fully understands her sister's pathology. She claims: 'Little sister, it's because of this France that you die, just like mother died of her Algeria. I, because of the impossibility of inventing another country' (185).[4] Here, the narrator sums up the impossibility of living in the past or in the present, in France or in Algeria – or even, in the real world, or in the realm of fiction. In its dismal conclusion, this story outlines a new and unexpected disease, one that is not associated with the immigrant. As the title suggests, *This Country I'm Dying Of*, we are to realize that, in fact, the nation itself is afflicted by a terminal and lethal disease.

Hunger Strikes All: Une difficile fin de moi

In contrast, Zitouni's *Un difficile fin de moi* transports starvation to a far more abstract level, that of human rights. By dying of hunger, the hero achieves a transcendent sense of identity and a collective identity with all the oppressed.

In the first part of Zitouni's novel, we observe the protagonist grossly gorge and then purge himself of all the negative influences of his past life, 'vomiting out the last crumb of infancy' (15). In a bulimic stream of consciousness, the narrator expels the maternal figure, who reflects a society of consumption and traditional passivity; the memory of his father, a 'terrorist' fighter, who exemplifies the fanaticism in Algeria and the oppressive patriarchal order (72); and his cynical lover, Matilde, who epitomizes the indifference and incomprehension of French society.

In hunger-starved hallucinations, the narrator forms new ideals for himself. He embodies all sorts of hungers-strikers (37–8): the figure of Fatiha, a 'virgin martyr' (27), who starved herself in his Algerian village to protest the treatment of widows in their country; political prisoners like Gerry Adams (99), and members of the Sinn Fein

(114–16). The book concludes with a union with the African *sans-papiers* to whom the novel is dedicated.

The narrator's fast is transformed into a cathartic, transcendental union with all the hungry, all the oppressed. In order to achieve this union, however, he must feed on all the stereotypes used to label the exploited – 'accidents,' 'stigmatized,' 'diseased' (36–7), and their bodily incarnations: 'Nothing but tools of the trade of flesh and blood [...] Broken bodies [...] Deteriorated bodies [...] Destroyed bodies' (41). In a climactic epiphany, the narrator realizes that these sick bodies are not symptoms of a disease that must be healed. Rather, they are signs of 'open conflict' and 'permanent rebellion' – they 'weren't in pain but in rebellion' (41). Only when the narrator achieves this *prise de conscience* – that the body in pain is the most basic form of resistance against the system – is he able to move beyond his body to a more abstract form of protest, in a struggle for universal human rights, a proletarian struggle, united with an all-inclusive community of the oppressed. This novel places the plight of immigrants in France on the level of universal human rights. It ends with the narrator's confession that his story is but a 'vapid excuse for those whom we crudely refer to as "the problem of immigration," although we owe them so much' (130). A personal purging of one's past, a cry of the oppressed, a rebellion against material culture, a tribute to immigrants, and a fight of solidarity against all global discrimination, Zitouni's novel offers an exhaustive exploration of the possible effects of self-starvation. Unfortunately, it also suggests that the only effective story that immigrants can tell is the story of their deaths by suicide.

Zouari and Zitouni's novels leave me perturbed. Both texts present hunger as a political act. Yet, the only resolution possible in this political performance is the annihilation of the subject in a final act of resistance. It seems a deeply solitary act that cannot impact society in any way.

These novels reflect a growing discourse of victimization, or 'wounded attachments,' as formulated by Wendy Brown with respect to the U.S. identity politics. Brown argues, in her article 'Wounded Attachments,' that in the politics of recognition, experiences of pain, trauma, and oppression increasingly become the basis of epistemological knowledge and moral authority. The result is that minority individuals are always assuming a victim position to confirm and legitimate identity for themselves. Clearly, these texts reflect this 'politics of pain'; their rhetoric fashions immigrants' identities out of victimhood, zeroism, and self-destruction.

These novels also point to some of the perils that this discourse of pain entails. Zouari uses anorexia and self-inflicted starvation to showcase a new and exceptional tragedy in the face of those often described in immigrant texts. The father's disability or the mother's death by exhaustion are not sufficient to translate the hardships of immigration; the author finds it necessary to sensationalize a tragic death by malnutrition to create a more pathos-laden story of utter suffering and sacrifice. In this case, the shock of the sensational, sacrificial anorexia eclipses more latent forms of social suffering, notably the family's poverty or its lack of social support. As feminist critics have argued, such is often the case in the politics of pain; this 'currency of distress has led to displacement whereby awareness of everyday structural adversity on a daily basis is eclipsed by the accounts of exceptional, personal, traumatic pain' (Skeggs 29).

Zitouni, on the other hand, finds it necessary to strip away any cultural or political elements that define individuals and to force them to a shared humanity. All traumas, afflictions, and oppressions are fused into a single image of the suffering body, seemingly the only vehicle oppressed individuals have with which to resist the social order. In Zitouni's humanist ideal, 'every difference counts as no difference,' as Wendy Brown might argue; every variety of subjugation – be it labour exploitation, political oppression, or racial discrimination – is neutralized to appeal to 'the universal ideal of juridical liberalism' (66). Zitouni's story engenders the opposite problem to Zouari's, that of relativizing the pain and reducing it to a common denominator, as a single reified narrative of victimization.

The immigrants' self-induced 'zeroic' victimization is perhaps the most disquieting element in these stories of suffering. The protagonists' subjectivity is seemingly not defined by their ability to act or work or think; rather, it is defined by the fact that they endure violence as passive victims. Since this violence is not inflicted on them by others, as physical injury, but rather structurally by their environment, as poverty or discrimination, they feel it necessary to harm themselves in order to become visible and legitimately in pain. Ultimately, however, both stories' struggle against oppression is lost – since liberation comes at the price of self-annihilation. This is a troubling disease/dis-ease, indeed.

Faking Pain to Claim a Name

In these novels, Maghrebi immigrant writers increasingly fictionalize their social dis-ease by textually embodying disease. To avoid annoying or stereotypical complaints of '*mal partout*,' they perform their pain with increasingly graphic and sickly performances, even hysterical theatrics. I have pointed to the ways that diseased texts attempt to resist their reification – by contaminating their hosts with a similarly infectious textual dis-ease (as in Kacem), by startling them from indifference with a heroic or zeroic act of self-sacrifice (as in Zouari), or by translating immigrant pain as a claim for universal human rights (as in Zitouni). I have also spotlighted some of the problems in this victim rhetoric: (1) the dis-eased self and other dichotomy that it replicates; (2) the agency possible for the sick, abject victim; (3) the shock of sensational trauma opposed to 'ordinary' suffering; and (4) the relativization of sufferings in an essentalizing universalist discourse.

In a last aside, I draw attention to a final problem: performing pain in order to claim a name. What happens when the author who assumes a marginalized victim position is not marginalized at all? What if a writer fakes pain to claim a literary name? What becomes of the abject – 'the immoral, sinister, shady,' 'that does not respect borders, positions, rules' (Kristeva, *Powers of Horror* 6)?

The case I am referring to (as those versed in Francophone studies have surely guessed) is the ficticious Paul Smaïl, who, in *Vivre me tue,* so smoothly replicated the conventional narrative of the healthy and hip immigrant. Yet, Paul Smaïl was not the Beur immigrant he pretended to be – supposedly the 30-year-old son of Moroccan immigrants, with a degree in comparative literature, writing under a pseudonym because of serious political problems. Upon the publication of his latest novel, *Ali le magnifique,* it was revealed that Paul Smaïl was a fraud: he was none other than Jacques-Alain Léger; a white, middle-aged novelist and former 1970s pop-star.

How can one analyse Paul Smaïl's work in light of this disclosure? Smaïl's fictionalized portrait of Beur culture has been taken to be a representation of actual Beur culture; some of his *verlan* was even officially institutionalized by dictionaries (Salles). *Vivre me tue* was hailed by critics as a work of literary style and a testament to personal and political engagement: 'a knife in the gut of contemporary French civilization' where 'personal and political themes intertwine' (Pascal).

Smaïl has even become such a 'classic' Beur writer that now, other novelists are accused of plagiarizing his 'authentic' style (Salles).

Even when the scandal of his impersonation erupted, Léger was
often placed in the position of a marginalized victim described as
alienated, embittered, or 'ashamed' – 'like a "project," like an "ethnic
minority"' (Mian). He was portrayed as representing the isolated,
abused rebel (Douin). Léger completely refutes any such alienation
and scoffed at the supposed suffering of the victim writer: 'When they
talk about the pain of writing, I am taken with a wild laughter ... I
don't suffer when writing. Writing is pleasure' (cited in Lelièvre).[5]

I am not saying that Smaïl/Léger became a successful writer
because he deftly adopted metaphors of disease. It is fair to say,
however, that *Vivre me tue* operates as a normative immigrant narrative and employs the conventional healthy and diseased and surviving
and suffering dichotomies: the 'healthy' Beur gains admission into
majority discourse by education and literacy and thus survives, while
the abject minority figure, the homosexual male, portrayed as diseased, suffers and dies. Similar is the case of Léger the writer, who
chooses not to conform to the proscribed roles of French identity politics. Instead of being viewed as a clever trickster adeptly performing a
role, the tendency is to place him, as a Beur writer, in the position of
the victim, the 'suffering rebel writer' even though he vociferously
denies any such assumptions.

The perils of diseased and dis-eased rhetoric are perhaps best exemplified by Smaïl's/Léger's 'fake fiction' and identity performance.
Ironically, Smaïl/Léger has recently accused another Beur writer,
Youcef M.D., of plagiarizing his style. Preposterously, as it turns out,
this supposed Beur author is yet another impostor – not a clandestine
Beur migrant, as reported by his publisher, but rather, an academic
from Strasbourg, named Claude Andrieux.[6] Pertinently and problematically, in his pseudo-autobiography, *Je rêve d'une autre vie: (Moi, le
clandestin de l'écriture)* (2002). Youcef M.D./Andrieux again writes of
'the sickness of being an Arab,' where 'you are branded with a hot-red
iron. You feel intense pain. It is a blow that strikes you every time your
name is pronounced' (47).[7] Youcef M.D.'s/Andrieux's summary statement here encapsulates many of the critical questions raised in this
chapter. Are Beur immigrants to be defined by 'pain' or the
'disease/dis-ease of being Arab?' What viable possibilities does this
pathological position offer immigrant writers?

The Ends of Bodily Rhetoric

On reading these chapters on Maghrebi immigrant fiction, one of my colleagues suggested that I should title this section '*Mal Partout*: Crips, Cunts, and Sickos,' because she felt that it best conveyed the sensationalist, graphic bodily rhetoric that I describe, and more importantly, she thought such a title would draw further readers to the book. I was a bit disquieted by these comments. In no way do I intend to convey that all Maghrebi immigrant fiction is rife with shocking bodily imagery or pain-filled stereotypes. Many Maghrebi immigrant texts do not deploy excessive bodily rhetoric. Moreover, most texts turn to other forms of expression such as cultural referents, traditional stories, humour, and satire to convey the immigrant experience in its variety; they do not merely dwell on immigrant suffering.

Nonetheless, as in ethnopsychology, there is a tendency for certain Maghrebi writers to turn to explicit bodily rhetoric to convey their social dis-ease. Such bodily rhetoric – characterized by brokenness, disability, mutilation, sexual violation, starvation, and disease – aptly translates these immigrants' suffering. On a fundamental level, the body is a universal signifier, shared and recognized by all human beings, and the expression of corporeal pain is perhaps the most direct way to communicate suffering so that it can be understood. Moreover, the body is the vehicle of traditional Arab culture, the sight and site of racial and ethnic stereotypes and perhaps the only stable referent that immigrants have. Throughout these chapters, I have shown how writers might also take up bodily rhetoric –as a strategy of resistance against cultural and social assimilation, as a symbol of socioeconomic exploitation, sexual oppression, or racial discrimination, and as a means of authenticating their suffering or even authorizing their identity.

In this chapter, focusing on the rhetoric of disease, I have pointed to particular problems related to this performance of pain. While such rhetoric resists dominant discourse, it also creates, performs, and reproduces immigrants' marginalized identities. Seemingly, this rhetoric of pain, in a groove of self-repetition and habituated resentment, grants writers *more* power and authority to speak. Finally, in such rhetorical performances, it becomes very difficult to distinguish 'real' immigrant suffering from a fictional performance of pain. Any clever imposter might take up this rhetoric of pain to gain a name in literary and social discourse.

In the end, must immigrant writers continue to claim pains, injuries, and suffering, always more explicit, always different, to maintain their authority and position? What will become of French-Maghrebi literature if it increasingly defines itself by bodily rhetoric, zeroism, victimization, and a politics of pain? If they are to perpetually perform bodily pain, French-Maghrebi writers risk becoming pathological victims. In so doing, their sufferings risk not being heard or heeded in the public forum. The epigraph to this chapter refers to Molière's risible 'Imaginary Patient' and to Fanon's dire warning about *mal partout* – the easiest response to repeated suffering is compassion-fatigue, and even, the denial of all suffering. Or in the extreme, as Fanon suggests, the victim will no longer be believed, but, rather, will stand accused.

PART III

Affective Cultural Translation:
Haitian *Vodou*

7 'Zombification': Hybrid Myth-Uses of *Vodou* from the West to Haiti

But Vodou is at once a religious and politico-social fact ... So much so, that
I dare say that the more one penetrates its mysteries, the more the history
of Haiti will reveal her secrets.[1]

– François Duvalier, *Oeuvres essentielles I*

In their article 'Working with Haitian-Canadian Families' (1998),
Canadian psychologists Gopaul-McNicol and colleagues discuss therapeutic interventions for Haitian immigrants referred to them for
mental health services. They explain that treatment should include
both 'assisting families with concrete needs' such as food, clothing,
shelter, and 'translation for those unable to communicate in English or
French' (235), but they also draw attention to the 'traumatic experiences' that these immigrants may have experienced as a result of sociopolitical and environmental conditions in Haiti (235). Most importantly, they emphasize the need to understand the cultural factors that
shape the psyches of Haitian-Canadian immigrants – in particular, the
religion of *vodou*, or 'the [Haitian] patient's spirituality which was his
greatest strength' (234). Gopaul-McNicol and colleagues urge thera-
pists working with Haitian immigrants to learn as much as possible
about the *vodou* religion; to work alongside Haitian psychologists who
understand Haitian religious practices; and even to seek the intervention of *vodou* priests in counselling their patients. In some cases, they
explain, Haitians' psychological problems – be they fear, depression,
or paranoia – might be linked to a problematical relationship with
vodou spirituality or, even, with the abusive use of *vodou* in Haitian
society.

In this part of the book, turning from psychology to literary studies, I explore how, in Haitian immigrant literature, cultural references to *vodou* beliefs and practices may be deployed to express the pain of immigration. Part II highlighted how Maghrebi authors increasingly stripped their suffering of cultural signifiers to exhibit their hardships through the universally shared referent of bodily pain. Part III, in contrary motion, delves into the difficulties of describing suffering with culturally specific connotations, such as those related to the complex cultural referent of Haitian *vodou*. In no way, however, does this focus imply that the body is absent from Haitian culture or Haitian immigrant texts. Quite conversely, the racialized, suffering, and politically traumatized body is explicitly visible both in Haitian literature and culture, in harrowing images of imprisoned bodies, tortured flesh, or the corpses of boat-people. Part III investigates to what extent these migrant bodies in pain might be represented not only with bodily referents, but with cultural signifiers as well, thus, delving into the possibilities and limits of a cultural rhetoric of pain.

This chapter thus draws attention to the complexity of cultural translation by showcasing the multivalent meanings ascribed to the cultural signifier of Haitian *vodou* in different political and historical contexts, both in the West and in Haiti. Haitian *vodou*, or 'voodoo'[2] in the West, has been largely misunderstood and misinterpreted in popular culture, and even in academic discourse. These Western cultural misconceptions reflect a form of 'zombification': in that they revive or evoke old preconceptions about Haitian *vodou* – be it racist depictions of *vodou* or deceptively 'resistant' appropriations of *vodou* – and ossify them into stereotypical depictions that have little to do with *vodou*, either in its cultural context, or in its political deployment. These misconceptions are largely propagated in literary and cultural productions that reflect particular political events and sociohistorical sentiments. Much like the immigrant narrative discussed in chapter 1 therefore, the trope of *vodou* has been assimilated by the West, as part of its cautionary pedagogical narrative, to further its hegemonic ends. In Haiti, as well, *vodou* has been inextricably linked to the Haitian national narrative. It has been appropriated to further various contentious nationalist agendas, including, saliently, that of François Duvalier's recent regime. As a result, *vodou* is for Haitian people a symbol of both resistance and oppression, of

freedom and suffering. While this chapter outlines the various literary and sociopolitical conventions associated with *vodou*, it is also
concerned with the emotional dimensions of these various cultural
translations. To discuss how immigrant writers might deploy *vodou*
to convey their sufferings of immigration (the subject of the next
chapter), it is crucial to understand not only the multiple cultural
translations of *vodou*, but also its polyvalent affective connotations.

Affective Cultural Translation

As Homi Bhabha has argued in *Location of Culture* (1994), 'the terms of
cultural engagement are produced performatively' (2) in 'insurgent
acts of cultural translation' (7). Bhabha's assertion urges us to consider
more seriously the underlying frameworks of such performative cultural translation. In its multiplicity of meanings and cultural contexts,
vodou resists transparent translation or any facile acts of insurgency.
Moreover, a focus on suffering draws attention to the emotional
dimensions of these cultural translations. It must be remembered that
culture, as a performance or rhetoric, is inherently affective – it relies
on and refers back to emotions, emotions associated with a particular
culture and, even, with a specific cultural signifier.

Currently, literary studies has a tendency to overlook the emotive
dimensions of culture. To illustrate, I refer to three of the canonical texts
of postcolonial, translation, and cultural studies: *The Cultural Studies
Reader* (*CSR*, edited by Simon During), *The Postcolonial Studies Reader*
(*PSR*, edited by Bill Ashcroft et al.), and *The Translation Studies Reader*
(*TSR*, edited by Lawrence Venuti). An examination of these texts
reveals that, while they all explore the socio-political dimensions of
culture, there are no in-depth analyses of its affective or emotional
dimensions; the words 'emotion' and 'pain,' for example, each occur
only twenty-four times in total in these three 500-page volumes, usually
idiomatically (such as in 'taking pains'). Only one article briefly discusses the role of emotions in popular culture (Naficy, in *CSR*) and only
one literary analysis fleetingly refers to pain (*PSR* 371). Ironically, in a
few places in these texts the authors urge the need for further study of
emotions: Richard Dyer stipulates that 'you have to learn what emotion
is embodied before you can respond to it,' while Rey Chow submits
that 'what we need, in other words, is a history of listening [...] and the
emotions that are involved in listening' (*CSR* 274, 396).

Translation theory has been instrumental in showing that the transmission of any source text to a target audience operates on several levels – linguistic, aesthetic, as well as cultural, and emotional. In other words, every text has a context, both cultural and situational (see Hall, *Beyond Culture*), that governs both its source origin and target reception. As translation theorist André Lefevere explains, in 'Composing the Other,' problems in translation are caused not only by discrepancies in languages, but also largely by 'discrepancies in conceptual and textual grids,' which 'in their interplay, may well determine how reality is constructed for the reader' (76). As Lefevere elaborates, translators and writers 'have to find ways of manipulating the grids in such a way that communication becomes not only possible, but interesting and attractive' (76). Lefevere broaches crucial questions in cross-cultural translation that also underlie this book: 'This brings us, of course, straight to the most important problem in all translating and in all attempts at cross-cultural understanding: can culture A ever really understand culture B on that culture's (i.e. B's) own terms? Or do the grids always define the ways in which cultures will be able to understand each other? Are the grids, to put it in terms that may well be too strong, the prerequisite for all understanding or not?' (77).

When taking up Haitian cultural themes such as *vodou* in their fiction, Haitian writers, like translators, are faced with the difficulties of negotiating complex conceptual grids, as well as narrative conventions. As translation scholar Susan Bassanett explains, 'translations are always embedded in cultural and political systems, and in history' (6). *Vodou*'s many sociohistorical, cultural, and political connotations are often convoluted and contradictory. Furthermore, as Lefevre points out, Haitian writers must also render their reappropriations of *vodou* 'interesting and attractive' (76), or engaging and aesthetic for the reader. The reader, of course, approaches these works of fiction with his or her own conceptual grids, which prompt various 'shifts' or gains and losses in translation (Popovic 78). What a Haitian reader might easily grasp as a political allusion might as easily be lost on the Western reader. By contrast, a trope that may be entertaining for the Western reader, such as zombies, might be deemed sensationalist and derogatory by the Haitian reader. Western readers, might approach Haitian literature with stereotypical narrative assumptions gleaned from such genres as horror movies, while misunderstanding Haitian narrative forms such as *pwovèbs* (proverbs) or *kont kreyòl* (oral storytelling). Because of these differing conceptual grids and resulting shifts in translation, much of the meaning of these *vodou* references might be lost on the target readership.

My objective here is not to emphasize the losses inherent in translation. Rather, I seek to examine what meaning might be gained or regained from such losses. In this chapter, by recovering some of the polyvalent historical and sociopolitical dimensions of *vodou*, I aim to reclaim some of its cultural, ideological, and emotional effects that otherwise might be lost in translation. In the next chapter, I seek to retrieve the lost cultural meaning of *vodou*, as reappropriated by Haitian writers to translate their immigrant experience, in particular their sufferings of immigration. For immigrants, the loss in translation aptly reflects the emotional loss of culture that they experience in immigration, given inevitable, necessary changes in acculturation. Given the inevitability of loss in cultural translation, my work is thus concerned with how such lost cultural elements may be reclaimed, reappropriated, or recreated.

My recuperative approach thus in many ways resembles Myriam Chancy's politics of representation, which in *Framing Silence: Revolutionary Novels by Haitian Women* she terms 'culture-lacune.' Like the many culturally alienated Maghrebis discussed in Part II, Haitian theorist Chancy also describes herself as a survivor of 'annihilation, both cultural and personal,' who once thought of herself 'as having no identity, or as having one filled with holes with what in French are referred to as *lacunes*' (*Framing Silence* 16). However, she survived 'by clinging to the vestiges of *creole* that lie dormant in my mind and by preserving a sense of self in an area of my consciousness that seems untranslatable' (16). She calls *culture-lacune* her move towards self-identity: 'By joining the word to culture, which connotes the positive presence of social, collective existence, I am implying that *lacune* can be read into the texts as a space of 'nothingness' that is transformed and affirmed through the politics of representation revealed in each' (16). My work aims to transform some of the *culture-lacunes* related to Haitian *vodou* into sites of cultural and affective meaning.

To discern discrete affective connotations of *vodou*, it is first necessary to understand *vodou* – most basically, as a religious practice, and then, more saliently, as a cultural representation. As I will show, as a cultural signifier, *vodou* has been translated, or 'zombified,' in numerous ways, each shaped by different historical contexts and sociopolitical agendas. Only by understanding these 'real-life' translations of *vodou* can the critic begin to reveal the ways in which, affectively and effectively, *vodou* has been recuperated and represented in immigrant fiction.

Vodou in Haiti

Haitian *vodou* is a religion, a set of spiritual beliefs and practices that seek to explain the world and give meaning to life. It is a syncretic religion, a fusion of ancient Dahomey traditions and Roman Catholic rites. The Haitian *vodou* belief system puts forth a good but indifferent god, *Bondye*, a series of spirits, or *lwa*, who are linked to Catholic saints. As ethnologist Maya Deren explains, people do not believe in the gods, they 'serve or obey the gods' (23) through their actions and participation in communal rituals. *Vodou* followers seek the advice of the *oungan* or *manbò*, the priest or priestess, who helps them understand and interpret these gods in their cult centre, the *ounfò*, with a series of rites, incantations, and *ouangas*, magical potions, and remedies. *Vodou* has a complex series of rites, such as the ceremony of initiation in which a person is possessed or 'mounted' by a spirit. *Vodou* is a secret, closed religion that one must be initiated into. There are different *vodou* sects, the most famous being the Petwo sect, associated with black magic, and Rara, associated with white magic.

Culturally, *vodou* is associated with the *kreyòl* language, which is a mixture of African and French languages, and is closely tied to the rich oral traditions of Haiti, which include such oral literary expressions as the *pwovèb* (proverbs) and *kont kreyòl* (folk tales). Many *vodou* elements have been incorporated into Haiti's rich oral folkore, such as the figures of the *bòkò* (sorcerors), *lougarous* (werewolves), and *marasa* (twins).

Historically, *vodou* was first practised by slaves in the French colony of St Domingue, Haiti's name as a colony. *Vodou* developed as a syncretic religion, a mix of African-based and Judeo-Christian religions, and as such, it both mimicked and subverted colonial authority. Despite its Christian symbology, under the Code Noir (1758–77) *vodou* was forbidden 'under penalty of death to be practised by day or by night' (Desmangles 26). Until its 1953 revision, various *vodou* practices were considered punishable offences in the Haitian Penal Code and carried the death sentence if practised in public. Even public performances of *vodou* or folklore rituals, as well as theatrical performances with ritualistic elements, were banned by laws promulgated in 1935 and 1943. These laws were imposed by the postoccupation, pro-Catholic, anti-superstition campaigns that followed after the U.S. invasion of Haiti. *Vodou* practitioners were thus persecuted during various periods of Haiti's history, most saliently: (1) during French colonialism, (2) under U.S. occupation (1915–34), (3) in the resulting Catholic Church's 'anti-superstition' campaign (1935–45), and recently, (4) after the fall of the Duvaliers' regime in 1986.

Despite these various legal prohibitions, however, *vodou* continued to be practised by much of the Haitian population throughout most of Haiti's history. Moreau de Saint-Méry, the first ethnographer of Haiti (1958 [1798]), testifies that despite the Code Noir, *vodou* ceremonies took place under the secrecy of the night in enclosed areas, hidden from all 'profane eyes' because the slaves feared the possible harsh punishments of local authorities (12–13). But some plantation owners also took part in *vodou* healing techniques: a certain M. Blaru states that once, when he was sick, slaves danced around him silently to obtain the healing power from their spirits (Desmangles 26).

Under slavery, *vodou* spirituality and its rich cultural imaginary existed in direct opposition to the physical brutality and racial subjugation inflicted on Haitian slaves, who otherwise had no rights. Slaves who were disrespectful of their masters were forced to eat their own excrement, had their bodies covered with molasses and were then tied to active beehives, or had hot irons or beeswax applied to their shoulders (James 11). In this economy of violence, *vodou* myths, oral traditions, and the *kreyòl* language perhaps granted slaves some meaning that transcended the violence imposed on them, and also strengthened the bonds of solidarity in the slave community.

Most importantly, *vodou* is also linked with the Haitian Revolution of 1791–1803. In 1757, *oungan* Makandal led a failed rebellion against the plantation masters; one of the *vodou* sects continues to be named in his honour. The rites conducted by *oungan* Boukman in Bois Caiman are reputed to have incited the uprising that ultimately led to the Revolution. The Haitian Revolution represents the only successful slave revolution in history; in 1804 it brought about the world's first Black Republic. For Napoleonic France, the defeat in Haiti signaled the loss of 40 per cent of its foreign trade. Although there is much doubt among historians about the veracity of this legendary ceremony,[3] in standard Haitian history, the onset of the Revolution has always been popularly associated with these *vodou* rituals.[4]

Many Haitians, therefore, associate Haitian culture and Haitian national identity with *vodou* practices, and view them as a symbol of resistance to imperialist oppression and colonial slavery. Even today *vodou*, at the grassroots level, continues to be a forum of public resistance, such as was seen in the late 1990s when *rara* demonstrations in New York City protested U.S. policies about Haitian refugees.

However, *vodou* does not only refer to ritual and resistance, a fact that is often glossed over in literary scholarship. When considered cross-culturally and transhistorically, it becomes evident that *vodou* also connotes cultural repression and political oppression. The cultural signifier of *vodou* has been deployed by both the Western and Haitian powers to legitimate authority and enforce totalitarian control.

Myth/Mis-understanding of *Vodou* in the West

Vodou has been largely misunderstood in the West; misinterpretations of *vodou* can be found everywhere, from popular culture to academic discourse. In popular culture, the word 'voodoo' conjures up images of voodoo-dolls, zombies, and spirit possession, as well as associations with primitivism and exoticism, the gothic macabre, or even satanic black magic. On the contrary, in academic treatises, the term *vodou* often prompts celebratory digressions about 'transcendental spirituality,' 'essential truths,' or more recently, triumphant 'syncretism,' 'creolism,' or 'hybrid resistance.' On one level, both of these interpretations of *vodou* are clearly distorted, if not exaggerated. Figuratively, they may be seen to represent a form of 'zombification' – or a revival and ossification of hackneyed clichés. On a deeper level, however, these Western cultural constructions of *vodou* also reflect circulating Western discourses: that of Western colonialism, specifically American imperialism, and more recently, that of cultural relativism or facile multiculturalism. For the Haitian immigrant, the writer in particular, both of these discourses, and their concomitant mistranslations of *vodou*, can prove equally problematical.

In the West, although the first ethnographic study of Haiti was published before the Haitian Revolution, in 1798, by Moreau de Saint-Méry, it is Sir Spenser St John's treatise, *Hayti or the Black Republic*, published in 1884, that captured the imagination of Western readers, precisely because St John described *vodou* in such a spectacular fashion. Like de Saint-Méry, St John reduces *vodou* beliefs to ophilatry, the worship of an all-powerful, supernatural serpent (186).

Although he admits to not having attended a *vodou* ceremony, St John reports on the dance of possession and other superstitions – such as black goats and *lougarous* (werewolves who kidnap children; 191, 184, 224).

More disturbing and more influential are St John's descriptions of *vodou* as human sacrifice and cannibalism. He describes child sacrifice, cites newspaper reports of people being fined for disinterring and eating corpses, and mentions midwives poisoning newborn babes so that they could be buried, revived, and eaten, and especially, he elaborates on the court case of Claircine, a young girl who was sacrificed and eaten in a stew (193–94, 198–204). For St John, 'it appears also to be an undoubted fact that human sacrifices are offered at Easter, Christmas Eve, New Year's Eve, and more particularly on Twelfth Night, or *Les Fêtes des Rois*' (198). He showcases juicy details of such cannibalism: 'packages of salted human flesh were found rolled up in leaves' (209); '[Haitians] were caught in the act of eating the flesh of a child raw' (having first sucked out its blood and then salted its flesh) (226); and a woman was taken hostage, dismembered, salted, and sealed in a cask in an outhouse (224). St John intimates that children often disappear not because of a mythical *lougarou*, but more prosaically, because of child sacrifice. St John's descriptions were clearly unfounded, based on hearsay and rumours. Yet, despite its factual shortcomings, St John's book spurred numerous articles about cannibalism, and, reprinted a number of times, it had a great impact on nineteenth-century beliefs about *vodou* and about Haiti.

St John's reading of *vodou* was certainly influenced by colonial prejudice. Although slavery had been abolished in most Black nations when St John's book was published, in 1884, starting, of course, with the Haitian Revolution in 1798[5] – racial prejudice and colonial primitivism had not disappeared, as is evidenced in St John's highly imperialistic discourse. By describing barbaric *vodou* practices, St John aims to show the failure of Blacks to govern themselves – he contends that every government since the Haitian Revolution has been implicated in *vodou* debauchery, such as bathing in the blood of goats (183–4).

Pursuing in St John's sensationalist tradition, William Seabrook, in his 1929 book *The Magic Island*, adds another element to the *vodou* repertoire: zombies. Interestingly, St John does not mention zombies, although he does report grave robberies and cases of people taking potions to simulate death or being poisoned to be later eaten (214–15). Seabrook offers a number of descriptions of zombies: 'corpses walking in the sunlight' or 'a band of ragged creatures [...] staring dumbly, like people walking in a daze [...] vacant-eyed like cattle' (99). He specifies superstitions such as that zombies must not eat salt or meat, and that with great pain, they would realize that they were dead. Most of Seabrook's zombie stories are hyped-up Gothic cemetery tales, for example, that of a mother watching her daughter shuffling to the cemetery among a horde of dead, clawing at the tombstone of her empty grave to be swallowed up like rotten carrion. Black and white photos and grotesque racist caricatures of Haitians granted readers added shock-value. Endnotes consisting of recipes for *wangas* and music used at voodoo ceremonies allege authorial credibility. Seabrook even justifies the presence of zombies by citing the Haitian Penal Code (Art. 249), when he warns that 'zombification' is a form of murder.

Seabrook's novel, published in 1929, was also influenced by political conditions, namely, the U.S. occupation of Haiti from 1915 to 1934. It reflects U.S. imperialist rhetoric about the occupation: to bring civilization and freedom to these backward peoples, while simultaneously exploiting their resources and pursuing American expansionist policies. The United States consolidated its military and financial control of Haiti by revoking certain Haitian laws and passing others. Haitian laws prohibiting sorcery (Art. 405–7 and 249 of the Penal Code) were particularly enforced during the U.S. occupation, and were the only ones translated into English in the U.S. Marine's version of the Haitian Penal Code (Ramsey 15). Article 249 specifically prohibits 'zombification,' as it was termed, as a form of attempted murder: 'Also shall be qualified as attempted murder the employment of drugs, hypnoses or any other occult practices which produce lethargic coma, or lifeless sleep and if the person (zombie) has been buried it shall be considered murder, no matter what result follows.'

In 1921–2, when American soldiers were called to testify in front of the U.S. Senate concerning military atrocities in Haiti, they repeatedly referred to the necessity of upholding these Haitian laws to curb the rampant spread of voodoo savagery (Ramsey 155). Seabrook's *Magic Island* further reinforces all the controversial stereotypes invoked about voodoo during the Senate Hearings. Hugely popular and influential, it was nominated for the Literary Guild Prize, reprinted and translated into many languages, and in particular, inspired the zombie horror film genre of the 1930s.

The 1930s saw the large-scale production of a number of Hollywood voodoo films. In 1932 the show *Zombie* made it to Broadway, and the first voodoo film, *White Zombie* (directed by Victor Halperin), hit theatres. This was followed by a whole series of such movies including: *Chloe* (1934), *Revolt of the Zombies* (1936), *King of the Zombies* (1941), and *I Walked with a Zombie* (1943). Notably, these films overlapped the Harlem Renaissance, when both Black and white American artists embraced Black culture and *négritude*, and expressionism in Europe; here Black culture was largely exoticized. In many ways, these zombie films emulated Seabrook's tawdry description of *vodou* religious practices, with numerous scenes of zombification, possession, and the like. Some also drew on the Haitian Penal Code to authenticate the presence of zombies. For instance, a promotional material for *White Zombie* reproduces Art. 249 of the Haitian Penal Code, and urges theatres to place this poster of 'tremendous interest' in their lobbies to attract crowds of people 'eager to read this novel display' (reprinted in Rhodes 81).

Although in the 1950s, better ethnographical texts appeared, such as Maya Deren's *The Divine Horsemen* (1953) and Alfred Métraux's *Le Voudou haïtien* (1958), fascination about 'voodoo' captivated Americans and even prompted a tourist boom to Haiti.[6] As Métraux quips, 'every American who disembarks there has but one word on his lips – "Voodoo"; and one wish – to see ceremonies which he imagines to be orgiastic and cruel' (56). During this time, traditional tawdry voodoo horror films continued to emerge, including: *Voodoo Woman* (1958), *The Incredible Creatures Who Stopped Living and Became Mixed Up Zombies* (1964), *Vengeance of Zombies* (1972), *Revenge of Zombies* (1972), and *Black Voodoo* (1977). As film theorist Tanya Krzywinska explains in her study of Hollywood voodoo films, most voodoo films operate within a framework of otherness; as part of the horror genre, they exploit otherness in the notion of the Gothic sublime, and as racialized films, they engage in epistemological and ethnic otherness (157). Krzywinska identifies three main types of voodoo films: (1) the 'nonsense' approach in which voodoo is denigrated, as childish superstition; (2) the 'satanic' variety, where voodoo, morally and culturally othered, is regarded as a form of anti-Christian black magic; and (3) the 'counter-discourse' genre, wherein voodoo is romanticized and exoticized, and

.is sanctioned and approved, in opposition to Western rationalism and imperialism. Most voodoo films deploy these three categories to different degrees and for various effects; however, their oppositional and binary parameters remain. As Krzywinska explains, these films are all 'structured around a central opposition between the primitive and the civilized' (158) and 'grounded in a dualistic approach to racial and cultural differences' (159).

In the late 1980s, Wade Davis's book *The Serpent and the Rainbow* prompted the latest wave of voodoo films. Davis led a scientific enquiry into the composition of Haitian 'zombie powder.' The film that followed, *The Serpent and the Rainbow* (1987), produced by Wes Craven, rarely departed from convention, but did introduce science and politics into the voodoo film genre. Notably, one of the film's plots was the overthrow of the dictator, again expressing the connection between *vodou* and politics. The U.S. intervention in Haiti occurred in 1994.

Clearly, representations of voodoo in Western popular culture are both literary and political constructs. St John's ethnography, characterized by racial prejudice and colonial primitivism, was influenced by colonialist discourses of imperialism. Seabrook's ethnographical novel, published in 1929 during the U.S. occupation of Haiti (1915–1934), reflects American imperialist rhetoric of that time: bringing civilization and freedom to backward barbarians. Likewise, cycles of Hollywood voodoo films can easily be correlated with the periods of heightened political relations between Haiti and the United States: the first voodoo film wave, ushered in by *White Zombie*, corresponded with the U.S. occupation of Haiti in 1915–1934, and the latest voodoo trend preceded the U.S. intervention in the 1990s.

Negative representations of *vodou* are not limited to only the literary and visual realm, but extend to other domains as well. Here I am referring briefly to their ramifications in scientific discourse, and by extension, problematically, in the sociopolitical sphere. In the mid-1980s, in the midst of the AIDS crisis, some scientists were quick to grant *vodou* a role in the transmission of AIDS. Moore and Lebaron, for example, in their scientific paper 'The Case for a Haitian Origin of the AIDS Epidemic,' claimed that blood used in sacrificial offerings might be infected with retroviruses closely related to HIV (Farmer, cited in *AIDS and Accusation* 340–2). They further suggested that many Haitian priests were homosexuals who abused their power to spread the infection. They justified their hypotheses with highly sensationalist rhetoric, akin to that used by St John and Seabrook.[7] In the political realm, such scientific evidence linking AIDS to Haiti was accompanied by deep-seated racism,[8] which spurred many Americans to support the 1992 rejection of thousands of Haitian boat-people by the United States.

Despite the blatantly racist depiction of *vodou* in popular culture, and its pernicious real-life effects on Haitian immigrants in the social and political arena, since the 1950s, *vodou* has also been skilfully studied in academic institutions. Various ethnographers, including Maya Deren, Alfred Métraux, and Leslie Desmangles, have been instrumental in accurately detailing the particularities of the Haitian *vodou* religion. But these scholars have largely limited their focus to the anthropology of Haitian *vodou* and have generally neglected its sociopolitical role. For instance, Harold Courlander, one of the fathers of Haitian ethnography, makes no mention of the politics of *vodou* in his work, although he visited President Duvalier several times (Abbott 91–2).

The study of *vodou* has received much favourable interest in academic institutions, and therein also lies one of its prevalent misinterpretations: until recently, *vodou* has often been studied rather uncritically, with little attention to its political context or its abuses in Haitian culture. As such, the translation of *vodou* in academic discourse often tells us more about prevailing theoretical trends within the institution, or sociopolitical discourses circulating at a particular time, than it does about *vodou* itself. Thus, it affords us little insight about the real-life uses of *vodou*, and concomitantly, the affective relationships that Haitian individuals may have to it.

To illustrate, when one surveys anthropological treatises of the mid-twentieth century, the contemporary scholar cannot miss the influence of such theories as structuralism or New Criticism, verging on New Historicism. Anthropologists tended to hypervalorize *vodou* as a means of transcending politics and structural violence. Willy Apollon, for example, concludes that *vodou* 'allows for survival in a mode of suspension. Death, sickness, socioeconomic exploitation, political powerlessness, police, moral and religious repression, finds in this domain of symbolic practices, a sense of meaning that is tolerable' (25–6). Others, influenced by Carl Jung's idea of the Collective Unconscious or Levi-Strauss' work on myths, universalize or relativize Haitian *vodou* as sacred wisdom or myths, which contrast with Western rationalism. Desmangles, for instance, declares that 'the complex truths' and 'unconscious wisdom of myths' reflect a different type of knowledge, one that transcends systematic logic and cannot be 'superseded by new scientific discoveries,' as it is 'immune to critical analysis' and 'empirical knowledge' (61). These universalizing academic theorizations tend to divest *vodou* of its sociopolitical associations and cultural context. As postcolonial theorist Emmanuel Eze argues, in his book *Beyond Dichotomies,* such binarism is dangerous: 'Most pernicious in such universalist discourse and in these mythic/scientific binaries are the side-effects. Even today, stereotypes about *vodou* myths have been used as a scientific rationalization of Haitians as backward barbarians' (49). As I have shown above, even in the 1980s, scientific validations linked AIDS to *vodou*. Eze advocates contextualization and particularization to curtail such universalism: 'The other is not a shadow or a mannequin, he [*sic*] belongs to a definite and concrete social-historical community. Concrete means particular' (49). When concretely particularized, it is clear that *vodou* has been repeatedly employed as a sociocultural rhetorical and political strategy, both in the West, and in Haiti.

In contemporary criticism, by contrast, Haitian *vodou* is often translated as an exemplary model of such concepts as syncretism,[9] creolization,[10] or hybridity. Although all of these anti-essentialist theoretical frameworks focus on the concrete, particular, and the different, in so doing, all too often they also adopt inflated, if not triumphalist, value statements. For instance, in Edouard Glissant's widely circulated definition, 'creolization is not a simple crossbreeding that would produce easily anticipated syntheses [...] the simple mechanics of a crude mixture of distinct things, it goes much farther – what it creates is new, unheard-of, and unexpected' (290–1). In no way am I suggesting that the mechanics of *vodou* are simple, and I would hope that my lengthy explanations of *vodou* suggest otherwise. It is an exaggeration, however, to consider creolization, hybridity, or syncretism, as always wholly novel and original or, concomitantly, as opaque or indecipherable. As Mikhael Bakhtin points out, in his application of the notion of hybridity to literary studies, all cultures and religions develop as organic hybrids (353). Similarly, 'creoles and creolization' are, according to George Lang, 'perfectly natural phenomena' in the development of societies (2); 'it would be mistaken to define creole literatures as being more dialogical, more fraught with exchange, than any others' (297).

In the case of Haitian *vodou*, rather than observing 'the unheard-of, unexpected,' we see replicated, albeit with a difference, various forms of racism, neocolonialism, or repeated cycles of violence. Overuse of such notions as hybridity, *métissage*, or difference risks assimilating *vodou* into a larger discourse of facile multicultural performance (as we have seen in the case of immigrant narratives in chapter 1) and completely evades issues of oppression, racial tension, and social stratification, which arise when *vodou* is examined in its social-political context.

Current academic discourse has a tendency to celebrate hybridity as a privileged form of resistance. Because of its origins in slavery and its role in the Haitian Revolution, *vodou* is often extolled as a model of 'intentional hybridity.' Bakhtin's concept of 'intentional hybridity' (359–60) – or hybridity as a cultural differential and a rhetorical strategy – represents one of the central, if not overtheorized, paradigms of postcolonial studies. All too often, such hybridity serves, in Bhabha's words, 'to celebrate the joyous power of the signifier' (112). Such 'joyous celebrations' of 'hybridity as resistance' habitually gloss over the fact that such hybridity often derives from contexts of great suffering. Along with connoting resistance to slavery and colonialism, Haitian *vodou* fundamentally represents an agonistic discourse: *vodou* is a signifier of suffering and oppression, a referent of the discourses of the power of French colonizers, American imperial forces, or even Haitian despots. In all, it is crucially important to acknowledge that concepts such as hybridity, creolization, and difference often originate from painful events such as colonization, repression, and interracial conflict, and reflexively refer back to them, revealing the difficulties of being othered – be it gendered, racialized, or socially stratified – in our global world.

Finally, in this celebratory discourse of cultural difference and resistance, it is seemingly forgotten that discourses of power can also engage in hybrid manipulations of culture, so as to gain and maintain their control and authority. There is a distinct tendency to equate hybridity, cultural performance, and 'insurgent acts of cultural translation' with the 'space of the people' (Bhabha 7, 146). Yet, hybridity does not always signal reversal, insurgency, or success for the people. On the contrary, when manipulated by institutions of power, hybrid cultural translations can become sites of oppression, defeat, and even death for the people. With the case of American imperialism, I have explored one such problematical political manipulation of *vodou*. Now let us turn to Haiti, to consider a final, abusive political translation of *vodou*.

Duvalier's Abusive Myth/Mis-use of *Vodou*

In Haiti *vodou* has been associated with politics from its very beginnings. As I have outlined, Haitian *vodou* emerged in opposition to colonial slavery. Throughout Haiti's history, *vodou* has represented a signifier of both suffering and resistance, whether under French colonialism, the U.S. occupation, or even recently, the *dechoukaj* – the period of political upheaval after the fall of the Duvalier regime in 1986. *Vodou* was banned throughout most of the nineteenth century. Nevertheless, early rulers of Haiti such as President Faustin Soulouque and President Antoine Simon associated themselves with *vodou* and even practised it, according to historians. Even Jean-Jacques Dessalines is popularly believed to have practised *vodou*, and is often associated with the god of war, Ogou, although in fact he openly hunted down *vodou* practitioners.

In recent history, however, no leader stands out more – as far as the political deployment of *vodou* is concerned – than François Duvalier, or 'Papa Doc,' whose regime lasted from 1957 to 1973, and who was followed by his son Jean-Claude or 'Baby Doc,' who was in power until 1986. The Duvalier regime manifestly exploited *vodou* as a political instrument and used it to oppress the Haitian people. Sadly, this fact is often glossed over in academic literature, especially in literary discourse or cultural anthropology. When I began my research on this subject, there were only a few history books (e.g., Laguerre) that explored this issue at some length.[11] Ironically, it is François Duvalier's own writing that best reveals his relationship to *vodou*. Markedly, many academic texts did not want to address Duvalier's association with *vodou*, because this political dimension of *vodou* would call into question its 'indigenous,' 'transcendental,' and 'resistant' associations. Unfortunately, like *vodou*, any cultural signifier may be deployed for oppressive ends, just as it can be a tool of resistance against oppression or persecution.

In Haiti's history, François Duvalier's regime signals the most salient shift in the hybrid translation of *vodou*: from a rhetoric of resistance to a rhetoric of repression. Duvalier deftly deployed the cultural meanings of *vodou*, in all of its ethnic connotations and historical denotations, to acquire and assure his political power. Scholars often gloss over the fact that, early in his career, Duvalier, along with Haiti's canonical writers Jacques Roumain, and Jean Price-Mars, were founding members of Haiti's Bureau d'Ethnologie. These intellectuals worked to counter the 1941 anti-superstition campaign by validating Haitian culture, and especially *vodou*. Moreover, Duvalier had also completed a degree in Public Health at the University of Michigan; during his stay in the United States, he surely became fully aware of the stereotypical depiction of *vodou* in American pop culture, from pulp fiction to zombie flix.

In his writings, Duvalier makes it clear that he seeks to reclaim authentic Haitian culture by recovering the lost and vilified practices of *vodou*. His writings thus reflect the 1930s *indigeniste* and *noiriste* movements, which sought to reclaim indigenous Black culture, and most notably, Jean Price-Mars' *Ainsi parla l'oncle...* (1928), the classic study of Haitian folklore and national heritage. For Duvalier, *vodou* is the 'crystallization of the origins and psychology of the Haitian nation' (225), 'authentic to the Haitian race' (177). He links this cultural practice intimately to nationalism, as the 'national and racial rise to consciousness' (167) and 'the supreme factor of Haitian unity' (177). He demonstrates full awareness of the pitfalls of Westernization or colonial mimicry: 'we do know that the archaic and apparently crude symbolism of Voodoo-worship is little to the taste of our high-brows smitten with Western culture' (176). To resist cultural reification, assimilation, and annihilation, Duvalier urges Haitians to uphold their culturally specific national identity, based in religious practices of *vodou*: 'As the mental make-up of any community is crystallized in the ways and customs, practices, beliefs and rites that are the extension of its religion, we will therefore consult Voodoo' (94). In many ways, Duvalier's nationalist rhetoric of ethnoreligious specificity resembles current cultural rhetoric, except that Duvalier deployed this rhetoric to perpetrate the genocide of his own people.

Duvalier gained power by allying himself with *vodou* priests, and, when elected, he made *vodou* Haiti's official religion. After seizing power, any opponents to Duvalier's regime, whether reluctant *oungans* or rival Christian clergy, were executed. To consolidate his power, Duvalier created a special militia force, the *tonton makoutes*, identified by red and blue neckties – the colours of the god of agriculture – to crush resistance. He himself dressed in black and wore a black top-hat, clothing associated with Baron Samedi – the malevolent deity of death and cemeteries – and claimed he was a reincarnation of the spirit of the revolutionary leader Dessalines. On the day he was instated as president, Duvalier drank pig's blood – to commemorate the ceremony at Bois Caiman and thus to inaugurate a new era of Haiti's history. Later, he performed ceremonies in cemeteries during which he smeared blood on the tombs of anti-Duvalierists. All of these allegedly *vodou* ceremonies were publicly broadcast on Haitian national radio, and this rhetoric of terror was transmitted to the entire Haitian public. The regime maintained control by publicizing gory spectacles of violence and by circulating rumours of further violence, or by institutionalizing some *vodou* practices, while maintaining certain other rites top secret, and punishable by death if disclosed (Johnson).

The climate during Duvalier's mad regime was therefore one of tremendous fear, rampant violence, and gruesome death. François Duvalier not only believed himself to be the god of death (*Gedè*), he also believed himself to be God. The 'pledge of allegiance' that every schoolchild had to recite about Duvalier was a perverted parody of the Lord's Prayer.[12] It is estimated that, during Duvalier's reign of terror, which was marked by violence, death, and *vodou* performances, between 20,000 and 80,000 people were massacred. An estimated 100,000 attempted to escape Haiti in makeshift rafts, as boat-people. From 1957 to 1986, one-fifth of the population of Haiti – and 80 per cent of the country's professionals or intellectuals – went into political or economic exile.

Duvalier's regime of terror, and his abusive deployment of *vodou*, went largely ignored in the Western world. In a weird twist of history, for instance, the Catholic Church excommunicated François Duvalier early in the 1960s, but repealed its decision in 1966, when Duvalier successfully convinced the Vatican of his devotion to the faith, as manifested in his 1969 book, *Mémoires d'un leader du Tiers-Monde: mes négotiations avec le Saint-Siège* (*Memoirs of a Leader of the Third World: My Negotiations with the Holy See*). While 'Baby Doc' (Jean-Claude Duvalier) was not as interested in *vodou* as his father was (he was largely a playboy puppet who plundered Haiti's coffers), during his rule, Haiti was basically a police state controlled by his father's minions and the Duvalierist militia, who would use any repressive means, including *vodou*, to preserve their power. After the fall of the Duvaliers, during the *dechoukaj*, there was a violent campaign against *vodou*, as the militia attempted to eliminate *oungans* or *manbòs* associated with the Duvaliers.

Yet *vodou* has not been eliminated from Haitian politics. When Jean-Bertrand Aristide came to power, he once again had to contend with the issue of *vodou* to gain public support and restore social order. Although formerly a Catholic priest, Aristide nonetheless realized the value of *vodou* in Haitian popular culture and thus its value in political discourse. In April 2003 he issued a decree stating that *vodou*, as Haiti's ancestral religion, is 'an essential element of Haiti's national identity,' intimately linked to Christian principles. His writings elaborate his understanding of the complexity of Haiti's syncretic culture and his attempts to reconcile *vodou* and Christian positions: 'I do not consider voodoo to be an antagonist or an enemy of the Christian faith. In the veins of voodoo flows a blood that is Christian. The two are complementary in their opposition to evil' (68). Interestingly, rather than stressing *vodou*'s historical or ethnic dimensions, as Duvalier does, Aristide emphasizes both religions' moral dimensions – he urges Haitians to espouse *vodou* to cultivate right action rather than *ressentiment*.

Translating Cultural Feelings

The signifier of Haitian *vodou* is laden with contradictory cultural and affective connotations. In the West, in certain academic discourses, an apolitical form of *vodou* is elevated to reflect the theoretical models of the day, be they structuralist myths or postcolonial hybridity. More generally, though, Haitian *vodou* is denigrated in popular Western culture, masking a dangerous binarism that reflects the imperialist policies of the United States. In Haiti, the affective attachments to *vodou* are far more complex. Certainly, as an indelible feature of Haiti's cultural heritage and an enduring symbol of Black resistance and survival, Haitian's *vodou* may stir up feelings of pride, patriotism, honor or faith. For many survivors of the Duvaliers' reign of terror, however, *vodou* may incite sentiments of dread, revulsion, and horror.

Understanding these manifold, emotion-laden, cultural translations of *vodou* is a necessary prerequisite to grasp the creative deployment of *vodou* in immigrant fiction. Haitian emigrants especially, who fled the Duvaliers' rule of terror, may experience a multiplicity of disparate affective responses to *vodou*. Some may view *vodou* practices with fond nostalgia; others may be repulsed by these signifiers of their past trauma. While some writers may share in some of François Duvalier's sentiments about *vodou* as an intrinsic part of Haitian culture, others may want to draw attention to the abusive translation of these religious beliefs. Just as some authors might wish to counter Western stereotypes about *vodou* and Haitian culture, others may refer to *vodou* to draw attention to their cultural alienation and immigrant hardships. How, then, do Haitian immigrant writers translate *vodou* in their texts? What can this cultural signifier tell us about the Haitian experience of immigration? Can it convey the sufferings of immigration? These are questions that I explore in the next chapter.

8 'Zombi Fictions':
Vodou Myth-Represented in Haitian Immigrant Fiction

Yon pakèt Ayisyin[...] ta vle fè ou kouè Vodou se sa minm, se klé solisyon problem nou yo. Yon lot pòsion Ayisyin [...] yo ékri: 'Vodou! Min pouazon an!'
— Anonymous 1975 Haitian editorial[1]

As we have seen in the previous chapter, the cultural signifier of Haitian *vodou* may connote a constellation of contradictory emotions. As a result, Haitian writers find themselves in a precarious position when espousing *vodou* themes in their fiction. Some writers might choose to affirm *vodou* in their work, as it represents Haiti's cultural heritage and is a symbol of Black resistance. Others, fully aware of the sensationalist depiction of voodoo in the West and the deprecation of Haiti as the 'poor,' 'barbarian' Black Republic, might seek to resist these stereotypes in their fiction. However, since 1957 *vodou* also is a symbol of much of the tyranny, oppression, and trauma of the Duvaliers' regime – the very reason many Haitians fled the country and sought refuge in exile. Thus, *vodou* may signal issues that writers might choose to avoid or to criticize in their writing. In Haitian immigrant literature, there exists a tension between nostalgic longing for *vodou*, emblematic of the Haitian immigrant's childhood home, culture, and heritage, and the association of *vodou* to tyrannical evil, trauma and oppression. This tension may be considered to be one of the characteristic features of Haitian immigrant fiction.

Cultural Translation

My untranslated *kreyòl* epigraph draws attention to the paradigm underlying this chapter: translation, particularly the role of cultural translation. In the previous chapter, I elaborated the ways in which the translation of *vodou* is shaped by the cultural, historical, and political contexts of the target audience, and how it thereby engenders different emotional responses. This chapter further elaborates the affective dimension of cultural translation, as I explore how immigrant authors deploy *vodou* as a form of persuasion – or rhetoric – to express the sufferings of immigration.

When reappropriating *vodou* myths in their fiction, Haitian immigrant writers rhetorically engage in 'insurgent acts of cultural translation' (Bhabha 7). Such rhetorical deployment of *vodou* reflects a manipulative translation, where 'the starting point [...] is not intended equivalence but admitted manipulation' (Snell-Hornby 23). Since their intended audience is largely French-speaking Westerners,[2] this type of translation may also be considered 'refractive,' defined by André Lefevere as 'the adaptation of a work of literature to a different audience, with the intention of influencing the way in which that audience reads the work' (*Translation* 4). In certain instances, this manipulative translation might even be viewed as 'abusive,' a term Philip Lewis uses in referring to a radical form of translation, where 'the translator's aim is to rearticulate analogically the abuse that occurs in the original text [... and] also to displace, remobilize, and extend this abuse in another milieu' (43).

Interestingly, in certain respects, the role of Haitian writers as critical cultural translators evokes the performance of *oungans* and *manbòs* during a *vodou* ritual. Ethnographers describe how, in *vodou* rituals and songs, *oungans* speak in *langaj* (Métraux 144), a mixture of Haitian *kreyòl*, bits of Latin or English, even invented phrases, as well as sounds that are often 'less accessible to translation' (Courlander, *Haiti Singing* 21). Similarly, Haitian writers' deploy a hybrid *langaj*, which might include Western stereotypes or Haitian *kreyòl*; it may be preformed explicitly or implicitly; and as a result, it may reflect either assimilation or rebellion, exilic nostalgia or existential suffering, cultural loss or artistic invention. Readers who approach Haitian texts as cultural interpreters must therefore learn to understand the different *langaj* these authors employ, as they appropriate or 'myth-appropriate' *vodou* in their fiction. Moreover, each of these writers' performative *langaj* has the power to influence or 'possess' its readers in some way.

Vodou in Haitian Literature:
From Price-Mars to Duvalier

The *langaj* that possesses a writer is often shaped by the literary tendencies circulating at a particular historical moment. Before considering the rhetoric of *vodou* in individual Haitian immigrant texts, it is therefore important to review its role in Haitian literature more generally, before and during the Duvaliers' regime.

Early twentieth-century Haitian cultural criticism sought to validate *vodou*. Jean Price-Mars' *Ainsi parla l'oncle...* (Thus Spoke the Uncle..., 1928), one of the founding texts of Haitian literature, exemplifies the cultural revival that took place in Haiti in the early twentieth century. Even before the Harlem Renaissance and the *négritude* movement, ethnologist Price-Mars penned this sociocultural history of Haiti, as a rebuttal to Western colonialism. In *Ainsi parla l'oncle...* he maintains that *vodou* is a religion, describes its rites and its origins, and links *vodou* to Africa and the Haitian Revolution. In a spirit of *noirisme* and *indigenisme*, he extols the subtlety of the *kreyòl* language[3] and advocates the promotion of the oral and ritual culture of Haiti as a means of creating an 'authentic' Haitian identity.

Price-Mars' validation of Haitian culture is later echoed by numerous Haitian writers, from François Duvalier in his essays (discussed in the previous chapter), to the creative fiction of writers in exile. René Depestre (b. 1926), who went into exile in 1959, in the early years of the Duvaliers' regime, for example, staunchly affirms the sociocultural value of *vodou* and its influence on his poetic work. In a 1992 interview he explained: 'on the cultural level – and there lies our hope – Haiti has succeeded in being a cultural nation. We have our own cultural identity, which is illustrated by Vodou. Vodou is the other presence of Haiti in me' (551). Depestre's work therefore generally describes *vodou* positively, with a mixture of nostalgia and humour, as a charming aspect of everyday life in rural Haiti. In *Alleluia pour une femme-jardin* (1981), for instance, Depestre describes how a mother takes her reluctant children to a *manbò* every year for purification healing rites and how this family consults a prophetess about the future. Yet, even in Depestre's novels, *vodou* acquires ominous and distressing undertones. In *Hadriana dans tous mes rêves* (1988), for example, Depestre explores the psyche of a zombified woman, using a first-person perspective. It is important to note, however, that Depestre's novels are most often set in Haiti, never in Cuba or France, to where he emigrated; as such, his fiction never expressly addresses the problem of immigration or the translation of *vodou* in a Western context.

During the Duvaliers' regime, there was a marked lack of Haitian scholarship on *vodou*. Although some Western scholars have drawn attention to François Duvalier's use of *vodou*,[4] I could not find any corresponding scholarship on *vodou*, especially on its political role, that was produced in Haiti itself. Perhaps because of the pejorative associations of *vodou* to tyranny and oppression, Haitian critics refer to *vodou* in the Duvalier/post-Duvalier era only in passing, and then usually negatively; more often, they avoid the topic altogether. The epigraph I have chosen – from a 1975 editorial – exemplifies the ambivalent feelings about *vodou* in Haiti during the Duvaliers' regime. It is written in Haiti, under censorship, thus anonymously, and hence evinces a markedly cautious tone in addressing the issue of *vodou*: 'Some Haitians would like to make you believe that *vodou* is precisely the solution to our problems. Others, the educated Haitians who make you believe that they could change the situation here, write "Vodou! There's the poison!"' (Anonymous 21). In this passage, the author sums up the contrast between official Haitian attitudes towards *vodou* (as the solution to Haiti's problems) and some Haitian intellectuals' contempt for it (as Duvalier's ideological toxin, or the opiate of the masses).

In the literature produced in Haiti at this time, *vodou* is often aligned with Duvalier's regime of terror, particularly in the figure of the zombie. Frankétienne's *Dezafi* (Challenge, 1975), for instance, the first novel written in Haitian *kreyòl*, is a story of zombification: the evil *oungan* Sintil, zombifies the young hero Klodonis to make him a slave. However, Klodonis revolts and frees himself, in a revolution that marks the end of the tyranny of the evil Sintil. This narrative of oppressive zombification and liberatory revolution can be read as an allegory of the Haitian situation under Duvalier. Similarly, in novels ranging from Marie Chauvet's *Folie* (Madness, 1968) to Francis Séjour Magloire's *Les Chroniques du macoutisme* (The Macoute Chronicles, 1986), Haitian writers adopt elements from popular tales, magic realism, and the fantastic to allegorically demonize Duvalier and his minions.[5]

In sum, the cultural elements of Haiti's oral, folkloric, and ritualistic traditions are a central feature in Haitian literature as it developed throughout the twentieth century, but their connotations were radically altered by Duvalier's manipulation of them. In 1928 Jean Price-

Mars asks whether, in light of its rich oral tradition, written Haitian literature could even come into being (173). By the 1960s, forty years later, Janheinz Jahn notes that perhaps the most salient evidence of the persistence of *vodou* in Haitian life is its manifestation in Haitian literature (56–7), as by then, *vodou* is a common trope in Haitian texts. Today, another forty years later, we may also ask – what is the role of *vodou* in Haitian literature, particularly in Haitian immigrant literature, after the Duvalier regime of terror forced so many Haitian writers to emigrate?

Ironically, in his own writings, François Duvalier suggests that the 'best hope of our [Haitian] generation' lies in 'the field of literature' – where he suggests that, 'like the Japanese and Jewish ethny [*sic*],' Black writers should 'assimilate white culture while preserving our spiritual framework, the only one capable of protecting our originality and the perenniality of our race' (63). How then are *vodou* myths reappropriated by Haitian writers in immigration – as 'white assimilation' or as 'originality'? Can the 'spiritual framework' of *vodou* translate the Haitian experience of immigration? What can these *vodou* myths tell us about the sufferings of immigration? These are the questions I will now consider, as I explore some of the leading, contemporary Haitian immigrant writers' use of *vodou* in their fiction.

Emile Ollivier: From Errance to Possession

Emile Ollivier (1940–2002), considered by many to be Haiti's foremost exiled writer because of his prize-winning nuanced, lyrical style, often introduces *vodou* into his texts. In his last collection of stories, *Regarde, regarde les lions* (See, See, the Lions, 2001), for example, Ollivier weaves magic realism into the everyday life of Montréal. In 'Lumière des Saisons,' a rosebush mysteriously blossoms after an ice-storm in the winter, and in 'Une nuit, un taxi,' a serpentlike woman haunts a taxi driver. Ollivier's autobiography, *Mille eaux* (A Thousand Waters, 1999), recounts the influence in his life of Evita, a courtesan's chambermaid; like the *vodou* goddess Ezuli, Evita awakened Emile's burgeoning sexuality and taught him everything he ever needed to know about *vodou*, the *lwa*, and *lougarous* (110). This exotic mulatto evokes one of the principal characters in his novel *Passages* (1991) – Amparo, a mulatto woman with whom the aging immigrant hero spends his last days in Miami. Amparo again reminds the reader of the *vodou* goddess Ezuli, who in her manifestations as Ezuli-Freda, represents seduction, love, and beauty, and is often depicted as a beautiful mulatto vested with the opulent accoutrements of the aristocracy. In many of his stories, then, Ollivier returns to the myths and traditions of *vodou* with lyricism and nostalgia.

In his novel *La Discorde aux cent voix* (Discord in a Hundred Voices, 1986), Ollivier presents a plurality of perspectives on traditional Haitian life, while also commenting on the immigrant experience. This novel depicts daily life in Les Cailles, described as a melting pot of the Christian religion, *vodou* rites, Western pop culture, and superstitious tall tales. On the one hand, the plot revolves around the failed attempts of a supercilious Haitian intellectual to gain power in this eccentric free-spirit village. On the other hand, the novel focuses on a despondent Haitian emigrant's return home from America. Ollivier uses *vodou* practices to contrast the rich cultural life in Haiti with the spiritual poverty of America.

As the title suggests, *La Discorde* presents a kaleidoscopic image of the cultural diversity in a Haitian village. The novel opens with the oracular voice of a prophetess, who predicts future doom to any spectators to the events in the village (13); in the next scene we observe some young boys, who seem to be disciples of Hare Krishna, wandering the streets (16). In another part of the novel, there is a solemn reading from the Catholic Liturgy of the Hours (206–8), while yet another section humorously plays with the traditional beginning of Haitian folk tales, 'krik! krak!' (38). *Vodou* is an important ingredient of this rich cultural mixture. Les Cailles is also depicted as an eerie 'land of zombies,' where 'everything is unwonted' (213). In other passages, however, such supernatural mysticism is countered by colourful vignettes of women prosaically going to the market, cooking dinner, or knitting away long into the night (110–11).

Ironically, the reader's perception of *vodou* is largely shaped by the grandiloquent intellectual narrator, Diogène Artheau. A scientist, political commentator and playwright, Diogène is constantly reading newspapers, political treatises, or esoteric texts. It is Diogène who most explicitly describes the *vodou* practices of Les Cailles. Vehemently opposed to these traditional rituals, Diogène scathingly characterizes Les Cailles as 'demonical' (58); as a cauldron brewing with strangeness, spiritualism, and sorcery (59), where the residents cohabit with the dead or are cursed and avenged by ghosts (59). He even scornfully dares the reader 'to find a village in the world where there is a greater density of demonologists per square metre, a greater ratio of frightening occultists and Satanist minions' (59). In Diogène's tirades, the reader recognizes many of the Western attitudes towards *vodou* as a barbaric rite. The novel also describes a number of *vodou*-related events in a much less spurious tone: stories of *oungans* (45), tales about the risen dead (73), and visions of the statue of a Madonna who cries (76), interlaced with the personal narratives of the villagers and the political events spanning a generation.

The central story follows the return of Denys Anselme from America to this village simmering with syncretism. Denys' return from '*errance*' is described with disillusionment. We are told that he is returning 'not from an America of chance of the gold rush, of the self-made man, but from an unnamed land, from an elsewhere, indefinable either by time, by place or by name' (147). In contrast to the vibrant town of Les Cailles, where the reader-spectator strolls effortlessly through a myriad of different cultural scenes, America is compared to a nonsensical existential no-man's land or a 'labyrinth,' where Denys experiences only 'fatigue' and 'despair' (129). Interestingly, Denys describes his alienation using Western references, including King Minos' labyrinth, the Sisyphean myth (129), and allusions to Sartre's play *No Exit* (129). Indeed, throughout *La Discorde*, it becomes apparent that, in immigration, Denys has lost much of his Haitian cultural heritage, only to acquire the existential suffering of the modern exile – namely, meaningless wandering.

Denys also feels that he has betrayed his country and his family by leaving Les Cailles (140), yet in the end his family and his village betray him. A rumour spreads, and is corroborated by a denunciatory official letter, which ultimately forces him to flee the village. He is told that, as an American citizen, any point on the globe belongs to him and that he must choose a different place to settle (170). This expulsion is clearly directed at the rejection that many Haitians might perhaps feel upon returning home. Ollivier points out, however, that his departure is unnatural and that the spiritual forces themselves rebel against this injustice. When Denys leaves, the village is stricken with a supernatural epidemic in which men lose their sexual prowess and stories of unexplainable infanticides and suicides spread like wildfire. Villagers suffer nightmares in which Denys returns to take his revenge. The magical reprisal eventually subsides, and Denys is forgotten until his sudden death in Vietnam years later (201). His death is mysteriously foreshadowed to his mother by a black butterfly, a *vodou* symbol of death, and literally announced in a telegram to Diogène, his father, manifestly distinguishing traditional maternal culture and the symbolic order through the father.

At the end of the novel, we learn that it was the intellectual Diogène, Denys' father, who wrote the letter condemning his son. In the final scene, we witness Diogène the scientist, and vehement critic of *vodou*, being possessed in an orgiastic *vodou* dance. Drunk with sugar cane, after sacrificing animals and drinking their blood, he lets himself be transformed morally and physically by the *vodou* gods in 'the purest of all ancestral rites' (262). Diogène's gestures translate his 'interior torment' (262) and expose 'the inner lining of his memory,' as he performatively unravels 'his whole battered life, his puzzle of solitude, and his perforated destiny now impossible to sew up,' as he finally brings 'the story out to the truth' (262). Stylistically, it would seem that Ollivier himself unweaves his tale, words giving in to dance, turning text into performance. This dramatic performance of pain reminds us of the powerful psychological dimensions of *vodou* called forth by Willy Apollon (1976). Drawing attention to the oral and preformative dimensions of *vodou*, Apollon claims that these practices counter Cartesian rationality, Western progress, and scholarly textuality. In Apollon's view, *vodou* offers its practitioners a unique means of gaining knowledge through sensual experience; possession even attains a surplus orgasmic value (82). Most importantly, *vodou* grants Haitians a means of expressing their ineffable pain through music, dance, and ritual language, while also cathartically purging, transforming, or healing it in a 'plural space of survival' (26).

In Ollivier's *La Discorde aux cent voix*, the carnivalesque traditions of village life, oral storytelling, and *vodou* performance represent the antithesis of intellectual rationalization: the letter of the father, the patriarchal attempt at civilized order and law. This hybrid cultural life contrasts with the culturally empty life in immigration. However, such a rich multicultural life seems possible only within this Haitian village. Unfortunately, for the Haitian emigrant Denys, successful return home proves impossible.

Gérard Etienne: Vituperating Violence

In contrast to Ollivier's multidimensional portrait of *vodou*, Gérard Etienne (b. 1936) puts forth a starkly and unequivocally negative depiction of *vodou*. As he explains in an interview: 'Vodou is not the immaculate virgin that is glorified by all the Haitian intellectuals for whom Catholicism remains an imperialist and colonial religion. Not at all. In my novels, *vodou* is seen as a hidden structure, but one that complements the feudal structure of Haiti [...] the violence and barbarism of the Haitian political system [...] our ideological superstructures, in this case, religious superstructures' ('Interview' 500). For Etienne, *vodou* connotes political, economic, and ideological oppression. In particular, it replicates the 'violence and barbarism' of the Duvalier regime.

Etienne's oeuvre can only be understood in relation to the trauma, imprisonment, and torture that he lived through during Duvalier's regime. In his first novel, *Le Nègre crucifié* (*The Crucified Negro*, 1974), the author remembers the torture he experienced in prison. The preface makes explicit that *Le Nègre crucifié* functions as 'a type of literary INDICTMENT of the institutionalized violence of Haitian society' (9). As such, the work reflects a manipulative form of translation. It also exemplifies George Lamming's rhetoric of violence (discussed in chapter 2)., Lamming advocates 'a certain kind of violence in the breaking,' 'a smashing,' as a form of 'therapeutic need' (45) to treat the psychic wounds of the individual subjected to violence.

Le Nègre crucifié delves into the traumatic memories of the narrator, who was pursued and captured by the *tonton makoutes*, Duvalier's militia. In prison he is tortured, both physically and mentally. In his delusions, the narrator imagines that demonic spirits, representative of the *tonton makoutes*, are chasing him; they want to possess him and turn him into a 'zombie of the Chief,' in a process that Etienne describes as 'zombification' (75).

Notably, to achieve such zombification, these malevolent entities exploit Haitians' self-loathing and their racial and colonial shame in order to gain authority over them: 'The gods hound the hate I have accumulated since my birth, since the day I realized I am a Negro from Haiti, colonized to the bones. The gods know I hate Negro zombies, that I hate my skin, the sun, the sea, everything that is reminds me I am from the race of those who kill'[6] (75). In contrast to Duvalier's writings, in which Haiti's glorious past and unique heritage are extolled, Etienne suggests that Duvalier was able to brainwash the Haitian population by drawing on their self-hatred and humiliation, which he then transformed into violence. Etienne's depiction of self-contempt here clearly reflects Fanon's notion of internalized oppression or Nietzsche's concept of negative *ressentiment*. Etienne's 'zombie' thus comes to symbolize the oppressed subject, first victim and then perpetrator of

institutionalized violence, who is caught in a perpetual cycle of bru-
talizing aggression.

To escape this zombifying cycle of violence, institutionalized by
physical and mental torture in prison, Etienne's hallucinating narrator
creates another persona for himself – his spirit-self, who wanders
throughout Haiti, while the narrator's real body rots in the prison cell.
The spirit-self attempts everything to escape the tyranny of Duvalier's
regime: he returns to nature, falls in love, rises up in rebellion, and
even takes part in *vodou* ceremonies. However, to his despair, nothing
can overturn the power of the Chief. In the end, the narrator's final act
of resistance is phallic self-mutilation: 'he lowers his pants and with a
nail immolates his member in two places' (33). Ultimately, the narrator
allows himself to be crucified rather than surrender and become a
zombie. In the end, there is no redemption or escape possible for the
expiatory victim in this cycle of inescapable violence.

Le Nègre crucifié thus draws on graphic, violent, and often painful
rhetoric to expose the brutality of Duvalier's *vodou*esque regime. For
instance, in a satirical repartee, Etienne compares the zombification to
the devastation caused by the atomic bomb: '[Haitian] Negroes believe
in zombies. Whites in the bomb [...] Behind the logic of the whites there
are the zombies of the Negroes [...] With the power of the dead, the
Negroes of Haiti will invent the H-bomb' (23).[7] Here Etienne takes up
a Western cultural equivalent to translate as clearly as he can to his
Western readers the enormous effects of such zombification: the genocide perpetrated by Duvalier resembles the mass death of nuclear war.
Etienne explains further that such zombification is only possible
because, in a culturally relavist perspective, the world refuses to recognize the horrors of Duvalier's regime: just as the United States
believes that 'Negro affairs are not White House affairs' (23), the
Vatican prefers 'a *vodou* Satan than the communist Satan' (74).

This reference to the atomic bomb is only one of the many instances
of hybridization in Etienne's text. His deployment of bloody Christian
tropes is also salient. As the title implies, *Le Nègre crucifié* revolves
around the narrators' crucifixion: the story defines itself as 'the cry of
one who was crucified and survived. A wound gashed into very bone
and hewn into a cross' (14). Etienne thus draws on a syncretic medley
of violent images drawn from differing cultural traditions to elaborate
the unimaginable cruelty of Duvalier's regime of terror.

Most forcefully, Etienne describes Duvalier's zombification using a
plethora of gruesome images, such as amputation: 'the new chapter in

the history opens with a resurrection of the heads, bodies with hacked arms, just heads' (22). Those who refuse to be zombies endure even more horrific fates: 'buried alive [...] a head bashed in with a hammer, a Negro forced to eat his excrement, a baby in an anthill, a paralyzed cripple covered with mosquitoes' (47). To the narrator's disgust, even his own father succumbs to Duvalier's *vodou* worship, and is described as 'sucking the member of the master, that dog of a master lying in a slough of pus' (30).

Etienne's most vehement attack is directed at Duvalier's militia, or 'the zombies of the Chief' (75), who 'make Haiti into a damned land. It's that simple' (122). In one scene, reminiscent of St John's ethnography, he describes the *tontons makoutes* at a depraved *vodou* ceremony: they light a ceremonial fire, get drunk on soursup tea, and end up sleeping with their own daughters on flea-infested rattan mats, near a basin of snakes, like 'a heap of flesh rotting in magic, hunger and orgies' (35). In another case, he refers to voodoo-dolls to show the *tontons makoutes'* aggression: they 'dispense death with needled voodoo-dolls' (84), or 'stick pieces of wood up the vaginas of the high-school girls of Port-au-Prince' (26). As for Duvalier, Chief of the Zombies, he transcends all violence by his ritualistic performance: 'all is well as long as he, the Chief, makes the sign of the cross four times above the corpses of his prisoners' (26).

Le Nègre crucifié employs graphically violent rhetoric to replicate the atrocities of the Duvalier regime, and to viscerally remember the trauma of the writer tortured in prison. As Keith Louis Walker explains, with his 'words proffered in pain,' Etienne exposes the 'repressed' and the 'unspeakable' aspects of torture (215). Similarly, he perhaps cathartically treats his past trauma in 'present exercises of anger' (Lamming 44). Rather than persuading readers of his pain, he struggles to make us *feel* it – with his hostile prose, his fragmentary psychic delusions, or his allusions to *vodou*. As a result, the reader almost viscerally experiences the writer's shattering, in body and spirit.

Intriguingly, in *Le Nègre crucifié, vodou* also offers the narrator a means of escaping his agony, while at the same time empathizing with others. As he splits off into his other, spirit-self, the narrator is able to endure his excruciating physical pain, as well as find comfort in sharing the torment of other victims of political oppression, and even in the daily martyrdom of ordinary Haitian people. In like manner, Etienne's powerful hybrid rhetoric, a mixture of Western, Christian, and *vodou* imagery, allows both Haitian and Western readers to enter into the psyche of the narrator, the author, and of the Haitian population tormented under Duvalier.

For some readers, however, Etienne's graphic imagery – as a form of abusive translation – may be too much to bear or empathize with. As Philip Lewis has defined it, 'abusive translation' aims 'to rearticulate analogically the abuse that occurs in the original text' and in so doing 'extend this abuse in another milieu' (43). *Le Nègre crucifié* is an obvious attempt to recreate Duvalier's vicious translation of *vodou*, while also further perpetrating this violence on readers, most often readers in a Western milieu. It is perhaps not coincidental that *Le Nègre crucifié* was not translated until 2006, more than thirty years after its original publication; translators and readers alike may be reluctant to be subjected to violence, aggression, or torture, even if rhetorically or aesthetically.

The traumatic sequelae of Etienne's torture continue to haunt his later work, set in immigration. Although Etienne's immigrant novels are never as graphically violent as *Le Nègre crucifié*, *vodou* tropes continue to be present, whether in relation to women (in *Une Femme muette* and *La Reine soilel levée*) or ex-Duvalierists abroad (*Un ambassadeur macoute à Montréal*). Although *vodou* most often alludes to violence or sociopolitical oppression in Haiti, it sometimes also relates to the immigrant experience.

Of all of Etienne's novels set in immigration, *La Pacotille* (The Trinket, 1991) most expressly explores the difficulties of the politically traumatized immigrant, in themes of disassociation, loss, amnesia, hallucination, and 'splitting' – between the past and the present, and between Haiti and Montreal. One of the novel's opening questions highlights the central theme of this book, 'How to make them understand exile inside, in a room overlooking Darlington Street closed off to Black Africa?' (14).

In *La Pacotille*, the narrator, Ben Shalom, suffers from paranoid schizophrenia; he is split, caught between his past crimes in Haiti and his present reality in Montreal. Plagued by nightmares, he has difficulty distinguishing reality from memory. He suffers panic attacks in the cold streets of Montreal, and is paralyzed by the indifference of the city and its inhabitants. At his work at the newspaper or the university, he feels shamed by an internalized inferiority complex, and feels reduced to a *pacotille*, a mere trinket. In all, '[his] suffering is not having an identity' (46).

In his mind, Shalom is similarly estranged, 'condemned to live with the beast' (163), an incarnation of his former oppression in Haiti. As in

Le Nègre crucifié, this narrator is pursued by this beast that attempts to reduce him to a zombie, 'whatever [he] does he remains a zombie of the beast. Wherever [he] is, the beast is hot on his trail' (224). This beast also indoctrinates him with violent, contemptuous thoughts of 'self-hatred, hatred of others and hatred of the world' (125). Yet again, the narrator finds himself split between his physical self and his *bon anj* – his spirit-self, which 'refuses to yield to the roars of the werewolves' (21). Once more, we are witness to the gruesome horrors in Haiti. For instance, in a shocking scene of delusion, brainwashing, or perhaps even reality, we watch Ben Shalom casually have intercourse with his mother (120). Repeatedly, Shalom struggles to express his mental torment, but ultimately fails. He cannot describe the tortures he has endured: the feeling of having his testicles hammered or the sensation of shivering, the nausea, and his corporal panic before the arrival of the beast. In all, 'words have not enough power to convey the unspeakable' (60).

Instead of being aimed at Duvalier's militia, Ben Shalom's vitriolic rhetoric is directed at immigration officials and bureaucratic institutions. Ben Shalom describes his repeated, harrowing visits to the immigration office, where he once even witnesses an unsuccessful applicant commit suicide (140). He points to the racist suspicions of immigration officials, their 'fears that their territory would be invaded by a colony of unidentifiable zombie-Negroes' (145). While, on the one hand, he congratulates himself that his mental condition – 'his beast' – has escaped medical examinations (99), on the other hand, he desperately seeks to make everyone aware of it, in vociferating crazy, caustic *vodou*esque tirades, such as, 'Allow me, Sir, to strangle you, to burn down your city and walk on your corpse. Permit me, Officer, to transport you to my stable with my magic wand, to do my Stations of the Cross, just like your Christ – under the claws of the beast, under the boots of an executioner [...] By strangling you, I'm doing you a great service. I'm ridding you of a most cruel disease that is destroying your race: hatred for another race'[8] (148). As reflected in this passage, Etienne mixes *vodou* imagery with Western and Christian tropes to remind the reader of the racialized violence inflicted on Haitians by various sociocultural translations, be they those of the Duvaliers, Christian colonizers, or even Canadian immigration officers. Ben Shalom thus tenaciously resists facile, forgetful, or comfortable assimilation, which he views as defeat: 'I don't want to simply give up as beaten by letting myself be assimilated in a new country' (101).

In the end, however, Ben Shalom realizes that no one will be able to understand his suffering: 'I understood. It's impossible for a white person from the outside to penetrate this universe, even with the most refined science in the world, even with the generosity of the saintliest of saint. Not because of indifference. Crazed minds articulate everywhere the same languages. In their cultural markers, in the superposition of worlds, in the self-reflection imposed by boundaries'[9] (244).

In his fiction, Etienne translates the universal language of the 'crazed minds' of many politically traumatized immigrants. In doing so, he exposes the 'cultural markers' of Haitian culture or *vodou*, as well as 'the superposition of worlds' of political violence and immigration procedures. Finally, he also poignantly reveals the 'boundaries' of personal pain that so often prevent even the most well-meaning individuals from penetrating the universe of suffering of traumatized immigrants.

In *La Pacotille*, Etienne's delusional hybrid appropriation of *vodou* again reflects Lewis' notion of 'abusive translation,' which Lewis further describes as a 'strong, forceful translation that values experimentation, tampers with usage, seeks to match the polyvalencies or plurivocities' with 'whatever might upset or force or abuse language and thought, might seek after the unthought or unthinkable in the unsaid or unsayable' (41). Clearly, Etienne's forceful, experimental, and polyvalent translation of *vodou* seeks to convey the ineffable violence inflicted on the Haitian people, be it by Duvalier's abusive cultural translation or the difficult cultural translation required in immigration. It is questionable whether such vitriolic violence is digestible by the target readership; the effects of Etienne's rhetoric of violence range from empathy to dismissal.

Stanley Péan: Detecting the Fantastic

Unlike Ollivier and Etienne, who generally associate *vodou* with a Haitian world-view, Stanley Péan cleverly translates *vodou* myths directly into immigrant life in the context of modern Western society. Péan reappropriates many *vodou* tropes – the kiss of death, possession, and zombies – in the macabre, gothic tone adopted by popular-culture to entice and seduce readers. Yet, through his tongue-in-cheek style he also satirizes these stereotypes and renders them humorous. One of his stories in *Noirs désirs* [Black Desires, 1999), follows a husband who must kill his wife not once, but repeatedly, because she keeps on reappearing as a zombie; in another story, a clairvoyant high school student sees corpses in biology class. Some of Péan's stories prove more ominous, though: from the grave, a mother urges her son to kill himself, and in another instance, a crazed mother kills her infant because he resembles a monster. Underlying most of Péan's stories are alienation and inescapable difference; the Haitian protagonists always carry a secret and are haunted by their cultural heritage.

Because of his often satirical and humorous tone and his use of the fantastic or detective genre, Péan has been largely dismissed by critics. Péan himself self-reflexively mocks his use of stereotypes and Haitian cultural elements in his own work. In his first novel, *Le Tumulte de mon sang* (Turmoil in My Blood, 1991), for instance, the Haitian poet protagonist is held captive by an ex-Duvalierist, who scorns his pathetic attempts at 'seasoning his poetry with *vodou* symbols, a *vèvè* here a *lwa* there,' in the clichéd style of 'any foreign writer in search of exoticism' (146). The ex-Duvalierist captor acerbically asks the poet: 'what can a mulatto from the Realm of Blueberries know about *vodou* or what need would he have to celebrate Mother-Guinea?' (146). The poor poet attempts to find a reply – some 'pseudo-metaphysical jargon' about 'a metaphor for "Haitianness"' (146) – but realizes that his captor does not want an answer. In this example, Péan points to some of the core issues of cultural deployment and questions the possible effects of such cultural rhetorics.

Literary scholars have yet to consider Péan's work in terms of Haitian immigration. In book reviews, Péan is more often described as a Québecois author than a Haitian-Canadian. I know of no serious literary analysis of Péan's work, certainly none that explores his subtle juxtaposition of *vodou* myth with immigration. Yet, I would argue that the connection, although implicit, is telling.

Some of Péan's stories overtly point to immigrant issues, as exemplified in his collection *La Plage des songes* (*PS*, Beach of Dreams). In 'Ce Nègre n'est qu'un Blanc, déguisé en Indien' (This Negro Is White, Disguised as an Indian), the Haitian immigrant protagonist is subjected to so much humiliation and racism, that he is transformed by his internalized rage into a crazed monster, and shreds everything in sight. Completely metamorphosed, he can neither control his wild instincts nor communicate with his loved ones. In another story, 'En prime avec ce coffret' (Free Gift Box), Péan challenges the myth of the American dream of success: Upon finding a magic box, an immigrant couple is finally able to thrive financially, but the price is seeped in gore and death. In 'Métempsychose' (Metempsychosis), Péan highlights the fears of Haitian immigrants when faced with Western medicine: when a couple visits a psychiatrist the two are confused with other patients, lose their identities, and are drawn into a crazy world of missing persons and misdiagnoses. Interspersed throughout all these stories are observations about the difficulties that Haitian immigrants experience abroad, with such remarks as, 'to be Haitian in the mid-1980s is no fun and is viewed even worse. The unemployment rate is more than 30 per cent. Those who work, work illegally' (PS 91). Moreover, Péan repeatedly draws attention to the fact that, while they are pursued by ghosts or demons in dreams or in fiction, in their real lives in Quebec, his Haitian heroes are haunted by material poverty or by a 'vague and anonymous sadness' that stems from their social exclusion (PS 61).

Péan's reappropriation of *vodou* imagery and Haitian folklore obliquely alerts readers to the perils of assimilation and cultural annihilation. For Haitians, estranging themselves from their culture might mean the death of their identity, a theme emphasized in 'Le Syndrome Kafka' (PS). In this story, a young Haitian, upon becoming involved with a white woman, starts to forget first his house and belongings, then who his friends and family are, and finally his own Haitian identity. He can no longer understand *kreyòl*, he cannot recall the taste of Haitian meals, and when he watches a television broadcast on Haiti, he feels nothing towards his native land. This bizarre amnesia reflects the cultural loss that many Haitians may suffer in immigration. Indeed, the weird voice echoing in his head presages as much: 'You have been absent from your native-land for too long a time; the metamorphosis is taking place; exile is making of you an intruder, a stranger everywhere, even at home, distance and time hollow out an abyss of indifference. From your troubled dreams, you will awaken crazed in your bed, transformed into God knows what, a mutant, a hybrid, something different, but no longer a Haitian'[10] (PS 111). In a series of weird Borgesian turns, the story ultimately reveals that this young Haitian does not exist at all, except in a dream fragment belonging to a stranger. While Péan is manifestly employing magic realism to create a fantastic story, it is also clear that he is commenting on the loss of Haitian identity that the Western dream of assimilation entails.

In his full-length detective novels, Péan shows even more forcefully that there is no way for the Haitian immigrant to escape *vodou*. His first novel, *Le Tumulte de mon sang,* relates the story of a couple who escape from Montreal to the countryside, only to find themselves in a house haunted by evil *vodou* spirits. A series of strange events and, ultimately, deaths ensue. In the end, the mystery is unravelled as the perpetrator is revealed: the murderer is an ex-Duvalierist officer. The plot of Péan's *Zombi Blues* revolves around a Haitian musician, who does not want to get involved in any Haitian 'stories' – be they of *vodou* or politics. However, when an ex-Duvalierist begins to terrorize the Haitian population of Montreal, the musician learns that he cannot escape: 'magic' power runs in his veins. In his novels, Péan suggests that the myths, politics, and trauma of the past must be dealt with in exile in the present. As cited in Toni Morrison's epigraph to *Zombi Blues*: 'Like in the blues, one must transform one's suffering and anxiety into something else, wisdom perhaps, without yielding to anger' (13). Here, again, we hear echoed the refrain of Lamming's 'exercices in anger' (44).

Thus, in his work, Péan urges us to learn to listen for the musical strains of this suffering Haitian reality, transposed into the hybrid harmonies of *vodou* myth. This premise is perhaps best exemplified in his short story 'L'Envers du silence' (*PS*, The Opposite of Silence). In this narrative, a woman-doctor sceptically confronts a man who claims to hear the voices of drowned boat-people in his head. Since she does not believe him, he smashes his head with a rock. As a result, the woman is then contaminated by the man's trauma and is herself plagued by a multitude of anguished voices: of those who have drowned, who were slaughtered by political violence, who died of hunger, and even who were incinerated during the Holocaust or killed by the atomic bomb. As in the fiction of Maghrebi immigrants, or in Etienne's *Le Nègre crucifié*, we again witness an act of drastic self-immolation to convey the sufferings of those who remain unheard. Tormented for the rest of her life by these anguished voices, the woman narrator of 'L'Envers du silence' urges readers to listen to the painful sounds of others, who might haunt us in dreams or in fiction. The story concludes with the invective *ou pa tande yo?* – 'do you not hear them?' (163) – a refrain that floats all through the narrative.

Throughout his supernatural stories, Péan seems to ask readers this same question: *Ou pa tande yo?* He encourages us to heed the implicit meaning behind his hybrid *vodou* rhetoric, which mingles together dream and horror, or stereotype and satire. As I have shown, couched in Péan's fantastic and humorous stories, are references to the harsh experiences of Haitian immigrants and the traumatic Haitian political situation. Although I find these connections between *vodou* myth and immigration to be rather overt, because of the conventions of the fantastic or detective story genre, the humour or satire, many of these allusions are too often missed and dismissed.

Edwidge Danticat: 'Survival Soup'

From Stanley Péan, whose fiction remains passed over by literary critics, I turn now to Edwidge Danticat. Danticat (b. 1969) is the best-known Haitian writer in North America, because, unlike the other authors considered here, she writes in English, and also because her work is acclaimed for its limpid style, engaging narratives, and vibrant imagery. Like Péan, Danticat adopts a creative approach to *vodou* myth, and in many ways, her work exemplifies an imaginative interpolation of Haitian cultural elements.

Danticat's hybrid deployment of *vodou* elements is perhaps epitomized in her story collection *Krik? Krak!* (1996), the work I will focus on here. *Krik? Krak!* manifestly derives its name from *kont kreyòl*, or Haitian storytelling, in which the stories begin with the dialogic interchange '*Krik?/ Krak!/ Tim-tim/ Bwa sèch.*' However, in her epilogue, Danticat suggests that she improvises on this standard oral form, saliently, by elaborating on its affective connotations: '"Krik? Krak! Pencil, paper. It sounds like someone is crying." Someone was crying. You and the writing demons in your head' (220). Manifestly, the associations that Danticat draws when describing this translation from oral to written form evoke some form of suffering, derived from cultural haunting.

In her epilogue, Danticat also likens her writing to the cooking up of 'survival soup,' as well as to the 'braiding of hair' (220), images of kitchen resistance and hybrid *métissage* that have captivated numerous literary critics. Without a doubt, Danticat concocts a potently mixed cultural brew for women survivors, one that simmers with ingredients from Haitian folklore, oral tradition, and *vodou* myth. It is important to recognize, however, that her hybrid 'survival soup,' while working to counteract suffering, is also distilled from suffering. As such, Danticat's writing may be likened to an antidote for the poison of institutionalized violence or cultural annihilation, which works by injecting readers with a small dose of this violence and cultural alienation. Danticat's stories are laden with suffering. Her work commemorates the agony of both Haitian writers – who were 'tortured,' 'killed,' 'raped,' 'covered in scalding tar,' or 'forced to eat their own waste'– as well as the anguish of young girls – 'who wake up one morning to find their panties gone' (221–2). In so doing, her writing interpolates recognizable traumatic historical events – the Haitian Revolution, the Trujillo massacre, the *dechoukaj* – with the stories of individuals, who have often been deemed 'nobodies,' including boat-people, prostitutes, or *restaveks* (child-maids). In all, Danticat not only braids together a diversity of stories, but she also reveals the 'unruly' and 'coarse' strands in these stories, or inassimilable experiences of suffering. Furthermore, Danticat's deployment of *vodou*, part of her hybrid 'survival soup,' reflects the cultural recuperation of suffering. *Vodou* themes sometimes reflect the poison of gendered violence, political oppression, or socioeconomic hardship; at other times, *vodou* symbology serves as a therapeutic antidote against such pain and violence.

Several stories in *Krik? Krak!* explore the associations of *vodou* with the political brutality, social exploitation, and oppression of women in Haiti. In the story 'Nineteen Thirty Seven,' for example, Danticat examines the life of a woman who survived the massacre of Dominican dictator Trujillo in 1937; she witnessed the gory death of her mother in the Massacre River. Traumatized, the woman lives as a recluse at the outskirts of a village, practising herbal healing, until she is condemned as a witch or *socouyant*[11] by the authorities. We witness the tortures that this woman, accused of being a witch, suffers in prison; every evening she is doused with ice-cold water, lest she fly away on her witchlike wings of flame during the night. In the story 'Between the Pool and the Gardenia,' another young woman is denounced as a witch when she adopts a dead baby, believing it to be alive. In this case, the deluded heroine, expelled from her village by her husband because she is infertile, is forced to work as a *restavek* (a child-maid) in a rich suburb, where she is taken advantage of by the other servants. In these cases, *vodou* myths are manifestly manipulated to justify sociopolitical oppression. Although ostensibly negative, these women's supposed demonic behaviour is implicitly symptomatic of their past trauma and gendered subjugation here further institutionalized by political oppression.

In other cases in *Krik? Krak!* Danticat's use of *vodou* stories point to the creative and healing power of myths and cultural traditions. In the story 'Night Women,' a prostitute invents wonderful stories for her son – visions of angels and ghost-women with stars in their hair (86) – to counter the sexual exploitation she experiences every night. In 'Seeing Things Simply,' a young Haitian girl is seduced by the classical painting of a French woman artist and starts sketching designs in the sand with her own blood. Her wounded sketches resemble *vèvè* drawings in *vodou* culture (Courlander, *Haiti Singing* 22) and sharply contrast with the bloody gore of the cock-fights between the macho men in the village. Finally, in 'A Wall of Fire Rising,' a destitute, unemployed father is so inspired by his son's recitation of *oungan* Boukman's revolutionary speech that he undertakes a suicide mission to protest his indentured labour at the hands of a sugar-cane factory owner. These stories, dreams, drawings, and declarations associated with *vodou* grant Danticat's heroes and heroines channels of self-expression, transcendence, and escape from their material hardships, as well as a means of resisting the violence of their oppression.

Sometimes Danticat's allusions to *vodou* are more subtle and can only be deciphered by the reader familiar with Haitian culture. For instance, *Krik? Krak!* consists of nine stories, and as such, the collection resembles the structure of a Haitian wake, which usually takes place over a span of nine days. This wake also alludes to the *vodou* funeral ceremony – of the reclamation of the souls of the deceased. The first and last stories of the collection, 'Children of the Sea' and 'Caroline's Wedding,' most clearly allude to this *vodou* practice. As I will show, in these two stories, numerous implicit references to *vodou* obliquely offer important insight into the Haitian experience of immigration.

In 'Children of the Sea,' Danticat draws attention to one of the greatest problems associated with Haitian immigration: the plight of Haitian 'boat-people.' Since 1972, tens of thousands of desperate people have attempted to flee the political brutality in Haiti by risking their lives on the high seas, a problem that culminated in the 1980s.[12] Under President Ronald Reagan, the United States adopted drastic measures to deter Haitians from taking to boats, including interdiction, repatriation, and detention.[13] In the 1990s, when a military coup forced President Aristide into exile, Haitians once again attempted to flee their country in rickety boats. As a result, the U.S. Coast Guard picked up nearly 70,000 Haitian boat-people in three years, most of whom were detained in Guantanamo in deplorable conditions for more than two years while awaiting processing. Today, U.S. policy-makers continue to practise simplistic discriminatory immigration policies regarding Haitians: they maintain that Haitians are all economic migrants, rather than political refugees or asylum seekers.[14]

In 'Children of the Sea,' Danticat delves into the experiences of one of these boatloads of people fleeing the political upheaval of the *dechoukaj* (uprooting). During *dechoukaj*, the post-Duvalier era, after

1986, the army controlled the country by force and again instigated anti-*vodou* scourges to justify their oppression. The story focuses on the tragic fate of two separated lovers: the young man, Kompé,[15] who witnesses the suffering on the high seas, and his unnamed female lover, who witnesses the violence in Haiti. Kompé describes the starvation and slow deaths of those on the boat, focusing in particular on the fate of a young woman who gives birth. The female lover correspondent, meanwhile, details the cruelty of the soldiers in Haiti: they 'imprison women, claiming they are witches' (19); kill demonstrating students and make parents pick up their children's severed heads (7); or make sons copulate with their mothers and then arrest them for immorality. We learn that the 15-year-old pregnant girl on the boat was raped by soldiers, after watching her mother be raped and murdered, under duress, by her brother (23). The lovers correspond with each other through letters that never reach their destination. Notably, the young woman sits writing her letters under a banyan tree, the resting place of the *vodou* family spirits, while Kompé voyages to the bottom of the sea, the final resting place of humans in *vodou* tradition.

The brutal violence depicted in this story is somewhat attenuated by allusions to *vodou* myth. The star-crossed lovers evoke the figures of Ezuli-La Sirene and Agwe, *lwas* (gods) of the seas. Just before dying, Kompé dreams of this underwater heaven, envisioning Agwe, starfish and mermaids dancing and singing in Latin, like priests in the cathedrals (28), or *oungans* at in vodou ritual. As Marie-José N'Zengou Tayo (1998) has shown, Haitian texts on boat-people[16] often refer to *lwa* Agwe. Moreover, Agwe is usually celebrated with a raft, called the *barque d'Agwé*, laden with sacrifices of rich food (Desmangles 184). In this case, the rickety raft does not carry food sacrifices but human ones. In *vodou* legends, glimpsing Agwe's 'beasts of the sea,' as Kompé does in his last hours, usually foreshadows death (Courlander, *Haiti Singing* 27); however, it is depicted as a delightful death, of dancing and rejoicing with mermaids.

Danticat guardedly references one of the major *vodou* ceremonies – *wete mò na ba dlo* – the reclamation of the souls of deceased ancestors, as described by numerous ethnographers. Haitians believe that the *lwa* and the spirits of the dead reside in a sacred dwelling place *en ba dlò*, 'in the watery deep' (Deren 36), or on *zilet en ba dlo*, the 'island beneath the sea' (Courlander, *The Drum* 19). *Wete mò nan ba dlo* ('extracting the dead from the waters of the abyss') is a death ritual in which the godlike life-force (*gwo-bon-anj*) of the deceased is separated from the community of the dead *en ba dlo*, and is reincorporated into the community of the living. Traditionally, this *vodou* rite is accompanied by a Roman Catholic wake, held for nine nights after the death (Richman 183). The celebratory ninth night, called *denye priè* ('last prayer'), concludes this death ritual.

Similarly, Danticat's collection also performs such ceremonial reclamation; her work reclaims the souls of these boat-people, as well as the spirits of many forgotten Haitians, including prostitutes, witches, widows, repudiated woman, and destitute labourers. The last story in the collection, the *denye priè*, is a celebration: 'Caroline's Wedding.' Moreover, the plot of 'Caroline's Wedding' features a Catholic memorial for the lost boat-people from 'Children of the Sea,' and thus completes the reclamatory *vodou* funeral ritual.

'Caroline's Wedding' explores how Haitian culture – both in its cultural heritage and legacy of suffering – may be reclaimed and celebrated in immigration. The story focuses on the Azile family at a crucial turning-point of their immigration experience: it begins as the older daughter Gracina finally receives her U.S. passport and as the younger American-born daughter Caroline prepares to marry a non-Haitian in an interracial marriage. Both of these changes unsettle the family dynamics, and force each woman to reconsider and resolve her personal relationship to Haitian culture.

The Azile family is characterized by sorrow, loss, and mourning. Family outings include attending memorial services, such as the one for the drowned boat-people in 'Children of the Sea.' Even a decade after their father's death, the girls in 'Caroline's Wedding' intentionally continue to grieve for him. Although their mother instructs them to wear red panties to ward off his dead spirit, the girls 'continue to wear black underpants as a sign of lingering grief' (172). Their family life is described as 'so heavy with disappointment' even on Sundays (174), which contrasts markedly with the Ruiz family's dancing next door – one of the reasons why Caroline may have chosen to marry a Latino man.

More markedly, both daughters are scarred by the wounds of immigration. Caroline, born in the United States, was born crippled, missing her left forearm because of the drugs her mother was given during her arrest in sweatshop raid (159). Figuratively, her missing limb may symbolize Caroline's missing past and her severed connection to Haiti. Gracina endures emotional sufferings of immigration. Upon gaining her passport, and thus her new American identity,

Gracina describes this acquisition in military terms: she gains 'a weapon' or a 'bullet-proof vest' for combat in the 'war-zone' or 'firing line' (213). Armoured by her new identity, Gracina finds herself plagued by nightmares in which she is visited by her father, who appears to her as a dancer wearing a mask, an incarnation of Guedé or Baron Samedi, the *lwa* of death.

The final story in *Krik? Krak!* suggests the healing of the sufferings of immigration can be achieved through recuperation of lost cultural elements. Both daughters successfully heal the wounds they've suffered in immigration through affective and effective narrative reclamation of Haitian culture. Upon encountering her father's spirit, narrator Gracina increasingly immerses herself in Haitian culture, in an effort to pierce her assimilative armour and re-member her broken, split self. As a result, Gracina's narrative is increasingly filled with more cultural references, stories, proverbs, and songs. For instance, at the beginning of the story, the girls play an association game that emphasizes their loss:

'Who are you?
I am the *lost* child of the night.
Where do you come from?
I come from the inside of the *lost* stone.' (164, italics mine)[17]

In contrast, after the wedding, they sing the classic song, 'Beloved Haiti there is no place like you. I had to leave you before I could understand you' (212), also intoned by the boat-people in 'Children of the Sea' (9). The story ends with the mother and Gracina playing this dialogic game: 'If we were painters what landscapes would we paint? What kind of legends will my daughter be told? What kinds of charms will I give her to ward off evil?' (216). In this game, there are no formulaic answers; rather, these open-ended questions elicit a multiplicity of possible responses. Similarly, immigration prompts Haitians to consider manifold ways of negotiating their cultural identity

Caroline's healing is even more tangible, as her narrative and cultural immersion is also accompanied by corporeal signifiers. We are told that Caroline 'liked to have her stub stroked' (174) while the girls shared stories. Her limb, described as a 'stuffed dumpling' (159), reflects a metaphor that Danticat develops further in her epilogue, where she describes women's stories as 'narrative dumplings' (220) immersed into her 'survival soup.' As the story progresses, Caroline reappropriates her missing limb through further stories, *pwovèb* (174), and even hybrid performance. For instance, she imagines her arm would come bursting out of her mother's stomach to the sound of rumbas (174). On her wedding day, her narrative transformation seems complete, as she appears wearing a prosthesis, thus no longer missing a limb. Yet, at the same time, she explains that strangely, she is experiencing 'phantom pain' (198), although she herself was never an amputee. Her mother, who had been previously estranged from Caroline, reconciles with her at this point, because she recognizes and empathizes with this imagined 'phantom pain' – as a form of cultural pain, characteristic of the immigrant condition (199).

Throughout this story, Danticat creatively reclaims a variety of Haitian cultural elements, *vodou* imagery included. As mentioned, Gracina's father appears to her as Baron Samedi. Similarly, because of her missing limb, Caroline may be associated with Gran Ezuli, or the Crone-Goddess of old age and wisdom. Danticat's elusive allusions to *vodou* are further exemplified in the recurring tropes of 'bones' and 'leaves.' In the story, the Haitian mother insistently makes 'bone soup'; however, on the morning Caroline's wedding, she transforms this ritual into a 'leaf bath.' The imagery of 'bones' and 'leaves' bears multiple meanings in *vodou* practices, and as such, it grants the culturally aware reader or critic a multiplicity of subtle yet powerful interpretations.

The mother's 'bone soup' simmers with rich cultural connotations. Narratively, it reminds us of Danticat's 'survival soup.' Thematically, it evokes Caroline's missing arm-bone; symbolically, her missing physical connection to her ancestral heritage. Interestingly, the first line of the Haitian national anthem refers to 'the bones of my people' (56). 'Bones' also call to mind a *pwoveb* about maternal love – '*Manman pa janm mode pitit li jouk nan zo*' (A mother never bites her children to the bone) – which appears in Danticat's story, translated as 'we're not like birds; we don't just kick our children out of our nest' (164).

In *vodou*, bones are most commonly associated with the *lwa* Legba (as *Legba Kafu* or *Gran Chimin*), the god of crossroads or gateways, often marked with old, dry bones. Songs to Legba include: 'Old bones, oh old bones [...] Oh Papa Legba can't you see that I have no bones' (Marcelin et al. 17). Legba himself is most often represented as an old man with a cane or crutch (Métraux 89). In the story, Legba's association with the aging mother, handicapped daughter, and the moment of transition seem rather clear. Legba is further associated with flags, sabres, and machetes (Courlander, *The Drum* 75), which call to mind Gracina's passport and its military connotations. Legba is also the god of 'chance' and 'accidents' (Herskovits 31) – which evokes Caroline's accident or her chance encounter with her husband. Most salient, however, is Legba's role in the *vodou* pantheon: Legba is the one who opens the gateway between the sacred and secular world and serves as the intermediary between humans and the gods. Legba thus incarnates the role of cultural interpreter. As Herskovits explains: 'To Legba was assigned the role of linguist between the kingdom of gods and gods and gods and men' (cited in Courlander, *The Drum* 36). Certainly, Legba's role adds further insight into the role of the Azile women, and by extension that of Danticat herself as writer: that of cultural interpreter.

Moreover, in *vodou*, Legba is also associated with trees in his manifestation of Gran Bwa (Deren 99), and thus subtly relates the imagery of 'bones' to 'leaves.' Furthermore, Gran Bwa[18] is the guardian of the forest of the spirits in *zile en ba dlò*, the island below the sea (Deren 100). The figure of Gran Bwa thus limberly connects 'Caroline's Wedding' to 'Children of the Sea,' where tree symbolism is also significant; for instance, the female lover writes under the banyan tree, describing the violence of *dechoukaj* ('uprooting' in *kreyòl*). The Azile women, and Danticat herself, might similarly be considered Legba–Gran Bwa, cultural interpreters, but also guardians of the spirits of the dead.

On her wedding day, the mother bathes Caroline in leaves, an act that might refer to a number of *vodou* rituals. Leaf baths are a common white magic ritual, serving to 'heal, reconcile enemies, get work and guardianship' (Métraux 275). Leaf baths are also important in both funeral and initiation ceremonies. In Haitian burials, which usually follow the ceremonial reclamation of the dead, the corpse is bathed in leaves to 'be thoroughly cleansed in order to make it acceptable to all the ancestral spirits' (Desmangles 73). In this way, the mother/daughter leaf bath might thus intimate reconciliation and closure with the past.

In another interpretation, leaf baths signify a new beginning and immersion for the Azile family. During the *vodou* initiation ceremony, *vodou ounsi* (initiates) must bathe in a leaf bath (Métraux 174), following a period of *djevo* (reclusion), to cleanse their heads in a *lave tet* (de-brainwashing). Caroline similarly shuts herself up in her room for a few days before her wedding. Moreover, Métraux notes that during the initiation period, *ounsis* eat only chicken bones and inner organs (180), perhaps another allusion to the mother's famous bone soup in Danticat's story.

Lastly, Courlander describes the use of leaves in the marriage ceremony commemorating the union of Met Gran Bwa and Fem Gran Bwa, *lwa* of the organic natural world (*The Drum* 66). At the end of this marriage ceremony, Courlander notes that bones are washed clean in sweet-scented leaves, in a mixture that then becomes a ritual lotion or bath. This marriage ceremony ends with the song: '*la famille vin paye sang / la famille vin paye sang / ceremoni la fini*' ('the family has paid its blood. The ceremony is finished'). When interpreted in light of this union, Caroline's interracial wedding might be considered to be the 'organic' conclusion of this immigrant story. In the end, the leaf bath – whether symbolic of rituals of burial, initiation, or marriage of the gods of Nature – denotes the Azile family's acceptance of change, their reconciliation with the past, and their immersion in and celebration of a hybrid multicultural future.

By elaborating on these manifold interpretations of 'bones' and 'leaves,' I have attempted to outline the many possible translations of Danticat's allusions to *vodou* myth – for the reader knowledgeable of *vodou* beliefs. While casual readers might not grasp the complexity of Danticat's implicit and hybrid cultural signifiers, they nonetheless discern its underlying meaning: that such a creative cultural reclamation can offer alienated and suffering immigrants some form of emotional healing. For literary critics as well, Danticat's imaginative use of *vodou* myths is curative: it urges them to delve further into the complexities of Haitian culture. Certainly, deciphering these subtle cultural signs offers a richer, multilayered interpretation of Danticat's fiction.

Dany Laferrière: Missing Gods (or *Vodou* on Ice)

I conclude my analysis of *vodou* with the most famous contemporary Haitian novelist writing in French: Dany Laferrière (b. 1953). In his first, ground-breaking book, *Comment faire l'amour avec un Nègre sans se fatiguer* (*How To Make Love to a Negro*, 1985) *vodou* is mentioned only once – when the main characters are making love, the ceiling shakes so terribly that the narrator comically quips that Ogoum, the god of fire and war, may be living upstairs (17). However, he notes that it might also be the wrath of Allah, or Beelzebub, or even the Apocalypse. In this novel, Laferrière creates a new, multicultural, and literate identity for the Haitian individual. Indeed, a book on *vodou vèvès* sits on the narrator's bookshelf – alongside esoteric books on Assyrian art, the English mystics, or Swinburn's 'Fata Morgana' (17). Clearly, Laferrière's hero is not the typical 'backward barbarian'; on the contrary, the well-read narrator reads Bukowski, Cendrars, or Miller, listens to jazz, and cites the Koran. These characteristics of high culture are perhaps one of the reasons that early critics doubted the book was written by a Black man. In fact, the only time the narrator overtly refers to Haitian culture – that Haitians eat cats – lands him in serious trouble with his feline-loving girlfriend (98–9).

By his omission of cultural referents specific to Haiti, Laferrière dispels preconceived stereotypes about Haitians. As he explains in an interview: 'I don't like what they say about me (I'm speaking of the Haitian that I am) in the West. For them, Haiti is only about poverty, voodoo and dictatorship. That's not all we're about. We are also living beings with goals and dreams. And particularly with a rich daily life' ('Interview').

Furthermore, when asked about his experiences of 'Haitian life,' 'diaspora,' and 'postcolonialism,' Laferrière retorts that he does not know 'what these expressions mean,' they are 'too vague,' 'imprecise.' As he says: 'I am an artist. I can't conceive life in any other way than the singular. The intellectual thinks in collective terms, the artist, about the individual' ('Interview'). Laferrière's use of *vodou* (or rather his missed use of it in this case), dismisses the reification of Haitian immigrants in the stereotypical collective lens of 'poverty, voodoo and dictatorship' and advocates a singular, artistic individuality.

Nevertheless, in *Le Cri des oiseaux fous* (*The Cry of the Crazy Birds*, 2000), the last volume of Laferrière's ten-work immigrant opus, his 'American autobiography,' as he calls it, *vodou* superstition seems to have the decisive last word. In this novel, Laferrière describes the last day before his departure from Haiti during which his best friend was killed, the event that prompted his decision to leave his country forever. The penultimate words of the novel (and of the whole opus) are those of his estranged father; whose last words to Laferrière were: 'I have no children since Duvalier has made all Haitians into zombies' (318). Thus, the legacy of political brutality, and its connotations with *vodou* superstition, clearly remain relevant for Laferrière.

In this last work, as a tribute to his heritage, Laferrière offers us a few subtle references to *vodou*. For example, just before getting on the plane, the narrator turns to face Legba, by whose intercession he passes through security. Legba in *vodou* mythology is the god of the crossroads, the god who joins the invisible to the real world, who is called upon first during any *vodou* ritual. Laferrière obliquely acknowledges Legba's saving power; as he explains, without Legba, 'who opens the gateway' (317), he would not have been able to pass to the other world. Similarly, his last meal in Haiti is a fish with the 'daughters of Agwe,' the god of the sea (308) – the sea being Haitians' final resting place in death. In another scene, we see a prostitute dressed in a bridal gown dappled with blood, in a bar filled with *tonton macoutes*. This is the image of Ezuli, the goddess of love, at times depicted as a seductress (Freda), and at other moments as an angry, vengeful bride (Ge Woug). When the narrator boards the plane, he remarks that he has passed out of evil, out of dictatorship, and into a different world bereft of gods. As he explains: 'the *vodou* gods do not travel North. They are too vulnerable to the cold' (317).[19] He is left alone, 'without guides, without gods,' to 'face the new world' and decipher new 'codes and symbols' (317).

In this last novel, Laferrière grants a subtle salute to *vodou* religious beliefs that perhaps only the reader sensitive to Haitian culture might be able to recognize. In Laferrière's novels focusing specifically on Haiti, *Pays sans chapeau* (*Country without a Hat*, 1996), for example, he turns to *vodou* traditions to reflect Haiti's rich cultural life. In his immigrant novels, however, Laferrière explores new codes and symbols, rather than referring to the clichés of *vodou* to describe the Haitian person not as a colonial or national subject but as a cosmopolitan individual.

Can the *Vodou* Gods Travel North?

In conclusion, can the *vodou* gods travel North? Or will they get lost? Are they too different? Certainly, in the Haitian texts analysed here, *vodou* signals difference and loss. Or rather, it gestures towards multiple differences, and speaks of multiple losses. Such cultural signifiers may become lost in the labyrinth of modernity (Ollivier) or in artistic hybridity (Danticat), just as they may be lost for the cosmopolitan individual (Laferrière) or for the victim traumatized by violence (Etienne). Allusions relating these *vodou* to the sufferings of immigration may also be dismissed because of *vodou*'s associations with the conventions of the fantastic or horror genre (Péan), because of abusively violent rhetoric (Etienne), or because of its multiple interpretations in the Haitian oral storytelling tradition (Danticat).

Can Haitian writers effectively take up *vodou* myths to refer to their pain of immigration, or should they look for new codes and symbols in immigration? Given all the different uses and abuses of *vodou*, will not any reference to it denote some sort of loss? In the end, does not such difference and loss best describe the immigrant condition and the suffering of immigration?

In the end it is up to the reader to judge the effects of this hybrid cultural rhetoric. Certainly, a cursory reader might miss or dismiss the manifold interpretations of *vodou* or its implicit allusions to the sufferings of immigration. The sensitive and careful critic, though, will gain much insight into the immigrant condition through the diverse translations of *vodou* presented here.

In Ollivier's *La discorde*, for example, we gain an understanding of immigrants' nostalgia for home, their disorienting dislocation abroad, and the precariousness of their return to their roots. *Vodou* becomes the symbol of a vibrant Haitian self, the antithesis to intellectual rationalization, an epistemological counter-discourse wherein orality and performance triumph over the literary word. In Etienne's texts, by contrast, all of *vodou*'s religious or cultural value is indeed destroyed in his dystopic portrait of a nation traumatized by tyrannical oppression, wherein any individual agency is lost, amputated, mutilated, tortured, or zombified in a cycle of perpetual violence. Yet, Etienne's visceral and graphic *vodou* imagery also enables us to penetrate the scarred psyches of traumatized political refugees, and their frustrations with ignorant and discriminatory immigration institutions. In Péan's stories, *vodou* transports us to a different, supernatural world, a world outside the experiential reality of poverty, alienation and discrimination, while also allegorically referring to the cultural transformations possible in immigration. As for Laferrière, he grants us insight into the complex motivations and hybrid cultural translations of the cosmopolitan individual. Finally, Danticat's reclamation of *vodou* myths, Haitian folklore, and oral storytelling offers readers a potent, therapeutic cultural remedy for the cultural and identitary loss inherent in immigration, in her 'survival soup' brimming with inventive, recuperative strategies. In the end, despite these numerous losses – perhaps inherent in the process of translation and in immigration – this chapter reveals what might be gained in translation and immigrant fiction, through a sensitive reading of Haitian *vodou* symbols. Ultimately, the final affective interpretation of these cultural elements depends on one's ability to read as a cultural translator.

Part III of this book showed how French-Maghrebi immigrant authors stripped their writing of cultural referents to turn to the body as a universal referent to signal their pain of immigration. I observed how these authors increasingly create graphic imagery to heighten the reader's awareness of their suffering, even going as far as translating themselves into pathological victims. In this part of the book, I have outlined how the suffering body might be cloaked in cultural connotations, specifically, those related to the hybrid cultural signifier of Haitian *vodou*. I have pointed to many myth/misinterpretations of Haitian *vodou* – both destructive and creative ones, both in politics and literature. In immigrant fiction, cultural rhetoric perhaps offers immigrant writers a more nuanced form of expression than corporal pain: not only can it denote their suffering of immigration, but it also suggests a space of creation, resistance, and perhaps release from their immigrant pain. What is more, cultural rhetoric even intimates a possible remedy for the suffering of immigration – through the vehicle of culture.

From bodily rhetoric and cultural rhetoric, let us now move to a last form of rhetoric to express the suffering of immigration – that of silence. From the shared experience of corporeal pain, to the culturally specific interpretation of suffering, let us now consider the possibility that the hardships of immigration may not be explicitly expressed at all, or they may be disguised in allusion, erasure, and understatement, or even, cloaked in silence. What happens when the sufferings of immigration are silenced, or apparently absent in immigrant fiction?

PART IV

Silencing Suffering:
The 'Painless' Czech Case

9 'Painless' Fictions?
Czech Exile and Return

The first years in exile were cruel, but we had chosen it, therefore we did not want to write home about our pain and hardship and today it 'returns' to us in the form of accusations.[1]

    – Anonymous émigré (quoted in Horáček and Šiklová, 9)

Here at home, we hold no love towards émigrés. We didn't like them before, and we don't like them now. Not that we don't concern ourselves with them, we just simply really don't like them. Seemingly it's some kind of tradition here [...] They can go ahead and complain, but since they have no political rights, let them whine, they pose no threat, as long as at home all is quiet.

    – Jiří Bigas, 'Our Relationship to Emigrants
    Is a Test of National Maturity'

'Painless' Rhetoric

These two quotes – one by a Czech émigré, the other by a Czech national – reveal the contradictory sentiments that I will elaborate in this chapter, as I focus on the problematical return of Czech emigrants 'home' to the Czech Republic after the fall of Communism. Under the communist regime, from 1948 to 1989, an estimated 550,000 people, or 3.5 per cent of the population, emigrated from Czechoslovakia, to become immigrants in other countries (Pehe 23). After the 1989 Velvet Revolution, thousands of these people returned, with high hopes of coming 'home.' Upon their return, however, they often faced resentment, xenophobia, and discrimination, both in the legal and the public forums. Now, almost two decades later, few of these individuals remain in the Czech Republic; they have left again, disillusioned by the negative reception they received.

My analysis in this chapter briefly sketches out the main issues of the Czech emigrant return, from both legal and symbolic perspectives, so as to focus on one aspect that has been completely overlooked in this debate: the literature written by them while in exile, while they were immigrants in other countries. I argue that a mistranslation of Czech exile literature largely informed the reception of Czechs' return after 1989. In Czech exile writing, these writers rarely voiced the 'pain and hardship' of immigration; instead, it was rhetorically silenced or avoided. Upon their return, their 'painless' experience was 'returned to [them] in the form of accusations' (Horáček and Šiklová 9). Here I will examine the multivalent sociocultural, historical, psychological, and literary reasons that may have prompted Czech immigrants to repress their sufferings in their writings. Most importantly, I examine the effects of this seeming absence of pain. What happens when the pain of immigration, or of emigration, is silenced? How is the reader to understand the silenced suffering in Czech exile literature? When emigrants can safely return home – are their difficulties of migration erased? How might the immigrant experience be translated in the public forum, if it is seemingly devoid of hardship?

These are some of the questions driving this chapter, which explores the 'painless rhetoric' surrounding the Czech emigrant experience, as translated in Czech social discourse and in Czech exile literature. This part of the book moves from an explicit rhetoric of pain (the body) and more implicit rhetorics of suffering (culture), to investigate an even more elusive form of rhetoric – that of silence. On the one hand, the absence of suffering attributed to Czechs who left may signify that their immigrant experience was relatively painless, in contrast to that of Maghrebis or Haitians, for instance. On the other hand, as I will argue, this absence of pain may denote a rhetoric – wherein suffering was denied, repressed, silenced, or avoided – that is chosen for a number of complex political or personal reasons. Certainly, as this chapter will show, a rhetoric of suffering based in differentials and hierarchies, played an important role in the reception of Czechs returning after 1989. The next chapter will reveal that a 'reticent' rhetoric of suffering continues to characterize postcommunist fiction written by Czech emigrants who returned 'home.'

Locating Difference: From Race to Return

Before delving into my analysis, it is perhaps necessary to stress a major difference between the Czechs and the other immigrants discussed in this book: White, Western privilege. Because of their unmarked appearance, Czech immigrants do not encounter the same type of discrimination and racism that Beurs endure in France or that Haitians experience in the United States; Czechs are not usually differentiated by their physical attributes. A further distinction must be emphasized: unlike Haitians or Maghrebis, Czech immigrants are unmarked by the destructive legacy of colonialism. Although it is true that the Czechoslovak Republic (CSR) did not exist as an independent country until 1918, the CSR never experienced the same economic, cultural, or political exploitation that Haiti or the Maghreb did, though the Czech lands did experience centuries of domination under the Habsburg Empire, six years under Hitler, and forty-one years of Soviet totalitarianism. Social class is also a critical consideration. Many Czech writers, especially those of the 1948 and 1968 generations, were prominent intellectuals and writers before they left their native land. Considered political exiles, they were not stigmatized as cheap labour in the same way that Algerian workers or Haitian boat-people were. Moreover, Czech culture has always been considered part of European high culture, and thus its literature may be more readily translatable than exoticized *vodou* rituals, for example. On the one hand, then, Czech immigrants, as well as their fiction, may be more easily integrated into the Western literary canon or into dominant Western culture. On the other hand, because of the lack of this difference, their sufferings – if expressed – could have been much more readily either dismissed as part of the universal human condition or conflated as post-modern angst, rather than being translated as the sufferings of immigration or of return.

White Western privilege, or the differing attitudes towards Czechs as opposed to other immigrant groups (such as Haitians or Maghrebians), is perhaps most explicit in the term generally used to describe Czechs living outside Czechoslovakia in the period 1948–1989. In the English or French language, these persons are usually termed 'émigrés,' rather than either 'emigrants' or 'immigrants.'[2] Even the *Oxford English Dictionary*, which defines 'émigré' as 'an emigrant of any nationality, esp. a political exile,' illustrates the term by specifically referring to 'Czechoslovakian *émigrés*, who were disaffected towards the then régime in Czechoslovakia' (*OED*, 2nd edition, emphasis in original). The term 'émigré' originated during the French Revolution, when Royalists fled France for political reasons, to seek asylum in neighbouring countries. While these Royalists included people of all classes, most of them were noblemen or clergy who fled France for fear of their lives. Moreover, during the French Revolutionary Wars (1792–1802), many émigré factions formed armies, and with the aid of neighbouring countries, such as Great Britain, aimed to overthrow the French government and restore the monarchy. The term 'émigré,' therefore, refers explicitly to a 'political exile,' to one who sees exile as a temporary expedient forced on him/her by political circumstances, and who wishes to return to his or her native land once there is a change of government. Furthermore, émigré bears connotations of a certain social standing, in the Czech case, that of the intellectual or writer class.

Czechoslovaks living outside their country during the Cold War were referred to as 'émigrés' by English and French speakers; thus, they were defined by their political circumstances, as well as by their involuntary 'push' to leave Czechoslovakia. As such, Czechoslovaks were differentiated from other, 'ordinary,' 'emigrants' or those 'who remove themselves from their own land to settle (permanently) in another' (*OED*) or from 'immigrants,' 'people who migrate into a country as a settler' (*OED*). Both of these more generic terms are ascribed to people who are lured by the 'pull' of another country, usually because of its economic prosperity. As I have discussed in chapter 1, these distinctions – between political refugees and economic migrants – are not always as clear-cut. Rather, the term 'émigré,' and its legal counterpart, 'political refugee,' more accurately reflect Western perspectives on Western and non-Western others. While political repression in White, Western countries is generally deemed 'political' (e.g., during the Cold War), such is not often the case in non-Western countries, those of 'the developing world' or the 'global South.' Instances of civil unrest and political oppression in non-Western countries are often not taken as seriously as those in Western contexts. For instance, I spent the summer of 2000 volunteering in a Liberian refugee camp in Ghana where, ten years into the brutal regime of Charles Taylor, refugees were still attempting to prove their Geneva Convention status as 'political refugees' in order to gain asylum in Western nations. More pertinently, just as many Czechoslovaks were fleeing totalitarian oppression in the years 1948–1989, during the same period, many Haitians were fleeing the tyrannical regime of the Duvaliers, yet the latter were rarely granted asylum as political refugees. During the Cold War, the Soviet Union was manifestly considered the West's political adversary, whereas the Duvalier dictatorial regime was concomitantly tolerated by the West (in contrast to Fidel Castro's socialist Cuba, for instance). The motivations of Czechs fleeing Czechoslovakia were not always political, however. Although some Czechs were indeed fleeing Czechoslovakia for political reasons, many of them left the country to seek better economic opportunities elsewhere, or to rejoin their families abroad, and ultimately, settled there permanently as immigrants.

In Czech, the word 'émigré' is rarely deployed; it is considered an archaic term referring to French Royalist émigrés. Rather, the English (or French) term 'émigré' is to be translated in current usage as 'political emigrant' (*politický emigrant*) or as 'refugee' (*uprchlík*; see *The Czech Academy's Comprehensive Czech-English Dictionary*, ed. Hais in 1991). Interestingly however, in Czech news reports of the 1990s, the term generally employed for returning Czechs was *emigrant*, not *politický emigrant*, in other words, the generic term devoid of any political connotations.

In this book, I choose to use the terms 'emigrant' and 'immigrant' to refer to the Czech migratory experience. By choosing these terms, I aim to disavow Western privilege, and to recognize that, in many ways, the Czech experience parallels that of other immigrant groups, as not all Czechs had political aspirations when leaving their country. I will only deploy the term 'émigré' to persons who specifically self-identify as leaving Czechoslovakia for political reasons.

Part IV differs from the rest of this book, however, in its focus on the 'emigrant' experience. My previous analyses examined the 'immigrant' experience, or the non-native's entry and integration into a new culture and society and his or her relation to the host country. While a section of Part IV examines the Czech immigrant experience ('The Silenced Suffering of Exile'), Part IV also investigates the 'emigrant' experience, or the former native's relation to the home country. Specifically, it focuses on the emigrant's permanent return home, and considers the reception and translation of the 'emigrant,' or former native, in the original homeland.

As Abdelmalek Sayad has powerfully argued in *Double Absence* (1999), the immigrant is always also an emigrant, split between past and present and between home and host country. In contrast to the copious number of psychological and sociological studies on immigration however, studies on emigration, or on the relation to the home country, are much scarcer. In our Western-centric world, the experience of immigration – in particular, that of non-Westerners assimilating into white, Western society – seems to be emphasized at the expense of the experience of emigration – or that of neo-Westerners relating to the 'old' '(read 'backward and undeveloped') country. Yet today, immigrants' ties to their former homeland are much stronger and much more complex than those of previous generations. In today's world of mass-transportation and global communication, a quick 'return home' is only a plane trip, phone call, Webcam or Email message away.

In literature, as in the social sciences, the immigrant condition has also garnered much more critical attention than the emigrant condition. While the immigrant novel has long been recognized as an established genre, and there are numerous studies of immigrant texts, there is, by contrast, no correlative genre of 'emigrant literature' and little literary criticism on immigrant's return to and relations with the former homeland. For instance, in the canonical 1981 formulation of the immigrant genre, Boelhower only briefly alludes to the immigrant's relation to the 'old world' (5). In one passage, he contrasts a previous 'monocultural world-view' (3) with the 'pluricultural reality' (13) of immigration. In another passage, he claims that, at the end of the traditional immigrant novel, the immigrant's relation to the 'old world' is one of 'idealized reality' (5), presumably one characterized by nostalgia, romanticism and embellishment.

Return home is nonetheless a common trope in contemporary immigrant literature, as we have already seen in Maghrebi women's writing (e.g., Zinai-Koudil, Ben Mansour, Boukhedenna) or in Haitian immigrant texts (e.g., Depestre, Ollivier, Laferrière). It is also clearly manifest in other immigrant literary traditions not developed in this book. The immigrant's return to the homeland is also a dominant theme in Iranian immigrant fiction (e.g., Satrapi, Rachlin, Bahrampour, Moaveni), in Asian-American narratives (e.g., Tan, Chong, Khu, Chai), or in the literature of the Indian diaspora (e.g., Mukherjee, Rushdie, Lahiri, Daswani, Kirchner), to cite a few examples. Such fictional returns in many ways reflect the in-betweenness of the immigrant condition, the precarious condition of being both an immigrant and an emigrant. The relation to one's homeland is not always as facile or as rosy as Boelhower contends. Just as Ollivier and Laferrière's descriptions of home reflect a hybrid, 'pluricultural reality,' Maghrebi women's writing showcases the ravages of civil war, not of some 'idealized reality.' In the Czech case, we will examine a return which incited painful differences between natives and emigrants, as well as between emigrants and émigrés.

This chapter considers a form of return that is perhaps more unusual in contemporary global politics and literary representations: the emigrant's permanent return home. In the Czech case, the prospect of returning home permanently was only made possible because of the surprising and unusual circumstances of the fall of the Berlin Wall. Ultimately, however, the possibility of permanent return also speaks to many temporary or idealized returns home by immigrant individuals. It prompts us to ask: what may be some of the generic features of emigrant narratives, or immigrant narratives focusing on emigration? Does a final return home signal the end of immigrant sufferings? How is the experience of immigration translated at home? What happens when the emigrant – or emigrants en masse – come home to stay?

The Return of the Czech Emigrant

Opustíš-li mne, nezahynu/ opustíš-li mne, zahyneš. (69)
(Should you leave me, I won't perish/ should you leave me, you will die.)
– Viktor Dyk, 69

This nationalist verse by Viktor Dyk is a classic for most Czechs. It represents the poetic political imaginary adopted by the former communist Czechoslovak regime: Mother Nation's warning against emigration and exile. Sadly, its threat seemed more relevant after the fall of communism than it did under communism.

Until 1999 commentators observed that an 'undeclared war was being waged' (Pecina) between Czechs who left and Czechs who stayed, a conflict that was even reflected in high political echelons. In 1990, for instance, Václav Klaus, the current president of the Czech Republic and then chairman of the Civic Forum party, was asked about the country's future relationship to Czech-Americans, to which he is reputed to have replied: 'Czech-Americans annoy me' (Bísek 35). In 1993, Peter Payne, chairman of the Czech Legislative Assembly, explained in a U.S. interview that émigrés have a 'bad reputation' because 'the public's logical feeling is that they are people who made their life better and easier by emigrating,' and opined that they should 'improve their image in the Czech Republic.'[3] Payne's remarks sparked outrage among many Czech intellectuals, as evidenced in many articles and op-eds on the subject.[4]

In reading the heated media responses in the mid-1990s, it becomes apparent that the debate about Czech returnees revolved around two issues: material rights and symbolic representation, both of which were inextricably linked. In his analysis of diasporic communities, William Safran describes the key features of expatriate minority groups, which he defines as diasporas: dispersed from their homeland, partially alienated from their host societies, they retain a collective vision or 'myth' of their homeland. Similarly, it may be argued that Czechs under totalitarianism also held an idealized vision of *krajané*, their Czech compatriots abroad in the West.

In 1989, with the possibility of return, after more than forty years of mystification and idealization, all such illusions were shattered. As Czech emigrants returned home, they became material persons, claiming rights such as citizenship, the vote, and restitution of their property. The Czech homeland was upturned by their return: it became necessary to transform them into Czech citizens, to translate their past into current events, and to transfer exile culture into national archives and museums. The emigrants' return forced Czechs to contemplate the meaning of Czechness itself, define Czech nationhood, re-evaluate their past, and forge a relationship with otherness in their present. The return coincided with a great move forward, towards a future democratic 'civil society,' capitalism, and market economy, just as the past was being erased, repressed, rectified, and rewritten.

Material Rights

Ostensibly, antagonism towards returning Czechs stemmed from their claims for national and material rights, namely, citizenship, the vote, and material restitution. When Czechoslovakia itself disappeared in 1993, with the formation of the Czech and Slovak Republics, so did the hyphenated position of the Czech abroad; dual citizenship became increasingly problematical. Czechs living abroad could not acquire Czech citizenship other than by the means accorded to any foreigner (via a work permit, residency requirements, and so on). A similar resolution accorded voting and property restitution rights; it was reserved only for those holding permanent residency or for those who had left before 1948. On the whole, returning Czechs were not particularly interested in reclaiming their lost land (only about 250 cases were heard by Czech courts; Kontra). Rather, they were upset by the requisite permanent residency provision that restricted restitution and the vote to people living in the Czech Republic. They considered it to be of symbolic (Bendová) or psychological (Nováček) value that they be included and recognized by the Czech state.

Ironically, at the same time Czechs abroad were stripped of rights within the Czech Republic, they were expected to help the country financially and politically, by financing Czech institutions and lobbying for Czech causes in other governments. Such help was considered their 'duty,' not actions deserving of quid pro quo rights or privileges (Povolný). These attitudes angered many Czech emigrants; as one put it, 'at first we were welcomed with open arms to later be told to stay out of Czech politics, while the Communist party members, at first rebuffed as criminals, were later allowed to participate in democracy' (Vrzala 21)

Throughout the 1990s Czech emigrants continued to voice their complaints about these issues, both at home and in the international forum. In 1997, for example, during a U.S. congressional debate on the expansion of NATO, some Czechs living in the United States vociferously sided against the Czech Republic's entry into NATO, most particularly the group calling itself the IAS, the International Association of Czechs for Dual Citizenship, Restitution, and Voting Rights (Shah). With its projected entry into NATO and the European Union, the Czech Republic was forced to reconsider its treatment of minorities, be they returning Czechs, or the Roma and Sinti (gypsies), who, because of the 1993 citizenship law, had become stateless. For example, a significant portion of the EU Commission's 1998 report on the Czech Republic was devoted to the situation of the Roma.[5] By the following autumn, the Czech Republic, eager to become a part of the global economy, yielded to international pressure, emigrant grievances, and their financial strangleholds and enacted law 193/1999. Law 193/1999 revoked the statutes of 1989 and 1993 and granted dual citizenship to returning Czechs and citizenship to stateless Roma, indeed, to all those who had been Czechoslovak citizens at some time between 1948 and 1989.

Symbolic Representation

It was perhaps on a symbolic level that Czech emigrants experienced most of the resentment and animosity directed towards them. The inhospitality, ill-will, and resentment towards them stemmed from 'tradition' (Bigas): certain sociohistorical structures – or 'myths' (Barthes) – propagated under communism, which persisted long after 1989. Perhaps the most basic of these myths was the belief that émigrés had betrayed the state. As one commentator sums up: 'exiles were considered either as deserters or traitors by the former communist regime. Perhaps it is the only thing that communists accomplished successfully' (Povolný). Along with this rhetoric, the communist state often took punitive action against émigrés' relatives: after these 'traitors' or 'defectors' left, members of their families were denied such rights as secondary school education or travel abroad.

Another misconception concerning Czechs who left was perhaps more banal, but much more widespread: the belief that they chose a 'better life' by leaving and that they enjoyed the 'good, easy life' abroad. This myth was not so much perpetrated by the state, as by emigrants themselves. In their letters back home, as well as in Czech exile literature, the life of Czechs abroad appears both painless and prosperous. As a result, 'serious misunderstandings arose,' as commentator Thomas Pecina put it: 'if there were a million émigrés, there were a million success stories.' Czechs at home contributed to such misunderstandings, often being completely seduced by the myth of the American dream, or of the Promised Land on the other side of the Iron Curtain.

After 1989 further misperceptions arose. Many guilt-ridden or well-meaning émigrés fostered the image of the poor, victimized, and deprived Czechs at home, and rushed to assist or even rescue them. Many homeland Czechs resented this paternalistic 'big brother' or even 'missionary' attitude, as well as the denigrating stereotypes of Czech natives as 'chalupáři,'[6] a 'bit greedy' or 'dumb' (Hanák). Children of Czech immigrants, or the second- and third-generation Czechs born abroad, earned the reputation of being 'spoiled brats,' who lacked cultural or linguistic skills and seemingly visited relatives on vacations only to shop or party. The return of Czech emigrants in the early 1990s coincided with an influx of other foreigners to the Czech Republic at that time, including European tourists and YAPS (Young Americans in Prague). By 1993 an estimated 7,000 to 30,000 American expatriates were living in Prague,[7] often as business entrepreneurs or as artistic bohemians. Many of these foreigners viewed Prague as either an investment opportunity or a cultural commodity.

Certainly, returning Czechs were not prepared for the resentment and even antagonism that they would experience in the homeland. Perhaps the greatest fantasy that these Czechs had nurtured was the illusion that their return would be a triumphant, happy homecoming. This was a hope they had harboured for decades, but this dream of an exultant return was shattered in the face of stereotypes, hostility, and discrimination.

The Value of Suffering

As Jan Drábek incisively points out, in the postcommunist Czech Republic 'the term emigrant does not designate a geographical dimension but a moral one.' ('Emigrant' 6). The returnee was either a traitor or a faithful patriot, either a self-indulgent charlatan entrepreneur or a do-good humanist intellectual. If, as emigrants, Czechs had abandoned their Czech homeland to 'go live better,' they deserved to remain emigrants. Only if they remained faithful to the afflicted Czech collective could they be considered citizens.

At the crux of this moral judgment lies the value of suffering. As Sasha Goluboff observes, 'the mythic charter for belonging in the Czech Republic [became] collective suffering.'[8] The pain of homeland Czechs, who had suffered under the totalitarian communist regime, was weighed against the seemingly 'painless' experience of those who left, who had supposedly lived happy, free lives abroad. No longer merely symbolic, suffering became a politically charged, material issue when returnees started claiming restitution for the pain and loss they had suffered, in this case, citizenship, the vote, and real estate. 'Justified suffering' became a question of legitimacy, national rights, and the key to national belonging.

Problematically, though, many Czechs chose to suppress any sufferings they experienced during immigration. As suggested by the interview cited in the epigraph at the beginning of this chapter, 'the first years in exile were cruel, but we had chosen it, therefore we did not want to write home about our pain and hardship, and today it 'returns' to us in the form of accusations' (cited in Horáček and Šiklová 9). In the postcommunist Czech Republic, this apparent absence of pain caused further misery for returnees. Many Czechs refused to believe that who left experienced any hardships while abroad, because many emigrants failed to say so. As Jiří Pehe, a former exile who worked as President Havel's chief political adviser, explains: 'The whole of society believed that they had suffered, while we in the West led a comfortable life. The people here simply don't understand that we lost everything and basically had to start from scratch' (cited in Hughes and Pardek 27).

The suppressed suffering of emigration and immigration is perhaps the most crucial, and the most misunderstood element of the Czech emigrant experience. Sociologist Jiřina Šiklová elaborates: 'Most of them [emigrants] wanted to justify their departure and so most of them never wrote home about their difficult beginnings, their despair, and hard work. They remained silent about it, and maybe that was a mistake. If people here only realized how really difficult were the beginnings of those who emigrated, they would not envy them. Today, we can no longer fill that gap' (11).

Despite Šiklová's admonitions, I will attempt to 'fill that gap' and explore some of the reasons that may have compelled Czech writers to silence their hardships of emigration and immigration in their fiction. Only by returning to the suffering of the past, albeit silent and repressed, can we hope to understand the Czech emigrant experience in the present.

The Silenced Suffering of Exile

In a comparative perspective, it becomes apparent that the hardships of Czech immigrants are muted or suppressed, both in the public forum and in exile literature. In stark contrast, for example, Maghrebi immigrants in France rioted in the autumn of 2005, publicly contesting their alienation and disenfranchisement in French society, and rendering their hardships of immigration explicit and agonizingly visible. Maghrebi immigrant writing is characterized by considerable references to immigrant suffering; some writers even somatize their psychological suffering by describing their estrangement, isolation or negative emotional states using bodily metaphors, metaphors of disability and disease. No such explicit agonistic rhetoric is to be found in Czech exile literature. These differences may be attributed to Czech immigrants' disparate racial and ethnic backgrounds, their socioeconomic status, and saliently, their relationship to the host country, given historical factors, such as colonialism. Furthermore, in some cultures it is considered polite to conceal one's hardships, while in others they are more readily verbalized. In the following section, I examine some of the sociohistorical, psychological, and literary reasons that might account for the suppression of pain in Czech exile literature.

Historical Concerns

Historically, it is important to account for different generational experiences of emigration. In the case of Czechs, there were three discrete waves of emigration, each driven by different political motives or philosophical beliefs: (1) the 1948 generation (60,000 in two years), *utíkali*, were 'running away,' for what they thought was a short while, in the firm belief that democracy would be reinstated in Czechoslovakia; (2) the 1968 wave (104,000 within two years to a total of 225,000 by 1970) *vycestovali*, were 'travelling out' of the CSR forever, as they viewed the Soviet occupation to be permanent.[9] As for the last wave, it *se vypařila*, 'evaporated' during normalization.

Saliently, the 1948 generation of Czech emigrants were *de facto* émigrés; their departure was clearly politically motivated and their sojourn abroad was deemed political exile. In Czech, members of this generation were also distinguished by the particular term *exulant*, or 'political exile.' *Exulants*, firmly believed that communism would soon fail, and thus they saw themselves charged with the important mission of safeguarding Czech national identity abroad. This meant that they had to remain strong and vibrant; any acknowledgment of suffering would be viewed as a sign of weakness. Pamphlets and articles produced by these early émigrés often celebrate the 'tragedy of exile' and warn exiled Czechs not to succumb to despair (Radimski 6). Ladislav Radimski, for example, devotes a chapter of his treatise on how to be an *exulant* to the problem of 'Healthy and Sickly Exile,' wherein he scathingly condemns 'people who are nervous, unsure, scared, unconfident, fearing denunciation; they are the adepts of the insane, candidates for suicide, unhappy people of the Kafkaesque type' (39). Ferdinand Peroutka, perhaps the most notable *exulant* of the 1948 generation, repeatedly emphasizes in his classic text, 'Jak být exulantem' (How to Be an *Exulant*, 1950), that 'it is necessary to consciously defend oneself from illness of the spirit' (213)

Later generations of emigrants, leaving after the Soviet invasion extinguished the Prague Spring of 1968, were fully convinced that communism would never fall, and that their departure was permanent. While the initial wave of 1968 emigrants were political exiles – or émigrés – as time progressed, many emigrants escaped Czechoslovakia for other reasons including for greater economic opportunity, social mobility, or to join their families abroad. Writers, however, were usually political dissidents, thus émigrés or writers in exile. Writers' self-reflections on exile, although varied, share a common theme: that of justifying their decision to leave Czechoslovakia and legitimating their exile. An exemplary case in point is, for instance, Jan Lukas' article entitled 'Why I chose Exile Only in 1966.' Some, like Ivan Jelínek, validate their exile as a 'loss and a gain' (6); others, like Jan Vladislav, as a 'responsibility and a freedom' (15). Yet others defend their Czechness despite their emigration. Zdena Salivarová, for instance, explains: 'I'm a Czech and never can be anything else, because it's impossible. Even if I lived two hundred years in Canada, and even if I liked this country as my own' (87–8). In these defences of exile, there is little mention of any suffering of exile and immigration. Jaroslav Vrzala explains that many of his fellow writers intentionally chose not to dwell on their hardships because they wished to resist communist rhetoric: 'Should we have complained crying about them? To write home about our difficulties and our fears meant playing into Communist propaganda' (21).

Psychological Factors

At this point, it is perhaps crucial to consider some psychological factors particular to Czech emigration. Like other immigrant groups, Czechs surely experienced psychological conditions associated with immigration, such as culture shock, isolation, anxiety, and alienation. However, they also suffered problems particular to their own socio-historical condition. Here I refer to the only two book-length studies concerned specifically with Czech emigration: Jiří Diamant's *Psychologické problémy emigrace* (Psychological Problems of Emigration, 1995) and Jacek Adolf's doctoral thesis (1977). Although these studies examine different immigrant groups in disparate contexts (Diamant examines Czech immigrants in the Netherlands in the 1980s, while Adolf surveys Czech and Polish political refugees in Toronto in the 1970s), both offer strikingly similar observations, as well as discerning insights into Czech exile writing.

To begin, both Diamant and Adolf emphasize the importance of 'the decision' to leave Czechoslovakia and the rationalization of this decision. Diamant argues that at the root of most of his patients' psychological problems was their inability to cope with their decision to emigrate. Likewise, Adolf summarizes the many interviews he conducted with Czech immigrants as characterized by their '(1) motivation to emigrate, (2) the validity of his [*sic*] perceptions of the circumstances that led to his decision to escape, and (3) the validity of his perception of the circumstances that motivate him to persist in exile' (212). The justification to emigrate is also a pervasive theme in autobiographical texts written by Czechs in exile.

More importantly, both Diamant and Adolf emphasize that Czech emigration can only be understood in the context of totalitarianism, which conditioned the behaviour of the second and third waves of emigrants. Both analyses expatiate on the oppression, dehumanization, and ruthlessness of the regime and elaborate on its damaging effects on people's psyches. Speaking of Czech and Polish political refugees, Adolf describes 'a prolonged crisis in which identity has been in doubt and in which there has been a painful dissonance between his values and his overt behaviour' (220). Both psychologists stress that many of these emigrants were forced to repress their negative emotions under totalitarianism, a society characterized by suspicion, lies, and betrayal. Even though in the West, as immigrants, they were free to express themselves, they continued to suppress their past experience, because it was generally misunderstood by the host society as 'idiosyncratic, exotic or completely irrelevant' (211). Many immigrants found this reception frustrating, and so they ceased to allude to their past altogether, as one of Adolf's interviewees explains: 'At first I used to become exasperated and infuriated anytime I tried to explain my decision to leave the country to anyone in Canada [...] Then I gave up. I came to understand that they have never experienced anything even remotely similar to what we had to go through' (212).

This tendency is again apparent in immigrants' autobiographies. Jan Lukas' defence of exile, for example, is primarily concerned with elaborating the evils of the communist regime; his only remark on his present life in New York City is his statement: 'What we have lived through in totalitarianism is to a certain extent incommunicable to Western audiences' (210). Adolf theorizes that, as a result of this duality, many immigrants experienced a state of what he characterizes as 'cognitive dissonance': on the one hand, they knew totalitarianism to be dangerous, a world-view upheld in their immigrant community; on the other hand, they were compelled to dismiss it as a mere inconvenience in their host society.

Finally, both Diamant and Adolf broach a problem that is perhaps more difficult to discern in written texts: the guilt that emigrants experienced because of their decision to leave their homeland. Both researchers point to the mixture of shame, self-reproach, and remorse that Czechs felt at having abandoned their friends and relatives to a precarious fate under totalitarianism. Diamant explains that his patients' inability to cope with their decision to emigrate was often their shameful view of it as an escape, a breach of solidarity, or an act of betrayal (33–4). Their ambivalent feelings were further exacerbated by any accusations of betrayal made by their families or the communist regime. One of Adolf interviewees' explains: 'The most painful and unfair accusation directed at escapees is that they are like rats deserting a sinking ship. That is not true. I believe that one can do more for one's country as a political émigré than as a political prisoner. Still, while accepting this on a rational level, I can never really get rid of a feeling of uneasiness, you might even call it guilt or something very similar, about the fact I left people who used to be close to me to their own devices and very likely I shall never see them again' (238).

Interestingly, referring to literature, Adolf characterizes this guilt as the 'Lord Jim complex' (238). The hero of Joseph Conrad's novel, *Lord Jim*, deserts his sinking ship and all of its passengers; the resulting guilt complex is the main driving force of the novel and of the hero's actions. Similarly, although exiled Czech writers rarely elaborate on their guilt, it may be the force driving them to repeatedly explain and justify their motivations for exile in their personal essays.

Literary Considerations

In novels and short fiction by exiled Czech writers, the hardships of immigration are even more elusive than in their autobiographical or essayistic reflections. Stylistically, any suffering of emigration or immigration in fictional texts is seemingly indirect or indefinable, connoted by allusion or intertextuality, or appearing in the guise of humour or satire. Such stylistic tendencies differ drastically from the current rhetoric of identity politics (discussed in chapters 2 and 6), which is governed by the 'politics of feeling,' where there is an overwhelming tendency to dramatize suffering, injury, and 'wounded attachments.'

Czech exile literature may perhaps be best characterized by its nuance, variety, and resistance to categorization. Even in the 1950s Peter Den (pseudonym for Ladislav Radimski) bemoans the fact that Czech exile literature from 1938 to 1950 is all too often subsumed under the rubric of 'literary escapism.' This is because it refuses to throw everything into the (Western) melting pot – be it atomic bombs, the United Nations, the Iron Curtain, the latest crop statistics or U.S.

opinion poll results – and does not 'nicely mix everything up according to the latest political trend, the five-year plan or *exulant* problem' (6). In his defence of Czech literature, he describes it as a nomad literature, as opposed to a hegemonic settler one, in that it resists cultural definitions by its flexibility, irony, and experimentation.

Some thirty years later, Mojmír Grygar makes similar observations in comparing Russian and Czech exile writing. In contrast to its Russian equivalent, Czech exile literature seems less personal and defensive in tone, and notably, much more critical and comparatively global in scope. Furthermore, as Grygar explains, Russian exiled writers often articulate their exile as a 'pain-filled uprooting and homelessness'; by contrast, Czech writers generally do not describe exile as 'a degradation, punishment or a pathological state,' he says while citing Kundera, who viewed his years in France as the best years of this life (94). Grygar ascribes some of these differences to those of 'big nations' as opposed to 'small nations,' and claims that the people of small nations such as Czechoslovakia adapt more easily to changing cultural contexts. Although Grygar's big/small thesis seems a bit specious when we consider the writing of Haitian or Maghrebi authors, who are also from 'small countries,' Grygar supports his argument by referring to the 'dual-perspective' (94) of such authors as Milan Kundera, Josef Škvorecký, Jaroslav Vejvoda, Jan Beneš or Sylvie Richterová.[10] Yet, he points out that certain works, such as the 'wild,' vulgar, or anarchistic texts of Pelc, Svoboda, or Novák, may only be understood in the context of resistance to totalitarian ideologies. Grygar also notes that some writers, such as Filip or Michal, express their pain, frustration, or anger using 'maximally expressive and opinionated forms' such as 'caricature, satire or hyperbole' (97).

In his bibliography of the varied spectrum of Czech literature, Jan Čulík deftly characterizes Czech exile literature, when he explains that '[Czech exile literature] is unusually sceptical of all systems of thought that offer a simplified and stereotypical interpretation of life [...] It is not only a criticism of 'socialist realism' but also of many aspects of life in Western societies' (39). Here, Čulík points to perhaps the most important factor affecting Czech exile literature: its scepticism of all forms of ideology, and of both communist and Western rhetoric.

In their opposition to communist rhetoric, Czech exile writers are resisting the main literary genre championed by the Soviets: socialist realism. Defined as art that was socialist in content and realistic in form, socialist realism sought to depict reality as it should be, not necessarily as it is (or was). Usually, socialist works depict the heroic struggles of proletarians in the face of capitalist oppression or happy life in collectivity. In many ways, the socialist realist narrative resembles the traditional immigrant model of 'poor-boy-does-good.' For this reason, perhaps, Czech exile writers avoid the generic immigrant hero model in their works. They are sceptical of any heroic, sentimental, or emotional depictions in the socialist-realist mode and cynical of any self-pitying, tragic victim heroes, because these are the characteristics of the genre espoused under communism.

Czech exile literature also resists generic Western literary models, most saliently the American 'immigrant novel,' and by extension, much of immigrant, diasporic, and minority literature. Very few Czech writers take up the genre of the immigrant novel,[11] and in so doing, perhaps dismiss any facile models of cultural integration or assimilation. Saliently, Czech exile writers avoid the genre of 'immigrant autobiography,' prominent in other diasporic literatures, and typified by memoirs by such exiled intellectuals as Eva Hoffman, André Aciman, or Edward Said.

Reading the Hardships of Exile

In the vast spectrum of Czech exile literature, some authors do describe their pain of emigration, however. Karel Michal, for example, characterizes his exile as 'a loss of the greater part of a person,' and Ivan Diviš, as a 'death penalty' (interviews in Hvížd'ala, 132, 224); Brousek calls exile an 'almost a suicidal step into the void' (quoted in Pfaff 856). Yet, rather than connoting any trials of immigration, for Czech writers exile signals an existential plight of universal human dimensions. Ivan Pfaff illustrates this point when self-reflexively citing a famous passage by Milan Kundera: 'You ask: *Heimweh*? Depression? Disillusion? Lack of adaptation? Giving up the fight? Stepping away from exile? No way. Just the simple credo of a person, to whom the dogged delusion of love and anger returns again and again: 'from the moment they expelled me from the circle, I am constantly falling, falling now, and then since they pushed me to it then, falling further, deeper, from my country into the empty space of the world'[12] (859).

The reader-response to Czech exile literature similarly translates the suffering of immigration as the condition of universal existential alienation. To cite but one example, Blanka Kubešová's *Romance pro Žoržínu* (Romance for Georgina, 1985), represents a standard immigrant text. It is the story of a young immigrant Czech who adapts to her new environment in the United States. Instead of reading this as a typical immi-grant novel, however, Czech readers seem to understand it from a more general perspective. The Czech reviewer transforms the 'trials' specific to immigration as the generalized feeling of estrangement, asking, 'Did we not all feel this state of being as adults or at least the vast majority of us?' (Strnad 181).

Problematically, the condition of exile is often reappropriated by writers living in Czechoslovakia to describe their own condition. Václav Jamek, for example, polemicizes that we all should live in a state of 'inner exile,' 'separate from society,' 'at its margins,' so as to be 'true to our convictions,' 'not handicapped by the demands of society' (1, 3). Similarly, Věra Linhartová, in her article 'Ontology of Exile,' concludes that everybody should live as an exile, 'out of one's place,' 'unsettled,' 'open in all directions' – as a nomad. Although she admits there is 'voluntary' and 'involuntary' exile, she urges everyone to view exile not as 'suffering' but to invite such inner exile as the opportunity for 'metamorphosis,' in a transformative cathartic pro-cess (1, 5).

By also taking up the condition of exile, writers within the home-land, in many ways, negate the particular experience of those writers living outside it as exiled émigrés. Their suffering becomes relativized and rendered equivalent to the pain of people living under totalitarian oppression. Such an equivalency is made poignant in this statement by Eva Kantůrková, penned shortly before the Velvet Revolution: 'I do not consider exile as a state, as a plight, trauma, as an uprooting from the roots and rights of home; those are perhaps the feelings of an *exulant* [...] It seems irrelevant to me whether one bears this burden at home or across the border. The only difference is the advantages of the living space' (79).

As far as their Czech readership was concerned, the hardships of Czech émigrés were comparable to a universal existential condition; in some cases, exile was even viewed analogous to their own hardships of living under totalitarianism. Little critical attention was paid to the specific hardships of emigration or immigration, or to the particular psychological, sociocultural, or historical dimensions of the Czech exile experience, either during their time abroad or upon their return.

Reading beyond Silences

The subject discussed in this chapter – the silencing of suffering – extends well beyond the case of Czech emigrants. It lays emphasis on the role of the immigrant as also always an emigrant, and problematizes the emigrant's relationship to the homeland. It draws attention to the phenomenon of emigration, re-emigration, and temporary return home in our contemporary global world. It invites comparisons – with other postcommunist countries, other diasporic communities, and other minority groups. Ultimately, this analysis points to the problematical role of suffering in the representation and performance of minority rights, and addresses a fundamental issue in contemporary discourse: how disenfranchised minorities might gain position, agency, and voice in our increasingly multicultural and globalized world.

The return of Czechs to the homeland poignantly shows the important role that suffering plays in social discourse, as previously outlined using Nietzsche's theorizations (in chapter 2). Furthermore, the struggles between Czechs who left and Czechs who stayed lucidly reveals the cultural differentials, *ressentiment*, and power dynamics that such a politics of pain engenders. This chapter suggests that a particularly effective, explicit, and performative rhetoric of pain is perhaps necessary to convey the grievances of a minority in the public forum.

This chapter also urges us to reconsider apparently 'silent' cultural representations – where suffering is seemingly absent, restrained, or indistinguishable. That pain is not readily transparent or easily translatable does not mean that it does not exist. As we have seen in the case of Czech exile literature, the pain of immigration was repressed for a number of historical, psychological, and literary reasons. Yet, even when generically explicit, it was mistranslated by the receiving audience, rendered universal, and relativized. Such suppression of pain invites us to consider other instances in which suffering may be repressed, denied, or generalized. It incites us to move 'in that reach of the beyond,' where we can listen to others' 'histories and silences, configure our cultural confusions, [so as to] meld memories of what remains untranslatable but no less telling' (Bhabha 32). Can a remedy be found by reaching for and listening to that beyond? If returning Czechs articulated their difficulties of return – in their fiction of return – would anyone hear their pain?

10 'The Suffering of Return': Painful Detours in Czech Novels of Return

They saw me as the embodiment of an émigré's suffering. Then the time came for me to confirm that suffering by my joyous return to the homeland. And that confirmation did not happen.

– Milan Kundera, *Ignorance*

Writing of Return

Novels about an immigrant's conclusive return home are rare. Rarely do political circumstances change so dramatically as to bring lasting peace and political and economic stability to enable immigrants to permanently return 'home.' Haitian or Algerian immigrant writers, for instance, cannot fathom permanently resettling in their war-torn, politically unstable, and economically deprived homelands. Even when the homeland is relatively stable, immigrants are reluctant to re-emigrate; they have settled in their new country. Most importantly, for writers, the literary institutions and readership that support their writing are located in the West. For example, one cannot imagine that such canonical immigrant writers as Amy Tan, Bharati Mukherjee, or Eva Hoffman would return to China, India, or Germany respectively, or that intellectuals such as Bhabha or Spivak would settle in India, although their work theorizes this postcolonial context. Yet, while permanent return may be untenable, temporary returns or visits are clearly possible in our age of global communication and mass transportation. Moreover, many immigrant texts do delve into the theme of return – in fiction.

The fall of communism in 1989 represents a unique moment in history, which granted Czech emigrant writers the opportunity to return home permanently. Many of them chose not to return – notably, Czech émigré writer Milan Kundera chose to remain in France – but many other dissident writers opted to go back home so as to continue writing in their native language and for their home readership.

A survey of Czech postcommunist writing reveals that very few returning authors directly address the experience of return in their postcommunist novels. Although a number of non-fiction essays inter-polate personal reflection with political commentary.[1] The return to the homeland is not a common trope in Czech fiction, cinematic or artistic production. In the case of Czech postcommunist literature, I know of only five fictional texts that may be considered 'novels of return.' Yet, as I will show, they do not address the return or, even less, the sufferings of return directly, using autobiographical references, generic narrative, or thematic tropes. Before examining these texts, however, I would like to deliberate on some of the reasons that return-ing Czech writers might not wish to broach the subject of return in their fiction.

Responding to Anti-Emigrant Sentiment

One reason that returning Czech writers were reluctant to expatiate their experience of return was because of the prevailing anti-emigrant sentiment in postcommunist Czech Republic. As we have seen in the previous chapter, returnees were greeted with a mixture of suspicion, resentment, and hostility, which was compounded or, as I have argued, perhaps even grounded, in the apparent absence of suffering in Czech exile literature.

The sufferings of Czechs who left were not only silenced upon their departure from Czechoslovakia, but were similarly stifled upon their return after 1989. In the numerous commentaries about returnees that I cited in the previous chapter, there is barely a mention of the painful adaptation that emigrants might have faced upon their return home – including isolation, alienation, discrimination, or difficult cultural adjustments. Some reports remark that for emigrants 'the spell of home was broken' (Troják 18), referring to their disillusionment and disappointment, but they never mention any of the psychological problems or socioeconomic hardships that they might have encoun-tered upon their return. In my private interviews with returning authors, however, issues of cultural readjustment, culture shock, and in particular, relationship and financial problems, were the main topics of conversation.

Even in public interviews, returning writers were reluctant to express their feelings about their return; their replies were usually kept curt and flippant. The following declaration by Ota Filip is an exemplary case in point. While Filip grants that life in exile can lead to 'chronic sickness,' like many Czech writers of his generation he refuses to expose his private pain publicly: 'I suppose all of us who live in exile are infected in some way with this sickness, manifest in outbreaks of tears, nostalgia, sentimental longing, even with self-destructive cynicism, as well as ordinary fits of sadness [...] But I am not willing to exhibit my wounds of my twenty-year exile to my foreign close ones, with reproaches and tears' (13). As in the past, returning writers, acting like stoic intellectuals, were reluctant to exhibit their sufferings of re-emigration agonistically in the public forum.

The Changing Role of the Writer and the Literary Market in Postcommunism

Writers' taciturn responses to their return may also have to do with the changed role of the writer in the postcommunist context. Under communism, exile writers – or dissident writers – were held in very high regard by Czechs, as by people in other countries of the Eastern Bloc. After communism, however, there was little or no place for 'dissident' writing in the Czech Republic: few people were interested in writings about the 'big questions about humanity,' whether questions of resistance, freedom, or solidarity; nor were they interested in the experiences of Czechs living 'on the other side.' As Kundera states in his novel *Ignorance* (2002): 'Just, I wasn't an émigré anymore. I wasn't interesting anymore' (170). On the contrary, in the new marketplace economy, 'politics and pornography [are] the two most popular subjects' in bookstores ('Freedom Is Hard' 73). Thus, former dissident writers faced the difficult task of adapting to new economic and socio-cultural conditions, while also maintaining their status as respected intellectuals or well-liked writers. Complaining about their hardships of return or berating Czechs about their hostile, xenophobic behaviours would certainly not endear these writers to their readership, but rather would cultivate further anger and resentment, while demoting these esteemed writers to 'cry-babies' or 'sour-pusses.'

In their essayistic or autobiographical writings, returning authors seem to cater to market demands – either politics or entertainment. For the most part, they avoid their personal issues of return, let alone lament or attempt to vindicate their hardships of return. As previously mentioned, several returning émigrés (e.g., Gruša, Chudožilov) have commented on their return in their political essays; however, such political reflections are devoid of any sentiment or pathos. Other writers and political commentators have taken to humour in their auto-biographical essays. Jan Drábek, in *Po uši postkommunismu* (Neck-Deep in Post-communism, 2000), satirically writes of his experiences as cultural attaché. Benjamin Kuras, in *Češi na vlásku* (Czechs on a String, 1996), parodies the founding myths of the Czech Republic: in his version, for example, Praotec Čech, the mythical founder of the Czech lands, establishes the nation at the foot of the noble mountain Říp, because it reminds him of a geographically succulent breast.

Writers of non-fiction and fiction alike have had to adapt to changing conditions in the Czech literary market. Andrew Wachtel has pointed out in his study of the postcommunist publishing industry, it is very difficult to sell 'serious literature' (597) in Eastern Europe, even though the number of publishing houses has grown dramatically. In the Czech Republic, there were thirty publishing houses under communism, 1,500 in the 1990s, but only 450 privately-run ones remain today. Most of these new publishing houses rarely publish new, original Czech material, because, just as translations of East European fiction are extremely difficult to market in the West, sales of original Czech writing also fell dramatically in the Czech Republic. Although Czechs still read an average of one book a month (617), comparatively a very high number, most of the books they read are in translation, and largely include American best-sellers or European literature. As Kundera points out in *Ignorance,* hardly anyone 'reads poetry these days,' although the Czech native in his novel still can recite it from memory (160).

Fiction writers have often adopted different topics and genres upon their return – perhaps to increase their marketability. Rarely do these authors even broach subjects related to their return. For instance, Jan Novák, in *Samet a pára* (Velvet and Vapour, 1992), described the 1989 turnover, and then he never wrote again. Others still, such as Jan Beneš, continue to comment on American life, but mention the Czech Republic only in passing. In some cases, established authors have started to write in more popular genres. The distinguished Canadian-Czech author Josef Škvorecký now writes detective stories,[2] and the well-known Czech writer Iva Pekárková now only writes humorous short stories and travelogues.[3] Yet, even successful Czech writers face financial difficulties. For instance, Pekárková, one of the most popular women writers in the Czech Republic post 1989, has been forced to become a 'ghost-translator' to make ends meet; though a feminist, she is forced to translate Harlequins under a pseudonym to support her writing career, a situation that would be unheard of for a best-selling author in the West.

If in their writing and public appearances, Czech writers who returned to the homeland rarely comment on their experience of return, in private interviews they are much more candid about this issue. Iva Pekárková readily admits that returning 'is not easy,' and even likens it to a 'personal grief.' Pekárková also explains, however, that problems of postcommunism often cannot be written about, because they are 'too difficult' or 'boring' for the reader: 'Yeah, sure, it's not easy to be back [...] The thing that bothers me the most? Perhaps the racism or the closed-mindedness. I came back because my [ex]husband wanted to live in Europe. But he doesn't really understand Czech. He's lucky. I sometimes wish I didn't understand what was being said! [...] Writing about it? It's too difficult maybe. [...] No, there is nothing to write about in the Czech Republic – the Czech Republic is boring. Besides, it's not a topic that interests people; it's not what they want to read, not what they want to buy.'[4]

Allegorical Detours

In Pekárková's latest books, written after her return to the Czech Republic, any explicit reference to the suffering of return is suppressed. The difficulties of belonging give way to the adventures of travelling, be it to India, Thailand, or Nigeria. Nonetheless, reading these texts closely, one realizes the return is there, referred to indirectly, in allegorical detours.

For instance, in Pekárková's novel *Třicet dva chwanů* (32 Khwan, 2000), set in Thailand in 1983, travelling and cultural assimilation relate thematically to the fate of the returning emigrant. The plot revolves around the narrator's attempts to visit a refugee camp, so as to understand and share the pain of 'real refugees.' Despite her efforts, she never makes it to one of the camps; a pass is denied her every time. However, she experiences pain of the private type when her friend Dao dies. Yet, she is forbidden to grieve this loss openly, because, for the Buddhist Thais, mourning or crying over the deceased people suggests that they did not live a worthwhile life. With great effort, the heroine Iva learns to mask her pain so as to conform to Thai cultural norms; later she escapes it by travelling some more. This is perhaps also Pekárková's fate: she is denied her suffering of emigration and return – she must learn to forget it, escape it, or set it travelling.

Novels of Return

Reading a Reticent Rhetoric of Pain

Few returning Czech writers therefore 'return home' in postcommunist fiction. By choosing different themes and genres for their narratives, they avoid commenting on the sociopolitical situation of emigrants in the 1990s. Such avoidance or evasion may be deemed a silent rhetoric of suffering. As revealed in Pekárková's travelogue, however, the difficulties of return may be intimated indirectly, whether analogically, allegorically, or thematically. Like exiled writers, then, returning writers often allude to their hardships using abstract asides, humorous satire, figurative language, or allegorical detours. The hardships of return are suppressed for similar reasons as the suffering of immigration, most notably because of the demands of the Czech readership. It is important to recognize that these returning writers' style – its aesthetics, narrative, themes, and structure – was shaped in exile, when the pain of migration was likewise exiled.

Reading returnees' novels of return requires the critic to engage with a 'reticent' rhetoric of pain – translated using a variety of indirect means, including allusion, comparison, understatement, humour, and satire – that connotes suppressed suffering. The critic must learn to interpret obliquely, as well as discerningly. In the following section, exploring five writers who are very different in style and theme, I would like to consider how one might begin to translate such a 'reticent' rhetoric of suffering.

I only know four 'texts of return' written in Czech: *Návraty* (Returns, 1998) by Josef Beneš; *...u výstupy do údolí* (...and Ascents into the Valley, 2000) by Jan Pelc; *Beze stop* (Without a Trace, 2001) by Jaroslav Formánek; and *Opilost z hloubky* (Drunkenness of Depths, 2000) by Lubomír Martínek, intriguingly all written by former immigrants to France. Set in postcommunist times, these texts indirectly reveal these returnees' observations on life in the Czech Republic in the early 1990s. Furthermore, all four of them also adopt mythical structures wherein suffering becomes a central, migrating motif. My analysis situates these texts within the context of Czech reviews, to discern how Czechs in the homeland have interpreted these disparate narratives of return. I also contrast these four Czech novels with Milan Kundera's novel, *Ignorance* (2002). Kundera is also a Czech living in France, but unlike the others, he chose not to return home permanently. In *Ignorance*, targeted for readers outside the Czech Republic, Kundera comments on the experience of failed return.

Beneš' Homecoming

The only novel that depicts the emigrant's return as a triumphant success is *Návraty* (Returns), by Josef D. Beneš, a relatively unknown Czech writer. In this final novel of Beneš' emigrant trilogy, which also includes *Dospívání: Smutek domu* (Adolescence: Sadness of Home) and *Útěky* (Flights), return represents the positive resolution of the emigrant's story. Immediately upon crossing the Czech border, protagonist Béd'a experiences a spiritual reunion with the natural beauty of his homeland, which has supposedly remained unchanged during communism (7). As Béd'a explains, his arrival is seemingly acknowledged by the nation itself: 'That is what they call a country. A place that recognizes you and talks to you' (33). Béd'a's return is heralded as a perpetual rebirth and rediscovery; he is likened to a phoenix, 'arising from the ashes of his scepticism, again and again' (12).

Idealistic in tone, *Návraty* hardly mentions any of the returnee's material problems. Béd'a's restitution claim is resolved in a matter of minutes (20), and his returnee friend's books are published almost as soon as he arrives in the Czech Republic, thus quickly restoring an engaged, recuperative dialogue with his lost compatriots (17). The novel then focuses on Béd'a's hard work, as he strives to rebuild his country-house, as well as his many attempts to educate his friends and family, who remain outdated in their ways. A Christlike figure, Béd'a looks with pity at the man in his cave, who is still a communist (47), and he remains 'patient' as he travels through towns where they hurl stones at him, insulting him as an 'economic migrant' (55).

This novel repeatedly describes the animosity that Béd'a faces upon his return. At one point, our hero asks a native Czech the reason for the hostility against him. In reply, incredibly, the Czech teenager actually bites his wrist (55) and hisses: 'Because you lived while we suffered!' (55). Yet, even then, our optimistic hero does not feel insulted or hurt by this remark. On the contrary, he wraps his wounded wrist, and explains to his readers that his attacker is merely an 'innocent victim of the unfortunate circumstances of our history, baleful propaganda and doubtful interpretations of our flight' (56).

The plot culminates when the townsfolk decide to construct a mall over a cemetery. Béd'a, firmly resisting such nihilistic commercialization, secretly exhumes the dead before the cemetery is destroyed and deposits their remains in his basement, which he converts into a chapel, thus completing, in a way, a second, personal 'exile.' As an erudite townsperson explains to Béd'a, the term 'exile' was first employed in medieval Europe to refer to graves that were transported from inside the church far out into the cemetery (152–3).[5] Here, our hero performs this ritualistic transport of the past, alone, into the entrails of his own house.

In all, Beneš melodramatic story of return does not seem credible; one wonders if the hero actually returned to a real Czech Republic. Even more implausible than Béd'a's return home is his lover Myriam's successful entry into Czech society. Myriam is a black Haitian who integrates without a single problem amid the white countryfolk, and learns to speak Czech fluently, simply by eagerly correcting all her mistakes (105).

Aside from its many flaws, *Návraty* nonetheless offers valuable commentary on the emigrant's return. In many ways, Béd'a's return represents the dream of the exultant return of the Czech 1948 generation, who until 1968, believed themselves to be saviours of the Czech nation in exile. Yet, Béd'a remains in exile when he returns to the Czech Republic, as he refuses any viable otherness, any actual change. His sanctimonious behaviour elevates him as the classic hero, harbinger of the modern and protector of the past. Yet, this heroization necessarily distances him from his Czech community. In the end, though, the central plot – the desecration and erasure of the past coinciding with rapid modernization and commercialization – reveals one of the central problems that the Czech Republic faced in the 1990s. Beneš nicely points to the fact that Czech émigrés remain the guardians of much of the Czech past, in this case symbolically located in their restituted yet modernized homes.

While there have never been any reviews of Beneš' trilogy – despite its ubiquity in Czech bookstores – recently, the literary journal *Prostor* published an autobiographical reflection by this little-known author, an evangelical priest who emigrated to Switzerland under communism. In this piece also titled 'Návraty...' Beneš again deliberates the issue of flight and return, apparently still consumed by these two dynamics. Departure is likened to 'point zero,' 'a feeling of dizziness,' and return is the 'great taboo,' the 'cause of so much misfortune and tragedies'('Návraty...' 130). Unlike the protagonist of his novel, Beneš himself seems not to have come to terms with either his exile or his return. However, referring to Biblical and literary epics, Beneš asserts his faith and his optimism in this process of change. The essay concludes with his concern about the new Europe that, much like the returning emigrant hero, must learn to escape from its heritage of communism and fascism and go back to its roots in Christianity.

Pelc's Violence

In stark contrast to Josef Beneš' utopian novel is Jan Pelc's dystopic ...*a výstupy do údolí* (...and Ascents into the Valley). In this semi-autobiographical story, the narrator crudely and often angrily works through the 'émigré schizophrenia' that he experienced when the Velvet Revolution dramatically 'shredded' his Parisian life. Olin, the hero of Pelc's previous dissident text entitled ...*a bude hůře* (...It'll Get Worse, 1985), is the owner of a prosperous firm in Paris, where he lives with a Frenchwoman. The end of the communist regime divides those who stay from those who return. Olin, unsure which camp to join, travels back and forth from Prague to Paris to Prague, always attracting the worst types, swindlers and thieves, who take advantage of him, rob him, and beat him up. To counter this chaos, Olin drinks himself into oblivion and falls into a hardened desperation, moving in his delusions from a sunny, colourful Paris to Czech lands of grey dirt and dilapidated walls, from a proud nation that has just won its freedom to one corrupted with Bolshevik fraud and theft. His personal life falls apart because he cannot decide between his two loves. In the end, Olin remains alone with his pain, in a nauseating and often revolting cycle of drinking and vaporous delirium of confessional digressions.

   Czech reviews of this novel focus ostensibly on Pelc's 'alcoholic passages,' his 'underground' themes and his style, which were considered 'shocking' under normalization[6] (Skrášek). Reviewers seem ambiguous, however, about the theme of return that drives the novel, describing it as the 'rough underside of the Velvet Revolution' or as a 'document' of the 1990s (Hrzalová, Kopáč). They never delve more deeply into the meaning of Olin's despair. For example, unsure how to analyse Olin's hopelessness and final return at the 'optimistic' (sic) conclusion of the text, one reviewer (Skrášek) simply reproduces it without further commentary: 'I bought a bottle and sat by the river. I stare at the Rudolfinum and I know that I have lost. Lost terribly. All those dreams that I left with and returned with, vanished like snow. I should emigrate again, somewhere. [...] But I can't; I am too old. [...]

Everything is fucked up. [...] Welcome home, Olin' (143). There is
clearly some form of visceral suffering of return in ...*a výstupy do údolí*,
made explicit in Pelc's tough, raucous rhetoric. While Pelc's drunken
harshness may be attributed to his anarchistic style, it is also an expression of the pain of a returning emigrant that, for Czech readers, cannot
be soberly understood, other than as a scream.

Formánek's Anonymity

Standing against Pelc's vociferous violence is the subtle and almost
transparent collection of stories *Beze stop* (Without a Trace), by Jaroslav
Formánek, who formerly lived in Paris and is now a reluctant resident
of the Czech Republic. The only Czech review of this collection does
not pick up on any of the many themes that subtly relate to immigration; the reviewer is actually unaware that Formánek has returned
from France (Haman, 'Formánek'). In *Beze stop*, unknown immigrant
heroes wander around in Prague and in Paris, interacting with the
jobless, the homeless, beggars, drunks, the destitute, all those people
who, like the immigrant, live outside of time and space – 'without a
trace,' as the title suggests. Exiled from the socioeconomic sphere,
these vagrants have no material presence at all and seemingly have
escaped the laws of physics, such as time: 'their bodies have passed the
thin shell of the present and pass through the veil of time' (15).

In some of Formánek's stories, these Czechs are invited back home,
but they are reluctant to return, even when offered money or contracts.
Thus, they only arrive by the night train and then depart at night
again, afraid of any definition or permanence. Certainly, Formánek is
wary of any binding identifications or categorizations. In 'Ved' ked' si
zapísaný,' for example, he compares all these migrants to the Indians
of North America, who once documented, became lost, ghettoized,
and imprisoned in categorizations. Through its deviations and
detours, this book questions the idea of a return to a fixed point of
origin – 'home' – which for the migrant, implies death: 'The return
home. A narrative about the return home [...]. Why in fact return? For
whom and why? [...] The time of the past is a different time. The desire
to live at home again, is barred by a minor detail – death' (22).

In 'Jeden podzimní den,' we return to Prague to observe this dead
'world of immobile marionettes and plaster cast angels' (117). In
'Rasputin,' the hero only feels comfortable with a drunk he does not
know; for the hero, like the drunk, clearly 'does not belong' (27) in the

Czech lands. The hero's drunken companion is the only lucid person in the city. Yet, when the narrator gives him some extra cash, the drunk kills himself. In Formánek's sad stories, the suffering of immigration, effaced and muted, almost without a trace, is likened to endless anonymous wandering, while the return home almost always signals death.

Martínek's Global Nomad

Opilost z hloubky (Drunkenness of Depths), by Lubomír Martínek, presents us with the most complex and nuanced examination of the emigrant's homecoming: it explores the problematical return of the cosmopolitan citizen of the world. As Martínek argues that, for the global nomad, 'return' is an 'impossible notion' (215). He clarifies that 'the return was much harder than departure. Departure was a momentary thing. Made easy by ugliness and disgust but also by the unknown and illusion' (150). Return, on the other hand, 'requires great strength and patience' (150). This philosophical text offers the reader no simplistic categorizations or easy answers, but rather delves into a stream of intermingling perspectives and possibilities, pointing to the murky complexity inherent in the notion of return in our postmodern, global world.

Martínek's novel comprises four interweaving narratives of return: Tahita, a Polynesian native, returns to his island after years of wandering the world; Rebeka, a Frenchwoman, settles in Prague to escape French conservatism; Victor, a Czech photographer, deals with his 'forced return' to the Czech Republic; and Bol, an émigré-wanderer, travels to Polynesia to purge himself of the bitterness he feels in the Czech Republic.

Each story offers powerful reflections on the notion of return. Tahita's tale, for instance, lyrically explores the conflicting forces of nature and culture on the cosmopolitan individual. While Tahita finds peace in the tropical beauty of his native island, and is generally happy to return to menial labour and daily subsistence, he also grieves for the more urbane and savvy parts of himself, which he must relinquish to live on his home island. Rebeka's story, on the other hand, sceptically deliberates on the rapidly modernizing postcommunist Czech society and Czech returnees, from the perspective of a newly arrived immigrant to the Czech Republic. Rebeka comfortably adjusts to life in Prague by accepting that she will always be considered the outsider there. By contrast, as she observes, returning Czechs seemingly cannot adjust back 'home,' which has profoundly changed during their absence; the time and space of their youth no longer exist. Rebeka posits that her Czech returnee friends seem to have depleted 'their meagre supply of adaptability' when they left and now can no longer further adapt to change (68). According to her, the suffering of these returnees stems from their attempts to 'halt change' and continue 'abiding in the painful, but recognizably predictable situations' of their departure (68).

In the two remaining narratives, we see most clearly the difficulties of the emigrant return. Both Victor and Bol must cope with a challenge faced by virtually all post-1968 Czech émigrés: they must come to terms with the fact that return home is now indeed possible. Unlike the 1948 generation, those who left after 1968 defined their lives by 'the non-returnable,' by the impossibility of return. Trapped in the 'forever and never' (215), many of them considered the Berlin Wall to be the only point of stability in their lives. The Wall vindicated their decision to leave, and justified their separation from their Czech community. When the Berlin Wall crumbled, many of them felt that the defining feature of their lives had collapsed with it, and were reluctant to relinquish it. As Martínek's narrator explains: 'The non-returnable, on which his friends had built their lives, that shaped them so deeply, was too difficult to give up. [...] Their private 'forever' expired and they missed it, for with it, their only point of stability vanished. Non-return, the basis of their existence. On which they had built their lives, from whence unwound their position and sprung back again to it. Non-return, the axis on which all revolved' (86). Here, Martínek points to a phenomenon that was never discussed in post-1989 emigrant debates, yet which exemplifies many émigrés' experiences: the need to grieve the loss of a defining part of their world-view – 'the non-returnable' – that for so long had determined their choices, attitudes, and lives.

In the lush Polynesian landscape, Bol faces another obstacle that precludes his return to the Czech Republic: the 'paralyzing and unsurpassable fear of boredom' (205). In contrast to other countries he has visited, the Czech Republic triggers no feelings for Bol; he feels no wonder, pleasure, or even disgust (215). As Bol remarks, for him, 'homesickness is not marked by nostalgia, frenzied emptiness or debilitating pain but merely by "lack"' (202). Yet, he also realizes that, given all of his experiences, he will always feel a lack somewhere (214). At the end of his reflection, contemplating the 'forever and never' of the past, he remains unsure whether in the future he can return home forever (215).

Victor is Martínek's only protagonist who returns home permanently. Because of an injury, he is forced home to seek medical attention. Thus, for Victor, return bears connotations of failure, weakness, and loss (87), and he must come to terms with his newly curtailed life. Like Bol or Tahita, Victor must adjust to the predictability, triviality, and ordinariness of Czech life, which contrasts markedly from his worldly adventures. Likening his condition to that of a scuba-diver adjusting to shallow surface depths (150) or a tightrope walker learning to perform with a safety net (86), he must now adapt to a banal life, 'bereft of tension, robbed of risk, cheated of dizziness' (86).

Saliently, Victor's narrative also offers a scathing portrait of Czech society in the early 1990s. He describes it as a sickened environment, scarred by past wounds and infected by present grievances: 'On every corner he heard regrets of shattered lives, lost youth, ruined careers, wasted talent [...] Their faces were worn and their bodies deformed, as if they were plagued by an unidentifiable disease. The air was poisoned with all their surrendered dreams and beliefs. Shame turned into envy and hatred. The shipwrecked mobs saved themselves by dirtying others as much as they could. Because every weakness could be held against them, they cast themselves in harsh masks. They confessed to pig-headedness and took shelter in intransigence' (125).

Victor finds that the Czech Republic in the 1990s is a country in stasis, paralyzed by its communist past. Time paradoxically flows backwards (118), as Czechs continue their past behaviours of either arrogance or servility (91). Victor's encounters with his former friends prove especially painful; they have become either traitors (153) or robots (157). He observes that the postcommunist environment is still characterized by 'eternal surveillance,' which results in either 'permanent charade' or 'complete numbness' (87).

For Victor, there is no escape or release from this corrupt, contaminated space. Even lovemaking is a 'contentious struggle [...] because masks were not taken off even in bed' (134). Only in his dreams, and in his conversations with Rebeka about his past, is he able to find some relief. Increasingly, Victor feels himself physically affected by this deceitful environment: he suffers insomnia, depression, and neurosis (87). He feels as if he is losing his individuality, becoming part of the featureless, apathetic Czech mob (90). More and more, Victor retreats to his darkroom, to find purpose and relief from torpor and numbness in his photography (146). His ultimate form of resistance, however, is silence – 'by remaining silent on his situation, that others were incessantly autopsying, he was denying their right to exist' (75). At the end of the story, we recognize Victor as the shadowy beggar on a street corner, completely ravaged by his return home.

In all, Martínek's labyrinthine *Opilost z hloubky* urges the reader to consider Czech returnees from both a global and a national point of view. In meandering reflections and a plurality of perspectives, Martínek considers the possibilities of return for the cosmopolitan nomad, the well-seasoned traveller, or adaptable individual, who in believing the non-returnable, is constantly experiencing multiple metamorphoses. Victor's rich life experiences contrast starkly with the narcissistic nationalism and stasis in the Czech Republic of the 1990s; it seems to him to be a country immobilized by self-pity, past griev- ances, and old communist myths and behaviours. Return 'home' to this environment is difficult and draining, if not wholly destructive for the cosmopolitan individual.

Czech reviewers have grappled with many of the complex themes in Martínek's text. Many concentrate mainly on his style, and most focus on the 'upheaval of the nineties' and the entrapment of 'the homo bohemicus' reflected in the novel (Šlajchrt). Some, however, do fully grasp the 'trauma of departure and return,' as exemplified in Martínek's work (Haman, 'Trauma'). Interestingly, a few seem disori- ented by Martínek's global perspective. As one reviewer explains, 'we experience suicidal dizziness from all the emptiness and the feeling of absolute futility of eternal flight' (Novotný 20). Most of all, though, reviewers are perturbed by Martínek's scathing comments about the Czech Republic, such as its 'stupidity beyond measure'; however, they attribute this phenomenon to the 'Czech condition of the nineties' or to the postmodern, global condition (Novotný 21).

The Great Return: The Pain of Ignorance

I turn now to perhaps the best-known Czech émigré writer, Milan Kundera. Like the other writers examined in this chapter, Kundera also emigrated to France, but unlike them, he chose not to return home after 1989. In his 2002 novel, *Ignorance*, Kundera directly addresses the 'Great Return' of the émigré, as he calls it, and attempts to destabilize the myths structuring this return, while also pointing to the possibili- ties open to the Czech emigrant in light of these myths. Given the mys- tique surrounding Kundera as a Czech émigré writer, this novel may be seen as his own defence for remaining in exile. Yet it is also another classic Kundera text, plaiting together myth and essay with a tragic- comic love story, interlacing such 'dualisms of being' as lyricism and kitsch, love and indifference, but most of all remembering and forgetting. The release of Kundera's novel garnered considerable attention in the Czech Republic, even though the book was not translated into Czech. Since readers were not able to read it in Czech, reviews summarize the French reception of the book or elaborate the text's central Odyssean myth in light of Kundera's work in emigration (Šmíd, Fischer). Only my own review, in Czech, discusses the novel in terms of the return of émigrés in the 1990s (Hronová and Brodská).

Kundera's first intervention in *Ignorance* is to undermine the mythic meaning of nostalgia, the longing for return but also *nostos algia*, the 'suffering' of 'return.' Marvelling at the manifold translations of this word (such as *homesickness, Sehnsucht, stýskat se*), Kundera points to the precariousness of this emotional state as purely affective, imaginary, and impossible to convey in language, least of all in a nationalized one. He himself takes pause at the Spanish *añoranza*,[7] 'which comes from the Catalan *enyorar*, itself derived from the Latin verb *ignorare*' (6), drawing the conclusion that, 'in that etymological light nostalgia seems something like the pain of ignorance, of not knowing' (6). For Kundera, the 'suffering' of 'return' is indeed painful, but most of all in its nescience, 'its lack or want of knowledge,' both for the émigré sufferer and the host witnessing this suffering. Kundera intimates that all narratives of return are but imaginary, nostalgic constructions; there are no returns in History or in one's life story.

Kundera then turns to Homer's *Odyssey*, the pivotal Western myth of return, to critique how this epic symbolically informs our understanding of Czech emigrant return. He scoffs at Homer, who 'glorified nostalgia with a laurel wreath and thereby laid out a moral hierarchy of emotions' (9). For Kundera, what is most significant in Ulysses' journey is not his symbolic return, which serves more as a pretext for the epic, or his emotional longing, a mere leitmotif in the text. Rather, it is the life of adventure and corporal pleasure that Ulysses and his companions lead on the journey. Kundera points to 'the genuine *dolce vita*' that Ulysses lived for six years with Calypso (8), and wonders if he had any such deep loving erotic relationship with his wife Penelope. Kundera emphasizes that Penelope did not recognize her husband at first; it was only in a sexual encounter that she, the faithful wife, realized his true identity (177). Nonetheless, it befits *The Odyssey* 'to extol Penelope's pain and sneer at Calypso's tears' (9).

Kundera perceptively points out that Ulysses' final, successful resolution in the end is possible only because his fellow-compatriots in Ithaca insist that he tell them the story of his adventures abroad:

'*Cuenta!!*' (Tell the story!!) (34). Only then is Ulysses able to remember, publicly, his past and his present. This invitation to recount one's past odyssey is certainly nowhere apparent, as Kundera transposes the myth into the postcommunist reality of the 1990s.

In counterpoint to Homer's mythical epic of return, Kundera describes the return of two Czech émigrés, Irena and Josef, after twenty years abroad. This homecoming, which Kundera epitomizes as 'The Great Return' (45), is shrouded in myth and offers only two roles for the actors: the oscillating polarities of the Great Victim or the Great Traitor (30). Kundera shows how Irena is always pitied by the French, viewed as 'a young woman in pain, banished from her country' (24). When they return to the Czech Republic, though, Irena and Josef are charged with the two mythic 'sins' I alluded to previously: (1) treason to the nation, and (2) having enjoyed a *dolce vita*, an 'easy life'; Josef represents the traitor; Irena, the opportunist.

In an aside, Kundera bluntly states that both the victimization and the guilt they feel are perpetrated by nationalistic sentiments and popular propaganda. He even goes so far as to claim that such anti-émigré feelings reflect the birth of the nation-state itself. He refers to the French Revolution, and the genesis of the first modern nation-state, where émigrés were viewed as traitors symbolically opposed to the loyal citizens. Kundera does not hesitate to relate these conditions to those in communist states: 'Loyal to the tradition of the French Revolution, the Communist countries hurled an anathema at emigration, deemed to be the most odious treason' (17).

To counter stereotypical assumptions, Kundera reveals the individual suffering of these two immigrants, exemplified by the deaths of Josef's wife and Irena's husband and their ensuing grief and solitude. These personal experiences demonstrate that pain is private: the most agonizing times of one's life remain incommunicable to others and can only be endured in silence, alone. Indeed, in Kundera's portrait, both Irena and Josef are to be pitied, not patronizingly and universally as Great Victims, but as individuals.

In Kundera's novel, Josef and Irena serve as the twin translations of the figure of 'the emigrant' to Czechs in the homeland, both in its symbolic and material connotations. Yet, they also translate the antithetical responses to the pain of immigration, that of the pragmatist and the idealist, or of the one who forgets and the one who is forgotten.

In Josef's story, deploying images of death, betrayal, and denial, Kundera describes what materially remains for the emigrant upon his return. The first place that Josef visits after getting back is a cemetery, itself almost gone, overgrown by new buildings. He sees death again, in the eyes of his brother when he meets him after twenty years. We learn that his brother considered Josef a deserter and a traitor, as dead to him. Like the biblical Joseph, Josef is envied by his brother, who – in a clear comment on restitution (58) – appropriated all of Josef's belongings except an old diary. On rereading his diary, Josef realizes that he has lost and forgotten the introspective and passionate young man he once was: 'the diary did not outlive the author's virginity' (87). Similarly in emigration, Josef survived because of his responses of loss and forgetting. He learned not to refer to his past or justify it (90), and abandoned any emotion or attachment to it. Returning to the Czech Republic, he even pathologizes his condition, claiming he is 'suffering from nostalgic insufficiency' (74) or from a 'masochistic distortion of memory' (74). However, in a passage that reiterates Kundera's famous 'unbearable lightness of being,' Josef realizes that forgetfulness ultimately frees him from his pain: 'Such is the law of masochistic memory: as segments of their lives melt into oblivion, men slough off whatever they dislike and feel lighter, freer' (76).

Irena's fate is more tragic: in word and in act she attempts to remember the past with the present, recreating it anew. On the personal level, Irena realizes that Josef was the love of her youth (actually, she is the addressee of Josef's discarded diary) and wishes to rekindle the love they once had. Ironically, however, when the couple finally makes love, Irena realizes that Josef does not know who she is. He was simply seduced by her because she used Czech swear-words, turning herself into the basest of prostitutes.

Irena symbolizes the narrative role of the emigrant, which is also denied and dismissed. Although Irena experiences 'unexpected joy' at speaking Czech (157), she realizes that her deformed, weakened accent seems foreign to her listeners. Most importantly, unlike in the case of Ulysses, no one is interested in listening to her odyssey; no one wants to hear about her experiences in France (19). The realization that no one cares about her past or present experiences is clearly painful for Irena. She describes her suffering with viscerally corporeal rhetoric, that of amputation: it is as if 'they amputated twenty years of her life' (43). Accused of leaving for a better life, Irena attempts to justify her decision by describing her personal story, confessing her private pain: 'You don't know how hard it is to carve out a little place for yourself in a foreign world. Can you imagine, leaving your country with a baby and with another in your belly? Losing your husband? Raising your two daughters with no money' (40). Her interlocutor friend, acting as both defence and prosecutor, judges her thus: 'Everybody wants to be acknowledged as the victim' (41). In all, there is no position, neither of hero nor of victim, for the returning emigrant in the narrative of the Czech nation. Irena even asks the crucial question: 'Is the epic of return pertinent to our time?' (54).

Ultimately, in Kundera's novel, only one position is possible in returning: that of the prostitute, a position he sardonically ascribes to his former homeland as well. *Ignorance* is no idyllic epic, wherein the Czech Republic, like a faithful Penelope, weaves while waiting for her hero. On the contrary, Prague is a commodity to be shared by all, where everyone wears T-shirts asserting 'Prague Is My Town.' Kundera makes his point rather crudely in the kinky penultimate scene, where Irena's mother, who represents 'the vitality of the Czech nation,' begins a perverse sexual relationship with Gustaf, Irena's boyfriend. For an instant, we wonder if this base encounter might not allude to Kundera's own ambiguous love-hate relationship with the mother-nation and his own fantasies. However, we prefer, like Josef in the last scene of the novel, to put a 'do not disturb' sign on the door, and forget what we just saw.

For a Happy Ending?

Kundera's novel *Ignorance* can be read from the context of an immigrant who chose not to return permanently to his native land, who like his character Irena, 'is saying her Great Farewells to the city that she loved more than any other and that she is prepared to lose once again, without regret, to be worthy of a life of her own' (138). But what of all the Czech emigrants who did return, who instead of regret bear hardships, and instead of Great Farewells faced Great Disillusionment? They cannot simply put a 'do not disturb' sign on the question of their return. Is indirect rhetoric – allegory, allusion, humour, avoidance – a way to respond to the suffering of return? Are detours – through drunkenness, violence, anonymity, migration, forgetting, and silence – the only possibility?

Now, almost a generation after the collapse of communism, it seems that the 'do not disturb' sign on the question of returning Czech émigrés is finally being lifted. Recently Czech psychologists and sociologists have started to seriously analyse the issue of Czech re-emigration. For example, in her 2004 article 'The Return from Emigration

Is Not Painless,' psychologist Olga Marlinová examines the various issues that returnees may have faced, such as the shattered 'fantasy of return,' the 'shock of return,' 'resentment,' and 'psychic splitting.' Similarly, in his 2005 sociological study, Zdeněk Nešpor examines the socioeconomic conditions of returnees, firmly grounding his analysis in multiculturalism and globalization. There is renewed interest in exile culture, manifested, for example, in Czech exile films, which have been the focus of film festivals in Jihlava or Pilsen. However, some grievances remain. English-Czech magazines continue to echo, in translation, some of the critiques that were intimated in Czech journals in the early and mid-1990s.[8] Nevertheless, these critiques also tend to conclude with moderate optimism. As we have seen in the previous chapter, in the new millennium, corresponding with the Czech Republic's entry into the European Union and its growing concerns with multiculturalism and immigration, there has been some reconciliation between the Czech government and returning emigrants.

Tensions between homeland Czechs and returnees have eased somewhat and there is renewed interest in emigrant experiences, especially on the part of the younger generations. Perhaps more open to difference because of increased mobility, this younger generation is eager to better understand the totalitarian period and the experiences of dissidents, many of whom are dying, leaving their stories untold. Exemplary of this trend is the documentary *Návrat Jana z pařížského exilu do Prahy* (The Return of Jan: From Parisian Exile to Prague, 2003), by young filmmaker Kateřina Krusová, which records the return in 2003 of dissident Jan Vladislav.[9]

Many of Vladislav's insights about his exile and return echo the issues I have outlined. In the documentary, Vladislav explains that, after 1989, he was not keen to return to the Czech Republic: 'he did not like the way things were going there.' For instance, he mentions that dissident solidarity, which had been so strong and cohesive under communism, altered and waned in postcommunism. The main reason, however, that Vladislav did not return to the Czech Republic was a legal one. As a dissident, he obviously had been stripped of his Czechoslovak citizenship by the totalitarian regime, and after 1989, he had no intention of 'begging' for its return. It was not until the law changed in 1999 that Vladislav's citizenship was restored to him, albeit through the intervention of his Czech friends and supporters. Ultimately, however, Vladislav's return 'home' was not political, but deeply personal: his wife was suffering from Alzheimer's disease, and he, in his early eighties, was her sole caregiver.

Now, Vladislav has settled in back home and has no regrets; on the contrary, he feels he has found welcome, especially among younger people, such as Krusová. Jan Vladislav's positive relationship with future generations is echoed by other returning émigrés, the cynical Jan Pelc, for example, who proclaimed in a 2000 interview: 'I believe in the next generation, the current fifteen-year-olds' ('Věřím').

In this chapter, one of my aims has been to offer these future generations a means to better understand the experiences of these returning writers, by elaborating on their reticent rhetoric, laden with oblique, implicit, and indirect references and allusions that may be sometimes difficult to discern or interpret. Only in Josef Beneš' *Návraty* is the reader faced with a traditional hero narrative, a sentimental Bildungsroman where the hero sacrifices himself in an attempt to educate and change the Czech lands after 1989. However, this mythical return proves to be an unconvincing failure. By contrast, in Iva Pekárková's travelogue we observe how the author deviates from graphic bodily pain in her immigrant fiction towards allegorical allusions in the works that she produced after returning to the Czech Republic. In *...a výstupy do údolí*, Pelc drowns the anger and grief of the excluded immigrant in alcohol and violence with writing so vociferous that one can barely read it. In *Beze stop*, Formánek conflates the immigrant with the jobless, the homeless, beggars, drunks, all those who, like the immigrant, live outside time and space – 'without a trace.' Martínek's *Opilost z hloubky* forces the reader to contemplate the role of immigrant as migrant or nomad, and incisively inverts the nationalist myth in his interrogation of the myth of globalization and cosmpolitanism. Finally, Kundera sums up this *nostos algia* or 'pain of return' by deconstructing the myth of return, and proposes forgetting as the only possible solution for the returning emigrant. Any other alternative, according to Kundera, intimates a prostitution of one's self, one's individuality, and one's past experiences.

As Kundera points out in his novel about the failed epic of the Great Return, what is needed is 'Cuenta!' – an interest in the immigrant or emigrant story. What is also required, as I have attempted to show in this chapter, is a better understanding of more indirect rhetorics of pain that point to suffering in implicit ways. It is only by understanding such 'reticent rhetoric' that we may be able to discern more latent forms of suffering, such as the immigrant experience, or other instances of structural violence or systemic inequality. Only by understanding the suffering of immigration – in its multiple fictional translations – can we hope to better respond to immigrant pain and perhaps resolve it, with a happy ending.

For a Responsive Conclusion

The physical and moral suffering the immigrant endures reveal to the attentive observer everything that native insertion into a nation and state buries in the innermost depth of minds and bodies.

      – Pierre Bourdieu, preface to *The Suffering of the Immigrant*

Moral life is the struggle to see – a struggle against the desire to deny the testimony of one's own eyes and ears.

      – Michael Ignatieff, *The Warrior's Honor*

In Real Life

Public perceptions and policies regarding immigration have changed dramatically since I began this book, some five years ago. During this time, twelve million people became new immigrants, and 150 million people worldwide became refugees (*International Migration Outlook*). The events of 9/11 and the subsequent 'War on Terror' have radically reshaped attitudes and laws concerning immigration.[1] In Europe, we observe increased anti-immigrant sentiment, with the rise of right-wing groups and leaders such as Vlaams Belang, Jörg Haider, Jean-Marie Le Pen, and the assassinated Pim Fortuyn; in Australia in 2004 there were anti-immigrant riots and in 2005 riots by disenfranchised Beur youth in France. U.S. anti-terrorist legislation[2] has severely affected legal immigration to the United States and exploited terrorism to criminalize illegal immigration.[3] In April 2006, for instance, millions of Americans took to the streets to protest Bill H.R. 4437, which classified unauthorized immigrants and anyone who helped them enter or remain in the United States as felons. U.S. terror policies have also affected immigrants in other countries. In Canada, for instance, anti-immigration measures range from tighter border security (the finger-printing and biometric scanning of Muslim-Canadians) to 'more secure' institutional practices (the Royal Bank suspending the U.S. bank accounts of Canadians from countries deemed a 'terror threat' by the United States). In the much-publicized case of Canadian Maher Arar, 'intelligence sharing' between Canada and the United States enabled U.S. authorities to export a Canadian citizen to be tortured in a torture-practising country (Syria) to extract (non-existent) intelligence information.

At the same time, in the past five years, more than 200 works of immigrant fiction, and scores of critical studies on immigration, have been published. Conspicuously, many of these focus on immigrant psychology;[4] psychologists are warning of the detrimental effects of terror policies on immigrant and refugee populations (Thomas, Pargeter). What effect might such scholarship have on policies or attitudes towards immigrants? How might we respond to these events, and to immigrant stories, be they in fiction or in real life?

Translating Pain

In *Translating Pain*, in a cross-cultural and interdisciplinary investigation, I have examined a story that cannot be told often enough: the immigrant narrative. In all of these narratives – from North Africa, Haiti, and Czechoslovakia – immigrant writers attempt to translate a certain lived experience: the difficulties of immigration. These immigrant hardships in many ways reflect psychological and sociological research about the immigrant experience. Yet, these immigrant sufferings are often denied, misunderstood, and misinterpreted in the public forum (in popular attitudes, public policies, and academic discourse) because, in many ways, these immigrant sufferings counter contemporary discourse about acculturation, multiculturalism, social order, integration, and cohesion. As Pierre Bourdieu explains, 'the physical and moral suffering the immigrant endures reveal to the attentive observer everything that native insertion into a nation and state buries in the innermost depth of minds and bodies' (xiv). In their literary works, immigrant writers confront these diverse sociocultural assumptions, as well as literary and generic conventions, which they then must creatively reproduce, reappropriate, and resist in fictional form.

Throughout *Translating Pain*, I have revealed how we, as attentive observers, might come to better understand the diverse sufferings of immigration by learning to better interpret diverse rhetorics of pain. In surveying French-Maghrebi, Haitian, and Czech immigrant texts, I have examined how writers might deploy bodily rhetoric, cultural rhetoric, and an even more subtly allusive rhetoric to communicate or translate their suffering of immigration. Each author, depending on his or her individual style or personal experiences, further engages the reader in his or her own particular form of agonistic expression. Thus, in some cases, the translation of immigrant pain may reflect unbearably violent rhetoric, reflective of past torture and trauma (Etienne) or inexorable social dis-ease (Kacem), which, in their abusive translations, may traumatize or infect readers. In other cases, more inviting rhetorics may playfully reappropriate stereotypes to entertain readers (Péan) or even work to heal cultural alienation through the use of creative or restorative techniques (Danticat).

In so doing, *Translating Pain* also explores the difficulties of translating immigrant pain. As we have seen in the case of Czechs, immigrants may repress certain sufferings of immigration, for a variety of historical, sociocultural, or political reasons. When these writers convey their hardships indirectly, whether through humour, analogy, or allusions, these signs of immigrant suffering may be easily dismissed, universalized, or relativized by readers. My analysis of Haitian immigrant texts reveals the difficulties of employing cultural elements, such as *vodou*, to translate immigrant hardships. Because of popular assumptions, political manipulations, or the cultural complexity connoted by a signifier such as *vodou*, much of the implicit meaning of such cultural translations may again be lost, refracted, or foreignized in translation.

The bodily pain in French-Maghrebi texts perhaps most effectively and explicitly translates the pain of immigration, as it refers to the universally understood referent of physical pain – in a rhetoric of somatic symptoms, injury, mutilation, and disease – to reflect the sociocultural suffering of immigration. However, I have pointed out the many problems inherent in this embodied rhetoric of pain. Notably, it reproduces the reification of immigrants as labouring, sexualized, and ethnic bodies. Most saliently, it entails a precarious performance of pain to satisfy the readership and its increasingly sensationalist or reductionist representations of bodily pain may easily engender the hierarchization and relativization of others' suffering.

Finally, *Translating Pain* demonstrates the importance of expressing the sufferings of immigration, both in fiction and in the public forum. We have seen in the case of Czech émigrés that their apparent absence of pain, manifested in Czech exile literature, has had significant consequences for these émigrés as they returned to the Czech Republic after 1989 to claim certain rights, such as citizenship, restitution, or recognition. The perils of the Czech case persuasively demonstrate that minorities must perhaps engage in an explicit, performative rhetoric of pain to affectively and effectively gain a greater role, voice, agency, or mobility in the public forum. Such a performative politics of pain is not without *caveats*, however, as we have seen in the case of some French-Maghrebi texts; it also risks furthering *ressentiment*, reproducing sociocultural hierarchiess or devolving into a discourse of 'zeroism' or pathological victimhood.

Translating Pain thus delineates both the possibilities and limits of translating immigrant pain in literary texts. Ultimately, however, the conclusions to be drawn from this critical study depend largely on each of our personal responses to this pedagogy of suffering. The translation of immigrant pain is not solely shaped by the 'source' text, be it in immigrant fiction or by immigrants themselves. Rather, the translation of immigrant pain – in fiction or in real life – fundamentally depends on the target audience, and its affective responses to immigrant sufferings. As discussed in chapter 1, it is the immigrant-recieving country that largely defines the immigrant or the generic immigrant story, just as it is the people in the target host nation who mainly read and publish immigrant fiction. It is this target audience that ultimately holds the power to translate the pain of immigration from fiction to real-life action. To conclude, therefore, I would like to briefly take pause to consider some of the different responses that we, as the target audience, might have to immigrant sufferings, and deliberate some of the possibilities, and limits, of our translation of immigrants' pain.

Compassion Avoidance

Interestingly, as we survey the many literary texts analysed in this book, we notice that nationals of the host country are conspicuously absent in them. Rarely do we encounter fully fleshed-out characters representative of the host country, and when we do, their responses are invariably negative, indifferent, or hostile. How to explain this absence, indifference, or even hostility on the part of the host audience? On the one hand, such indifference might stem from a lack of knowledge about immigrant suffering, which in many ways, this book seeks to remedy. On the other hand, such lack of concern may paradoxically stem from an excess of suffering.

Numerous media theorists have pointed to the fact that human suffering has become a commodity in our contemporary age of mass media: we are bombarded with a plethora of stories and images of human suffering, cruelty, violence, disasters, or war to the point that we have become 'voyeurs of the suffering of others, tourists in their landscapes of anguish' (Ignatieff 10). As a result we may suffer from 'compassion-fatigue' (Moeller), a term coined to refer to the stress experienced by journalists or psychologists who are too overwhelmed by the trauma they witness to feel any emotion whatsoever, but that is currently employed to describe the unresponsiveness of the general population to atrocities in the media. In light of so many shocking images, it may be argued that our cognitive processes suffer from 'information overload, input overload or saturation' that train our brains to 'filter' or 'tune out' disturbing images (Cohen 187). More problematically, because of the quantity of suffering we observe daily, certain forms of suffering may become 'normalized' or 'routine' (189); just as we may become increasingly 'desensitized' or 'psychically numbed' to certain forms of suffering (191). As Susan Moeller explains, in *Compassion Fatigue: How the Media Sell Disease, Famine, War and Death* (1999), 'our moral fatigue and exhausted empathy is, in some degree, a survival mechanism' (53). Or to paraphrase Stanley Cohen, we're not unaware of the truth, 'we are just tired of the truth' (187).

In *States of Denial* (2001), however, psychologist Cohen disputes many of the claims underlying the populist thesis of compassion fatigue, such as information overload, normalization, or desensitization, to argue that the excess of suffering in the contemporary media speaks more of 'media fatigue' (192) and 'compassion avoidance' (193), than it does of compassion fatigue. Rather, Cohen argues that 'the problem with multiple images of distant suffering is not their multiplicity but their psychological and moral distance' (194). To curb the effects of compassion avoidance, Cohen suggests getting closer to subjects in pain – by learning more about their stories.

Yet, as we have seen in a number of these immigrant narratives, the receiving audience is often unwilling to listen to the immigrant story. Most saliently, the Czech case outlines one of the obstacles impeding a receptive response from the target audience: the hierarchization or relativization of others' pain, because of an excess of one's own personal suffering. As Kundera points out in *Ignorance*, no one was interested in Irena's immigrant story because, as her host explains, 'everybody wants to be acknowledged as the victim' (41). As I have shown in examples ranging from French-Maghrebi fiction to Czech politics, a politics of pain often engenders hierarchies of suffering, which either denigrate or universalize others' pain, so as to gain authority, voice, and power for one's self.

Towards Sympathy and Affective Action

Given these various reasons for compassion avoidance, how might we formulate a sympathetic reader-response? What might such a position entail? Unfortunately, none of the literary texts offer us a model of a compassionate reader-response. To posit such a position, we must turn to literary, philosophical, or ethical theories about pity, compassion, and empathy.

Since the time of the Ancient Greeks, literary theorists have delved into what conditions may incite sympathetic feelings towards another person. For instance, Aristotle theorized that feelings of pity are aroused when (1) we believe that a serious misfortune has befallen another person whom we consider to be important; (2) we must deem that the individual was not entirely responsible for the misfortune; and lastly (3) we apprehend that we too are vulnerable to such misfortune ourselves (R1386a). Furthermore, Aristotle argued that experiencing pity, specifically in response to the performance of a tragedy, would purge the audience of violent emotions (*catharsis*), which as a result, would lead to a 'good life' of sensible moderation of these emotive states.

Aristotle's observations are particularly fruitful when we consider our responses to immigrant suffering. Do we consider immigrants as equals, and thus worthy of sympathy? Or do social differentials separate us from their misery? Aristotle points out that it is much easier to pity those who 'are like us in age, character, disposition, social standing, or birth' (1386a).[5] Do categories such as social class, gender, and nationality hinder our understanding of immigrants' hardships? Likewise, Aristotle reminds us that, to elicit pity from the audience, a hero's misfortunes should seem significant and inadvertent. Do we view immigrant sufferings as note-worthy, or do we blame immigrants for their plight? Interestingly, the 'painful and destructive evils' that Aristotle cites as 'serious' and 'unintentional' (1386a) are much more common sites of suffering than the crises that we might expect: death, disease, injury, old age, and hunger, as well as isolation, friendlessness, or disappointment (1386a). These misfortunes are hardships that immigrants face, but that could also be dismissed as a normal part of life in general. What types of immigrant suffering would be 'serious enough' to warrant our attention?

Finally, we might ask ourselves what effects such a sympathetic reader-response might have in the social order. While Aristotle argued that experiencing pity might lead to sensible moderation, other literary and ethical theorists have attributed even greater social potential to it. For instance, in the eighteenth century, Lessing, a major dramatist of the German Enlightenment, developed a theory of 'tragic pity' (*tragisches Mitleid*, *Hamburg* 75), in which he argued that the goal of tragedy was to transform 'passions into virtuous actions' (78, 193).[6] For Lessing, pity is the noblest of human emotions, which can also lead to the greatest human good: '*The man who pities most is the best of men*, the one who is most open to social virtues and to all forms of generosity' (*Letter* 195, emphasis in original).[7] Unlike Aristotle, Lessing believes that any type of misfortune has the potential for arousing pity in a morally upstanding bystander. Moreover, theater representations of tragedy 'should intensify our powers of empathy to the point that we are touched by misfortune [...] experiencing it directly ourselves' (*Letter* 195), and thus serve to further our sense of social responsibility and activism. Might reading texts of immigrant suffering similarly cultivate our sense of empathy and foster a global ethics of care and concern?

Much like Lessing, many ethical theorists in the eighteenth century, such as Smith, Hume, or Schopenhauer, refer to pity as a common social good in their works on sympathy or compassion. Adam Smith (1723–90), for example, best known for his foundational treatise on capitalism, *On the Wealth of Nations* (1776), also examines sympathy. In his treatise on social morality, *The Theory of Moral Sentiments* (1759), Smith posits sympathy as the key to our moral sense and social cohesion.[8] Similarly, Schopenhauer (1788–1860) suggests that 'sympathy shows itself in the sincere participation in [another person's] joy and grief, and the disinterested sacrifices made in respect of the latter' (386).

Contemporary literary theorists have similarly promulgated the ethical values of pity and compassion. Classical scholar Martha Nussbaum translates Aristotle's term of 'pity' as 'compassion,' and, through her analysis of this emotion, advances compassion as a 'cosmopolitan emotion' that can help 'cultivate our humanity.'[9] Werner Krieglstein posits compassion as the 'new philosophy of the other' in contemporary society.[10] Finally, Fred Alford, in his article 'Greek Tragedy and Civilization: The Cultivation of Pity,' argues that love and pity are 'civilizing' emotions. In his view, pity is a 'recipe for civilization,' not merely because it offers 'consolation for man's isolation and pain' to make victims feel better, but because 'the connections of pity also help to contain the aggressive acting out by which men, women and nations otherwise seek to overcome their pain' (274). In Alford's view, the civilizing emotions of love and pity, if channelled correctly, might actually be able to quell the resentment, greed, rage, and violence in society to foster a more decent and peaceful civilization (259) – a thought-provoking claim indeed.

According to ethical theories based on pity, a compassionate reader-response might possibly lead to greater social concern. Indeed, might a sympathetic reading of immigrant texts provoke greater understanding and compassion for the immigrant condition? Might such pity develop our moral and ethical sense, as Lessing argues? Might experiencing such sympathy lead to action, as Schopenhauer suggests? Might hostility and aggression be prevented by a cultivation of pity, as Alford claims? If so, should we define pity as the new 'cosmopolitan emotion,' the 'philosophy of the other' or 'the recipe for civilization'?

Against Pity

Although there are many theoretical validations of pity or compassion, it is also crucial to concede that there are many opponents of pity or compassion. Until the sixteenth century, for instance, pity, derived from the Latin *pietas*, signified both 'the virtue of piety' as well as 'the quality of being pitiful' (*OED*). The 'quality of being pitiful' was further defined as '1. the disposition to mercy or compassion; clemency, mercy, mildness, tenderness' or '2. a feeling or emotion of tenderness aroused by the suffering, distress, or misfortune of another, and prompting a desire for its relief; compassion, sympathy.' In modern usage, however, pity is associated with the pitiful and the pathetic, and usually means 'to commiserate, be sorry for' and, as the *Oxford English Dictionary* warns, implies 'slight contempt for a person on account of some intellectual or moral inferiority attributed to him.'[11]

This negative attitude towards pity in Western philosophy might stem from the historical separation of reason from emotion, a perspective developed first by the Greeks, and later reappropriated during the

Enlightenment, when science and objective rationalization tended to set aside subjective feelings. An ethics based on emotions such as pity has been opposed by numerous thinkers including Plato, the Stoics, and Christian writers such as Thomas Aquinas, or Kant and Spinoza during the Enlightenment. A salient example of the denigration of pity is Plato's depiction of Socrates' death in the *Apology*, where, facing death, Socrates stoically refuses to engage in 'pitiful dramatics' or a dramatic appeal to pity to save his life (34c–35c). We see this tendency in the texts analysed herein, especially in those by Czech intellectuals. As Ota Filip concisely sums up: 'I am not willing to exhibit my wounds of my twenty-year exile to my foreign close ones, with reproaches and tears' (13).

It is Nietzsche who makes what is perhaps the strongest claim against pity. Indeed, according to Nietzsche, society's greatest danger lies in *Mitleiden*,[12] pity or compassion (*The Gay Science*, sec. 271). Nietzsche contends that pity intensifies the suffering of victims by further scorning or shaming them (*Beyond Good*, sec. 30), while also fuelling suffering for those pitying them (*Daybreak*, sec.133). By thus multiplying suffering, pity therefore also increases evil in the world (*Will to Power*, sec. 368). Furthermore, pity promotes weakness in those responding with pity: pity acts as a 'depressant. A man loses force when he pities' (*Anti-Christ*, sec. 7). Those who pity demonstrate numerous deficiencies – a lack of strength, endurance, and stoicism or susceptibility to fear, weakness, and suffering – that clearly counter Nietzsche's notion of the superman. By thus promoting weakness, 'pity thwarts the whole law of evolution, which is the law of natural selection' (*Anti-Christ*, sec. 7). In all, Nietzsche dismisses pity on two counts: first, by validating pain, pity promotes the suffering of all parties concerned, and second, by cultivating weakness pity counters natural selection.

Nietzsche's disturbing remarks on pity are reflected in certain contemporary negative attitudes towards immigrants. Some people continue to view immigrant complaints as signs of weakness or inadequacy, just as others continue to believe that immigrants need to face certain hardships in order to become strong, sensible, and productive members of society. Certainly, many of the literary texts I have analysed in this book reproduce the model of the stoic, adaptable, immigrant-citizen.

Nietzsche also puts forth another important observation about the appeal to pity – that it is a performative act, if not a staged performance. Significantly, he remarks that 'whenever we are *noticed* to be suffering, our suffering is superficially construed' (*Gay Science*, sec. 338). Some demonstrations of pain are not necessarily pain-induced, Nietzsche contends, citing the case of children or invalids, who 'make a spectacle of themselves' just so that they might be noticed and to assert their power over the observer (*Human*, sec. 50). In so doing, Nietzsche's cautions echo those of numerous theorists, such as Spinoza, who objects to pity because it is unverifiable and can easily be deceiving (Book 4, 225). Is pain a 'truth' that can be verified – either with proof, tangible evidence, argument, or logic? Or will any expression of pain always necessarily remain a representation or performance?

The many problems associated with the performance of pain bring us to one of the central issues of *Translating Pain* – how to prove or legitimate suffering in words? In a court of law, to claim a grievance or substantiate a claim, one usually needs to resort to proof or evidence. Rarely, one can legally engage in an *argumentum ad misericordiam* or an 'appeal to pity,' although such an argument continues to be an important basis of judgment in the stages of sentencing, for instance, and it remains significant in humanitarian claims or charitable appeals. Refugee claimants, for example, rely largely on an *argumentum ad misericordiam* when applying for asylum, especially when they have few elements of tangible proof to substantiate their fear of persecution.

Establishing 'proof' of one's pain becomes even more difficult in literary fiction, especially when one considers such a nebulous form of pain as immigrant suffering. Manifestly, writers cannot refer to physical evidence of their pain, but must reproduce it in narrative, imagery, linguistic and cultural signs: they must convince readers of their experience with rhetoric. Throughout this work, I have examined numerous rhetorical strategies that immigrant writers might employ to legitimate their suffering in words. Yet, were any of these strategies substantial enough to 'prove' to us as readers that immigrants do indeed experience a variety of hardships in the process of immigration? Were we more convinced by writers' 'appeals to pity'? Or did we simply dismiss these immigrants' claims as posturing or performance? Weakness and inadequacy? Irrationality or lack of stoicism? Or failure to achieve successful integration?

Furthermore, contemporary theorists have drawn on Nietzsche's critique of pity to argue that instead of relativizing suffering or eliciting empathetic feelings of mutuality, pity, in fact, only reaffirms social hierarchies. For instance, Brian Massumi warns that 'having pity for someone who occupies a category that is not socially valorised, or expressing moral outrage on their behalf, is not necessarily helpful in the long run, because it maintains the category and simply inverts its value sign, from negative to positive. It's a kind of piety, a moralizing approach.' While Massumi describes this pietous pity as another form of self-justifying domination, Charles Altieri goes so far as to suggest that we may derive pleasure 'in identifying with other people's suffering, since nothing secures bourgeois self-satisfaction, so well as sympathy with those who lack the same possessions' (41). These remarks translate pity into moralizing piety and self-laudatory classist paternalism. They prompt us to turn from the object of our pity, the immigrant, to consider ourselves – as members of the hospitable host country or as the subject who pities – and discerningly probe the motives for our compassion or pity. What moral ground, or position of piety, do we gain by pitying the immigrant? Or, taking Altieri's remark seriously, what pleasures does pitying have for us?

These various claims against pity perhaps inform us more about our own cultural values – about 'rationality,' 'truth,' 'performance,' 'strength,' 'success,' or 'immigration' – and our role as the 'morally upstanding,' 'well-off,' citizen, than they do about pity itself. Whereas the ethical theorists on sympathy, whom I alluded to in the previous section, argue that compassion has the potential of transcending difference, in these examples, we find those cultural values that maintain distinctions, partiality, and hierarchies, and in turn, shape our culture of indifference and difference.

Into Real Life

The pedagogy of suffering presented in this book not only teaches us to better understand immigrant sufferings or discern different rhetorics and politics of pain, but significantly, also informs us about our own responses to the suffering of others. What rhetoric does it take for us to respond with compassion or concern? What might strip away our indifference, our differences, our egotism, or our 'compassion fatigue'?

Interestingly, many contemporary ethical theorists of 'compassion fatigue,' 'denial' or 'modern conscience,' such as Moeller, Cohen, Ignatieff, all contend that to better engage with the sufferings of others, we must first learn to listen to their stories. According to Ignatieff, the minimal requirement to engage with others' suffering is to spend time with them: it is necessary to have 'enough time to pierce the carapace of self-absorption and estrangement that separates us from the moral world of others' (29). Reading is a way of spending time with others, of vicariously participating in their experiences, in our imaginations. Therein, perhaps, lies the ethical value of literature: it offers us an intimate way of sharing the life of another, and may thereby lead us to greater awareness and responsiveness to social concerns around us. Thus, *Translating Pain* invites us, as readers, to consider the role of literature, and its value, in the real world.

Yet, as I have emphasized throughout this book, reading about the other, or vicariously spending time with others in the virtual world of fiction, is neither transparent nor facile. Rather, it requires cautious and discerning acts of translation – both of the other and of ourselves. In particular, reading about the suffering of others, impels us to ponder the translation of these literary fictions in 'the Real, either in the form of cultural materialism or communal responsibility.'[13]

Throughout *Translating Pain* I have advocated the role of the cultural translator. To truly grasp the experiences of others, especially those of immigrants, I have argued that it is first necessary to understand their culture – which shapes all of their experiences, including their use of language or their expression of pain. Similarly, it is just as fundamental to understand our own cultural language, or that of the host nation, as it inflects our understanding of immigration, and of suffering, as well as our responses to others' differences or others' pain. While in this conclusion I call for a sympathetic reader-response to immigrant suffering, such a response can only be grounded in a form of complex compassion, one that translates the nuances of cultural differences from culture to culture, but also, in so doing, from literary fictions to 'real life.'

Ultimately, it is up to the reader to respond to the many questions raised by this work. Examples of rising discrimination and hostility towards immigrants are all around us in public policies and attitudes, as are stories of increasing immigrant hardship. How will we respond to these stories of immigrant suffering – be they in fiction or in 'real' life'? Can we learn to translate these stories affectively? Can we transform these politics of pain into an effective politics of compassion? In the end, it is up to all of us to translate the pain of immigration – with effective action. So – how will we translate the pain of immigration?

Notes

An Affective Introduction

1 All names referring to real immigrants in this book are fictional, so as to protect the privacy of real people. *Azadeh* means 'freedom' in Farsi; *desta* means 'happiness' in Amharic, and *ti moun* is the Haitian *kreyòl* term for 'children.'

2 Notable exceptions in immigrant literary studies include Andreea Ritivoi's *Yesterday's Self* (2002) and Matthew Jacobson's *Special Sorrows* (1995), which explore immigrant nostalgia and nationalistic sentiments respectively.

3 For psychiatric conditions related to immigration, see, e.g., Hutchinson and Haasan on immigrants to Europe; Smith et al. on European immigrants to Canada; Ortega et al. on Hispanics in the U.S.; Cooper on Blacks in the U.K.; Haasen et al. on immigrants to Germany; Cantor-Graae et al. on immigrants to Norway; Zolkowska et al. and Hjern et al. on immigrants to Sweden.

4 *Folie à deux* refers to a rare psychiatric disorder, wherein two people share the same paranoia or delusion. For a clinical example related to immigrants, Israeli women and daughters in particular, see Lerner et al. (1996). The Persephone syndrome refers to neurotic anxiety and depression, brought about by extreme attachment and separation of mothers and daughters; it has been particularly noted among Greek immigrants (see Dunkas and Nikelly).

1 'Perversely through Pain'

1 All translations from French are mine, unless noted otherwise. Originals of lengthier quotes (as in this case) will be provided: 'Peut-on être

étranger et heureux? L'étranger suscite une idée neuve du bonheur. Entre fugue et origine: une limite fragile, une homéostase provisoire [...]. Le bonheur étrange de l'étranger est de maintenir cette éternité en fuite ou ce transitoire perpétuel' (55).

2 In 1994, e.g., 43,302 individuals from 74 different countries were intercepted for trying to cross the Czech-German border illegally ('New Trade' 45).

3 See various reports on EUMC's website http://eumc.eu.int/eumc/index.php.

4 Private interview with author, taped.

5 The French word 'étranger' may be translated as either 'stranger' or 'foreigner.' In the context of the conference, Kristeva also refers to the migrant or immigrant.

6 For further examples, see Kristeva's *Étrangers à nous-mêmes*, *Lettre à Harlem Désir*.

7 For more information on nostalgia as a disease, see George Rosen's article 'Nostalgia: A 'Forgotten' Psychological Disorder' or chapter 1 in Ritivoi's *Yesterday's Self*.

8 See, e.g., Grinberg and Grinberg, Akhtar or Haour-Knipe.

9 Knafo and Yaari, e.g., divide the immigrant journey into (1) the planning phase, (2) the adjustment phase, (3) the mourning phase, (4) the acceptance or assimilation phase.

10 Olga Marlin structures immigration into the following personal and familial phases: (1) separation from the family and home, (2) identification with parents, (3) creation of new inner parents, and finally (4) acceptance through mourning for lost family and lingering nostalgia.

11 Meaders describes the following phases of adjustment and cultural transformation: (1) survival of identity to (2) bicultural identity to a (3) transcultural identity.

12 In 'In-Car-Ceration or Auto-Mobility? Ethnic Minorities in the Space of the Car' (2005), I explore the space of the car in films about immigration to show that the closed transient space of the car exemplifies this space of immobile in-betweenness for ethnic minorities.

13 See, e.g., Cole et al. or Williams and Westermeyer.

14 Ben-Sira defines 'stress' as a prolonged disturbance of an individual's emotional homeostasis, while 'readjustment' refers to the restoration of emotional homeostasis as a result of successful coping with stress.

15 'Dissociation' is a psychological term referring to sudden temporary alterations in the normal functions of consciousness. In common usage, it is known as 'splitting.'

16 See, e.g., Zborowski, Kleinman, Waitzkin and Magaña, and Leenaars et al. Leenaars et al. examine the high rates of suicides among immigrants and explore the somatization of immigrant suffering in a cultural perspective.

17 In his early 1960s study of immigrants in Norway, Eitinger suggested that their higher incidence of mental disease could be attributed to their exposure to isolation, helplessness, language difficulties, hostility, and indifference from the host population.

18 Medical researchers have only just begun to observe the variables that language differences and deep-seated linguistic structures create in such disorders as aphasia, dysphasia, or dysgraphia. See, e.g., 41st Annual Meeting of Academy of Aphasia, Vienna, 19–21 October 2003, papers collected in *Brain and Language* 87:1, 2003; or Raman and Weekes.

2 'Suffering Matters'

1 There is a rare genetic disorder, congenital analgesia, that prevents people from feeling any pain whatsoever.

2 Here I refer to Robert Kugelman's famous formulation 'pain is an "it," but also what "I" am' (342).

3 Ben-Sira specifically categorizes these demands as instrumental (economic roles and expectations), cognitive demands (sociocultural roles and expectations), and affective (related to family, friends, interracial and intergenerational roles and expectations).

4 *Saudade* and *dor* exemplify the difficulty of translating emotive states across languages and cultures. *Saudade* has been alternately translated as 'sad longing,' 'yearning,' 'nostalgia,' or 'homesickness' (Taylor's *English-Portuguese Dictionary*, 571), or as 'more or less a melancholy sense of incompleteness, linked by memory to situations where one is missing the presence of someone or something; or of being far away from some place and thing; or of the absence of certain prior life experiences or pleasures; all conditions which seem desirable to the affected individual' (my translation of Houaiss' *Portuguese Dictionary*, 2525). These definitions do not capture this complex feeling which among other things, requires 'a mastery of Portuguese and Brazilian poetry,' and which Brazilians consider 'the purest expression of the Brazilian soul, of their heightened sensibility and awareness of the natural and social environment [...] of their acute sensitivity to the human condition and to its tragedies and losses, longing and in particular, memory itself' (Scheper-Hughes 436). Similarly, *dor* is an untranslatable Romanian concept of suffering, a painful longing

and future-oriented nostalgia, which renowned poet Lucian Blaga describes in relation to Romanian identity: 'Existence for Romanian is *dor*, aspiration across horizons, existence which in its entirety flows towards "something"' (164, translated in Boia 147).

5 Again, these terms denote nuanced cultural concepts, but simplistically translated, in Haitian *vodou* a *bokò* is a 'black magic sorcerer' and in Arab-Muslim contexts, a *djinn* is a 'spirit that can assume animal or human form.'

3 'Mal Partout'

1 His stomach hurts; his head hurts; his back hurts; he has pain everywhere. He suffers terribly; his face is eloquent; suffering imposes itself on it.
'What's wrong my friend?'
'I'm going to die, Doctor'
His voice is broken, imperceptible.
'Where does it hurt?'
'Everywhere, Doctor.'

2 Throughout his article, Jarret plays on the various meanings of 'representation,' which may be translated as 'theatrical performance,' 'representation,' or in psychology, as 'perception.'

3 'Je ne m'étendrai pas sur ce « mal partout » que nous avons tous eu l'occasion de constater chez les migrants maghrébins. La plainte est monotone, stéréotypée, lancinante, agaçante, l'expression verbale est souvent pauvre, l'imagerie quasi nulle.'

4 See Groselle, Bennani, or Bendjalli.

5 'Problèmes affectifs et sexuels de travailleurs nord-africains en France,' doctoral dissertation, University of Paris VII-Jussieu, 1975.

6 Here, my work refers to Yamina Benguigui's *Mémoires d'immigrés* (1997), a series of interviews that offers an excellent overview of the concerns facing various Maghrebi groups, or immigrant 'fathers,' 'mothers,' and 'children,' as Benguigui terms them.

7 'Je m'ennuie, j'en ai marre de voir le temps passer. Je voudrais mieux vivre, être bien dans ma peau. D'ailleurs je ne sais pas pourquoi je suis si mal en moi. J'en ai assez d'essayer de me faire comprendre. Je sais que ça ne marche pas. Pourquoi faut-il toujours faire semblant aux gens qui s'en foutent de ce que je raconte? C'est un jeu très dur, moi je ne tiens plus le coup. J'en ai ma claque. J'ai vingt ans, y en a qui disent que c'est le bel âge. Je suis instable à tous les niveaux.'

8 'La peinture craquelée, disparue par endroits, faisait ressortir les fêlures du béton, comme un visage qui aurait trop vieilli, avant de naître. Les trous béants marquaient la façade, telle la lèpre un visage déjà malade.'

9 Sebbar's rather optimistic novel *Shérazade*, e.g., ends with a fatal accident, while Kessas' inconclusive *Beur's Story* culminates with Farida's suicide.

10 Smaïl's book has been translated into English under the title *Smile* (Serpent's Tail, 2000.)

11 'Il y aura toujours un autre candidat moins basané que moi, le cheveu moins crépu, la peau moins grenue, le nez moins busqué. [...] Je ne suis pas une ressource humaine; j'ai trop sale gueule.'

12 For an interesting analysis of such exoticization in popular culture, see Lionnet's article 'Immigration, Poster Art, and Transgressive Citizenship' (1995).

13 For further examples, see Gilroy 123; Eisenstein 65; Walters 269; Suleri's novel *Meatless Days*.

14 'J'eus l'impression que tous les pays me claquaient la porte au nez. Ils étaient privés. Il fallait la carte pour entrer. J'étais condamné à vivre dans les no man's lands que j'imaginais comme des couloirs froids où le vent soufflait à tout rompre.'

15 'La somatisation vient signifier le *défaut* (par défaut) de l'inscription et de l'identification à la nouvelle culture par la langue. Quand la langue maternelle fait défaut, ne permet plus l'inscription culturelle et sociale ni l'identification à la nouvelle situation il y a recours à la somatisation pour mieux dire la souffrance.'

16 'On a mal, on veut dire quelque chose, il y a un manque. L'écriture vient avec ce manque. Une blessure intime, ouverte' (cited in Bonn and Boualit 29–30).

4 'In the Maim of the Father'

1 'Handicapé et reclus chez lui, mon père n'existait plus aux yeux des autres [...] Je n'osais pas le fixer trop longtemps.'

2 C'est ainsi que j'assistai à ma première opération à cœur ouvert. Ils ont branché les électrodes. Non, non. Ce n'est pas cette fois-là qu'ils ont branché les électrodes. Ils ont ouvert mon coeur. Non, je me trompe. Non, cette fois-là, c'est le cœur de la terre qu'ils ont ouvert, le cœur de la terre et d'un fleuve.

3 Ce qui a été terrible, c'est le jour où je suis devenu inapte au travail. [...] J'avais toujours travaillé, deux fois plus que les autres, d'abord pour évoluer, ensuite pour être considéré comme les Français qui avaient les

mêmes qualifications que moi, enfin pour mes enfants, pour mes fils, pour qu'ils soient fiers de leur père, pour qu'ils comprennent que j'avais tout fait pour m'intégrer. [...] Je ne comprends pas ce que cela veut dire, au fond, s'intégrer.'

4 'Ceux qui perdent un membre du fait d'un accident du travail s'estiment souvent touchés par la grâce de Dieu, car ils en finissent une fois pour toutes avec l'exil.'

5 'Ce qui étonne et fait problème (voire scandale) au point d'être mis au compte de la pathologie, c'est-à-dire de l'anormalité, c'est la manière dont l'immigré malade use de sa maladie (et de l'instance médicale) pour régler un litige qui est, dit-on, d'ordre social.'

6 'Il s'était assis sans un mot. Et ils s'étaient tous penchés au-dessus de sa main. Leurs têtes n'avaient jamais été aussi proches de la sienne. Un état d'immobilité les avait tous saisis là.'

7 'Un père disparu dans un accident banal. Une mère malade de son pays. Une vie sans joie. Les crises anorexiques d'Amira. L'argent qui manque comme chez tous les pauvres. Rien qui ne pourrait permettre d'espérer.'

8 'Il n'osait plus lever la voix sur nous, ni nous commander. Improductif, il se persuada très vite que son autorité, à l'image de la moitié inférieure de son corps, ne faisait plus effet.'

9 'Je n'osais pas le fixer trop longtemps. Un hâle sombre, cuivré, imprégnait son visage figé, comme les réminiscences d'un soleil antérieur, devenu cendre.'

5 'Ni Putes Ni Soumises?'

1 Nous, femmes vivant dans les banlieues, issues de toutes origines, croyantes ou non, lançons cet appel pour nos droits à la liberté et à l'émancipation. Oppressées socialement par une société qui nous enferme dans les ghettos où s'accumulent misère et exclusion. Etouffées par le machisme des hommes de nos quartiers qui au nom d'une «tradition» nient nos droits les plus élémentaires [...]
  • Assez de leçons de morale [...]
  • Assez de misérabilisme [...]
  • Assez de justifications pour notre oppression [...]
  • Assez de silence [...]
Personne ne nous libérera de cette double oppression si ce n'est nous-mêmes.

2 See the previous chapters for discussions of Houari or Zemouri. Other notable fiction of this genre includes Ben Jelloun's *La Réclusion solitaire*

and *La Plus Haute des Solitudes*, Chraïbi's *Les Boucs* and Boudjedra's *Topographie idéale pour une agression caractérisée* (1975).

3 Ireland, however, has pointed to a couple of biographical accounts about the female first-generation, including: Dalila Kerouani's *Une fille d'Algérie, éprise de liberté* and Nedjma Plantade's *L'Honneur et l'amertume: le destin ordinaire d'une femme kabyle.*

4 La fille au consulat [...] je lui ai répondu sans me gêner : 'Ma grosse, quand tu auras la chatte déchirée par six accouchements, que ton mari t'aura larguée pareil qu'un morceau de viande pourrie pour en prendre une plus fraîche, quand tu iras mendier le pain de tes enfants auprès des Français et qu'en plus ils te le donnent avec tous les égards tandis que tes compatriotes mettent un double verrou à leur cœur, on verra alors si tu auras encore l'envie de rentrer au bled y manger des croûtons imbibés d'une mauvaise huile d'olive en priant le ciel qu'un voisin charitable veuille bien te niquer en échange d'une poignée de patates à faire bouillir aux enfants.'

5 La violence et la détresse qui m'habitent ont besoin d'exploser. Mon corps trouve une solution. C'est intelligent, un corps! Il se met à faire des cris d'épilepsie. Pas n'importe quoi ! Parfois, il faut sept ou huit personnes pour me contenir [...] Alors mes crises deviennent un nouveau mode d'expression.

6 Je vous ai livré, ici, ce qu'on peut y vivre dans la banlieue. Ce pire qui a fait basculer toute ma jeunesse dans l'horreur.

7 Devant mon mutisme, ils choisirent de se venger sur moi de la manière la plus inhumaine qui soit. D'abord ils me violèrent brutalement à tour de rôle; à présent je ne me souviens plus s'ils étaient quatre ou cinq, ensuite, et, alors que j'étais à demi consciente, ils m'attachèrent les pieds, m'écartelant ainsi entre deux arbres et, ôtant la muselière au chien, ils lui donnèrent l'ordre d'attaquer. C'est alors que l'horreur totale fut consommée. Hurlant à me faire éclater les poumons, je sentis les puissants crocs de la bête s'enfoncer férocement dans mon sexe, emportant dans sa gueule des morceaux entiers de chair ensanglantée, et je m'évanouis.

8 Front Islamique du Salut, or roughly translated, the Algerian Islamist Party.

9 See, e.g., 30, 37, 42, 92, 96, 131, 133, 137, 171.

6 'Pathologically Sick'

1 'What, you hussy? Of course, I am sick! I'm sick, you, insolent you!'

2 'Faced with this pain without lesion, this sickness spread all over and

within the body, this continuous suffering, the easiest attitude [...] is the denial of all morbidity. In the extreme, the North African is a pretender, a liar, a malingerer, a lazy-ass, a thief.'

3 'Un père disparu dans un accident banal. Une mère malade de son pays. Une vie sans joie. Les crises anorexiques d'Amira. L'argent qui manque comme chez tous les pauvres. Rien qui ne pourrait permettre d'espérer.'

4 'Petite soeur c'est de cette France que tu meurs, comme ma mère est morte de son Algérie. Moi de l'impossibilité où je fus d'inventer un autre pays.'

5 'Lorsqu'on me parle de la douleur d'écrire, je suis pris de fou rire ... Je ne souffre pas d'écrire. Écrire, c'est un plaisir.'

6 Although a French-born Moroccan, Andrieux does not speak *verlan* and has never lived in a *cité*, but rather teaches French and Arabic in Strasbourg. However, even this claim is suspect, according to *Libération* (Perrignon).

7 'La maladie d'être arabe ... T'es marqué par un fer rouge. Tu ressens une intense douleur. C'est un coup qu'on te porte à chaque fois que l'on prononce ton nom.'

7 'Zombification'

1 'Mais le Vodou est à la fois un fait religieux et politico-social ... Au point qu'il n'est osé d'affirmer que plus on pénètrera les mystères, mieux l'histoire d'Haïti nous livrera ses secrets' (163).

2 In this chapter, I distinguish the Haitian religion of *vodou* (*kreyòl* orthography) from its Western counterpart, by referring to the latter as 'voodoo.'

3 The two historical sources usually serve to corroborate the event (which was to have occurred between 14 and 21 August 1791): Antoine Dalma's *History of the Revolution*, supposedly written in 1793–4 but published in 1814 (cited in Geggus, 82), and an oral report by Cécile Fatiman, a *manbò* who witnessed the event, published in her grandson's Étienne Charlier's writings.

4 Especially after the publication of Jean Price-Mars' influential *Ainsi parla l'oncle ...* (1928), discussed in the next chapter.

5 Then in most British Caribbean colonies in 1838; in the French ones in 1848; in the U.S. in 1865; and only recently, when St John wrote his text, in Puerto Rico (1873) and Cuba (1880).

6 This travel boom was compounded with the brief period of stability

prompted by the rise to power of Paul Magloire, a Black leader sympathetic to U.S. policies.

7 An example of this rhetoric: 'In frenzied trance, the priest lets blood [...] The priest bites out the chicken's tongue with his teeth and may suck on the bloody stump of the neck. These sacrifices, infected with one of the Type C oncogenic retroviruses, which is closely related to HTLV, are [...] repeatedly sacrificed [*sic*] in voodoo ceremonies, and their blood is directly ingested by priests and their assistants' (cited in Farmer, *AIDS and Accusation* 81).

8 Such racism is clearly manifested in this letter to an editor cited by Farmer: 'Thank God there are men like President Bush who have the moral strength to take a stand. Haitians are worthless, genetically inferior scum [...] The elimination of the nigger with the AIDS virus is the greatest thing that has happened to the world [...] The U.S. Navy should use the Haitian boats for target practice' (342).

9 *Vodou* is manifestly a syncretic religion, 'syncretism' generally referring to the mixing or fusing of different religious traditions. However, as my brief synopsis reveals, this syncretism continues to be further modified in different sociopolitical and historical contexts. Thus, *vodou* should be viewed in terms of 'engaged' or 'inventive' syncretism, as defined by Christopher Balme (13).

10 'Creolization' refers to the dialectical interaction between cultures within a wider intercultural process, and has been associated with chaos theory (Benítez Rojo), as well with the carnivalesque (Bakhtin).

11 Several historical analyses, especially Paul Johnson's and Julie Heath's brilliant articles on the subject, have explored this topic further.

12 Excerpts of this prayer, as well as radio broadcasts of Duvalier's *vodou* ceremonies, are featured in Avila and Gee's *Krik Krak: Tales of a Nightmare*.

8 'Zombi Fictions'

1 All translations from French and *kreyòl* are mine. Please note that this editorial does not follow standard orthography, as it was published before 1985, when *kreyòl* was standardized. A translation of this epigraph is provided later in the chapter.

2 It is important to recognize that most of the works discussed in this chapter would not be read by readers in Haiti. Western books are not easily accessible and are exorbitantly expensive for the average Haitian, whose income is approximately U.S.$350 per annum. As well, a large

proportion of ordinary Haitians are illiterate (50 per cent according to U.N. statistics) or do not read French.

3 This subtlety is nicely revealed by the classic proverb *'palè frasè pa espri'* (just because you speak French, does not mean you are intelligent).

4 See, e.g., Hurbon and Bébel-Gisler (111–13), Hoffman (196–7), Laguerre (101–21), Dash (16–22, 82–5), and Saint-Louis and Houtart (108–67).

5 For more information on these Haitian novels and their appropriations from oral literature, magic realism, and the gothic fantastic, see Maximilien Laroche's *La double scène de représentation* (2000), or for a shorter overview of the zombie figure in Haitian, his article, 'Imaginaire populaire et littérature: Le hougan, le zombie et le mécréant.'

6 Les dieux courent après la haine que j'accumule en moi depuis ma naissance, depuis le jour où je me suis rendu compte que je suis un nègre d'Haïti, colonisé jusqu'aux os. Les dieux savent que je hais les zombis nègres, que je hais ma peau, le soleil, la mer, tout ce qui me fait songer que je suis de la race de ceux qui tuent.

7 Les Nègres croient aux zombis. Les Blancs à la bombe. Les Nègres ressuscitent des morts [...] Derrière la logique du Blanc il y a les zombis du Nègre [...] Par le pouvoir des morts, les nègres d'Haïti inventeront la bombe H (23).

8 Obsession quotidienne, l'Immigration canadienne. Permettez monsieur que je vous étrangle, que j'incendie votre ville, que je marche sur votre cadavre. Permettez monsieur l'Officier qu'avec mon bâton magique je vous transporte dans mon écurie pour faire mon chemin de croix, de la même façon que votre Christ sous les griffes d'une bête, sous les bottes d'un bourreau [...] Je vous rends un grand service en vous étranglant. Je vous débarrasse de la plus cruelle maladie qui détruit votre race, la haine d'une espèce (148).

9 J'avais compris. Impossible pour un Blanc de l'extérieur de pénétrer dans un tel univers, même avec la science la plus raffinée de la terre, même avec la générosité du saint le plus saint du ciel. Non par indifférence. Les cervelles détraquées articulent partout les mêmes langages. Par les marques culturelles, la superposition des mondes, le repli sur soi imposé par des frontières (244).

10 Tu t'absentes de la patrie trop longtemps, la métamorphose s'opère, l'exil fait de toi un intrus, un étranger partout même chez toi, la distance et les années creusent un gouffre-indifférence, au sortir de rêves agités, l'insensé réveil dans ton lit transformé en Dieu sait quoi, un mutant, un hybride, enfin quelqu'un, quelque chose d'autre, mais plus un Haïtien (111).

11 In her story, the woman is termed a *lougarou* or werewolf, a demonic form inhabited by men. Women would be considered *soucouyant* or witches, as depicted by Danticat. This translation from *soucouyant* to *lougarou* exemplifies one of the many creative 'cultural translations' Danticat performs in her work.

12 In July 1981 alone, more than 4,000 Haitians reached the coast of Florida alive, while thousands more dead washed up along the U.S. coasts.

13 Under Reagan's administration, an agreement between the U.S. and Haiti enabled the U.S. Coast Guard to stop boatloads of Haitians and return them to Haiti – to face political persecution, imprisonment, and even death. Between 1981 and 1991 more than 25,000 migrants were thus inter-dicted; only six were 'screened in' to the U.S. By comparison, 75,000 Cuban refugees were picked up in that same period, and all of them, including convicted criminals, were granted immediate asylum. In 1992 President Bush Sr reinstated a policy of interdiction and repatriation, which prevented Haitians from applying for asylum, a policy that was later continued by President Clinton in 1993. Although in recent years, Haitians have been granted better treatment, the policy of detention in Krone prison continues. According to a 23 April 2003 ruling by Attorney General Ashcroft, any illegal immigrant can be detained indefinitely to address national security concerns.

14 In 2002 only 27,000 Haitians were admitted to the U.S., most of them as immediate family. Only 200 were admitted on employment preferences and 735 as asylum seekers.

15 *Konpe* means 'godfather' in *kreyòl*, but it also refers to a traditional folk-tale figure, *Konpe* Lapin, a figure of cleverness and cunning.

16 I am very much indebted to N'Zengou-Tayo's article (1998), one of the rare articles on the use of *vodou* in a number of Haitian and American texts.

17 This song may reflect a standardized Haitian song of complaint: 'I cried/ Oh when I lost my mother I cried!' It is described by Courlander, in *Haiti Singing* (60).

18 In other incarnations, Gran Bwa/Legba is also linked to Loko Atisò, a wise old man pictured sitting under tree with a cane, invoked in times of sickness or bad fortune, as well as Loko Ayizan, a healer associated with vegetation.

19 Les dieux du vaudou ne voyagent pas dans le Nord. Ces dieux sont trop frileux. Je serai donc seul pour affronter ce nouveau monde. Un univers avec ses codes, ses symboles.

9 'Painless' Fictions

1 All translations from the Czech are mine.
2 As a case in point, a portion of Part IV was published in the *Slavic and East European Journal* (85.1) as 'The Czech Emigré Experience of Return after 1989.'
3 Jiří Payne, 'Vzkaz krajanům.' *Československý týdeník*, 29 July 1993, reprinted in *Listy* 23:5 (1993): 89–91.
4 Most of *Listy* 23:5 (1993) is devoted to this issue, as is *Český dialog* 3:21 (1993).
5 European Commission Regular Report from the Commission on Progress towards Accession, Brussels, 1998.
6 *Chalupáři* refers to those people who, in communist times, took up dilapidated country houses (*chalupy*), fixed them up for years on end, and lived in them on weekends, thus escaping from the city and politics.
7 'Y(oung) A(mericans in) P(rague).' *New York Times Magazine* (12 Dec. 1993): 671.
8 Goluboff is responding to an earlier version of this chapter, which I presented at a conference.
9 Estimates from Česká tisková kancelář,'Historie české emigrace se píše téměř čtyři století.' *Mladá fronta dnes* 4 May (1998): 7. Actual figures remain unknown.
10 The oeuvre of these exiled Czech writers is vast and varied. Grygar presumes that the reader is familiar with both these writers' works, and those of other Czech exiled writers. Some of the seminal novels by these particular authors include Kundera's *Žert* (*The Joke*) and *Valčík na rozloučenou* (*The Farewell Party*); Josef Škvorecký's *Mirákl* (*Miracle Game*) and *Příběh inženýra lidských duší* (*The Engineer of Human Souls*); Jaroslav Vejvoda's *Zelené víno* (Green Wine) and *Osel aneb splynutí* (The Ass or Metamorphosis); Jan Beneš' *Zelenou nahoru* (*Kiss Me, I Am Bohemian*), and Sylvie Richterová's *Návraty a jiné ztráty* (Returns and Other Losses).
11 Some notable exceptions include Jan Novák's *Striptease Chicago* and *Willy's Dream Kit*; Iva Pekárková's *Gimme the Money* and *Gang zjizvených*; or Jan Beneš' *Zelenou nahoru*. Note that several of these texts were published in English.
12 In his description of being 'outside the circle,' Pfaff cites Milan Kundera's *Kniha smíchu a zapomnění* (*The Book of Laughter and Forgetting*; Toronto: 68 Publishers, 1981), 84.

10 'The Suffering of Return'

1 In the Czech case, e.g., see Drábek's *Po uši postkomunismu*; Gruša's *Česko – návod k použití*; Chudožilov's *Proč necítím národní hrdost*, and Kotas, *Klaus a jeho éra*.

2 See Josef Škvorecký's *Dvě vraždy v mém dvojím životě*, or his series with Zdena Salivarová, *Krátké setkání, s vraždou*; *Setkání po letech, s vraždou*; *Setkání na konci éry, s vraždou*.

3 See, e.g., Pekárková's *Do Indie kam jinam, Třicet dva chwanů*; *Najdža hvězdy v srdci*.

4 From a personal interview with the author, Prague, 2000.

5 Interestingly, the medieval term 'translatio' or 'translation' referred to the ritualistic deposit of remains in the church.

6 In Czechoslovakia, 'normalization' generally refers to the period 1969–87. At this time, no reforms or deviations from the Soviet socialist model were allowed.

7 Kundera's etymological fondness here was one of the reasons the novel was first published in Spanish.

8 See, e.g., the special edition 'Émigrés: Exiled at Home and Abroad' of *New Presence* (Winter 2003).

9 Poet, translator, and essayist Jan Vladislav was a renowned dissident, a signatory of Charta 77, and importantly, the publisher of the samizdat press Kvart.

For a Responsive Conclusion

1 Interestingly, already in October 2001, a special issue of the Catholic periodical *America* (185 no. 13), 'Immigration and Terrorism,' showed the inextricable link between these paradigms. In his article 'The Issues Have Become Blurred and Entangled' (8–9), Robert McChesney points out that in the U.S., more than 20,000 non-citizens, including 5,000 minors are detained because of the Illegal Immigration Reform and Immigrant Responsibility Act (IIRIRA), passed in 1996 – more than five times the number in the mid-1990s. Indeed, the number of people detained and deported because of the Patriot Act and accompanying immigration legislation has only increased; however, exact numbers are unknown because of 'security' and 'intelligence' reasons.

2 Examples of such legislation include the Patriot Act (Oct. 2001), the Enhanced Border Security and Visa Entry Reform Act (2002), the creation

of the Department of Homeland Security (2001), and the consequent dismantling of the Immigration and Naturalization Service (2003).

3 Examples include the creation of the 370-mile triple-layered fence along the Mexican border, deportation, incarceration of illegal workers, and the proposed bill H.R. 4437.

4 Notably, the collected writings of the late Abdelmalek Sayad, whose seminal ethnopsychological studies of the immigrant condition inspired much of my research, have recently been translated into English under the *a propos* title, *The Suffering of the Immigrant* (2004).

5 Rousseau, in his *Emile*, also draws his account from Aristotle's classical tradition, and argues that an awareness of vulnerability is a requirement for pity. I cite this marvellous quote to illustrate this point: 'Why are kings without pity for their subjects? Because they count on never being human beings. Why are the rich so hard towards the poor? It is because they have no fear of being poor. Why does a noble have such contempt for a peasant? It is because he never will be a peasant' (224).

6 Lessing's remarks on the affective role of theater nicely echo Frye's famous deliberation on the value of literature: 'What good is the study of literature? Does it help us to think more clearly, or feel more sensitively, or live a better life?' (1).

7 *Der mitleidigste Mensch ist der beste Mensch,* zu allen gesellschaftlichen Tugenden, zu allen Arten der Großmuth der aufgelegteste (italics in original).

8 Smith perceived sympathy as an instinctive relationship wherein the interests of the actor and the spectator are in mutual concord. He even believed that 'by the imagination,' the spectator can empathically place himself or herself in the situation of those suffering, even experiencing their pain as if physically, and he also pointed to instances in which the spectator commiserates with those who are not even conscious of their pain, such as the mentally ill, infants, or the dead.

9 Here I refer to Martha Nussbaum's article 'Cosmopolitan Emotions?' in the *New Humanist,* and her book *Cultivating Humanity.* She elaborates on the ethical value of compassion in her book, especially in chapter 3, 'Narrative Imagination.'

10 In *Compassion: A New Philosophy of the Other,* Krieglstein develops a theory of transcendental perspectivism 'learning to see and experience the world through the eyes of others' (7).

11 Citations from *Oxford English Dictionary* (*OED*), 2nd ed., eds. Simpson and Weiner (Oxford: Oxford University Press, 1989).

12 Nietzsche's 'Mitleiden' is generally translated as 'pity' (Kaufman 220);
    however, Nauckhoff's recent translation (2001) translates it as 'compas-
    sion' (152).
13 For further insight on the connections between literature, ethics, and
    affect, I urge readers to browse the summer 2007 issue of the *University of
    Toronto Quarterly*, 'The Ethical Turn in Canadian Literature and Criticism'
    (Goldman and Pysen, eds., 2007). Scholars in this volume elaborate on
    many of the theorists addressed in this conclusion (Nussbaum, Frye,
    Massumi, Altieri) and in so doing, they point to the 'opacity,' 'complexity
    and messiness' (823) of reading literatures of the other, as well as to the
    ambiguity of our responses and motives as readers and critics. Particu-
    larly valuable is the discussion on compassionate reader-responses: for
    instance, empathetic reading may 'refine our sensibilities' (821), lead us
    'in the direction of greater human solidarity' (824), just as it can lead to
    'narcissism,' 'ethical egoism,' and even 'excessive empathy as pathology'
    (951–2).

References

Abbott, Elizabeth. *Haiti: The Duvaliers and Their Legacy*. New York: McGraw-Hill, 1988.

Abe, Jennifer, and Zane Nolan. 'Psychological Maladjustment among Asian and White College Students: Controlling for Confounds.' *Journal of Counseling Psychology* 37 (1990): 437–44.

Abu-Lughod, Lila, and Catherine Lutz. *Language and the Politics of Emotion*. Cambridge and New York: Cambridge University Press, 1990.

Aciman, André. *Out of Egypt: A Memoir*. New York: Farrar, Straus and Giroux, 1994.

Adda, Bouabdellah. *L'Entre-Deux Vies*. Paris: Marsa, 1999.

Adolf, Jacek. 'Adaptation of East European Refugees and Political Émigrés in Toronto with Special Reference to Immigrants from Poland and Czechoslovakia.' Unpublished doctoral dissertation, York University, Toronto, 1977.

Ahmed, Sara. *The Cultural Politics of Emotion*. New York: Routledge, 2004.

Akhtar, Salman July. *Immigration and Identity: Turmoil, Treatment, and Transformation*. Northvale, NJ: Jason Aronson, 1999.

Alford, C. Fred. 'Greek Tragedy and Civilization: The Cultivation of Pity.' *Political Research Quarterly* 46 (1993): 259–90.

Alger, Horatio. *Struggling Upward; and Other Works*. New York: Crown Publishers, [1890] 1945.

Altieri, Charles. 'Lyrical Ethics and Literary Experience.' *Mapping the Ethical Turn : A Reader in Ethics, Culture, and Literary Theory*. Eds. Todd Davis and Kenneth Womack. Charlottesville: University Press of Virginia, 2001. 30–58.

Amara, Fadela Zappi Sylvia. *Ni putes ni soumises*. Paris: Découverte, 2003.

Andrieux, Claude (Youcef M.D.). *Je rêve d'une autre vie: (Moi, le clandestin de l'écriture)*. Vauvert: Au diable Vauvert, 2002.

– *Le Ghost Writer*. Vauvert: Au diable Vauvert, 2003.

Anonymous. 'Min sèl 41.' *Sèl* 6.41 (1978): 21.

Antin, Mary. *The Promised Land*. Boston, New York: Houghton Mifflin, 1912.

Apollon, Willy. *Le Vaudou: un espace pour les voix*. Paris: Galilée, 1976.

Aristide, Jean-Bertrand. *Aristide: An Autobiography*. Trans. Christophe Wargny. Maryknoll, NY: Orbis, 1993.

Aristotle. *Rhetoric*. Trans. Rhys Roberts. Internet Classics Archive.

Ashcroft, Bill, ed. *The Postcolonial Studies Reader*. London: Routledge, 1995.

Avila, Jac, and Vanyoska Gee. *Krik Krak: Tales of a Nightmare*. Chicago: Facets Video, [1997], 2000.

Bahrampour, Tara. *To See and See Again: A Life in Iran and America*. New York: Farrar, Straus and Giroux, 1999.

Bahri, Hamid. 'Patriarchy and the Figure of the Father in the Francophone Maghrebian Novel from the Nineteen Fifties to the End of the Twentieth Century.' Unpublished doctoral dissertation, City University of New York, 2004.

Bakhtin, Mikhael. *The Dialogic Imagination: Four Essays*. Trans. Michael Holquist. Austin: University of Texas Press, 1981.

Balme, Christopher. 'Inventive Syncretism. The Concept of the Syncretic in Intercultural Discourse.' *Fusion of Cultures?* Eds. Peter Stummer and Christopher Balme. Amsterdam and Atlanta, GA: Rodopi, 1996. 9–18.

Barthes, Roland. *Mythologies*. Paris: Seuil, 1957.

Bassnett, Susan, and Harish Trivedi. *Post-Colonial Translation: Theory and Practice*. London and New York: Routledge, 1999.

BBC. *Profile: Jean-Marie Le Pen*. http://news.bbc.co.uk/2/hi/europe/3658399.stm.

Begag, Azouz. *Le Gone du Chaâba*. France: Seuil, 1986.

Bell, Vicki. 'Owned Suffering: Thinking the Feminist Political Imagination with Simone de Beauvoir and Richard Wright.' *Transformations: Thinking through Feminism*. Ed. Sara Ahmed. New York: Routledge, 2000, 61–77.

Bellil, Samira Stoquart Josée. *Dans l'enfer des tournantes*. Paris: Denoël, 2002.

Ben, Myriam. 'L'Emigré.' *Ainsi naquit un homme: nouvelles*. Paris: L'Harmattan, 1993. 135–73.

Ben Jelloun, Tahar. *La Plus Haute des Solitudes: Misère sexuelle d'émigrés nord-africains*. Paris: Seuil, 1977.

– 'Problèmes affectifs et sexuels de travailleurs nord-africains en France.' Doctoral dissertation. University of Paris VII-Jussieu, 1975.

– *La Réclusion solitaire*. Paris: Denoël, 1976.

Ben Mansour, Latifa. *L'Année de l'éclipse*. Paris: Calmann-Lévy, 2000.

Bendahman, Hossaïn. *Travail culturel de la pulsion et rapport à l'altérité: Langue, corps et inconscient*. Paris: L'Harmattan, 2000.

Bending, Lucy. *The Representation of Bodily Pain in Late Nineteenth-Century English Culture*. New York: Oxford University Press, 2000.

Bendová, Jana. 'Klikaté cesty k srdci krajanů.' *Mladá fronta dnes* 5 Feb. 1994: 6.

Beneš, Jan. *Zelenou nahoru : Kiss Me, I Am Bohemian : Kriminaloidní sci-fiction přítomné minulé budoucnosti*. Toronto: Sixty-Eight Publishers, 1977.

Beneš, Josef D. *Návraty*. Prague: Primus, 1998.

– *Dospívání: Smutek domu*. Prague: Primus, 1993

– 'Návraty...' *Prostor* 67/68 (2005): 127–35.

– *Útěky*. Prague: Primus, 1993.

Benguigui, Yamina. *Mémoires d'immigrés*. Paris: Canal+, 1997.

Benjamin, Walter. 'The Task of the Translator.' Trans. Harry Zohn. *Illuminations*. New York: Harcourt and Brace, 1968. 69–82.

Benítez Rojo, Antonio. *The Repeating Island: The Caribbean and the Postmodern Perspective*. Durham: Duke University Press, 1992.

Ben-Sira, Zeev. *Immigration, Stress, and Readjustment*. Westport, CN: Praeger, 1997.

Berger, John. *And Our Faces, My Heart, Brief as Photos*. London: Writers and Readers, 1984.

Berlant, Lauren. *Compassion: The Culture and Politics of an Emotion*. New York: Routledge, 2004.

– 'The Subject of True Feeling: Pain, Privacy and Politics.' *Transformations: Thinking through Feminism*. Ed. Beverley Skeggs. London: New York, 2000, 33–48.

Bhabha, Homi K. *The Location of Culture*. London and New York: Routledge, 1994.

Bigas, Jiří. 'Vztah k vlastním emigrantům je zkouškou národní zralosti.' *Mladá fronta dnes* 4 May 1998: 7.

Bísek, Petr. 'Are Czechs Outside of the Country Foreigners?' *New Presence* 2.3 (2000): 35.

Blaga, Lucian. *Spaţiul mioritic*. Bucharest: Cartea Româneasca, 1936.

Boelhower, William. 'The Immigrant Novel as Genre.' *Melus* 8.1 (1981): 3–13.

Boia, Lucian. *History and Myth in Romanian Consciousness*. Budapest: Central European University Press, 2001.

Bonn, Charles. *La Littérature algérienne de langue française et ses lectures: Imaginaire et discours d'idées*. Sherbrooke: Naaman, 1974.

Bonn, Charles, and Farida Boualit. *Paysages littéraires algériens des années 90: Témoigner d'une tragédie?* Paris: L'Harmattan, 1999.

Booth, Wayne. *The Rhetoric of Fiction*. Chicago: University of Chicago Press, 1961.

Boubeker, Ahmed. *Les Mondes de l'ethnicité: La communauté d'expérience des héritiers de l'immigration maghrébine*. Paris: Balland, 2003.

Boudjedra, Rachid. *Topographie idéale pour une agression caractérisée*. Paris: Denoël, 1975.

Boukhedenna, Sakinna. *Journal 'Nationalité: immigré(e).'* Paris: L'Harmattan, 1987.

Bourdieu, Pierre. 'Preface.' Abdelmalek Sayad, *The Suffering of the Immigrant*. Trans. David Macey. Cambridge: Polity Press, 2004. xi–xv.

Bouzid. *La Marche: Traversée de la France profonde*. Paris: Sindbad, 1984.

Bravo, Irene, and Ondina Arrufat. 'The Illness Attitude Scales: Adaptation and Translation into Spanish for Use with Older Adults.' *Journal of Applied Gerontology* 24.4 (2005): 355–71.

Brown, Wendy. *States of Injury: Power and Freedom in Late Modernity*. Princeton, NJ: Princeton University Press, 1995.

Brueggemann, Brenda Jo. *Lend Me Your Ear: Rhetorical Constructions of Deafness*. Washington, DC: Gallaudet University Press, 1999.

Burke, Kenneth. *A Grammar of Motives*. Berkeley: University of California Press, 1969.

Burnett, Angela. 'Care of Refugees and Asylum Seekers.' *Ethnicity, Health and Primary Care*. Ed. Joe Kai. Oxford: Oxford University Press, 2003, 195–205.

Cahan, Abraham. *The Rise of David Levinsky*. New York and London: Harper, 1917.

Cantor-Graae, Elizabeth, et al. 'Migration as a Risk Factor for Schizophrenia: A Danish Population-Based Cohort Study.' *British Journal of Psychiatry* 182.2 (2003): 117–22.

Caron, David. *AIDS in French Culture: Social Ills, Literary Cures*. Madison: University of Wisconsin Press, 2001.

Caruth, Cathy. *Trauma: Explorations in Memory*. Baltimore: Johns Hopkins University Press, 1995.

Cernovsky, Zach. 'Refugees' Repetitive Nightmares.' *Journal of Clinical Psychology* 44.5 (1988): 702–7.

Chai, Arlene J. *The Last Time I Saw Mother*. New York: Fawcett Columbine, 1995.

Chambers, Ross. *Facing It: AIDS Diaries and the Death of the Author*. Ann Arbor: University of Michigan Press, 1998.

– *Room for Maneuver: Reading (the) Oppositional (in) Narrative*. Chicago: University of Chicago Press, 1991.

Chancy, Myriam. *Framing Silence: Revolutionary Novels by Haitian Women*. New Brunswick: Rutgers University Press, 1997.

– *Searching for Safe Spaces: Afro-Caribbean Women Writers in Exile*. Philadelphia: Temple University Press, 1997.

Charef, Mehdi. *Le Thé au harem d'Archi Ahmed*. Paris: Mercure de France, 1983.

Charlier, Etienne D. *Aperçu sur la formation historique de la nation haïtienne*. Port-au-Prince: Presses libres, 1954.

Chauvet, Marie. *Amour, colère et folie*. [Paris]: Gallimard, 1968.

Chong, Denise. *The Concubine's Children: Portrait of a Family Divided*. New York: Viking, 1994.

Chraïbi, Driss. *Les Boucs*. Paris: Denoël, 1955.

– *Passé simple*. Paris: Denoël, [1954] 1986.

Christenfeld, Timothy. 'Alien Expressions: Wretched Refuse Is Just the Start.' *New York Times* 10 Mar. 1996: Sec. 4, 4.

Chudožilov, Petr. *Proč necítím národní hrdost*. Prague: Dauphin, 1999.

Cohen, Stanley. *States of Denial: Knowing about Suffering and Atrocity*. Malden, MA: Polity Press, 2001.

Cole, Ellen, et al., eds. *Refugee Women and Their Mental Health: Shattered Societies, Shattered Lives*. New York: Haworth, 1992.

Cooper, Brian. 'Immigration and Schizophrenia: The Social Causation Hypothesis Revisited.' *British Journal of Psychiatry* 186.5 (2005): 361–63.

Courlander, Harold. *The Drum and the Hoe; Life and Lore of the Haitian People*. Berkeley: University of California Press, 1960.

– *Haiti Singing*. Chapel Hill: University of North Carolina Press, 1939.

Čulík, Jan. *Knihy za ohradou: česká literatura v exilových nakladatelstvích, 1971–1989*. Prague: Trizonia, 1991.

Danticat, Edwidge. *Krik? Krak!* New York: Vintage, 1996.

– 'Let My People Stay.' *Essence* July (1994): 124.

Dash, J. Michael. *Culture and Customs of Haiti*. Westport, CN: Greenwood, 2001.

Daswani, Kavita. *For Matrimonial Purposes*. New York: Putnam, 2003.

Davis, Wade. *The Serpent and the Rainbow*. New York: Simon and Schuster, 1985.

Déjeux, Jean *Littérature maghrébine de langue française: Introduction générale et auteurs*. Sherbrooke: Naaman, 1978.

Den, Peter. 'V zamyšlení nad tak zvanou únikovou literaturou.' *Sklizeň* 3(1).25 (1955): 6–7.

Deng, Alephonsion, et al. *They Poured Fire on Us from the Sky: The True Story of Three Lost Boys from Sudan*. New York: Public Affairs, 2005.

Depestre, René. *Alléluia pour une femme-jardin*. Paris: Gallimard, 1981.

– *Hadriana dans tous mes rêves*. Paris: Gallimard, 1988.

- 'Interview.' *Callaloo* 15.2 (1992): 550–4.
Derrida, Jacques. 'The Law of Genre.' Trans. A. Ronnell. *Glyph* 7 (1980): 176–232.
Deren, Maya. *Divine Horsemen; Voodoo Gods of Haiti*. New York: Chelsea House, [1953] 1970.
Desmangles, Leslie Gérald. *The Faces of the Gods: Vodou and Roman Catholicism in Haiti*. Chapel Hill: University of North Carolina Press, 1992.
Diamant, Jiří. *Psychologické problémy emigrace*. Olomouc: Matice Cyrilometodejská, 1995.
Djaïdani, Rachid. *Boumcœur*. Paris: Seuil, 1999.
Djemaï, Abdelkader. *31, rue de l'aigle*. Paris: Editions Michalon, 1998.
Doudier, Samira. 'Littératures maghrébines et subsahariennes de langue française: L'Image du père.' *Littérature comparée et didactique du texte francophone*. Paris: L'Harmattan, 1999.
Douin, Jean-Luc. 'La Cabale contre Paul Smaïl.' *Le Monde* 2 Mar. 2001 http://www.lexis-nexis.com.
Drábek, Jan. *Po uši postkomunismu*. Prague: Knižní klub Ikar, 2000.
- 'Emigrant není označení morální, ale geographické.' *Mladá fronta dnes* 9 May 1994: 6.
Dunkas, Nicholas, and Arthur G. Nikelly. 'The Persephone Syndrome: A Study of Conflict in the Adaptive Process of Married Greek Female Immigrants in the U.S.A.' *Social Psychiatry* 7.4 (1972): 211–16.
During, Simon, ed. *The Cultural Studies Reader*, 2nd ed. London: Routledge, 1999.
Duvalier, François. *Mémoires d'un leader du tiers monde: Mes négociations avec le Saint-Siège; ou, une tranche d'histoire*. Paris: Hachette, 1969.
- *Oeuvres essentielles*. Port-au-Prince: Presses Nationales d'Haïti, 1968.
Dyk, Viktor 'Země mluví.' *Česká poezie dvacátého století*. Ed. Milan Blahynka. Prague: Český Spisovatel, 1980. 69.
Edmondson, Belinda. *Making Men: Gender, Literary Authority, and Women's Writing in Caribbean Narrative*. Durham: Duke University Press, 1999.
Eggers, Dave. *What is the What: The Autobiography of Valentino Achak Deng: A Novel*. San Francisco: McSweeney's, 2006.
Eisenstein, Zillah R. *Against Empire: Feminisms, Racism, and the West*. New York: Palgrave Macmillan, 2004.
Eitinger, Leo, and David Schwarz. *Strangers in the World*. Bern: Huber, 1981.
Etienne, Gérard. 'Interview.' *Callaloo* 15.2 (1992): 498–500.
- *La Pacotille*. Montréal, Québec: Hexagone, 1991.
- *Le Nègre crucifié: récit*. Montréal: Éditions Balzac, [1974] 1994.
Eze, Emmanuel Chukwudi. 'Beyond Dichotomies: Communicative Action

and Cultural Hegemony.' *Beyond Dichotomies: Histories, Identities, Cultures, and the Challenge of Globalization*. Ed. M. Elisabeth Mudimbe-Boyi. Albany: State University of New York (SUNY) Press, 2002, 49–68.

Fanon, Frantz. *Black Skin, White Masks*. London: MacGibbon and Kee, 1968.

– 'Le "syndrome nord-africain."' *Esprit* 20.2 (1952): 237–51.

– *Peau noire, masques blancs*. Paris: Seuil, 1965.

Farmer, Paul. *AIDS and Accusation: Haiti and the Geography of Blame*. Berkeley: University of California Press, 1992.

– 'On Suffering and Structural Violence: A View from Below.' *Daedalus* 125.1 (1996): 261–83.

– *Pathologies of Power: Health, Human Rights, and the New War on the Poor*. Berkeley: University of California Press, 2003.

Felman, Shoshana, and Dori Laub. *Testimony: Crises of Witnessing in Literature, Psychoanalysis, and History*. New York: Routledge, 1991.

Filip, Ota. 'Identita v cizině.' *Tvar* 11 Nov. 1995: 13.

– *Poskvrněné početí*. Toronto: 68 Publishers, 1976.

Fischer, Petr. 'Kunderovy marné návraty.' *Lidové noviny* 15 Feb. 2003: 13.

Formánek, Jaroslav. *Beze stop*. Prague: Torst, 2001.

Frankétienne. *Dézafi*. Port-au-Prince, Haiti: Fardin, 1975.

Franklin, Benjamin. *Way to Wealth*. Middletown, CN: Hart and Lincoln, 1814.

Fraser, Nancy. 'From Redistribution to Recognition? Dilemmas of Justice in a "Post-Socialist" Age.' *New Left Review* 212 (1995): 68–93.

'Freedom Is Hard to Handle (East European Writers).' *Economist* 316.7665 (1990): 73–4.

Frye, Northrop. *The Educated Imagination*. Toronto: CBC Publications, 1963.

Gans, Eric. 'The Culture of Resentment.' *Philosophy and Literature* 8.1 (1984): 55–66.

Geggus, David. *Haitian Revolutionary Studies*. Bloomington: Indiana University Press, 2002.

Genette, Gérard. *Théorie des genres*. Paris: Seuil, 1986.

Gilroy, Paul. *Against Race: Imagining Political Culture Beyond the Color Line*. Cambridge, MA.: Belknap Press of Harvard University Press, 2000.

Girard, René. *Violence and the Sacred*. Trans. Patrick Gregory. Baltimore: Johns Hopkins University Press, 1977.

Glissant, Edouard. 'The Unforeseeable Diversity of the World.' *Beyond Dichotomies: Histories, Identities, Cultures, and the Challenge of Globalization*. Ed. M. Elisabeth Mudimbe-Boyi. Albany: SUNY Press, 2002. 287–95.

God Grew Tired of Us. Dir. Christopher Quinn. DVD. Sony Pictures Home Entertainment, 2007.

Goldman, Marlene, and Kristina Kyser, eds. 'The Ethical Turn in Canadian

Literature and Criticism.' *University of Toronto Quarterly* 76.3 Special issue (2007): 809–1006.

Goluboff, Sasha. 'Discussant Remarks: Mobility, Labor and the Ties That Bind.' *Anthropology of East Europe Review (AEER)* 2002. Accessed 14 June 2005. http://condor.depaul.edu/~rrotenbe/aeer/v20n2/Goluboff.pdf.

Gopaul-McNicol, Sharon, et al. 'Working With Haitian-Canadian Families.' *International Journal for the Advancement of Counselling* 20 (1998): 231–42.

Gorlée, Dinda. *On Translating Signs: Exploring Text and Semio-Translation.* Amsterdam and New York: Rodopi, 2004.

Groleau, Danielle. 'La détresse et l'enfantement: l'hyperemesis gravidarum revisité en contexte migratoire.' *Évolution Psychiatrique* 70.3 (2005): 623–41.

Grinberg, León, and Rebeca Grinberg. *Psychoanalytic Perspectives on Migration and Exile.* New Haven: Yale University Press, 1989.

Grosselle, Jean. 'Le Mal partout.' Doctoral dissertation. Université de Marseille, 1979.

Gruša, Jiří. *Česko – návod k použití* Prague: Barrister and Principal, 2001.

Grygar, Mojmír. 'Proměny spisovatele v exilu.' *Listy* 13.3 (1988): 93–101.

Haasen, Christian, et al. 'Impact of Ethnicity on the Prevalence of Psychiatric Disorders among Migrants in Germany.' *Ethnicity and Health* 3.3 (1998): 159–65.

Hais, Karel. *Velký anglicko-český slovník.* 4 vols. Prague: Academia, 1991.

Halimi, Serge. 'Les Terroirs de l'extrême droite.' *Le Monde diplomatique.* May 1998. Accessed 21 Sept. 2001 http://www.monde-diplomatique.fr/1998/05/HALIMI/10472

Hall, Edward Twitchell. *The Silent Language.* Westport, CN: Greenwood, [1959] 1980.

– *Beyond Culture.* Garden City, NY: Anchor, 1976.

Haman, Aleš. 'Jaroslav Formánek je stopař prchavých okamžiků.' *Lidové noviny* 26 June 2001: 20.

– 'Trauma odchodů a návratů.' *Nové knihy* 40.47 (2001): 38.

Hanák, Jiří. 'Exil, emigrace a my domácí.' *Český dialog* 7/8 (1995): 6.

Handlin, Oscar. *The Uprooted.* Boston: Little Brown, [1952] 1990.

Haour-Knipe, Mary. *Moving Families: Expatriation, Stress and Coping.* London: New York, 2001.

Hardt, Michael, and Antonio Negri. *Empire.* Cambridge, MA: Harvard University Press, 2000.

Hargreaves, Alec. 'Perception of Ethnic Differences in Post-War France.' *Immigrant Narratives in Contemporary France.* Eds. Susan Ireland and Patrice J. Proulx. Westport, CN: Greenwood, 2001. 7–23.

Heath, Julie. 'Representing Haiti: Vodou and Nationalism in the Writings of

François Duvalier and Jean-Bertrand Aristide.' *Midwestern Folklore* 25.1 (1999): 22–41.

Herman, Judith Lewis. *Trauma and Recovery*. New York: Basic, 1992.

Herskovits, Melville J. *Life in a Haitian Valley*. Garden City, NY,: Anchor, [1937] 1971.

Heywood, Leslie. *Dedication to Hunger: The Anorexic Aesthetic in Modern Culture*. Berkeley: University of California, 1996.

Hjern, Anders, et al. 'Social Adversity Contributes to High Morbidity in Psychoses in Immigrants – a National Cohort Study in Two Generations of Swedish Residents.' *Psychological Medicine* 34.6 (2006): 1025–33.

Hoffman, Eva. *Lost in Translation: A Life in a New Language*. New York: Dutton, 1989.

Hoffmann, Léon-François. *Haïti: couleurs, croyances, créole*. Montreal: CIDIHCA, 1990.

Horáček, Milan, and Jiřina Šiklová. 'Introduction to Conference 'Home/Exile."' *Listy* 22.6 (1992): 1–9.

Houaiss, Antônio, et al. *Dicionário Houaiss da língua portuguesa*. Rio de Janeiro: Editora Objetiva, 2001.

Houari, Kassa. *Confessions d'un immigré: Un Algérien à Paris*. Paris: Lieu Commun, 1988.

Houari, Leïla. *Zeïda de nulle part*. Paris: L'Harmattan, 1985.

Hron, Madelaine. 'In-Car-Ceration or Auto-Mobility?: Ethnic Minorities in the Space of the Car.' *On the Move: Identity and Mobility*. Eds. Krysztof Knauer and Tadeusz Rachwal. Bielsko-Biala: Wyedawnictwo ATH, 2005, 81–98.

Hronová, Madelaine, and Zdena Brodská. 'Kundera a mýtus návratu: *La Ignorancia*.' *Host* 19.4 (2003): 36–8.

Hrzalová, Hana. 'Jan Pelc napsal další prózu o drsném rubu "něžného" sametu.' *Haló Noviny* 21 Mar. 2000: 9.

Hughes, Nicole, and Simon Pardek. 'Coming Back or Coming Home?' *New Presence* (Summer 2005): 27–9.

Hurbon, Laënnec, and Dany Bébel-Gisler. *Cultures et pouvoir dans la Caraïbe: Langue créole, vaudou, sectes religieuses en Guadeloupe et en Haïti*. Paris: L'Harmattan, 1975.

Hutchinson, Gerard, and Christian Haasen. 'Migration and Schizophrenia: The Challenges for European Psychiatry and Implications for the Future.' *Social Psychiatry and Psychiatric Epidemiology* 39.5 (2004): 350–7.

Hvížd'ala, Karel. *České rozhovory ve světě*. Kolín nad Rýnem: Index, 1991.

IASP (International Association for the Study of Pain Subcommittee on Classification). 'Pain Terms: A Current List with Definitions and Notes on Usage.' *Pain* (Suppl 3) (1996): S216–S221.

Ignatieff, Michael. *The Warrior's Honor: Ethnic War and the Modern Conscience*. New York: Holt, 1997.

Imache, Tassadit. *Une fille sans histoire*. Paris: Calmann-Levy, 1989.

International Migration Outlook: Annual Report. Paris: Organisation for Economic Co-operation and Development, 2006.

Ireland, Susan. 'First Generation Immigrant Narratives.' *Immigrant Narratives in Contemporary France*. Eds. Susan Ireland and Patrice Proulx. Westport, CT: Greenwood, 2001. 23–46.

Jacobson, Matthew Frye. *Special Sorrows: The Diasporic Imagination of Irish, Polish, and Jewish Immigrants in the United States*. Cambridge: Harvard University Press, 1995.

Jakobson, Roman. 'On Linguistic Aspects of Translation.' *On Translation*. Ed. Reuben Brower. Cambridge: Harvard University Press, 1959. 232–9.

Jahn, Janheinz. *Muntu: African Culture and the Western World*. New York: Grove Press, 1990.

Jamek, Václav. 'Pěkně divný exil.' *Literární Noviny* 5.12 (1994): 1, 3.

James, C.L.R. *Les Jacobins noirs; Toussaint Louverture et la révolution de Saint-Domingue*. Paris: Gallimard, 1949.

Jarret, Robert. 'Représentation du corps chez le migrant' *Psychologie Médicale* 13.11 (1981): 1719–23.

Jelínek, Ivan. 'Ztráta a zisk.' *Proměny* 104 (1973): 6–10.

Johnson, Paul. 'Secretism and the Apotheosis of Duvalier.' *Journal of the American Academy of Religion* 74.2 (2006): 420–45.

Kacem, Mehdi Belhaj. *Cancer*. Mayenne, France: Tristram, 1994.

Kantůrková, Eva, and Filip Ota. 'Rozhovor na dálku s Evou.' *Listy* 19.2 (1989): 79–81.

Kassovitz, Mathieu. *La Haine*. VHS. PolyGram Video, 1996 [1995].

Kerouani, Dalila. *Une fille d'Algérie, éprise de liberté*. Paris: Laffont, 1991.

Kessas, Ferrudja. *Beur's Story*. Paris: L'Harmattan, 1990.

Kettane, Nacer. *Le Sourire de Brahim*. Paris: Denoël, 1985.

Khaïr-Eddine, Mohammed. *Corps négatif, suivi de histoire d'un bon dieu*. Paris: Éditions du Seuil, 1968.

Khu, Josephine M.T. *Cultural Curiosity: Thirteen Stories about the Search for Chinese Roots*. Berkeley: University of California Press, 2001.

Khuri, Fuad Ishaq Jad. *The Body in Islamic Culture*. London: Saqi, 2001.

Kirchner, Bharti. *Darjeeling*. New York: St Martin's Press, 2002.

Kleinman, Arthur, Veena Das, and Margaret M. Lock. *Social Suffering*. Berkeley: University of California Press, 1997.

Knafo, Daniella, and Ariel Yaari. 'Leaving the Promised Land.' *Immigrant Experiences: Personal Narrative and Psychological Analysis*. Eds. Paul H.

Elovitz and Charlotte Kahn. Madison, NJ: Associated University Presses, 1997. 221–40.

Kontra, Martin. 'Pozor na emigranty.' *Respekt* 6 Mar. 1995: 4.

Kopáč, Radim. 'Pelcova próza je víc dokumentem než uměním.' *Mladá fronta dnes* 2 Mar. 2000: 18.

Kotas, Jiří. *Klaus a jeho éra.* Prague: Adonai, 2003.

Kraut, Alan M. *Silent Travelers: Germs, Genes, and the 'Immigrant Menace.'* New York: Basic, 1994.

Krieglstein, Werner. *Compassion: A New Philosophy of the Other.* Amsterdam and New York: Rodopi, 2002.

Kristeva, Julia. *Black Sun: Depression and Melancholia.* New York: Columbia University Press, 1989.

– *Etrangers à nous-mêmes.* Paris: Fayard, 1988.

– *Lettre Ouverte à Harlem Désir.* Paris: Rivages, 1990.

– *Powers of Horror: An Essay on Abjection.* New York: Columbia University Press, 1982.

– 'Y a-t-il des étrangers heureux?' In *Migrations et errances: Forum international.* Proceedings of UNESCO conference, 8/9 June 2000. Paris: Grasset, 2000. 53–66.

Krzywinska, Tanya. *A Skin for Dancing In: Possession, Witchcraft and Voodoo in Film.* Trowbridge, England: Flicks Books, 2000.

Kubešová, Blanka. *Romance pro Žoržínu.* Zurich: Konfrontace, 1985.

Kugelman, Robert. 'A Phenomenological Analysis of Mental and Physical Pain.' *Problems of Theoretical Psychology.* Ed. Tolman Captus. North York, ON: Captus, 1996.

Kundera, Milan. *Ignorance.* Trans. Linda Asher. New York: HarperCollins, 2002.

– *Kniha smíchu a zapomnění* (The Book of Laughter and Forgetting). Toronto: 68 Publishers, 1981.

– *Valčík na rozloučenou.* Toronto: 68 Publishers, 1979.

– *Žert.* Prague: Československý spisovatel, (Rudé právo), 1968.

Kuo, Wen H., and Yung-Mei Tsai. 'Social Networking and Immigrant's Mental Health.' *Journal of Health and Social Behaviour* 27 (1986): 133–49.

Kuras, Benjamin. *Češi na vlásku: příručka národního přežívání.* Prague: Baronet, 1996.

Kusher, Howard. *Self-Destruction in the Promised Land: A Psychocultural Biology of American Suicide.* New Brunswick, NJ: Rutgers University Press, 1989.

LaCapra, Dominick. *Representing the Holocaust: History, Theory, Trauma.* Ithaca: Cornell University Press, 1994.

Laferrière, Dany. *Comment faire l'amour avec un Nègre sans se fatiguer*. Montréal: VLB, 1985.

– 'Interview.' *Discover Haiti: Literature-Dany Laferrière*. 15 Oct. 2003. http://www.discoverhaiti.com/culture_danylaferriere.htm.

– *Le Cri des oiseaux fous*. Outremont, Quebec: Lanctôt, 2000.

– *Pays sans chapeau*. Outremont, Quebec: Lanctôt, 1996.

Laguerre, Michel S. *Voodoo and Politics in Haiti*. New York: St Martin's Press, 1989.

Lahiri, Jhumpa. *Interpreter of Maladies: Stories*. Boston: Houghton Mifflin, 1999.

Lamming, George. *The Pleasures of Exile*. Ann Arbor: University of Michigan Press, [1960] 1992.

Lang, George. *Entwisted Tongues: Comparative Creole Literatures*. Amsterdam: Rodopi, 2000.

Laroche, Maximilien. *La double scène de la représentation: Oraliture et littérature dans la Caraïbe*. Port-au-Prince, Haïti: Mémoire, 2000.

– 'Imaginaire populaire et littérature: Le hougan, le zombie et le mécréant.' *Notre Libraire* 133 (1998): 82–9.

Laronde, Michel. *Autour du roman beur: Immigration et identité*. Paris: L'Harmattan, 1993.

Lazarus, Emma. 'New Colossus.' New York, NY, (Statue of Liberty), 1883.

Leenaars, Antoon, et al. 'Special issue: Suicide: Individual, Cultural, International Perspectives.' *Suicide and Life-Threatening Behavior* 27.1 (1997).

Lefevere, André. 'Composing the Other.' In *Post-Colonial Translation: Theory and Practice*. Eds. Susan Bassnett and Harish Trivedi. New York: Routledge, 1999. 75–94.

– *Translation, Rewriting, and the Manipulation of Literary Fame*. London and New York: Routledge, 1992.

Lelièvre, Marie Dominique. 'Profil: Comme une plume; Jack-Alain Léger, 53 ans.' *Libération* 23 Sept. 2000: 64.

Lerner,Vladimir, David Greenberg, and Josef Bergman. 'Daughter-Mother *Folie à deux*: Immigration as a Trigger for Role Reversal and the Development of *Folie à deux*.' *Israel Journal of Psychiatry and Related Sciences* 33.4 (1996): 260–4.

Lessing, Gotthold Ephraim. *Hamburg Dramaturgy* (Hamburgische Dramaturgie). Trans. Helen Zimmern. New York: Dover, 1962.

– 'Letter to Nicolai (on Tragedy), 13 Nov. 1756.' Trans. J.P Payne. *The Theory of Criticism from Plato to the Present: A Reader*. Ed. Raman Selden. London: Longman, 1998. 194–5.

Lewis, Philip E. 'The Measure of Translation Effects.' In *Difference in Translation*. Eds. Joseph F. Graham. Ithaca: Cornell University Press, 1985. 253.

Linhartová, Věra. 'Za ontologii exilu.' *Literární Noviny* 9.49 (1998): 1, 5.

Lionnet, Françoise. 'Geographies of Pain: Captive Bodies and Violent Acts in the Fictions of Myriam Warner-Vieyra, Gayl Jones, and Bessie Head.' *Callaloo* 16.1 (1993): 132–52.

– 'Immigration, Poster Art, and Transgressive Citizenship: France 1968–1988.' *Sub-Stance* 76–77 (1995): 93–108.

Listopad, František. 'Z referátu na sjezdu kulturních pracovníků v Paříži.' *Sklizeň* 4.44 (Aug. 1956): 6–7.

Lost Boys of Sudan. Dir. Megan Mylan. DVD. Actual Films, Principe Productions, 2003.

Lukas, Jan. 'Proč jsem zvolil exil až v roce 1966.' *Svědectví* 8.30 (1966): 207–12.

Magloire, Francis Séjour. *Les Chroniques du macoutisme.* Port au Prince: Haïti-Progrès 1986.

Mander, Gertrud. 'The Women's Therapy Centre Language Project: Evaluation.' *British Journal of Psychotherapy* 20.1 (2003): 97–102.

Marcelin, Pierre, Philippe Thoby-Marcelin, and George Cephas Ford. *The Singing Turtle, and Other Tales from Haiti.* New York: Farrar, Straus and Giroux, 1971.

Marks, Deborah. 'Disability and Cultural Citizenship: Exclusion, 'Integration' and Resistance.' *Culture and Citizenship.* Ed. Nick Stevenson. London: Sage, 2001. 167–80.

Marlin, Olga. 'Fleeing toward the New and Yearning for the Old.' *Immigrant Experiences: Personal Narrative and Psychological Analysis.* Eds. Paul H. Elovitz and Charlotte Kahn. Madison, NJ: Fairleigh Dickinson University Press, 1997. 241–55.

Marlinová, Olga. 'Návrat z emigrace není bezbolestný.' *Psychologie dnes* 10.1 (2004): 16–17.

Martínek, Lubomír. *Nomads Land.* Prague: Prostor, 1994.

– *Opilost z hloubky.* Prague: Prostor, 2000.

Massumi, Brian. 'Navigating Movements: An Interview with Brian Massumi.' *21C Magazine.* 20 Aug. 2007. www.21cmagazine.com/issue2/massumi.html.

McNally, David. *Bodies of Meaning: Studies on Language, Labor, and Liberation.* Albany: SUNY Press, 2000.

Meaders, Nobuko. 'The Transcultural Self.' *Immigrant Experiences: Personal Narrative and Psychological Analysis.* Eds. Paul H. Elovitz and Charlotte Kahn. Madison, NJ: Fairleigh Dickinson University Press, 1997, 47–60.

Méliane, Loubna. *Vivre libre.* Paris: Oh, 2003.

Mesmin, Claude. *Les Enfants de migrants à l'école: réussite, échec.* Grenoble: Pensée sauvage, 1993.

– *Psychothérapie des enfants de migrants.* Grenoble: Pensée sauvage, 1995.

Mesmin, Claude, and Tobie Nathan. *La Prise en charge éthnoclinique de l'enfant de migrants.* Paris: Dunod, 2001.

Métraux, Alfred. *Le Vaudou haïtien.* Paris: Gallimard, 1958.

Mian, Emran. 'Smile.' *Herald* (Glasgow) (Culture Section) (2000): 1.

Michal, Karel. *Rodný kraj.* Cologne: Index, 1977.

Mitchell, David T., and Sharon Snyder. *Narrative Prosthesis: Disability and the Dependencies of Discourse.* Ann Arbor: University of Michigan Press, 2000.

Moaveni, Azadeh. *Lipstick Jihad: A Memoir of Growing up Iranian in America and American in Iran.* New York: Public Affairs, 2005.

Moeller, Susan. *Compassion Fatigue: How the Media Sell Disease, Famine, War, and Death.* New York: Routledge, 1999.

Mokeddem, Malika. *Des rêves et des assassins.* Paris: Grasset, 1995.

Moreau de Saint-Méry. *Description topographique, physique, civile, politique et historique de la partie française de l'isle Saint Domingue.* Paris: Société de l'histoire des colonies françaises, [1798] 1958.

Morris, David B. *The Culture of Pain.* Berkeley: University of California Press, 1991.

Mortimer, Mildred P. *Maghrebian Mosaic: A Literature in Transition.* Boulder, CO: L. Rienner, 2001.

Mossallenejed, Ezat. *Torture in the Age of Fear.* Hamilton: Seraphim, 2005.

Mukherjee, Bharati. *Jasmine.* New York: Grove Weidenfeld, 1989.

Nafisi, Azar. *Reading Lolita in Tehran: A Memoir in Books.* New York: Random House, 2003.

Nathan, Tobie. *La Folie des autres: Traité d'ethnopsychiatrie clinique.* Paris: Dunod, 1986.

– *Le Sperme du diable: Éléments d'ethnopsychothérapie.* Paris: Presses universitaires de France, 1988.

Návrat Jana z pařížského exilu do Prahy. Dir. Kateřina Krusová. VHS, FAMU, 2003.

Nešpor, Zdeněk R. 'Reemigrace českých západních emigrantů v 90. letech 20. století z hlediska ekonomické sociologie.' *Sociologický časopis* 41.1 (2005): 31–55.

'The New Trade in Humans.' *Economist,* 5 Aug. 1995: 45–7.

Nhial, Abraham Mills DiAnn. *Lost Boy No More: A True Story of Survival and Salvation.* Nashville: Broadman and Holman, 2004.

Nida, Eugene , and Charles Taber. *The Theory and Practice of Translation.* Leiden: Brill, 1969.

Nietzsche, Friedrich. *Anti-Christ*. Trans. H.L. Mencken. Tuscon AZ: See Sharp Press, 1999.

– *Beyond Good and Evil: Prelude to a Philosophy of the Future*. Trans. W.A. Kaufmann. New York: Vintage Books, 1989.

– *Daybreak: Thoughts on the Prejudices of Morality*. Trans. Maudemarie Clark and Brian Leiter. Cambridge: Cambridge University Press, 1997.

– *The Gay Science; With a Prelude in Rhymes and an Appendix of Songs*. Trans. Walter Arnold Kaufmann. New York: Random House, 1974.

– *Human, All Too Human*. Trans. R.J. Hollingdale. Cambridge U.K.: Cambridge University Press, 1996.

– *On the Genealogy of Morals: A Polemic*. Trans. Douglas Smith. Oxford: Oxford University Press, 1996.

– *Thus Spoke Zarathustra: A Book for Everyone and No One*. Trans. Reginald John Hollingdale. Harmondsworth: Penguin, 1961.

– *Will to Power*. Trans. W.A. Kaufmann and R.J. Hollingdale. New York: Random House, 1967.

Nixon, Rob. *London Calling: V.S. Naipaul, Postcolonial Mandarin*. New York: Oxford University Press, 1992.

Nováček, Petr. 'Je načase integrovat náš exil do národa.' *Mladá fronta dnes* 7 June 1994: 6.

Novák, Jan. *Samet a pára*. Brno: Atlantis, 1992.

– *Willy's Dream Kit*. New York: Harcourt Brace, 1985.

– *Striptease Chicago*. Toronto: 68 Publishers, 1983.

Novikova, Irina. 'Women in Amber and Mothers in Songs: Instruments in Women's Memories (Wakako Yamuchi and Agate Nesaule).' *Literature on the Move: Comparing Diasporic Identities in Europe and the Americas*. Heidelberg: Universitätsverlag, forthcoming.

Novotný, Vladimír. 'O bytostech, které neustále odkládají život na později.' *Tvar* 12.2 (2001): 20–1.

Nussbaum, Martha. 'Cosmopolitan Emotions.' *New Humanist*. Dec 2001. Accessed 6 Mar. 2005. http://www.newhumanist.org.uk/volume116 issue4.php.

– *Cultivating Humanity: A Classical Defense of Reform in Liberal Education*. Cambridge, MA: Harvard University Press, 1997.

N'Zengou-Tayo, Marie-José. 'Vodou et migration dans les romans haïtiens sur la migration populaire des boat-people.' *Conjonction: Bulletin de l'Institut français d'Haïti*. 203 (1998): 33–45.

OECD (Organization for Economic Co-operation and Development). *International Migration Outlook: Annual Report*. 2006. Accessed 10 Dec. 2006. http://www.oecd.org/document/2/0,2340,en_2825_494553_38060354_1_1_1_1,00.html.

Ollivier, Émile. *La Discorde aux cent voix*. Paris: Michel, 1986.
- *Passages*. Montreal: L'Hexagone, 1991.
- *Mille eaux*. Paris: Gallimard, 1999.
- *Regarde, regarde les lions: nouvelles*. Paris: Michel, 2001.
Ortega, Alexander, et al. 'Acculturation and the Lifetime Risk of Psychiatric and Substance Use Disorders among Hispanics.' *Journal of Nervous and Mental Disease* 188.11 (2000): 728–35.
Ovid (Publius Ovidius Naso). *Tristia*. 10 A.D. Accessed 20 March 2005 http://www.ancienttexts.org/library/latinlibrary/ovid/ovid.tristia.html.
Palinkas, L.A. 'Ethnicity, Identity, and Mental Health: The Use of Rhetoric in an Immigrant Chinese Church.' *Journal of Psychoanalytic Anthropology* 5 (1982): 235–58.
Pargeter, Alison. 'North African Immigrants in Europe and Political Violence.' *Studies in Conflict and Terrorism* 29.8 (2006): 731–47.
Pascal, Julia. 'A Beur with a Sore Head.' *Independent* 29 Jan. 2000, sec. (London): 11.
Peale, Norman Vincent. *The Power of Positive Thinking*. New York: Prentice-Hall, 1952.
Péan, Stanley. *Noirs désirs*. Montreal: Leméac, 1999.
- *La Plage des songes et autres récits d'exil*. Saint-Laurent, Quebec: BQ, 1998.
- *Le Tumulte de mon sang*. Montreal: Québec/Amérique, 1991.
- *Sombres allées et autres endroits peu hospitaliers: Treize excursions en territoire de l'insolite*. Montreal: Voix du Sud/CIDIHCA, 1992.
- *Zombi Blues*. Montreal: Courte échelle, 1996.
Pecina, Thomas. 'When Czechs Fight Czechs.' *Central European Review.* 19 July 1999. Accessed 3 Jan. 2005. http://www.ce-review.org/99/4/pecina4.html.
Pehe, Jiří. 'Uprchlíci v moderních českých dějinách.' *Útěk a exil v umění.* Prague: UNHCR, 2003. 22–4.
Pekárková, Iva. *Do Indie kam jinam*. Prague: LN, 2001.
- *Gang zjizvených*. Prague: Mata, 1998.
- *Gimme the Money*. London: Serpent's Tail, 2000.
- *Najdža hvězdy v srdci*. Praha: LN, 2003.
- *Péra a perutě*. Toronto: 68 Publishers, 1989.
- *Třicet dva chwanů*. Prague: MATA, 2000.
- *Truck Stop Rainbows*. New York: Farrar, Straus and Giroux, 1992.
- *The World is Round*. New York: Farrar, Straus and Giroux, 1994.
Pelc, Jan. *...a bude hůře*. Cologne: Index, 1985.
- 'Věřím příští generaci, dnešním patnáctiletým.' *Právo* 7 Dec. 2000, sec. Salon addition: 1–2.
- *...a výstupy do údolí*. Prague: Mata, 2000.

Peroutka, Ferdinand. 'Jak být exulantem.' *Skutečnost* 2.11/12 (1950): 213–16.

Petersen, William. *Japanese Americans: Oppression and Success*. New York: Random House, 1971.

PEW Research Center. *World Publics Welcome Global Trade, But Not Immigration: A 47 Nation Pew Global Attitudes Survey*. Washington, Oct. 2007.

Pfaff, Ivan. 'Zmatky kolem růžového paloučku.' *Svědectví* 19.76 (1984/85): 855–9.

Plantade, Nedjima. *L'Honneur et l'amertume: Le Destin ordinaire d'une femme kabyle*. Paris: Balland, 1993.

Plato. 'Apology.' In *The Trial and Death of Socrates*. Trans. G.M.A. Grube. Indianapolis: Hacket, 1975.

Popovic, Anton. 'The Concept 'Shift of Expression' in Translation Analysis.' *The Nature of Translation*. Ed. James Holmes. The Hague and Paris: Mouton de Gruyter, 1970. 78–87.

Portes, Alejandro, and Rubén Rumbaut. *Legacies: The Story of the Immigrant Second Generation*. Berkeley: University of California Press, 2001.

Povolný, Mojmír. 'Exil a české politické instituce.' *Lidové noviny* 28 June 1995: 8.

Price-Mars, Jean. *Ainsi parla l'oncle...* Port-au-Prince: Imprimerie de Compiègne, 1928.

Propp, Vladimir. *Morphology of the Folktale*. Trans. Louis A. Wagner. Austin: University of Texas Press, 1968.

Rachlin, Nahid. *Foreigner*. New York: Norton, 1978.

Radimski, Ladislav. *Skloňuj tvé jméno exulante!* samizdat, 1967.

Radstone, Susannah. 'Screening Trauma: *Forrest Gump*.' *Memory and Methodology*. Oxford and New York: Berg, 2000. 188–93.

Raïth, Mustapha. *Palpitations intra-muros*. Paris: L'Harmattan, 1986.

Ramsey, Kate. 'Performances of Prohibition: Law, "Superstition," and National Modernity in Haiti.' Doctoral dissertation, New York, Columbia University, 2002.

Rapport, Nigel, and Andrew Dawson. *Migrants of Identity: Perceptions of Home in a World of Movement*. Oxford: Berg, 1998.

Rhodes, Gary Don. *White Zombie: Anatomy of a Horror Film*. Jefferson, NC: McFarland, 2001.

Richards, Ivor A. *The Philosophy of Rhetoric*. New York: Oxford University Press, [1936] 1950.

Richman, Karen. *Migration and Vodou*. Gainesville: University Press of Florida, 2005.

Richterová, Sylvie. *Návraty a jiné ztráty*. Toronto: 68 Publishers, 1978.

Ritivoi, Andreea Deciu. *Yesterday's Self: Nostalgia and the Immigrant Identity*. Lanham, MD: Rowman and Littlefield, 2002.

Rosen, George 'Nostalgia: A 'Forgotten' Psychological Disorder.' *Clio Medica* 10.1 (1975): 29–51.

Rousseau, Jean-Jacques. *Emile*. Trans. Allan Bloom. New York: Basic, 1976.

Rushdie, Salman. *The Satanic Verses*. New York: Viking, 1989.

Safran, William. 'Diasporas in Modern Societies: Myths of Homeland and Return.' *Diaspora* 1 (1991): 83–99.

Said, Edward. *Reflections on Exile*. Cambridge, MA: Harvard University Press, 1990.

Saint-Louis, Fridolin, and François Houtart. *Le Vodou haïtien: Reflet d'une société bloquée*. Paris and Montreal: L'Harmattan, 2000.

Salivarová, Zdena. 'Rozhovor před oceánem.' *Benefice*. Ed. Karel Hvížd'ala. Toronto: 68 Publishers, 1990. 84–101.

Salles, Alain. 'Duel d'écrivains polymorphes.' *Le Monde* 12 Apr. 2002 (sec. Le Monde Des Livres). http://www.lexis-nexis.com.

Satrapi, Marjane. *Persepolis 2: The Story of a Return*. New York: Pantheon Books, 2004.

Sayad, Abdelmalek. *La Double Absence: Des illusions de l'émigré aux souffrances de l'immigré*. Paris: Seuil, 1999.

– *The Suffering of the Immigrant*. Trans. David Macey. Cambridge: Polity, 2004.

Scarry, Elaine. *The Body in Pain: The Making and Unmaking of the World*. New York: Oxford University Press, 1985.

Scheper-Hughes, Nancy. *Death without Weeping: The Violence of Everyday Life in Brazil*. Berkeley: University of California Press, 1992.

Schutz, Alfred. 'The Stranger: An Essay in Social Psychology.' *American Journal of Sociology* 49.6 (1944): 499–507.

Seabrook, William. *The Magic Island*. New York: Harcourt Brace, 1929.

Sebbar, Leïla. *Shérazade: 17 ans, brune, frisée, les yeux verts*. Paris: Stock, 1982.

Shah, Andy. 'Czech-Americans Seek Return of Homeland Citizenship.' *Daily Bruin* 19 Nov. 1997. Accessed 3 Jan. 2005. http://www.dailybruin.ucla.edu/DB/issues/97/11.18/news.czech.html.

Siebers, Tobin. 'Disability as Masquerade.' *Literature and Medicine* 23.1 (2004): 1–22.

– 'Resentment and the Genealogy of Morals: From Nietzsche to Girard.' *The Ethics of Criticism*. Ithaca and London: Cornell University Press, 1988, 124–57.

Sif, Minna. *Méchamment berbère*. Paris: Ramsay, 1997.

Šiklová, Jiřina. 'O exilu pro Český dialog: Rozhovor s Jiřinou Šiklovou.' *Český dialog* 3 (1994): 10–11.

Silverman, Kaja. *Male Subjectivity at the Margins*. New York: Routledge, 1992.

Skeggs, Beverley. 'The Rhetorical Affects of Feminism: Introduction.' *Transformations: Thinking through Feminism*. Ed. Sara Ahmed. London and New York, 2000. 25–33.

Škrášek, Petr. '– a Olin se vrací.' *Literární noviny* 11.13 (2000): 9.

Škvorecký, Josef. *Dvě vraždy v mém dvojím životě*. Prague: Ivo Železný, 1996.

– *Mirákl: politická detektivka*. Toronto: 68 Publishers, 1978.

– *Příběh inženýra lidských duší*. Toronto: 68 Publishers, 1977.

Škvorecký, Josef, and Zdena Salivarová. *Setkání na konci éry, s vraždou*. Prague: Ivo Železný, 2001.

– *Setkání po letech, s vraždou*. Prague: Ivo Železný, 2000.

– *Krátké setkání, s vraždou*. Prague: Ivo Železný, 1999.

Šlajchrt, Viktor. 'Bol na ostrově.' *Respekt* 11.50 (2000): 21.

Smaïl, Paul. *Ali le magnifique*. Paris: Denoël, 2001.

– 'Qui est l'auteur de *Ali le magnifique* ?... L'énigmatique Paul Smaïl répond au *Figaro*.' *Figaro* 5 Jan. 2001. http://www.lexis-nexis.com.

– *Smile*. Trans. Simon Pleasance and Fronza Woods. London: Serpent's Tail, 2000.

– *Vivre me tue*. Paris: Balland, 1997.

Šmíd, Jan. 'Francouzský návrat *Nevědomosti*.' *Lidové noviny* 14 Apr. 2003: 11.

Smith, Geoff N., et al. 'The Incidence of Schizophrenia in European Immigrants to Canada.' *Schizophrenia Research* 87.1–3 (2006): 205–11.

Snell-Hornby, Mary. *Translation Studies: An Integrated Approach*. Amsterdam and Philadelphia: Benjamins, 1995.

Sontag, Susan. *Illness as Metaphor; And, AIDS and Its Metaphors*. New York: Doubleday, 1990.

Spinoza, Benedictus. *The Ethics: Part IV*. Trans. R.H.M. Elwes. Boulder: NetLibrary. 1990. Available: http://www.netLibrary.com/

St John, Spenser. *Hayti or the Black Republic*. London: Smith Elder, 1884.

Strnad, Jan. 'Exil jako nemoc – Blanka Kubešová: romance pro Žoržínu.' *Promený* 23.1 (1986): 180–1.

Suleri, Sara. *Meatless Days*. New York: HarperCollins, 1991.

Svoboda, Jiří. *Autostopem kolem světa*. Scarborough: Autostop, 1979.

Tadjer, Akli. *Les ANI du 'Tassili.'* Paris; Seuil, 1984.

Tan, Amy. *The Joy Luck Club*. New York: Putnam's, 1989.

Taylor, James. *Portuguese-English Dictionary*. Stanford: Stanford University Press, 1987.

Thomas, Nina K. 'Efforts to Prevent Terrorism: Impact on Immigrant Groups.' In *Collateral Damage: The Psychological Consequences of America's*

War on Terrorism. Eds. Paul Kimmel and Chris Stout. Westport, CT: Praeger, 2006, 131–44.

Thomson, Rosemarie Garland. *Extraordinary Bodies: Figuring Physical Disability in American Culture and Literature*. New York: Columbia University Press, 1996.

Todorov, Tzvetan. *The Conquest of America: The Question of the Other*. New York: Harper and Row, 1984.

Troják, Jan. 'Image domova.' *Český dialog* 3.2 (1993): 18–19.

UNHCR. *2005 Global Refugee Trends*. Geneva: Author, 6 June 2006.

Vasse, Denis. *Le Poids du réel, la souffrance*. Paris: Seuil, 1983.

Vejvoda, Jaroslav. *Osel aneb splynutí*. Toronto: 68 Publishers, 1977.

– *Zelené víno*. Toronto: 68 Publishers, 1986.

Venuti, Lawrence, ed. *The Translation Studies Reader*. London: Routledge, 2000.

Vikanes, Ase, et al. 'Variations in Prevalence of Hyperemesis Gravidarum by Country of Birth: A Study of 900,074 Pregnancies in Norway, 1967–2005.' *Scandinavian Journal of Public Health* 36.2 (2008): 135–42.

Vladislav, Jan. 'Exile, Responsibility, Destiny.' In *Literature in Exile*. Ed. John Glad. London and Durham: Duke University Press, 1990. 14–27.

Vrzala, Jaroslav. 'Paní profesorce Jiřině Šiklové.' *Český dialog* 9 (1995): 20–1.

Wachtel, Andrew. 'Writers and Society in Eastern Europe, 1989–2000: The End of the Golden Age.' *East European Politics and Societies* 17.4 (2003): 583–621.

Waitzkin, Howard, and Holly Magaña. 'The Black Box in Somatization: Unexplained Physical Symptoms, Culture, and Narratives of Trauma.' *Social Science and Medicine* 45 (1997): 811–25.

Walker, Janet. *Trauma Cinema: Documenting Incest and the Holocaust*. Berkeley: University of California Press, 2005.

Walker, Keith Louis. 'Words Proffered in Pain: Gérard Etienne, Shame, and the Counter-Confession.' *Countermodernism and Francophone Literary Culture: The Game of Slipknot*. Durham, NC: Duke University Press, 1999. 213–66.

Walters, Wendy. 'Writing the Diaspora in Black International Literature "With Wider Hope, in Some More Benign Fluid..." Diaspora Consciousness and Literary Expression.' *Diasporic Africa: A Reader*. Ed. Michael Gomez. New York: New York University Press, 2006. 271–89.

Weekes, Raman Ilhan, and Brendan Stuart. 'Deep Dysphasia in Turkish.' *Brain and Language* 87.1 (Oct. 2003): 38–9.

Weiss, Richard. *The American Myth of Success: From Horatio Alger to Norman Vincent Peale*. New York: Basic, 1969.

Williams, Carolyn, and Joseph Westermeyer. *Refugee Mental Health in Resettlement Countries*. Washington: Hemisphere, 1986.

Wittgenstein, Ludwig. *Preliminary Studies for the 'Philosophical investigations.'* Also known as the *Blue and Brown Books*. Oxford: Blackwell, 1958.

Woodman, Marion. *The Owl Was a Baker's Daughter: Obesity, Anorexia Nervosa and the Repressed Feminine: A Psychological Study*. Toronto: Inner City Books, 1980.

Woolf, Virginia. 'On Being Ill.' *The Essays of Virginia Woolf*. Ed. Andrew McNeillie. London: Hogarth Press, [1926], vol. 4, 1994, 317–32.

Yahyaoui, Abdessalem. *Corps, espace-temps, et traces de l'exil: Incidences cliniques*. Grenoble: La pensée sauvage, 1989.

Yezierska, Anzia. 'How I Found America.' *Hungry Hearts*. Ed. Blanche Gelfant. New York: Penguin Classics, [1920] 1997. 152–74.

– *Bread Givers*. Garden City, NY: Doubleday Page, 1925.

Young, Richard E., and Kenneth Pike, eds. *Rhetoric: Discovery and Change*. New York: Harcourt Brace and World, 1970.

Zborowski, Mark. *People in Pain*. San Francisco: Jossey-Bass, 1969.

Zemouri, Kamal. *Le Jardin de l'intrus*. Alger: Enal, 1986.

Zinai-Koudil, Hafsa. *Sans voix*. Paris: Plon, 1997.

Zitouni, Ahmed. *Une difficile fin de moi*. Paris: Cherche midi, 1998.

Zolkowska, Krystyna, et al. 'Increased Rates of Psychosis among Immigrants to Sweden: Is Migration a Risk Factor for Psychosis?' *Psychological Medicine* 31.4 (2001): 669–78.

Zouari, Fawzia. *Ce pays dont je meurs*. Paris: Ramsay, 1999.

Index

global, 192, 207; vocabulary of culture and, 32

communism, 27, 187, 189, 197, 199, 201, 207–8

compassion: avoidance, 231; fatigue, 231; pity as, 233–4

Compassion Fatigue (Moeller), 231

Confessions d'un immigré (Houari), 88, 89, 90

Conrad, Joseph: *Lord Jim,* 202

Courlander, Harold, 147, 156, 174, 175, 179, 249n17

creolization, 23, 148, 149

Cri des oiseaux fous, Le (Laferrière), 181–2

Cubans, 30, 191, 249n13

Čulík, Jan, 203

cultural rhetoric, 49, 136, 148, 151, 183, 184, 229

Cultural Studies Reader, The (During), 137

cultural translation, 229, 238; and acculturation, 41, 42–3; affective, 137–40; in critical theory, 42, 43, 149, 156; and identity, 43; by immigrant writers, 41–2, 153, 167, 183, 229, 249; in immigration, 41, 167, 168; and target culture, 42, 238; of *vodou,* 136–7, 153, 155–6, 183

culture: and body, 74, 75, 80; Czech, 189; in expression of immigrant suffering, 41–3, 49, 139, 229; Haitian, 135, 142, 147, 160, 161, 168, 172, 177–82; of host nation, 16, 42, 45, 46; Maghrebi, 75, 78, 80, 87, 97, 102, 106, 107, 108, 125; and politics of pain, 55, 56; and rhetorical strategies, 48, 49; *vodou* and, 135, 136, 142–7, 151, 161, 168.

See also acculturation; target culture

Culture of Pain, The (Morris), 34, 41

culture-lacune, 139

Czech emigrant literature, 202–4; avoidance of heroic in, 204; during vs after communism, 209; as dissident/émigré literature, 11; dual perspective in, 203; lack of hardships in, 198; as literary escapism, 202–3; nature of, 202–3; reader-responses to, 204–5; Russian compared to, 203; scepticism of, 203–4; style of, 202; suffering in, 60, 188, 204, 229, 230; tone of, 203

Czech emigrants: absence of suffering, 188, 198; assistance for Czechs at home, 196; as betrayers of state, 196; and communism, 27, 189; decision to leave homeland, 200–2; differences from other groups, 189; economic motives, 191; as émigrés, 189–90, 199; fall of Berlin Wall and, 193; films, 225; as guardians of Czech past, 214; guilt of, 30, 201–2; homeland Czechs vs, 193–4; loss of 'non-returnability,' 218; in Netherlands, 200; 1948 generation, 199, 214, 218; 1968 wave of, 199, 218; pain of, 187; as political exiles, 11, 189–90, 199; as political refugees, 8, 11; psychological factors, 200–2; punitive action against relatives of, 196; as refugees, 30; return of, 193–8; social class, 189; success stories, 196; suppression of suffering by, 197–8; in Toronto, 200–2;

126; suffering as ascetic ideal and, 54; totalitarianism and, 201. *See also* national identity

identity politics: disabled Maghrebi immigrants and, 84; disabled workers and, 97; feminist studies and, 57; pain and, 51; politics of pain and, 57; rhetoric of, 202; rhetoric of pain and, 57–9; and victimhood, 57–62, 127–8

Ignatieff, Michael, 227, 231, 237–8

Ignorance (Kundera), 207, 209, 210, 212–13, 220–4, 232

illegal immigrants: absence from immigrant narratives, 60; labourers, 60; Maghrebi, 78–9; suffering of, 60, 78–9; in U.S., 227–8

Illegal Immigration Reform and Immigrant Responsibility Act (U.S.), 251n1

Illness as Metaphor (Sontag), 120

Imache, Tassadit: *Une fille sans histoire*, 93

immigrant heroes, 44; avoidance in Czech exile literature, 204; in Maghrebi texts, 67, 113; otherness of, 15, 17; social skills, 17

immigrant literature, 10, 11, 15–24; acculturation in, 45; early, 16; emigrant literature vs, 10, 192; expressions of pain in (*see* translation[s]); generic, 15; genre of, 43–5; heroes of, 15; as host country narrative, 45; journeys in, 15–16; and pluriculturalism, 16, 18, 44; *ressentiment* and, 56; as series of trials, 16, 54; as success stories, 18–19; suffering within, 17–18; as survival strategy, 81; target audience of, 45; target languages and, 45–7

immigrant mothers, daughters' views of, 107

Immigrant Novel as Genre,' 'The (Boelhower), 15–16

immigrant pain and suffering, xii, 25; absence of, 184; as adaptation, 24; body and, 74, 80–1, 108–9; causes of, 26–8; and citizenship, 4; corporeal pain and, 131; cultural rhetoric and, 184; culture in expression of, 41–3; definition of, 25; difference originating from, 23; dismissal of, 20; final return home and, 193; generic conventions around, 5; healing through cultural reclamation, 173, 176–7, 180; host society and, 45–6; and hybridity, 23; immigration process and, 27–8, 44; importance of expressing, 230; and individualism, 4; institutional interpretation of, 53; internalization of, 18; lack of knowledge of, 231; language difficulties in conveying, 32; legitimation of, 236; linguistic problems, 31–2; and minority rights, 206; normalization of, 33–4; particularization of, 24; and power, 57; and privileged identity, 59; psychological symptoms, 29–31, 114; real vs fictional, 131; and redemption, 41, 46; as series of trials, 44; silent expression of, 184, 205–6; social interpretations of, 56–7; somatic, 31, 109; as structural violence, 28; suppression of, 60, 197–8, 206, 208, 229; sympathetic reader-response to, 232–4, 238; translation of, 39, 41, 43, 47–9, 229, 230; universaliza-